FOR HIS EYES ONLY

UNIVERSITY OF CHICHESTER

FOR HIS EYES ONLY

The Women of James Bond

edited by
LISA FUNNELL

WALLFLOWER PRESS
LONDON & NEW YORK

A Wallflower Press Book
Published by
Columbia University Press
Publishers Since 1893
New York • Chichester, West Sussex
cup.columbia.edu

Cover image:
© Danjaq/Eon Productions

A complete CIP record is available from the Library of Congress

ISBN 978-0-231-17614-9 (cloth : alk. paper)
ISBN 978-0-231-17615-6 (pbk. : alk. paper)
ISBN 978-0-231-85092-6 (e-book)

Columbia University Press books are printed on permanent
and durable acid-free paper.
This book is printed on paper with recycled content.
Printed in the United States of America

c 10 9 8 7 6 5 4 3 2 1
p 10 9 8 7 6 5 4 3 2 1

TABLE OF CONTENTS

SECTION 3: FEMINIST CRITIQUES AND MOVEMENTS

SECTION 4: GENDERED CONVENTIONS

SECTION 5: FEMALE AGENCY AND GENDER ROLES

SECTION 6: JUDI DENCH'S TENURE AS M

ACKNOWLEDGMENTS

This book is dedicated to my family. First, I must thank my partner, Dr. Travis Gliedt, for encouraging me to pursue this project. You are a source of inspiration and incredibly supportive of all my research endeavors. Second, I need to thank my dad, Lorne, for introducing me to the Bond franchise and sharing with me his love for the series. Your enthusiasm for this anthology and constant inquiries into its progress served as a great motivation for its completion. I also must thank my mom, Mary, for enduring Sunday dinners in front of the television where we watched the same Bond films over and over. Your indulgence gave me the opportunity to develop my research passion. Finally, I need to thank my brother Dave, his wife Caren, and especially their three children Tailor, Harrison, and Daniel who are always thrilled to see their names mentioned in my books (even though, as Harrison has told me, there are too many words and not enough pictures). You are a source of love and laughter in my life.

Although *For Your Eyes Only: The Women of James Bond* has been a personal labor of love, this book has benefited from the support of various people. First, I must thank my contributors whose insightful work is featured throughout this book. Second, I need to thank Yoram Allon, Commissioning Editor at Wallflower Press, for your suggestions and support throughout the various phases of publication. Third, I need to thank my research assistant Jordyn Snow for helping to compile and edit the collection. Finally, I must thank Christoph Lindner for writing a compelling foreword for the book.

I am also grateful for receiving permission to reproduce selections from the following copyrighted material:

An earlier version of Chapter 14 by Sabine Planka—"Female Bodies in James Bond Title Sequences"—appeared as Planka, Sabine. "Weiblichkeit als Appetizer. Frauenkörper in den James Bond-Title Sequences." *Gendered Bodies: Körper, Gender und Medien*. Eds. Lisa Kleinberger and Marcus Stiglegger. Siegen: universi – Universitätsverlag, 2013. 47-72. Reproduced with the permission of the editors.

CONTRIBUTOR LIST

THOMAS M. BARRETT is Professor of History at St. Mary's College of Maryland. He is the author of *At the Edge of Empire: The Terek Cossacks and the North Caucasus Frontier* (1999). He has published articles on the history of Cossacks, the North Caucasus, Russian themes in American culture, and American science fiction during the cold war. He is currently writing a book on the image of Russia and Eastern Europe in American popular culture. He is the original conceptualizer, researcher, and writer for the Library of Congress's multimedia digital library, Meeting of Frontiers (frontiers.loc.gov).

FERNANDO GABRIEL PAGNONI BERNS currently works at Universidad de Buenos Aires (UBA) as Graduate Teaching Assistant of "Literatura de las Artes Combinadas II." He teaches seminars on American Horror Cinema and Euro Horror. He is director of the research group on horror cinema "Grite" and has published essays in the books *Undead in the West* (2012), *The Ages of Wonder Woman: Essays on the Amazon Princess in Changing Times* (2014), and *Heroines of Comic Books and Literature* (2014), among others.

MICHAEL W. BOYCE is Associate Professor and Program Chair of English and Film Studies at Booth University College in Winnipeg, Manitoba. He is the author of *The Lasting Influence of the War on Postwar British Film* (2012). In his current project, he examines the representation of crime and criminals in post-war British film.

JEFFREY A. BROWN is Professor in the Department of Popular Culture and the School of Critical and Cultural Studies at Bowling Green State University. He is the author of numerous academic articles about gender, ethnicity and sexuality in contemporary media, as well as three books: *Black Superheroes, Milestone Comics, and Their Fans* (2000), *Dangerous Curves: Action Heroines, Gender, Fetishism and Popular Culture* (2011), and *Beyond Bombshells: The New Action Heroine in Popular Culture* (2015). He is currently completing a book about live action superheroes in film and television in post-9/11 American culture.

CHARLES BURNETTS teaches film in the Department of Philosophy and Religious Studies at Kings University College, University of Western Ontario. He is the author of *Improving Passions: Sentimental Aesthetics and American Film* (2015). He has published articles in *Journal of Film and Video, New Review of Film and Television Studies* and *Scope*.

JAMES CHAPMAN is Professor of Film Studies at the University of Leicester, UK, and author of *Licence to Thrill: A Cultural History of the James Bond Films* (2007), as well as other works on film and television history including *Saints and Avengers: British Adventure Series of the 1960s* (2002), *War and Film* (2008), *Inside the Tardis: The Worlds of "Doctor Who"* (2013), and *Film and History* (2013).

ROBERT VON DASSANOWSKY is Professor of German and Film, Director of Film Studies at the University of Colorado, Colorado Springs and works as an independent film producer. He is a member of the European Academy of Sciences and Arts, the European Film Academy, and a Fellow of the Royal Historical Society. His recent books include *Austrian Cinema: A History* (2005), *New Austrian Film* (2011), *Quentin Tarantino's Inglourious Basterds: A Manipulation of Metacinema* (2012), *World Film Locations: Vienna* (2012) and *Screening Transcendence: Film under Austrofascism and the Hollywood Hope 1933–38* (2015).

KLAUS DODDS is Professor of Geopolitics at Royal Holloway, University of London and Editor of *The Geographical Journal*. He has written numerous articles on the popular geopolitics of James Bond and other spies/assassins including Jason Bourne, and his work has appeared in such journals as *Geopolitics, Journal of Popular Film and Television, Environment and Planning D: Society and Space, Third World Quarterly, Critical Studies on Terrorism, Critical Studies on Security, Transactions of the Institute of British Geographers, Geographical Review,* and *Popular Communication*. He is the co-author, with Sean Carter, of *International Politics and Film: Space, Vision, Power* (2014).

LISA FUNNELL is Assistant Professor in the Women's and Gender Studies Program at the University of Oklahoma. She has published numerous articles on gender and feminism in the Bond franchise. She also researches Hong Kong martial arts films and Hollywood blockbusters. Her book *Warrior Women: Gender, Race, and the Transnational Chinese Action Star* (2014) won the Emily Toth Award for Best Single Work in Women's Studies from the Popular Culture Association/American Culture Association in 2015. She is also the co-editor of *Transnational Asian Identities in Pan-Pacific Cinemas: The Reel Asian Exchange* (2012) and *American and Chinese-Language Cinemas: Examining Cultural Flows* (2015).

CATHERINE HAWORTH is Lecturer in Music at the University of Huddersfield. Her research focuses on musical practices of representation and identity construction across various media, with a particular focus on film and television music. Recent publications include articles on identity and the soundtrack in female detective films and the female gothic genre; guest editorship of the gender and sexuality special issue of *Music, Sound and the Moving Image*; and the co-edited collection *Gender, Age and Musical Creativity* (2015).

CHRISTOPHER HOLLIDAY currently teaches Film Studies at King's College London and London South Bank University, and has previously been visiting lecturer in animation at the University of Kent. He has published several book chapters and journal articles on computer-animated films and, most recently, written on the performance of British actors in contemporary US television drama for the *Journal of British Cinema and Television*. His research interests include popular Hollywood cinema, histories of British film and television, as well as nuances of film style, fictional world creation and acting within the context of digital media and traditional animated forms.

STEPHANIE JONES is Teaching Fellow at the Department of Theatre, Film and Television Studies in the Institute of Literature, Languages and Creative Arts at Aberystwyth University in the UK. In 2012, she completed a PhD on representations of masculinity within the Bond franchise including an analysis of notions of masculinity within Fleet Street Press responses to James Bond films. Stephanie is the editorial assistant for the Routledge journal *Media History*.

ROSS KARLAN is a PhD candidate in Hispanic Literature and Cultural Studies at Georgetown University, and holds a Bachelor of Arts from the University of Pennsylvania in Cinema Studies, Hispanic Studies, and Art History. He has always been a fan of James Bond, and has studied magic since he was a child. In addition to his academic interests in Latin America, much of Ross's research investigates the intersections of magic, film, literature, and art.

PETER C. KUNZE completed a PhD in English at Florida State University in 2012 and is current working on a second PhD, in Media Studies, at the University of Texas at Austin. His research examines masculinity, comedy, and childhood across literature, film, and new media. Recent interests include sincerity in contemporary American culture and the industrial history of the Animation Renaissance. He is the editor of *The Films of Wes Anderson: Critical Essays on an Indiewood Icon* (2014) as well as the forthcoming collection *Conversations with Maurice Sendak*.

JIM LEACH is Professor Emeritus in the Department of Communication, Popular

Culture and Film at Brock University, St. Catharines, Ontario. His research and teaching interests include Canadian cinema, British cinema, popular cinema, and film and cultural theory. He has published books on the films of Alain Tanner and Claude Jutra, on British cinema and Canadian cinema, co-edited a critical anthology on Canadian documentary films, and developed a Canadian edition of an introductory film studies textbook. His latest book is a monograph on *Doctor Who* for Wayne State University Press.

CHRISTOPH LINDNER is Professor of Media and Culture at the University of Amsterdam and Director of the Netherlands Institute for Cultural Analysis. His work on Bond includes the edited volumes *Revisioning 007: James Bond and Casino Royale* (2009) and *The James Bond Phenomenon: A Critical Reader* (2009).

DAN MILLS has a PhD. in English from Georgia State University where he wrote his dissertation on early modern utopian literature. He has published articles in the journals *Pedagogy, Cahiers Élisabéthains,* and *In-Between: Essays and Studies in Literary Criticism* and has forthcoming articles in edited collections on critical theory and early modern literature and Western encounters with the East.

STEPHEN NEPA currently teaches history at Temple University, Moore College of Art and Design, and Rowan University. He has written for *Planning Perspectives, Environmental History, Buildings and Landscapes, New York History,* and other publications. He is also contributing essays to the forthcoming volumes *The 100 Greatest Bands of All Time: A Guide to the Legends who Rocked the World* and *A Greene Country Towne: Philadelphia, Ecology, and the Material Imagination.*

LORI L. PARKS is Visiting Assistant Professor of Art History at Miami University, Ohio. Recent publications include entries in *The Cultural Encyclopedia of the Breast* (2014) and essays in the forthcoming collections *Tim Burton: Works, Characters, Themes* and *Relentless Seeking: Contemporary Art and Addiction in Global Contexts.* She is also co-editing with Drs. Neumann and Yamashiro a special issue on food for the *European Journal of American Culture.*

BRIAN PATTON is Associate Professor of English and Film Studies in the Department of Modern Languages at King's University College at Western University in London, Canada. His published work includes contributions to *Ian Fleming & James Bond: The Cultural Politics of 007* (2005), *100 Entertainers Who Changed America: An Encyclopedia of Pop Culture Luminaries* (2013) and *James Bond and Popular Culture: Essays on the Influence of the Fictional Superspy* (2014).

ANNA G. PIOTROWSKA is Associate Professor in the Institute of Musicology at Jagiellonian University in Kraków, Poland. In 2010, she was a Fulbright Fellow in Boston University, USA and in 2005 she held the Mellon fellowship in Edinburg University, UK. She is the author of *Gypsy Music in European Culture* (2013) and four books in Polish, including *On Music and Film: An Introduction to Film Musicology* (2014).

SABINE PLANKA currently works at the University of Siegen as a coordinator for administrative matters and as a researcher in the Department German Studies. She is editor of *Die Zeitreise. Ein Motiv in Literatur und Film für Kinder und Jugendliche* (2014). She has published an article in *Film International* and essays in the collections *Der skandinavische Horrorfilm* (2013) and *Writing Worlds: Welten- und Raummodelle der Fantastik* (2014) .

EILEEN ROSITZKA is a PhD candidate in Film Studies at the University of St Andrews, Scotland. She is currently Co-Editor-in-Chief of *Frames Cinema Journal* and has written essays in *Bigger Than Life: Ken Adam's Film Design* (2014) accompanying an exhibition of the same title at the Deutsche Kinemathek, as well as in the collections *The Sound of Genre* (2015) and *Genre und Serie* (2015).

MARLISA SANTOS is Associate Professor in the Farquhar College of Arts and Sciences at Nova Southeastern University in Fort Lauderdale, Florida. She is the author of *The Dark Mirror: Psychiatry and Film Noir* (2010) and the editor of *Verse, Voice, and Vision: Poetry and the Cinema* (2013). She has also published numerous essays in peer-reviewed anthologies on various topics such as food and film and contemporary southern film, and on directors such as Martin Scorsese, Edgar G. Ulmer, and Joseph H. Lewis.

ALEXANDER SERGEANT is a PhD candidate within the Department of Film Studies at King's College London. His thesis examines issues of spectatorship in relation to the Hollywood fantasy genre and was supported by a grant from the UK Arts and Humanities Research Council. His research interests include the history of Hollywood cinema in the twenty and twenty first centuries, film theory, theories of film spectatorship, film philosophy and psychoanalysis. He has published on these subjects in a variety of academic journals and edited collections.

ANDREA SEVERSON has two Master of Arts degrees, in Media Arts from the University of Arizona and in English: Rhetoric & Composition from Arizona State University, and is now working towards a PhD in rhetoric at ASU, focusing on fashion rhetoric. She has been teaching at Arizona State University and Maricopa County Community Colleges since 2010. For the past ten years, she has also worked as a freelance costume designer on various theatrical and film projects. She has been a member of the Arizona Costume Institute since 2010 and served on its Board of Directors from 2011 to 2014.

KRISTEN SHAW is a doctoral candidate in the English and Cultural Studies Program at McMaster University. Her major research interests include representations of gender and race in popular culture, including film, television, and literature, as well as studies of science fiction and fantasy. She has been published in *Inquire: Journal of Comparative Literature* and is currently the assistant editor of an upcoming essay collection on Canadian science fiction. She is currently writing her dissertation entitled *Strangers in Strange New Lands: Feminist Spatial Politics in Science Fiction.*

BOEL ULFSDOTTER is Senior Lecturer in Media Studies at Skövde University College, Sweden. She completed her PhD in Film Studies at the University of Reading in 2008. Her areas of research specialization include popular film and culture, screen costuming, fashion history and consumption, and museum culture.

TRAVIS L. WAGNER is completing a Master of Library and Information Science degree and a Women's and Gender Studies Graduate Certificate at the University of South Carolina. He is an instructional assistant within the Women's and Gender Program with a focus on images of women, particularly in South Korean cinema. He has published in *Cinephile: The University of British Columbia's Film Journal* (2014).

FOREWORD

Christoph Lindner

This book is urgently needed. The place and significance of women in the world of James Bond (in literature, film, gaming, and beyond) has been under-examined to date. Yes, individual articles on women and James Bond have been published periodically over the years and, for quite a different readership, a number of coffee-table books on the "Bond girls" exist, but we have been missing a sustained, focused, and critical study of the topic until now. And yet, as critics and fans alike have always recognized, women are integral to the 007 series in many different ways - as necessary to the James Bond formula as Bond himself. As this book demonstrates in relation to a rich variety of examples and from a full range of critical and theoretical perspectives, women not only enable and help to define the extreme masculinism of the Bondian multiverse, but also figure as sites of contestation and experiment over the cultural politics of the body, gender, sexuality, race, nationality, and more.

Tony Bennett and Janet Woollacott have long maintained that 007 functions as a floating signifier, periodically getting updated to reflect changing attitudes in society. This book shows just how much that process of signification depends on Bond's relationship with women, ranging from his sexual conquests (and failures) in the form of so-called "Bond girls," to his increasingly charged flirtations with office co-workers like Miss Moneypenny, to his oedipal conflicts with the hybrid mother-father figure of Judi Dench's M. Much more important, however, is that this book demonstrates the ways in which women in the 007 series also function as floating signifiers in their own right, reflecting but also sometimes anticipating or undermining mainstream constructions of identity, agency, and power.

The challenge of writing about women and James Bond, and perhaps one of the reasons why the topic has remained under-examined for so long, is captured in the book's title *For His Eyes Only: The Women of James Bond*. As this grammar of possession suggests, women in the 007 series have largely been defined by their relationship with Bond, just as Bond himself has often been defined by his relationship with women. The difference, as captured in the wording of the title, is that Bond is named, identified, singularized, whereas women remain generic, interchangeable, dependent.

This not only reflects how women have figured in the 007 series from the beginning, but also the difficulty of studying "the women of James Bond" without the overshadowing, controlling presence of Bond.

But what happens if we study the women *of* James Bond in terms that defy or transcend their relationship of dependence *with* James Bond? What is a "Bond girl" when she is understood as being neither a possession nor a "girl"? In short, what happens when we re-conceptualize women in the 007 series in terms other than those inherited from, or operating within, the series itself? These are among the many pressing questions addressed by the authors in the chapters that follow. So although Bond looms large in this book (and necessarily so) women loom much larger. The result is a radically different vision of the world of James Bond that has not been possible or available before. As a consequence, *For His Eyes Only: The Women of James Bond* changes how we see and understand the 007 series as whole, including our own relationship to it.

INTRODUCTION

THE WOMEN OF JAMES BOND

Lisa Funnell

The release of *Skyfall* (Sam Mendes 2012) marked the fiftieth anniversary of the James Bond film franchise. The 23rd film in the series, *Skyfall* earned over $1 billion dollars (USD) at the worldwide box-office and won two Academy Awards. Amidst such popular and critical acclaim, many have questioned the representation of women in the film, viewing *Skyfall* in relation to the Bond franchise at large. From the representation of an aging and disempowered M, to the limited role of the Bond Girl, to the characterization of Miss Moneypenny as a defunct field agent, *Skyfall* arguably develops the legacy of Bond at the expense of women in the film. Although some might argue that the Bond franchise has adjusted its politics of representation—a notion promoted through a 2011 video celebrating International Women's Day featuring Daniel Craig and Judi Dench in their Bond roles discussing gender equality—the most recent film *Skyfall* is decidedly regressive in its narrative treatment of female characters.

Bond has historically been defined by his relationships with women and particularly through heterosexual romantic conquest. As noted by Jeremy Black, Bond's sexual partners provide a "visual guarantee of the maleness of the Secret Service" and these conquests offer "tipping point[s]" in the narrative (107-9). By indiscriminately sleeping with multiple women in each film, Bond helps to ensure the success of his mission by aligning his lovers with his moral plight. In light of Bond's treatment of women—seducing, bedding, and discarding them—the franchise has been accused of being sexist and misogynistic. Although some might argue that the franchise has progressed in terms of gender equality, as Craig's Bond sleeps with fewer women than his predecessors, the problematic representation of women in *Skyfall* recalls the media-driven backlash against feminist gains in the 1970s, which impacted the depiction of women in the series. Indeed, Tony Bennett and Janet Woollacott note that Bond films of the 1970s featured the "putting-back-into-place" of women by "fictitiously rolling back the advances of feminism to restore an imaginarily more secure phallocentric conception of gender relations" ("The Moments" 28). Since *Casino Royale* (Martin Campbell 2006) and its sequels *Quantum of Solace* (Marc Forster 2008) and *Skyfall* constitute a rebooting of the series, it leads many scholars, like myself, to question if

1

there a place for women in the new world of James Bond and, if so, what role will these women play in the future of the franchise?

For His Eyes Only: The Women of James Bond seeks to answer these questions by examining the role that women have historically played in the franchise, which greatly contributed to the international success of the films. This anthology constitutes an important academic study on the women in the Bond franchise as it moves beyond the discussion of a single character (e.g. Honey Ryder), character type (e.g. the Bond Girl), or group of films (e.g. the Connery era). While scholars have examined this subject in previous works, their arguments can be found in broader studies on the Bond franchise (see Black [2001], Chapman [2007]) and edited collections (see Lindner [2003], Weiner et al. [2010]). This book redresses this critical oversight by providing a comprehensive examination of femininity and feminism in the Bond series. It covers all 23 Eon productions as well as the spoof *Casino Royale* (Val Guest et al. 1967) and considers a range of Bond women from primary characters to secondary figures to the women who lend their voices to the title tracks. More importantly, this book moves beyond a cursory discussion of casting and characterization to consider a range of factors that have helped to shape the representation of women in the franchise, including female characterization in Ian Fleming's novels, the vision of producer Albert R. Broccoli and other creative personnel, the influence of feminism and other social and political factors, and broader changes/trends in British and American film and television. This anthology provides a timely and retrospective look at the depiction of women in the franchise, in light of the 50-year anniversary of the series, and offers new scholarly perspectives on the subject.

The anthology is divided into six sections. The first, *From Novel to Film*, considers the representation of women in the Bond novels and explores how these characters are adapted into the films. James Chapman argues that the representation of women is at once more conservative and progressive in the novels than the films. He contends that while the novels may be criticized for their casual sexism and misogyny, they provide greater scope for female agency as "the girl" often possesses skills and knowledge that Bond does not, and even rescues him on occasion. Boel Ulfsdotter examines the character design of Tiffany Case in Fleming's novel *Diamonds Are Forever* (1956) and discusses the factors that influenced her transposition into the 1971 film. She argues that the filmic Case is a transitory figure as the series shifts from one Bond Girl concept to another, a situation that influenced the development of her screen persona. Jim Leach considers the performance of Judi Dench as M in relation to her novel and film counterparts. He argues that the presence of a female M unsettles the basic formula of the series and the extent of this disruption is not just a question of her gender but also one of political and technological developments in the world in which she exercises her authority.

The second section, *Desiring the Other*, examines how the intersection of gender with race, ethnicity, and/or nationality impacts the narrative treatment of women in the franchise. Thomas Barrett examines the characterization of Tatiana Romanova in *From Russia with Love* (Terence Young 1963) in relation to the shifting discursive terrain as the Soviet Union began opening up to the West. He argues that Bond, by escorting Romanova to the West, enacts a contemporary conversion fantasy that renders Soviet women ripe for Western consumption. Travis Wagner examines the relationship of Bond, a privileged white colonial figure, with the various black women who appear over the course of the series. He explores how racial stereotypes are mobilized in the representation of black women and how their treatment by Bond works to reaffirm and entrench his privilege. Charles Burnetts explores how the secondary woman or "fluffer" character is set up as a tool/commodity in the narrative to be exploited by Bond and/or the villain. He discusses the preponderance of black fluffer characters in the franchise and the ways in which this fluffer typology sits in tension with contemporary mandates for "positive" representation. Kristen Shaw examines the disciplinary process that is initiated when Moneypenny accidentally shoots Bond in *Skyfall*. She argues that Moneypenny is put into her "proper" place as a racial and gendered "Other," effectively transforming her from Bond's equal to a supportive sidekick. Lisa Funnell examines the depiction of Asian women across three key phases of the Bond franchise. She argues that Asian femininity is depicted through the use of antiquated stereotypes; the films foreground the distinction of unacceptable and acceptable femininity in relation to the white status quo, that being James Bond.

The third part, *Feminist Critiques and Movements*, explores female representation through the lens of feminism. Robert von Dassanowsky examines Ursula Andress' Vesper Lynd in *Casino Royale* (1967), arguing that she is the most remarkable female character of the decade's espionage genre for her vast independent power and wealth. He contends that the character intertexts with the Eon Bond series and especially *Dr. No* (Terence Young 1962), and conflates the other sexually domineering figures Andress previously portrayed. Marlisa Santos suggests that *On Her Majesty's Secret Service* (Peter Hunt 1969) fits the formula of the Hollywood Golden Age "woman's film." She explores how the film breaks the androcentric mold of the Bond film by centralizing the role of women, defining Bond through the main female character of Tracy di Vicenzo, as well as the symbolic female influence of Queen Elizabeth II, the locus of Bond's professional identity. Dan Mills examines the representation of women in *On Her Majesty's Secret Service*, arguing that the film breaks generic conventions by depicting strong female characters (Tracy di Vicenzo, Irma Bunt, Moneypenny) who are more actively involved in the development of the narrative than their male counterparts (Bond, Blofeld, M). He contends that the depiction of women reverses gender roles in the Bond canon in a way that makes *On Her Majesty's Secret Service* an aberration in the series. Fernando Gabriel Pagnoni Berns argues that the representation of Bond women in the early 1980s is influenced by the radical feminist movement. He explores how *For Your Eyes Only* (John Glen 1981) and

Octopussy (John Glen 1983) register the impact of second-wave feminism through a consideration of the Sisterhood communities that emerged in places like the United States and India. Alexander Sergeant examines the depiction of Electra King in *The World is Not Enough* (Michael Apted 1999) and the various attempts made within the film to domesticate desire under the domain of the phallus. He argues that King both embodies and problematizes traditional gender roles, and through the use of masquerade she manages to hold Bond's phallic authority at a distance.

The fourth section, *Gendered Conventions*, considers a variety of female-focused or feminine elements that have helped to define the Bond generic tradition. Sabine Planka examines the form and function of the Bond title sequence, an element that has helped producers to integrate more women and especially female sexuality into the franchise. She argues that the semi-nude female body is served up as an appetizer to a presumed male audience in order to peak their interest in the forthcoming film. Eileen Rositzka examines the representation of "Secondary Girls," emphasizing the importance of mystique to female characterization in the franchise. She notes that once the (female) enigma is solved, she is rendered unremarkable and new enigmas are produced to take her place. Catherine Haworth considers the interplay of music with the representation of women in *Goldfinger* (Guy Hamilton 1964). She argues that the musical and visual motifs of the title sequence spill over into the film's narrative proper and create spaces within which female desire and agency can be articulated. Anna Piotrowska notes that while there is no Bond Girl musical theme, a female perspective is forwarded in the films through the song lyrics and female voices featured in the title tracks. She argues that, through the soundtrack, women remain immortalized in the form of disembodied voices and their eternal presence is asserted as voices of consciousness. Andrea Severson utilizes costume theory to explore the representation of femininity and power, particularly in relation to the Bond Girl. Two films serve as case studies for her analysis: *Dr. No* (1962), which marks the beginning of the series, and *Casino Royale* (2006), which marks the re-conceptualization of the franchise.

The fifth section, *Female Agency and Gender Roles*, examines gender equality in various facets of the Bond film. Stephen Nepa examines the relationship between Bond and Tracy di Vicenzo in *On Her Majesty's Secret Service*, focusing on the messages being relayed about gender through their secret agent nuptials. He explores how shifting gender roles in the film influence the representation of Bond women in subsequent films and 007's relationships with them. Ross Karlan discusses how the Bond Girl operates like a magician's assistant, as her performance is largely defined by her relationship with Bond and the audience of the films. He argues that when viewed through the lens of magic, the Bond Girl takes on a more active role in the Bond universe. Stephanie Jones examines how the car in Bond films serves as an object that reflects changing ideas about the role of women and technology. She examines three similar scenes in which Bond receives a new car from Q and traces the shift change in gender ideologies. Klaus Dodds explores the re-introduction of Moneypenny in *Skyfall* and the ways in which her character is different from earlier incarnations. He argues that *Skyfall* puts forward the impression that (older/experienced) male agents belong in the field over (younger/less experienced) female agents who serve better as sidekicks rather than professional colleagues. Jeffrey Brown explores how *Salt* (Phillip Noyce 2010), an action film starring Angelina Jolie, is a self-conscious attempt to create a female Bond franchise and examines the ways that key Bond conventions are reconfigured due to the gender change of the superspy. In particular, Brown explores how Salt is de-sexualized in order to avoid the hero being diminished by objectification.

The sixth section, *Judi Dench's Tenure as M*, offers critical perspectives on the representation and character trajectory of Dench's M. Peter Kunze reads Dench's portrayal of M through the lens of feminist critiques of postfeminist discourse and culture. He argues that while a female M gestures toward a productive revision of the traditionally sexist franchise, patriarchal logic persists in the so-called updated Bond films. Brian Patton maps the transformation of M as well as the Bond/M relationship over the course of seven films released between 1995 and 2012. He argues that the advent of a female M brings to the fore a new emphasis on female authority as the series' producers work to situate Bond in a world where a woman in a position of power might be greeted with something other than contempt. Lori Parks examines the characterization of women in *Skyfall* focusing specifically on the intersection between age and gender. She argues that the representation of M, an aging woman, contrasts with the typical depiction of the Bond Girl, and that the introduction of Moneypenny, as an inexperienced agent who trades in field work for a desk job, influences the perception of Dench's M. Christopher Holliday notes that while the maternal overtones between Bond and M have gained momentum during the Craig era, the representation of M in *Skyfall* is also reflective of the Bond Girl. He argues that the irresolvable tension between M's maternal weight and her iconography as "lover" instigates the character's demise in *Skyfall*, and marks the culmination of Dench in the role. Michael Boyce examines the shift in the representation of Dench's M from an unusually complex female character in the Brosnan era Bond films, to a domesticated, neutered mother-figure in the Craig era Bond films. He argues that within the limited gender perspective of the Bond world, mothers (like wives) are unnecessary and undesirable, and her exit is foreshadowed and required.

Section 1

FROM NOVEL
TO FILM

CHAPTER 1

"WOMEN WERE FOR RECREATION"

The Gender Politics of Ian Fleming's James Bond

James Chapman

[Bond] sighed. Women were for recreation. On a job, they got in the way and fogged things up with sex and hurt feelings and all the emotional baggage they carried around. One had to look out for them and take care of them. (*Casino Royale* 27)[1]

The 12 James Bond novels and eight short stories written by Ian Fleming between 1953 and his death in 1964 are the foundational texts of the Bond franchise. However, Bond's literary origins have too often been overlooked in Bond scholarship, which has largely focused on the series of films produced continuously by Eon Productions since 1962. The international popularity of the films, combined with their extraordinary longevity, has established Bond as a global brand whose cultural reach has entirely transcended the original source texts in which he first appeared. For the authors of one of the many popular studies of the Bond films, indeed, the character's iconic status "owes everything to his incarnation on the cinema screen, and little to the novels of Fleming" whom they regard as "tangential" to the films (Barnes and Hearn 5). To read the Fleming stories today is to discover a James Bond who is both like and unlike the popular hero of the films. Nowhere is this more evident than in their gender politics: the Bond novels are paradoxically more sexist in their attitudes yet at the same time allow greater narrative agency for their female characters than most of the films that have been spun from them. This essay will explore the gender politics of Fleming's Bond stories, examining first the social and cultural politics of the texts with particular regard to their attitudes towards women, and then the representation and characterization of female characters in the stories themselves.

To analyze any cultural texts it is essential to understand them in relation to their historical contexts. This is especially the case for popular fiction, which is more sensitive to the demands of the market and the tastes of consumers than high-brow culture. Like all products of popular culture, the Bond stories are tracts for their times: they are informed by and respond to the ideological climate in which they were produced and consumed. The first Bond novel, *Casino Royale*, was published in April 1953 and thereafter the books appeared regularly at one-year intervals until 1965, with the last novel, *The Man with the Golden Gun*. The short-story anthology *Octopussy and The Living Daylights* was published after Fleming's death. Sales of the early hardbacks were respectable if not spectacular (the first hardback edition of *Casino Royale* had a print run of only 4,750) but the popularity of Bond began to take off in the later 1950s. Tony Bennett and Janet Woollacott, in their cultural studies analysis of the Bond phenomenon, identify 1957—the year *From Russia, with Love* was serialized in the *Daily Express*, a popular mass-circulation newspaper—as "the first stage in the transformation of Bond from a character within a set of fictional texts into a household name" (*Bond* 24). Since 1955, the Bond books were published in paperback: combined sales of all Bond paperbacks rose from 41,000 in 1955 to 58,000 in 1956, 72,000 in 1957, 105,000 in 1958, 237,000 in 1959, 323,000 in 1960 and 670,000 in 1961 (ibid. 26-7). It was in 1962—the year that the first Bond film was released in Britain—that combined sales first passed one million. For literary historian John Sutherland, the Bond books were a landmark in publishing because "they revealed a new reliable market for a certain kind of book that was not trash and could be marketed as a 'brand name' (i.e. 'the latest Bond')" (176).

Contemporary critical responses to the Bond novels were divided between those who admired them as superior entertainments and those who disliked them on the grounds of what they saw as excessive sex and violence. The reviewer of *The Times Literary Supplement*, for example, found *Casino Royale* "an extremely engaging affair, dealing with espionage in the 'Sapper' manner, but with a hero who, although taking a great many cold showers and never letting sex interfere with work, is somewhat more sophisticated" ("An Extremely Engaging Affair" 249). Fleming also found an admirer in Kingsley Amis, who felt the Bond books "were more than simple cloak-and-dagger stories with a bit of fashionable affluence and sex thrown in" (9) and were imbued with "a sense of our time" (144). Other commentators, however, were entirely hostile. The criticism of Fleming for peddling sex and violence reached a crescendo with the publication of *Dr. No* in 1958. The broadside was led by Bernard Bergonzi, who detected "a strongly marked streak of voyeurism and sado-masochism in his books" and deplored "the complete lack of any ethical frame of reference" (220). And Paul Johnson described *Dr. No* as "the nastiest book I have ever read" on account of its unhealthy combination of "the sadism of a schoolboy bully, the mechanical, two-dimensional sex-longings of a frustrated adolescent, and the crude snob-cravings of a suburban adult" (431).

David Cannadine has explained the different critical reactions to the Bond novels as reactions to the decline of British power after the Second World War. He points out that the publication history of the novels spans the period from the Coronation of Queen Elizabeth II in 1953—"a retrospectively unconvincing reaffirmation of Britain's continued great-power status"—to the funeral of Winston Churchill in 1965, an event that represented "not only the last rites of the great man himself, but was also self-consciously recognized as being a requiem for Britain as a great power" (46). The debacle of the Suez Crisis in 1956 and the hurried retreat from empire between 1957 and 1965 rudely drove home the lesson that Britain's standing in the world was in seemingly terminal decline. There was a strong critique, from both the political right and the political left, that Britain's decline as a global power was a consequence of declining moral standards at home. The Bond novels, with their emphasis on sex and conspicuous consumption, were seen by some commentators as visible symptoms of this decline. To this extent they can be placed within the same cultural contexts as John Osborne's play *Look Back in Anger*, first performed at the Royal Court Theatre in 1956, and the "northern realist" novels of authors such as John Braine (*Room at the Top*) and Alan Sillitoe (*Saturday Night and Sunday Morning*).

While, on the face of it, the politics of the Bond novels would seem far removed from the "Angry Young Men", on closer reading they prove to be highly equivocal about changes in British society.[2] On the one hand, the social politics of the books are conservative in the extreme. Fleming's Britain, as Amis suggests, is "substantially right of centre" (96). Thus, *The Times* is "the only paper Bond ever read" (*From Russia, with Love* 96) and his mental image of his country is "a world of tennis courts and lily ponds and kings and queens, of London, of people being photographed with pigeons on their heads in Trafalgar Square" (*Dr. No* 224). Bond's attachment to the past is indicated by his choice of car (a 1930s Bentley) and his sentimental affection for the old five-pound note—"the most beautiful money in the world" (*Goldfinger* 66). Bond dislikes the consequences of social change: he takes an instinctive dislike to a taxi-driver whom he considers "typical of the cheap self-assertiveness of young labour since the war" (*Thunderball* 9) and, somewhat hysterically it must be said, believes that homosexuality is "a direct consequence of giving votes to woman and 'sex equality'" (*Goldfinger* 222). Bond himself is characterized as an unequivocal patriot, as the title of the twelfth book, (*On Her Majesty's Secret Service*) attests, and is often cast in the role of a national champion. His response to the Head of the Japanese Secret Service (who has "formed an unsatisfactory opinion about the British people since the war") perfectly sums up Bond's (and Fleming's) politics: "England may have been bled pretty thin by a couple of World Wars, our Welfare State politics may have made us expect too much for free, and the liberation of our Colonies may have gone too fast, but we still climb Everest and beat plenty of the world at plenty of sports and win Nobel Prizes" (*You Only Live Twice* 81).

On the other hand, however, the Bond novels embrace certain aspects of social and cultural change. Fleming is at some pains to present Bond as a modern, even classless hero. He differs from the clubland heroes of the pre-war British thriller, such as Sapper's Bulldog Drummond and John Buchan's Richard Hannay, in so far as he is not a talented amateur—the Drummond stories, especially, tend to give the impression that fighting diabolical criminal masterminds is just another form of "sport" to be fitted in between rubbers or bridge or hearty games of rugger—but a ruthless professional assassin. Time and again the books emphasize Bond's professionalism, whether getting into peak physical shape for an arduous assignment (*Live and Let Die, Dr. No*) or acquainting himself with all the known methods of cheating at cards (*Moonraker*). His attitude towards his job reveals the ultimate professional: "It was his profession to kill people. He had never liked doing it and when he had to kill he did it as well as he knew how and forgot about it. As a secret agent who held the rare double-O prefix—the licence to kill in the Secret Service—it was his duty to be as cool about death as a surgeon" (*Goldfinger* 3). Bond exemplifies what the social historian Harold Perkin called "the rise of professional society", one that is "structured around career hierarchies rather than classes, one in which people find their place according to trained expertise and the service they provide rather than the possession or lack of inherited wealth or acquired capital" (359). Contrary to some accounts, Bond is not a quintessentially British gentleman hero: he feels out of place in the cozy clubland world of his generic forbears ("Doesn't look the sort of chap one usually sees in Blades") and knows "that there was something alien and un-English about himself" (*Moonraker* 34). As the critic James Price observed: "It is the fact of his not being a gentleman—both in this sense and in the chivalric meaning of the word—which immediately distinguishes him from Buchan's Richard Hannay" (69).

The social politics of the Bond novels—which, it seems reasonable to assume, broadly reflect Fleming's own views—are essential to understanding the role and representation of women in the stories. One of the features that most obviously distinguished the Bond stories from previous generations of British thrillers was the greater visibility of women both in narrative terms and as sexualized objects. Bulldog Drummond and Richard Hannay, for example, had little room for women: both seemed more comfortable in homosocial relationships with close groups of male friends than in their marriages to Phyllis Benton and Mary Lamington. Bond, in contrast, meets a different girl in each novel—Fleming invariably refers to the heroine as "the girl"—and usually enjoys a sexual union with her by the story's end. (*Moonraker* is the exception to this rule: Bond does not sleep with Gala Brand who is engaged to a police officer.) While Bond's sexual conquests in the books do not match the numbers in the films—in most stories there is just the one main girl—he was nevertheless the first protagonist of spy fiction to indulge his sexual appetite so openly and frequently.[3]

The graphic (for the time) accounts of sex in the Bond books have caused some critics to see them in the context of the emergence of mass-market pornography during the 1950s. In his study of British spy literature, for example, Michael Denning avers that "the James Bond tales can rightly be seen as an important early form of the mass pornography that characterizes the consumer society, the society of the spectacle, that emerges in Western Europe and North America in the wake of post-war reconstruction" (*Cover* 109-10). Fleming lent credence to this view when he remarked that "the target of my books [...] lay somewhere between the solar plexus and, well, the upper thigh" ("How To Write A Thriller" 14). There are many instances of erotic spectacle in the Bond novels: the gypsy-girl fight in *From Russia, with Love* and the performance of the strip-tease artiste in *The Man with the Golden Gun* are just two. It is symbolic that the publication of the first Bond novel came in the same year as the launch (in America) of *Playboy*, the first mainstream pornographic men's magazine. While it was not until the 1960s that the link between Bond and *Playboy* was institutionalized, when the magazine serialized some of the later stories as well as running photo-spreads of starlets from the Bond films, from the outset there was a clear parallel in their representation of sexuality. Like *Playboy*, the Bond novels construct a male fantasy world of sexually available females and guilt-free sexual relationships. Fleming's somewhat *outré* names for his female characters—including Tiffany Case, Honeychile Rider, Kissy Suzuki, Mary Goodnight and most notoriously Pussy Galore—have sometimes been seen as a parody, though they serve to reinforce the association between femininity and sexuality.

The women of the Bond novels conform to the *Playboy* ideal of sexuality in two particular ways. The first is their representation as erotic spectacle. Fleming's descriptions of his female characters construct them unashamedly as sexualized objects: they are usually tall, athletic, and toned, while their most frequently commented on physical characteristics are their "fine", "firm" or "splendid" breasts. Like *Playboy* models they are often wearing a swimsuit (such as Tracy in *On Her Majesty's Secret Service*) or underwear (Tiffany Case in *Diamonds Are Forever*, Jill Masterton in *Goldfinger*) when Bond first sets eyes on them, or might even be naked (Tatiana Romanova in *From Russia, with Love*, Honeychile Rider in *Dr. No*). Bond's first glimpse of Honeychile Rider on a Caribbean beach exemplifies the strategy of what one critic called "the technique of the erotic distraction" (Bear 24):

> It was a naked girl, with her back to him. She was not quite naked. She wore a broad leather belt round her waist with a hunting knife in a leather sheath at her right hip. The belt made her nakedness extraordinarily erotic [...] She stood in the classical relaxed pose of the nude, all the weight on the right leg and the left knee bent and turning slightly inwards, the head to one side as she examined the things in her hand. (*Dr. No* 79)

Bond is thus represented as a voyeur and the woman as an object of "to-be-looked-at-ness" (Mulvey, "Visual" 837). Bond is endowed not only with a license to kill but a "licence to look" (Denning, *Cover* 110). And the reader, implicitly male, is associated with Bond's point of view.

The other way in which the Bond novels exemplify the *Playboy* ethos is in their representation of guilt-free sexual relationships. Sex in the Bond stories is something to be enjoyed rather than regarded as a sordid affair. As Bond reflects on his night of passion with Jill Masterton in *Goldfinger*: "It hadn't been love [...] Neither had had regrets. Had they committed a sin? If so, which one?" (48). This emphasis on guilt-free sex is associated with female as well as male desire. The Bond Girl is usually characterized as being independent and willful. Domino Vitali, for example, is "an independent girl, a girl of authority and character [...] She might sleep with men, obviously did, but it would be on her terms and not on theirs" (*Thunderball* 115). The emphasis here on the woman's freedom to make her own sexual choices can be seen as an early stirring of the greater social and sexual freedom that emerged in Britain during the "cultural revolution" of the 1960s, especially following the availability of the contraceptive pill (Marwick 21). This is not to say, however, that the Bond stories reflect a particularly progressive view of women's sexuality. Indeed Fleming's view of what women really want from sex would surely be enough to leave some readers apoplectic with rage: "All women love semi-rape. They love to be taken. It was his sweet brutality against my bruised body that had made his act of love so piercingly wonderful" (*The Spy Who Loved Me* 148). Even an otherwise assertive and independent woman such as Tracy in *On Her Majesty's Secret Service* "knows" that her proper position is laying on her back: "Make love to me [...] Do anything you like. And tell me what you like and what you would like from me. Be rough with me. Treat me like the lowest whore in creation" (*On Her Majesty's Secret Service* 31). To this extent the Bond stories reassert a traditional—and culturally problematic—male fantasy of women's sexuality.

The caricatured and one-dimensional characterization of women in the books (unlike some of the male characters like Quarrel and Kerim Bey who are particularly well-drawn) has led cultural theorists to suggest that women should be seen less as characters and more as functions of narrative. Umberto Eco's structuralist analysis of the Fleming novels employs the metaphor of a game of chess in which the characters all play out familiar situations: Bond is assigned a mission by M (Head of the British Secret Service); he travels to an overseas location where he meets friends and allies, and makes his first acquaintance with "the girl"; Bond gives first check to the villain, or the villain gives first check to Bond; Bond seduces the girl, or begins the process of doing so; Bond and the girl are captured by the villain, who tortures Bond; but Bond escapes, vanquishes the villain and possesses the girl (Eco, "Narrative" 52). This narrative structure can be seen, with minor variations, in most of the novels, including *Casino Royale*; *Live and Let Die*; *Diamonds Are Forever*; *From Russia, with Love*; *Dr. No*; *Goldfinger*; *Thunderball*; *On Her Majesty's Secret Service*; *You Only Live Twice*; and *The Man with the Golden Gun*. *Moonraker* is a partial and unusual exception in that it is set wholly in England and Bond does not possess the girl at the end.

Tony Bennett has modified Eco's reading of the Bond stories by analyzing them in terms of a set of narrative codes—the "sexist code", the "imperialist code", and the

14

"phallic code"—which regulate the relationships between characters. The imperialist code, for example, regulates the relations between Bond (British) and his allies (foreign), who are presented in subordinate roles, while the phallic code informs the relationships between Bond and M (who endows him with authority: his "licence to kill") and between Bond and the villain (who threatens Bond with castration through torture: literally so in the case of Le Chiffre in *Casino Royale*). The sexist code is posited on the notion that the girl is usually "out of place" either ideologically, in that she is in the service of the villain (as in *Live and Let Die*, *Diamonds Are Forever*, *From Russia, with Love*, *Thunderball* and *Goldfinger*), and/or sexually, in that she is either physically or emotionally "damaged", and is initially resistant to Bond (as in *Casino Royale*, *Diamonds Are Forever*, *Dr. No*, and *Goldfinger*). In this reading Bond's seduction of the girl serves an ideological purpose as he "repositions" her into the "correct" place: he seduces her away from the villain and/or restores her normative heterosexuality. As Bennett argues: "In thus replacing the girl in a subordinate position in relation to men, Bond simultaneously repositions her within the sphere of ideology in general, detaching her from the service of the villain and recruiting her in support of his own mission" ("James Bond as Popular Hero" 13). This interpretation of the gender relations of the books also explains why Bond does *not* sleep with Gala Brand in *Moonraker*: she is neither working for the villain (she is an undercover policewoman) nor is she emotionally damaged.

Yet to interpret the Bond Girls merely as passive and waiting to be "repositioned" by the dominant male hero does not entirely fit some of the stories. There are several occasions in the books when Fleming allows the girl a much greater degree of narrative agency. Indeed on several occasions it is the girl who comes to Bond's rescue. In *Diamonds Are Forever*, for example, it is Tiffany Case who effects their escape when she knows how to drive a railroad handcar. Domino Vitali saves Bond's life at the end of *Thunderball* when she shoots villain Largo with a spear gun. And in *On Her Majesty's Secret Service* Bond—physically exhausted, surrounded by enemies and at the end of his tether—is saved by the arrival of Tracy: "What a girl! [...] He had gathered enough strength, mostly from the girl, to have one more bash at them" (172). On other occasions the girl possesses superior knowledge that assists Bond in his mission. Honeychile Rider is able to escape the fate devised for her by the evil genius Dr. No—staked out as "white meat" for black crabs—on account of her knowledge of nature: "That man thought he knew everything. Silly old fool [...] The whole point is that they don't really like meat. They live mostly on plants and things" (*Dr. No* 220). Elsewhere the girl sometimes exercises her own narrative agency entirely independent of Bond. In the short story "For Your Eyes Only", Judy Havelock sets out to kill the gangsters responsible for her parents' murder. She rejects Bond's assertion that killing is "man's work": "You go to hell. And keep out of this. It was my mother and father they killed. Not yours" (*For Your Eyes Only* 67).

It may have been partly as a response to the criticisms of sexism levelled against his books that Fleming once tried to place the girl at the center of a Bond narrative. The ninth novel, *The Spy Who Loved Me,* is unusual in that it is written in the first person from the perspective of heroine Vivienne Michel and that James Bond enters only two-thirds of the way into the book. Eco excludes *The Spy Who Loved Me* from his analysis on the grounds that it "seems quite untypical" ("Narrative" 38). Yet the novel is part of the corpus of Bond texts and cannot be left aside simply because it does not conform to a particular theoretical framework. It would be fair to say that Fleming's attempt to present a woman's point-of-view is less than wholly successful. The book was not well received and Fleming never wrote another one like it (Lycett 401-2). Jeremy Black has suggested that *The Spy Who Loved Me* was more in the tradition of the so-called "kitchen sink" realism exemplified by John Braine's *Room at the Top* (which had been filmed to great acclaim in 1959) than the imperialist spy thriller (71-2). Fleming's account of how Vivienne loses her virginity at the back of a dingy cinema includes the sort of sordid detail that characterizes the social realist novels of the time. Nevertheless there is some evidence that Fleming was attempting to say something more serious about attitudes towards women in 1950s Britain. Vivienne's first sexual experience with her boyfriend Derek presents her not as the instigator but as a woman who has been exploited: "Now I couldn't refuse him! He would come back and it would be messy and horrible in this filthy little box in this filthy little back-street cinema and it was going to hurt and he would despise me afterwards for giving in" (*The Spy Who Loved Me* 28). The book is particularly notable for its unsympathetic representation of men. Vivienne's first boyfriend Derek is a wealthy public schoolboy who dumps her after having his way with her because his parents disapprove of her. Her second lover is a German called Kurt who makes her have an abortion when she becomes pregnant. While the first half of the book is successful in presenting Vivienne as a more rounded character than other Bond Girls, in the second half she resorts to type. Vivienne is running a motel in upstate New York when the owner sends two gangsters to burn it down as part of an insurance fraud. The two "hoods" are about to rape Vivienne when, miraculously, James Bond arrives. He immediately understands the situation, rescues Vivienne, kills the gangsters, makes love to her, and leaves in the morning. Vivienne constructs a romantic fantasy of Bond as a man who "had come from nowhere, like the prince in the fairy tales, and he had saved me from the dragon [...] And then, when the dragon was dead, he had taken me as his own reward" (*The Spy Who Loved Me* 147).

The Spy Who Loved Me should be seen as a flawed but genuine attempt to identify with the woman's point of view. However, it was bound by the extent of its difference from the other stories to remain a one-off experiment, hence its marginalization in most accounts of Fleming's stories. Yet in its own curious way it exemplifies the paradoxical nature of the gender politics of Fleming's Bond. On the one hand Fleming sought to present women as independent and in control of their own sexuality. The emphasis in his books on sexual freedom for both men *and* women can be seen as anticipating the emergence of the "permissive society" in the 1960s. This would be taken further in the James Bond films, which began in 1962. But on the other hand the perpetuation of gender stereotypes and the representation of women as sexualized objects means that the books are unable to explore the social consequences of this independence in a realistic way. Ultimately what the Bond books seem to suggest is that greater sexual freedom for women amounted to greater sexual opportunities for men. At their worst they pander to male fantasies that women are "easy" and willing sexual partners. This tension between the progressive and the conservative (in some cases even downright reactionary) is a constant feature of the books and it is this tension that makes them such fascinating cultural artefacts.

NOTES

1   Reference to the Penguin publication of the novels.
2   "Angry Young Men" was a term that gained currency in theatrical and literary circles following the production of John Osborne's *Look Back in Anger* in 1956 and referred to a group of dramatists and writers whose work was characterized by its broadly "anti-establishment" outlook.
3   The exceptions are *Goldfinger* and *On Her Majesty's Secret Service*, where Bond sleeps with two women.

CHAPTER 2

THE BOND GIRL WHO IS NOT THERE

The Tiffany Case

Boel Ulfsdotter

This chapter focuses on the problematic character design of Tiffany Case, James Bond's female companion in *Diamonds Are Forever* (novel, Ian Fleming 1956; film, Guy Hamilton 1971).[1] To date, there has been limited scholarly attention directed towards examining the conceptualization and representation of Case in the novel or film. It is my argument that Case is regularly passed over in academic works because her persona reflects a different agenda of feminine performativity than normally debated in contemporary Bond studies, including the Bond Girl discourse. My chapter aims to explore why Fleming's characterization of Case was found wanting when transposed from novel to screen in the early 1970s.

Tom Mankiewicz was hired to help rework Richard Maibaum's original script for *Diamonds Are Forever*. One factor that influenced his adaptation was the 15 years that separate the novel (1956) and the film (1971). During this time, Western countries had experienced significant social, cultural, and political changes including the widespread influence of second-wave feminism, which promoted gender equality in the family and workplace. However, (proto)feminist values had already been incorporated into the literary persona of Case, given Fleming's description of her as being a hardworking, independent, and single woman in the novel. This representation should have simplified her transposition from novel to film regardless of the impact of second-wave feminist discourse on the entertainment industry in the 1960s and 1970s. Instead, her character appears to be watered down by it and the question is why?

The Bond Girl concept did not exist prior to the establishment of the James Bond film franchise in the early 1960s; it was developed soon after into a recurring character type that became the object of Bond's gaze and affection, helping to confirm his masculinity and sexual virility. Broader changes to the social standing of women in the 1960s made it necessary to change the initial Bond Girl formula. Producers decided that a new type of female companion should be paired with Bond around the time when the script for *Diamonds Are Forever* was being developed (Chapman 123). Thus,

Case serves as a transitory figure as the series shifts from one Bond Girl concept to another, a situation that may have influenced the development of her screen persona.

FLEMING'S (TIFFANY) CASE

In his seminal analysis of the Bond novels, Umberto Eco notes that Fleming used stock characters based on a Manichean ideology of clear cut dichotomies like good/bad, hero/villain, and beautiful/ugly as a foundation for his literary technique ("Narrative" 45-7). This mythological structure resulted in a series of oppositional character relationships in the novels—Bond-M, Bond-Villain, Villain-Woman, and Woman-Bond (ibid. 36). According to Eco, the relationship between the Woman and Bond in the novels is based on five prerequisites: first, the girl is beautiful and good; second, she has been made frigid and unhappy by severe trials she suffered in adolescence; third, these experiences have conditioned her to the service of the Villain; fourth, through meeting Bond she appreciates her positive human chances; and fifth, Bond possesses her but in the end loses her (ibid. 44). According to Eco, all of Bond's relationships with women follow this pattern in Fleming's novels, including Case (ibid.).

The literary Case appears to deviate from Eco's expected criteria in all areas except for the first one. While Bond does not admire Case for her beauty or goodness, he is attracted to her "brazen sexiness" (44) and the reader is made aware that she is good looking. Interestingly, Case is characterized, above all else, as a woman of ambition and intelligence, and so while she meets the first criterion, her character extends well beyond it. In relation to the second criterion, there is an obvious discrepancy between Felix Leiter's melodramatic backstory of Case, including her gang rape and subsequent alcohol abuse, and the actual behavior of Case as well as her personal account of her own history. For instance, Leiter claims that Case is a recovering alcoholic and member of Alcoholics Anonymous, a claim that is contradicted by the depiction of Case ordering cocktails and drinking pink champagne with Bond. Fleming never mentions that Case has "fallen off the wagon" or is engaging in destructive behavior. Another poignant example occurs when Case whispers to Bond that she has "never what you'd call 'slept with a man' in my life" (265) in spite of Leiter stating the opposite (90-1). One explanation for these discrepancies resides in the fact that Case had lied during her previous dealings with the authorities and Leiter may have been fed false information. Given Fleming's overall characterization of Case, one is more likely to believe her first-person account than the details relayed by Leiter.

Case does not meet the expectations for the remaining criterion. She is not compelled by her past to work for the Villain; instead, she decides to work for the Spang brothers in order to improve her socioeconomic status. Fleming writes that after her first meeting with Bond, Case "thought to herself, with sudden angry despair, another damn crook. Couldn't she ever get away from them?" (52-3). She seems to be motivated by money and social mobility rather than by her jaded past. This leads into her subversion of the fourth criterion: Case is self-reliant as to her positive human chances. She does not associate her future plans with Bond until the end of the narrative when they have fallen in love and she learns his true identity. Contrary to Eco's fifth criterion, Bond does not lose Case in the end but instead brings her back to his flat in England (301-2). Hence Case is not the typical "Woman" featured in a Fleming novel given these discrepancies with Eco's matrix.

One feature that defines the Woman in the Bond novels is the use of a double entendre for her name (e.g. Pussy Galore), a phrase that can be understood in two different ways and traditionally helps to position her as an erotic object of Bond's gaze. The name of Tiffany Case is an exception to this tradition as it was not created to meet this sexist convention. Instead, Eco suggests that Case's name is primarily reflective of her vanity (Tiffany and vanity being anagrams)[2] and interest in beautiful things. Eco also writes that her name brings to mind "the beauty case of the mannequin" ("Narrative" 47), which is very fitting since Case is a diamond smuggler in need of different identities that a beauty box can provide. Given the depth of her characterization, however, she does not seem to be defined by her vanity. Instead, her name might actually be a false identity or persona (much like those used by Bond in various novels including *Diamonds Are Forever*), another lie that she perpetuates when communicating with the authorities. While Fleming does not suggest that her name is fake, he also does not correct any of the other discrepancies in the novel relating to her character. This might lead the reader to question the divergence between her name and her actual depiction in the novel.

In light of her desire to improve her socioeconomic status, Case can be included among the young, urban, post-war generation of the 1950s, which Michael Denning refers to as the self-made New Aristocrats (*Cover* 94-6). Placing Case alongside Bond in this respect helps to explain her Bond-like sensibility towards self-development and different expression of material culture. Denning also suggests that Fleming's novels should be read as narrative codes of tourism and pornography rather than imperialism and sexism, thus emphasizing Bond's "licence to look" rather than his "licence to kill" (ibid. 102). Bennett and Woollacott similarly observe that Bond is a key representative of a "licence to consume" (*Bond* 247), thus explaining his flair for conspicuous consumption and how "his style and expensive tastes identified him as a well-heeled bachelor with no strings" (150). This discussion of Bond's "licences" can also be applied to Case since she too is presented as a New Aristocrat.

As a female character, Case exercises the same rights to look and consume as Bond, as she has made her own future through consistently reinventing her persona. His most detailed description of Case consequently portrays her as both a style icon and a woman of means, which implicitly denotes willingness to move up socially through consumption:

She was dressed to go out except for her hat, a small black affair that swung from her free hand. She wore a smart black tailor-made over a deep olive-green shirt [sic] buttoned at the neck, golden-tan nylons and black, square-toed crocodile shoes that looked very expensive. There was a slim gold [Cartier] wrist-watch on a black strap at one wrist and a heavy gold chain bracelet at the other. One large baguette-cut diamond flared on the third finger of her right hand and a flat pearl ear-ring in twisted gold showed on her right ear where the heavy pale gold hair fell away from it. (46)

Fleming's characterization of Case through her clothing and accessories indicates that she, like Bond, is construed primarily through material tastes. While Case is never described from Bond's voyeuristic point of view, Bond does account for her appearance implicitly, thus neutralizing all blatant expressions of a male gaze. Fleming writes, "'And as for the frock,' Bond continued, 'it's a dream, and you know it is. I love black velvet, especially against a sunburnt skin, and I'm glad you don't wear too much jewellery, and I'm glad you don't paint your fingernails'" (97). From a narrative point of view, Bond's description of Case is altogether based on her exterior or material assets—her look, as it were—and lacks all signs of intimacy.

A similar detachment is apparent when Fleming describes the naked body of Case. His description of Bond seeing her "sitting, half-naked, astride a chair" with an arched spine is close to pornographic. Fleming writes, "The black string of her brassiere across the naked back, the tight black lace pants and the splay of her legs whipped at Bond's senses" (43). Fleming's use of this pornographic stereotype to introduce Case can either be understood as completely unwarranted and therefore an expression of mere voyeurism when related to her forthcoming performance in the narrative, or, the reader must admit that Case is a woman who is in complete control of her own integrity and therefore unwavering even if seen semi-naked by a complete stranger (Denning, *Cover* 109). In my view, Fleming's unwillingness to connect Case's material attributes more intimately to her person may be a result of the overall detached writing style of Fleming in *Diamonds Are Forever*. As a result, Fleming's literary remediation of Case and Bond are executed in exactly the same way.

Fleming's preoccupation with visual and material values results in a literary technique based on semiotic branding—describing well-known objects and everyday situations that are completely irrelevant to the narrative. Eco suggests that Fleming's "technique of the aimless glance" is the key to his literary style because it gives the reader an opportunity to identify with the story, instead of rejecting the entire narrative because of the excessive action scenes ("Narrative" 51-2). What Eco does not mention, however, is that Fleming's literary technique only has a male reader in mind, which explains Denning's suggestion of the presence of "a discourse of the spectacle" (*Cover* 104) in relation to Bond's female companions as a necessary secondary requisite.

Most of Fleming's descriptions of Case give the impression that she is in full control of her appearance when she interacts with Bond. There are, however, two passages in *Diamonds Are Forever* where Case becomes subject to a blatant discourse of visual spectacle. The first is a scene situated at "The Tiara" nightclub where she works at the blackjack table dressed in a "smart Western outfit in grey and black—short grey skirt with a wide black metal-studded belt, grey blouse with a black handkerchief round the neck, a grey sombrero hanging down the back by a black cord, black half-Wellingtons over flesh-coloured nylons" (189-90). The second involves Case dressed up in a Western costume while in the company of a gangster boss in his Western town mock-up. Bond notices that it makes her look "like something out of *Annie Get Your Gun*" (219) and the reference to a staged musical show confirms Denning's idea of the spectacular view and the woman as spectacle in Fleming's narrative construct (*Cover* 104). On both these occasions, Case has been commanded to wear a certain costume in order for her "to-be-looked-at-ness" (Mulvey, "Visual" 835) to please the villain above all else and that this takes place without her approval. The rest of the time, Fleming presents Case a self-reliant woman of the 1950s through her own choice of clothes and attitude towards individual prosperity.

THE SCREEN CASE

As a New Aristocrat, the literary Case reflects the "affluence, fashion [and] modernity" of the 1950s (Denning, *Cover* 96). This might be one reason why screenwriter Tom Mankiewicz felt it was necessary to update, and in some ways, reinvent the character for the film adaption being produced 15 years later. Andrew Sarris argues that the success of the film adaptation resides in its "cockily contemporaneous screenplay" (79) and acknowledges the extent to which Mankiewicz updated and revised Fleming's novel. While Sarris mentions the allusion to Howard Hughes and the Cold War rhetoric featured in the dialogue, he does not discuss the adaptation of Case or her role in the film.

Similar to her literary counterpart, the filmic Case is a self-made, professional diamond smuggler who is on par with Bond in her fondness for all forms of material culture. However, the film begins to diverge from the novel in terms of Case's image. When Case is introduced, she is seen wearing wigs of different lengths and colors. The Women featured in Fleming's novels were typically presented with blonde or dark brown/black hair with no intermediary shades (Amis 55). Funnell notes that Bond Girls appearing in the first decade of the film series adhered to these color expectations. When the franchise shifted its representation of Bond Girls in the 1970s, they also adjusted the imaging conventions. Funnell notes that Case appears in the same scene wearing a blonde and brown wig, before emerging with her natural red hair. She writes: "this play on hair color is intentional, ironic and self-reflective. By physically embodying and subsequently poking fun at the conventions restricting the appearance of English Bond Girls, the American Bond Girl of the "future" frees herself from the set expectations of Ian Fleming's novels transposed to the film series" ("From English" 72). Thus, the image of Case, as noted by Funnell, plays a key role in understanding her character. While conforming to a new Bond Girl formula, the filmic Case is also distanced from the literary character, who appears blond in the novel.

The struggle to develop the screen persona of Case is also reflected in the difficult strategy of having her "film costumes conform to notions of realism but also [their] need to employ notions of cinematic spectacle" (Street, *Costume* 9). All of the costumes for Case were designed by Donfeld (aka Don Feld, 1934-2007) whose key characteristic as costume designer was an aim for a contemporary ready-to-wear look. And yet, Donfeld also infused some of Case's costumes with a more spectacular look that reflects the influx of French haute couture and especially Yves Saint Laurent's Rive Gauche label. It seems that Donfeld, like many other costume designers, was deeply impressed by Saint Laurent's controversial fashion collection in 1968, which announced that the modern woman's wardrobe should be based around a trouser suit and a black, transparent evening dress (Drake 62-3). Donfeld's fashionable outfits for Case confirm the difficult dichotomy of film costume inspired by haute couture fashion in that the "creation of clothes as spectacle is the prerogative of the couturier; the overriding ethos of the costume designer is conversely to fabricate clothes which serve the purpose of the narrative" (Bruzzi 3). Donfeld's choice of iconic designs for the outfits worn by both Case and Bond in the honeymoon suite sequence of *Diamonds Are Forever* are exemplary of this binary purpose. In view of Eco's remark that Fleming used his "technique of the aimless glance" to punctuate the narrative unfolding (*The Role* 166), Bruzzi writes that iconic clothes have "an independent, prior meaning; they function as interjections or disruptions of the normative reality of the text" (18). This statement echoes Denning's notion of a discourse of the spectacle, and relates directly to the up-beat chic and theatrical excess that characterize the costuming of Case in *Diamonds Are Forever*. Although the transposition of Case to film resulted in an ambivalent design of her character, Donfeld's costuming serves the film's narrative demands and responds to the audience's expectations of spectacle. While emphasizing her free agency as a woman in professional life, these costumes cannot prevent the film from further diluting the narrative agency of her character.

Case's most memorable costumes include a white three-piece trouser suit and a variety of lingerie and bathing suits. Both garment groups and their performativity belong to the most important markers of liberated female fashion during the late twentieth century, since they became hallmarks of Yves Saint Laurent's Rive Gauche label (Drake 63). In the late 1960s and early 1970s, the trouser suit was still an ideological statement in the modern woman's wardrobe, confirmed by Saint Laurent's comment that it was the new epitome of "a practical, modern, easy world" (Drake 63). Key female celebrities like Bianca Jagger, Jerry Hall, and Yoko Ono had just started wearing them so the appearance of Case in a white trouser suit came as no surprise. White was also a central color during the 1970s, as intimated in the scene in which Case appears on the white chaise longue in the bridal suite of Howard Hughes' hotel. The scene connotes a nostalgic return to the Art Déco-inspired black-and-white visions of the 1930s musical films such as *Top Hat* (Mark Sandrich 1935), which featured extravagant costumes worn by Fred Astaire and Ginger Rogers. The underlying iconographical references to a newlywed couple are fully endorsed by Case's extravagant dress, and Bond sporting his hallmark black tuxedo. This scene is thus in tune with the overall amorous mood of Fleming's novel.

The costuming of Case in lingerie and a bikini relates to a far more complicated dress code since it serves two purposes. The first is voyeuristic as it places her body on display and attracts the attention of male onlookers (both on and off the screen). The second is indicated by their implicit statements in relation to the film narrative and their correlation to the aforementioned pseudo-pornographic scenes in the novel. Early in the film, Case has just come back to her flat when Bond, under the pretext of being her new smuggling partner, rings her doorbell. She invites him into her salon and then immediately proceeds to the bedroom. On her return into the frame, Case is dressed in champagne colored underwear and a transparent negligée. This outfit is worn with a brown wig, altogether changing her earlier appearance as a blond. Given the implications underpinning her image, it takes a minute for the audience to realize that Case is *not* wearing this particular outfit because she intends to lure Bond into the bedroom, an important signal of her unique standing in the narrative since the audience would be expecting this to happen given that *Diamonds Are Forever* is a Bond film after all. On the contrary, Case remains in control of her identity and her costuming becomes nothing less than a statement of power. She willfully turns herself into an object for the male gaze (Mulvey, "Visual" 837) and engages in a masquerade of femininity (Doane, *Femmes* 25) in order conceal the fact that she is actually the boss of the visiting smuggler.

Her body language and performativity firmly superimpose her screen persona onto the 1970s view of the liberated woman's social status and tastes in fashion. This would seem to indicate that Case was designed to come across as the leading female character through her costuming and narrative agency. This suggestion is confirmed by the extreme backlash she receives when she is kidnapped and not in control of her standing in the film. She is turned into an object of the male gaze by Blofeld, who forces her to wear a small bikini despite the fact that she is involved in an action sequence. This works to limit her narrative agency since she can do little to help Bond fight the bad guys wearing such a skimpy outfit. What is interesting about this sequence is that a costume very similar to Case's own tour de force (the underwear/negligée combo) now connotes her own state of powerlessness.

TIFFANY CASE VS. THE BOND GIRL MOLD

In her discussion of the Bond Girl typology, Lisa Funnell argues that "the image of the Bond Girl strongly adhered to the character template outlined by Ian Fleming in the James Bond novels" ("Negotiating" 201). Her discussion is quite similar to the one proposed by Eco in relation to the novels. Much like her novel counterpart, the filmic Case departs from the traditional Bond Girl mold. I would argue that Case's reduced performativity on screen is directly related to the film's offering of a supplementary image of femininity in order to meet audience expectations for the Bond Girl.

The character Plenty O'Toole was added to the film script for *Diamonds Are Forever* by Mankiewicz. Although Case is the only female character in the novel, Mankiewicz extrapolated and developed O'Toole from the so called casino 'shills' described by Fleming as attractive girls in tantalizing evening gowns who had "been given fifty dollars [by the management...] to warm up the dead tables" (189). O'Toole thus conforms to Fleming's manifold images of casino girls given that these women "have always been constructed primarily in terms of male desire and pleasure" (Bennett and Woollacott, *Bond* 193) and many have served as "peripheral romantic interest[s]" for Bond (Bold 171).

As expected, O'Toole runs into Bond at the casino, his defining locale in the novels and films. Since his encounter with Sylvia Trench in the first Bond film *Dr. No* (Terence Young 1962), Bond has met with (and picked up) potential Bond Girls at the casino like Domino Derval (Claudine Auger) in *Thunderball* (Terence Young 1965) and Tracy di Vicenzo (Diana Rigg) in *On Her Majesty's Secret Service* (Peter Hunt 1969). Unlike these other women, O'Toole adds neither escort nor mystery to the film, and I would argue that O'Toole was invented merely as an erotic object for the male gaze. Her mission is clearly expressed when she leans across the gambling table and offers to help Bond win the game. She introduces herself as Plenty O'Toole, a double entendre name that can easily be made out as *plenty of tool*. Bond's cynical answer, "Of course you are!" is meant to further emphasize the literary and sexist pun while confirming her limited importance to the narrative.

The second scene that identifies O'Toole as a deeply confusing romantic intermezzo is her ensuing dinner at a fancy restaurant with Bond. These intimate scenes occur frequently in both the novels and films, and normally represent a step further towards to the bedroom. However, this particular scene was scrapped by the production team behind *Diamonds Are Forever*, possibly because it complicated the underlying love affair between Bond and Case. So, instead of being seduced by him, she gets thrown out the window of Bond's hotel room by the hoodlums waiting for Bond. Although she survives the fall by landing in the swimming pool below her window, her hasty demise from view confirms her insignificance to Bond and the narrative at large. Still,

O'Toole made her appearance on the screen and performed her to-be-looked-at-ness according to the ordinary Bond regime of appetizer and sex object, and ultimately ends up being disposable. The appearance of O'Toole as a "peripheral romantic interest" and voyeuristic spectacle has the potential to create confusion as the audience might begin to question which woman constitutes the traditional Bond Girl.

Mankiewicz' voyeuristic intentions with O'Toole are bluntly displayed in the casino scene especially when compared to Case's action-oriented behavior. Although the casino is generally presented in the Bond franchise as a male arena of latent sexual and fetishist interplay, both women decidedly step out of it for professional reasons. The difference in narrative agency between the women is signaled through their costumes. While Case is dressed in a three-piece trouser suit, an image that indicates a professional motivation, O'Toole is wearing an evening gown complete with luxurious jewelry and a décolletage that leaves little to the imagination, as she is obviously waiting to be picked up. The difference in their images relates directly to their positioning in the narrative, with Case stating her importance from the very beginning of the film. I therefore suggest that Mankiewicz's decision to have O'Toole 'double' as the "Bond Girl" in *Diamonds Are Forever* effectively works to dilute the character frame of Case.

CONCLUSION

The addition of O'Toole to the film has resulted in Case's more ambivalent screen persona and subsequent oversight in the discussions of the Bond franchise. The literary Case was already an anomaly given that she does not fulfil the prerequisites for the Woman according to Umberto Eco's matrix. Instead, she seems to be presented as a mirror reflection of Bond, given Fleming's ambition to have them represent the same consumerist ideal as image producers of a new, affluent post-war aristocracy through material culture. These aspirations are indicated mainly through material assets and artefacts that add to the credibility of Case's capability to survive, which Fleming accentuates by having her repeatedly reinventing her persona through different identity regimes and showing off her economic ability to consume. Unfortunately, these "Bondian" characteristics of the literary Case were a cause for concern when the novel was adapted into a film. As a result, Mankiewicz introduced a second female character into the narrative despite Case's visual excess, pronounced female agenda through costuming, and self-reliant performativity, which all clearly indicate that she could have played O'Toole's part as well. The ambivalence caused by O'Toole is further confirmed by the production team's decision to scrap the amorous scenes between her and Bond. It is therefore O'Toole that heavily reduces the overall credibility of the filmic Case and prevents her from becoming the film's Bond Girl proper. The literary Case was set against the franchise's initial Bond Girl formula and found wanting.

Perhaps Fleming's most Bondian female character has not yet been given the opportunity to firmly change the Bond Girl template.

NOTES

1 Reference to the Vintage Books publication of the novel.
2 The letters V and F have been interchangeable in European language for hundreds of years and belong to the same group of phonemes when articulated.

CHAPTER 3

JAMES BOND AND FEMALE AUTHORITY

The Female M in the Bond Novels and Films

Jim Leach

In this chapter, I will examine the introduction of a female head of the British secret service and its implications for the Bond phenomenon. My main concern will be with the tenure of Judi Dench as M in seven films from 1995 to 2012, but, in order to discuss her performance in context, I will first examine the representation of the male M in the earlier novels and films, as well as that of the female M who appeared shortly afterwards in the continuing novel series. Any assessment of Dench's M must attend to the interaction of the actor's persona and performance with the apparent ideological projects of the films in which she appears. By exploring the continuities and differences between her character, the former male M, and the female M of the novels, I will argue that the presence of a female M disrupts the basic formula of the series and that the extent of this disruption is not just a question of her gender but also of political and technological developments in the world in which she exercises her authority.

THE BOND-M RELATIONSHIP

Most of the components of the Bond formula were already in place in Ian Fleming's first novel, *Casino Royale* (1953).[1] These include the characters with whom the secret agent interacts inside his home base before and during his missions: M, the head of the British secret service who gives Bond his missions; his personal assistant, Miss Moneypenny, with whom Bond flirts on his way in and out of M's office; and Q, the quartermaster, who equips Bond with the weapons and gadgets he needs in each adventure. Their presence in the novels and films creates a sense of stability in contrast to the exotic, dangerous, and usually foreign settings in which Bond carries out his missions. In the films, they were embodied by actors who became firmly associated with the characters for many years: Bernard Lee appeared as M until his death in 1981, Lois Maxwell was Miss Moneypenny until 1985, and Desmond Llewellyn continued as Q until 1999.

According to Umberto Eco's structural analysis of Fleming's novels, the Bond-M relationship is one of "a series of oppositions which allow a limited number of permutations and interactions" (*The Role* 147). Its meaning depends on other oppositions, notably between Bond and the Villain and Bond and the Woman, but, for the purposes of this chapter, I will focus mainly on the effects of introducing a female M into this structure.

In Fleming's novels and the early Bond films, the depiction of M's patriarchal middle-aged masculinity is clearly a conservative strategy at a time when all forms of authority were beginning to be called into question in post-war Britain and other Western countries. However, while M serves to anchor the texts as representations of traditional and imperial values, far more attention is paid to Bond's less inhibited youthful masculinity, especially his relations with women and his frequent disregard of official channels during his missions. Although Eco describes it as a "love-hate" relationship (148), it is always clear that Bond respects M and that M recognizes that Bond's unorthodox methods get results. This basic structure was carried over into the films in which M, as played by Lee and then by Robert Brown, was in effect a "straight man" to Sean Connery and the other actors who embodied Bond.

Understandably, M was often seen as a father-figure to Bond (Antony and Friedman 60; Bennett and Woollacott, *Bond* 131), and yet M's function within the formula is not quite as stable as this would suggest. M was apparently Fleming's code name for his mother (Richler 346), and, in Fleming's novel *Diamonds Are Forever* (1956), Bond tells Tiffany Case that their relationship cannot be permanent because he is "almost married already" to a man whose "name begins with M" (163). The older man's attitude to the newer type of masculinity represented by Bond is also highly ambivalent: in *From Russia, with Love* (1957), Fleming explains that M "disapproved of Bond's 'womanizing'" but also recognized that "his prejudice was the relic of a Victorian upbringing" (84-5).

M thus represents a type of masculinity associated with the old British Empire and most recently embodied in the figure of Winston Churchill. While Bond shared with M a background in the wartime navy, his appeal stemmed from a fusion of traits derived from the traditional image of the British gentleman with those of a more modern type of masculinity, attuned to the emerging consumer and youth cultures, which led to comparisons with John F. Kennedy, who indeed admired the Bond books and once invited Fleming to a dinner at his home (Willman, "The Kennedys" 178). The relationship between the two male characters thus embodies "the tension between the old and the new" that has always been central to the Bond phenomenon (Leach, "The Spymaster" 226).

"THE NEW M'S A WOMAN":
INTRODUCING THE FEMALE M

In 1985, when the production team decided that she was too old to make Miss Moneypenny's flirtations with Bond convincing, Lois Maxwell suggested that she should be allowed to play M instead, but "the idea was rejected on the grounds that the public would not accept a female in the role" (Pfeiffer and Worrell 147). Ten years later, the producers thought the public was ready, and Judi Dench made her debut as M in *GoldenEye* (Martin Campbell 1995), which was also the first film for Pierce Brosnan as Bond. There was speculation about how the introduction of a female M would affect the successful formula, but Dench's performance was much admired, and she continued in the role for six additional films until her character's death in *Skyfall* (Sam Mendes 2012), which ends with the installation of a new male M.

Shortly after the introduction of Dench, the novel series followed suit. Fleming died in 1964, but Bond novels continued to appear, more or less independent from the film series (apart from novelizations based on the film scripts). The most prolific contributors were John Gardner, who wrote 14 novels between 1981 and 1996, and Raymond Benson, who wrote six between 1997 and 2002. At the end of Gardner's *COLD* (1996), Bond learns that "M's retired, and the new M's a woman" (275), and she first appears in *Zero Minus Ten* (1997), the first novel written by Benson, who has explained that he was directed to "make the character of M a woman (to stay in synchronization with the current Pierce Brosnan/Judi Dench films)" ("Introduction" vii). However, although they are about the same age, the new M in the novels is different in many ways from her cinematic counterpart. Through passing comments, it is revealed that Dench's M is married with a family (that never appears onscreen), and by *Skyfall* we learn that she is now a widow. Her name, which is not revealed until after her death, is Olivia Mansfield. In the novels, M's name is Barbara Mawdsley, and she is a divorcee.

Just as the Bond phenomenon has always managed to accommodate itself to the political upheavals of the past 60 years, the introduction of a female M can be seen as a belated attempt to adjust to the changes in gender roles and representations that had occurred during this period. If so, critics and scholars have been divided about the franchise's success in achieving this goal, with some agreeing that "changing attitudes towards women were reflected in the casting of Judi Dench as a feminist 'M'" (Street, "Contemporary" 185-7), and others pointing out that the female M's "feminine sympathies" often prove to be "a liability" (Woodward 184). Although the novels have not received as much critical attention, Benson's depiction of the female M raises similar questions about its ideological implications.

Of course, Britain has had a female head of state ever since Bond first came on the scene, but it was the appointment of Stella Rimington as Director General of MI5 in

1992 that apparently convinced the producers of the film series that a female M would seem credible to audiences. However, the woman most prominently in their minds would have been Margaret Thatcher, Britain's first, and still only, woman Prime Minister (1979-90). Thatcher's determination to make Britain great again echoed the nationalist wish-fulfillment fantasy in the Bond texts, which depict Britain as the dominant partner in the "special relationship" with the US. However, her reputation as the "iron lady," implementing economic policies that caused widespread unemployment and promoting traditional family values, suggested that her goal was to reinstate, rather than question, old patriarchal values, as did her frequent admiring references to Churchill, especially during the Falklands War (1982).

During the 1980s, Bond's commander in chief, to whom M reported, would thus have been a woman, but this was addressed only once in the film series, at the end of *For Your Eyes Only* (John Glen 1981), when Thatcher (impersonated by Janet Brown) appears on a television monitor to congratulate Bond on the success of his mission while he is making love to his latest conquest. This caricature left open the question of how Thatcher fits into the ideological coordinates of the Bond phenomenon, but the novel series suggests that Bond sympathizes with her political views. In Gardner's 1990 novel *Win, Lose or Die*, Bond is in charge of security arrangements when Thatcher visits a battleship, and he clearly knows and admires her. She acknowledges that they are "old friends" and that he was "instrumental in saving not only my life, but that of ex-President Reagan, some time ago" (162). Although Thatcher was no longer in power when Dench became M, her controversial legacy would inevitably color perceptions of M as a female authority figure in both the films and novels.

In the novels, unlike the films, there is no need to adjust to new actors taking over as Bond. Although the novelists may choose to emphasize different aspects of the character, he remains, even more so than in the films, an "ageless and timeless 'mobile signifier'" (Scheibel 28). Similarly, the assumption, in both the novels and the films, is that the same male M occupied the position for over 30 years, until his retirement and replacement by an obviously different character. The films never mention what happened to the old M, but, in the novels, the new M must prove herself despite the continued presence of the old M, with whom Bond remains "close friends" (Benson *Zero* 26). This information is relayed by the omniscient narrator who, through the use of "free indirect style," also provides access to "the subjective thoughts and feelings" of characters (Macey 141), and in this case, mainly from Bond's perspective.

Thus, before M gives Bond his assignment in *Zero Minus Ten*, the reader is told that "he wasn't even sure if he liked her, but he respected her," and that, when she calls him a "chauvinist," he "didn't hold it against her because, for one thing, she was right" (27). They settle into a steady, if uneasy, professional relationship, much like that of Bond and the male M, and neither Bond nor the narrator ever questions her authority on the basis of her gender. The only time her femininity becomes an issue is in Benson's second novel, *The Facts of Death* (1998). After it is revealed that the new M is "more vocal than her predecessor had been in criticizing Bond's womanizing and sometimes unorthodox methods" (21), she turns up at a party given by the old M in "a formal black evening gown that was low-cut in a V, revealing more of their boss than anyone at the office had ever seen" (35). She is with a man, and Bond has to get over the shock of "realizing M had a sex life" (38), and he is even more disturbed when he begins to suspect that her lover is a traitor. As it turns out, Bond is wrong, but the man is being blackmailed because of his criminal past. After he is murdered, M is distraught not only at her loss but also at her poor judgment, and Bond empathizes with her because he knows what it is like "when a lover betrayed everything you stood for and believed in" (242).

M's affair temporarily complicates the Bond-M relationship by pushing her character into the unstable territory usually occupied by Bond, and Benson underlines this shift through a sub-plot in which Bond becomes involved in an affair with Helen Marksbury, his personal assistant, who, in the next novel, is blackmailed into helping the villains. At the end of *The Facts of Death* Bond comes to think that M is "beginning to act like old Sir Miles after all" (289), and, in Benson's later novels, she reverts mainly to the basic functions of sending Bond on his missions and calling him to task when he disobeys orders. In the novels published since Benson's last in 2002, M is once again male, with no mention of what happened to Barbara Mawdsley, and it is as if the female M never happened.

"A WOMAN IN A MAN'S PROFESSION": ASSESSING JUDI DENCH'S M

In the film series, the casting of Dench, whose background was mainly in theater and television, helped to make her a film star with the stature to embody the regal authority of Queen Victoria in *Mrs. Brown* (John Madden 1997) and Elizabeth I in *Shakespeare in Love* (John Madden 1998). With the evolution of her star persona, M becomes a greater focus of attention than her predecessor, with the result that she is sometimes drawn into the main action, requiring Bond to rescue her. Like the female M of the novels, she becomes a much less stable element in the Bond-M relationship than the male M was, and the pressures of the narratives in which she becomes involved ensure that Dench's M behaves somewhat differently from film to film. For those who felt that the films offered a negative depiction of female authority, these inconsistencies result in "a schizophrenic character whose shifting values are another sign of her incompetence" (McNeely, "The Feminization" 160).

Instead of two kinds of masculinity, old and new, facing each other, the meetings between Bond and the new M place his athletic and seductive masculinity opposite "a woman in a man's profession," to quote Dench's Queen Elizabeth. All the other positions of authority—in the secret service, the military, and the government—are occupied by men, and M's diminutive stature makes her seem vulnerable in this environment. Dench responds by heightening the intensity and determination that were already part of her stage and television persona, and, when she denounces Bond as "a sexist misogynist dinosaur" in *GoldenEye*, the old M's "Victorian values" become a statement of feminist principles, and it is Bond who now represents the past rather than M.

The characterization of M was further complicated when the producers decided to replace Brosnan with Daniel Craig, so that in her last three films Dench was interacting with a very different Bond. While Brosnan's Bond was often compared to Sean Connery's, and has a similar sophisticated urbanity, Craig's Bond is much more crudely physical. As with the response to the depiction of a female M in general, critical response to the effects of this change on the representation of M was much divided. On the one hand were those who felt that, while "feminist ideals became accepted as the norm in the Brosnan films," the Craig films took "the Bond universe a step backwards," making M one of many women who "had their agency stripped away from them by the end of the film" (Amacker and Moore 154, 150). On the other hand, Tom McNeely, who stressed M's incompetence in the Brosnan films, asserted, "The relationship between the new Bond and the female M places more real power in the hands of M" ("The Feminization" 160). I would question both of these claims, which downplay the contradictions at work in both sets of films, but, since Dench was the only regular actor carried over into the Craig films, a comparison of her interactions with Brosnan and Craig in each actor's debut films will bring out some of the implications of the change for her character.

In her first appearance in *GoldenEye*, Dench's M performs the usual function of giving Bond his assignment. Her evident hostility toward Bond is clearly that of a woman asserting her authority in a virtually all-male environment. She has just overheard Tanner, her chief of staff, refer to her as "the evil queen of numbers," referring to her reliance on statistics and her concern to cut budgets. After denouncing Bond for his sexism and "cavalier attitude to life," she objects to his reliance on his "instincts" and warns him not to think she "doesn't have the balls to send a man to his death." The film thus undercuts traditional gender stereotypes, but it remains unclear to what extent the tension between them is due to her gender or to her methods. Brosnan's Bond adopts a coolly ironic attitude in the face of M's attacks, leaving the viewer to infer what he is actually thinking, but M does soften somewhat as he leaves, telling him to "come back alive."

Craig's Bond was introduced in *Casino Royale* (Martin Campbell 2006), based on the first Bond novel, which had been filmed only in a parodic version that stands outside the official canon. The film loosely adapts the novel's plot, which is presented as Bond's first outing as an agent with a license to kill, but the story is moved forward into the present, and Dench continues in the role of M, creating a temporal paradox that raised questions about whether this is still the same character or a "new woman" (Amacker and Moore 149). As in *GoldenEye*, the pre-credits sequence establishes the new Bond as an action hero, but the emphasis is on his physical endurance rather than the nonchalant poise of the Brosnan Bond. When he shoots an unarmed suspect in a foreign embassy, he creates a diplomatic incident that leaves M wondering if she has promoted him too soon. The film omits the usual scene in which M gives Bond his assignment, and the first time they meet onscreen is when he breaks into her house and uses a sophisticated program on her computer to trace a code word used by the villain to a club in the Bahamas. When she finds him there, she calls his intrusion a "bloody cheek" and denounces him as a "blunt instrument." She tells him, "I have to know if I can trust you and that you know who to trust." Treating him like a wayward son, she warns him not to break into her house again, to which he responds with a blank look and a curt, "Ma'am."

This sequence brings out the extent to which the Bond formula has been destabilized, with Bond's actions so far threatening to push him into the territory of the Villain in Eco's model. It also articulates the problems of trust associated with the rise of international terrorism, which are linked in the films to technological developments that erode the boundaries between public and private space. Whereas, in Benson's *High Time to Kill*, the old M is described as having been "computer illiterate" and reluctant to approve "funding to update technology at MI6" (46), new communications technologies are prominent in the latest films, and increasingly affect the relations of Dench's M with the activities of Bond in the field. Of course, the emphasis on these issues is not unique to the Bond films, since they are very much signs of the times, but the issue of trust, and its relation to the impact of new technology, complicated the adjustments that had to be made to accommodate the new M.

The mutual distrust between M and Bond disappears completely in Dench's second film, *Tomorrow Never Dies* (Roger Spottiswoode 1997), in which she stands up to her male superiors in the military and government and allows Bond to follow his instincts in search of evidence to expose the plot of a media mogul who uses satellite technology in an attempt to provoke World War III. However, when she follows her own instincts in *The World is Not Enough* (Michael Apted 1999), *Die Another Day* (Lee Tamahori 2002), and *Casino Royale* by trusting younger women, they betray her trust. Yet deceptive appearances are everywhere in these films, and in *Die Another Day* and *Quantum of Solace* (Marc Forster 2008), apparently public-spirited businessmen turn out to be the villains, and in the latter film the CIA is actively helping the villain. In *GoldenEye* and *Skyfall*, the villains are former British agents.

The extent to which M's misjudgments undermine her position as an authority figure will depend on how viewers respond to Dench's performance in the context of the films' narratives. In an apparent reversion to the gender stereotypes called into question in *GoldenEye*, the new M becomes vulnerable because she follows her instincts (as she had earlier blamed Bond for doing), but Dench's performance suggests M is struggling to balance authority and humanity in a complex world in which traditional moral values no longer operate. In *Skyfall*, she appears before a parliamentary committee and tells them, "The world is not more transparent now, it's more opaque" and points out that "we" do not know our enemies because "they" are not nations but individuals. Of course, the individual villain, working for his own ends rather than for any nation, has long been a staple of the Bond films, but the effect here is to suggest that international terrorism is a phenomenon that makes the world in which M operates an even more unstable one than the Cold War environment in which the old M exercised his authority.

M's argument that the modern world is not more "transparent" is an implicit rejection of the idea that new surveillance technology can control the threat of terrorism. This technology, which has become an increasingly familiar presence in everyday life as well as in the world of espionage, is associated with the new M from the beginning. When she first appears in *GoldenEye*, Bond and Tanner are watching a large video screen showing satellite images of a remote part of Russia. At the beginning of *Tomorrow Never Dies*, a caption introduces "A Terrorist Arms Bazaar on the Russian Border" that, we soon discover, Bond is filming and transmitting to MI6 headquarters in London, where it is watched by M and a group of her staff and military officers. These surveillance images provide useful information, but they soon give way to the richer cinematic experience that allows the viewer to become involved with Bond's activities in the field.

However, the evolution of digital media technology in the new millennium means that it increasingly infiltrates the cinematic experience. Alongside the shift from celluloid to digital projection, digital readouts are now often juxtaposed with, or superimposed on, the film images. The emphasis on virtual reality tends to create a sense of disembodiment, an effect that the films try to counter with the graphic violence of torture sequences like those in *Die Another Day* and *Casino Royale*, which insist on the physically real suffering to which Bond is subjected. As M discovers, however, while the new technology allows her to view the action from a distance, it also breaks down the distinction between home base and field of action that had been central to the Bond formula. She is now able to intervene more directly in Bond's missions, as she does in the opening sequence of *Skyfall* in which she relays instructions from London to Bond and a female agent during an elaborate chase sequence through the streets of Istanbul. But the reverse is also true since the action can also invade the previously secure world from which M operates, as it does to catastrophic effect in *Skyfall*.

In Dench's last film as M, both the villain and the new Q (played by Ben Whishaw as a computer nerd) boast that they can cause more destruction with their computers than Bond can in the field. When M's computer is hacked and her office bombed, Bond tries to save her by proving his continued relevance as a field operative in this new hi-tech environment. M has lost the trust of her superiors, and Bond takes her to his childhood home (after which the film is named) to escape from the city and its surveillance cameras. When the terrorists track them down, M is, in effect, drawn into the territory of Eco's Woman (or Bond Girl), helping him to defeat the enemy in a spectacular battle and losing her life in doing so.

In *GoldenEye* M called Bond "a relic of the Cold War," but the complexities caused by his mistakes at the beginning of *Casino Royale* prompt her to declare, "Christ, I miss the Cold War." The films effectively endorse the pleasures of nostalgia by stressing that surveillance technology complicates the issues as much as it clarifies them. Nostalgia is also invoked at the end of *Skyfall*, when Gareth Mallory who, as Chairman of the Intelligence and Security Committee, was one of the female M's fiercest critics, replaces her as M. As his administrative assistant, he hires the young female agent whose shot almost killed Bond, and for the first time we learn that her name is Eve Moneypenny. It is not clear whether she is related to the old Moneypenny, who has not appeared in the Craig films, but, much like the novel series, the new arrangements represent a self-conscious return to the home base situation that existed before the female M took over. The implications of this apparent regression remain to be seen, but the effects will probably prove to be as complicated and contradictory as those associated with Dench's tenure as M.

CONCLUSION

The relationships defined in Eco's model were never as stable in the films as they were (perhaps) in Fleming's novels. The function of the Woman, for example, was split between two (or more) Bond Girls in each film, with one of them sometimes working for the Villain. In the recent films, the Bond-Woman relationship has come under pressure but has changed only superficially, with the women becoming more active in furthering the plot, and, similarly, the reworking of Bond with different actors does not really affect his function as a dashing and resourceful male. However, in the films, Bond frequently becomes, in his quieter moments, the object of the gaze in a way that is more conventionally associated with the Woman, and Lisa Funnell has suggested that in *Casino Royale* this tendency is heightened to the point that "Craig is presented [...] through iconography associated with the Bond Girl and *not* James Bond" ("I Know" 467). It is arguable, however, that the introduction of a female M has had the most destabilizing effect on the Bond formula.

While this effect is also apparent in the novels, it is intensified in the films by the ways in which specific actors inflect the Bond-M relationship. Whereas the Dench-Brosnan relationship was one in which trust cannot be taken for granted (as it usually was with the male M), the Dench-Craig interactions often evoke a mother-son relationship that refers back to, and partially subverts, the original relationship between Bond and the male M. Craig has stated adamantly, "She's his mum" ("Daniel Craig" 15), although Bond qualifies this in *Quantum of Solace* by saying, "She likes to think she is." Yet, if Fleming's Bond felt that he was "almost married" to the male M, the virtual transformation of the female M from mother-figure to Bond Girl in *Skyfall* underlines the perversity that was always present in the supposedly stable relationships that support the Bond formula.

NOTE

1   Reference to the Penguin publication of the novels.

Section 2

DESIRING THE OTHER

CHAPTER 4

DESIRING THE SOVIET WOMAN

Tatiana Romanova and *From Russia, with Love*

Thomas M. Barrett

Tatiana Romanova, the "Bond Girl" in *From Russia, with Love* (novel, 1957; film, Terence Young 1963),[1] holds a crucial position in the western re-visioning of Soviet and Russian women. The story tells of a plot in which the beautiful Romanova, who has a decoding machine in her possession, lures Bond onto the Orient Express where he will be assassinated. Bond prevails over this and a second attempt to kill him and, after much lovemaking, Romanova falls for the British spy and follows him to the West. What gave *From Russia, with Love* its charge was its emergence amidst a shifting discursive terrain when the Soviet Union began to open to the West and Soviet women were discovered, through travel accounts and magazine reportage, as objects of desire. By escorting Romanova to the West, Bond enacts a contemporary conversion fantasy that makes Soviet women ripe for Western consumption.

Umberto Eco has stressed the Manichean, binary nature of the Fleming novels, with a world "made up of good and evil forces in conflict" (*The Role* 162). In *From Russia, with Love*, this plays out on an extremely liminal terrain, one that supports Romanova's crossing of thresholds. First, she is framed in the narrative by all sorts of inside/Western Others, including gypsies, Turks, half-Turks, Bulgarians, and a half-Irishman. These figures are not entirely "civilized" Westerners, but they are also not Russians or purely Easterners either; while some of them help out Bond, others try to hurt him. They reside in a liminal space between East and West and sometimes it is hard to tell where their loyalties lie. Or their liminality provides Bond insight into the confused terrain. Darko Kerim, the head of the British secret service in Turkey, has a "strong Western handshake of operative fingers," but a gypsy-like face, and a great appreciation for all things English, but also expert local knowledge on which Gypsies and Bulgars not to trust (92). The narrative itself describes a trip along that nineteenth century transverser of cultures, the Orient Express. As Bond experiences it, the political frontier reinforces the cultural and this is most notable when Fleming writes: "Soon they would be out of Turkey. But would Greece be any easier? No love lost between Greece and England. And Yugoslavia? Whose side was Tito on? Probably both" (146-7). The trip facilitated a great transition: Romanova's journey from East to West, as she moves from Istanbul to Paris, and in the process is transformed by sex with Bond from an enemy to an émigré, a Soviet to a Westerner, and a communist to a consumer. The train trip also straddles time. As a Romanova, that is with a name that links her to the imperial royal family, she harkens back to an earlier era when Russian royals and nobles fled the revolution to a West where they were always a bit out of place; she too escapes, but with her youth, beauty, and contemporary sheen, she points to the future, and there is no doubt that she will fit in comfortably.

The contexts of the novel and film also enhanced this liminality. The novel was published at a transitional period, when the Soviet Union was emerging from the shadow of Stalin and embarking on a reform experiment that included peaceful engagement with the West and a new stress on consumerism. Of course Bond was cynical about Khrushchev's new direction, remarking, "I'm not sure how they're going to react to the scraps of carrot they're being fed by K and Co." (130). Coming on the heels of the Soviet invasion of Hungary in 1956, the novel is regarded as strongly anti-Soviet (Black 28). Yet the story also offered its own version of peaceful engagement: although this was not the last time Fleming fingered the Soviets, with the positive figure of Romanova the novel anticipated his future benign attitude. The film marked the first substitution of SPECTRE for the old Communist bad guys.

Lisa Dresner has noticed that almost every character in the Bond novels occupies a liminal space and operates as "signifiers of displacement, miscegenation, and boundary crossing. [...] This radically overdetermined liminality ultimately reflects Britain's Cold War-era paranoia about a world in which racial, national, economic, and sexual boundaries are all being blurred" (271). The main liminal character in *From Russia, with Love* is Romanova; this Russian who is bringing love does not reflect paranoia but rather hope and desire, which ultimately works to the advantage of the West.

As a fictional character, Romanova had many predecessors in the *femmes fatales* and amazons that have populated the Western image of Russia. Russian women were often coded as dangerous because of their non-normative sexuality. They either used their feminine allures for political ends, such as the image of Catherine the Great with her enormous sexual appetites and the bomb-throwing, dagger-wielding Russian nihilist women who also lured their political prey with irresistible beauty (see Alexander 289-92, 329-41; Barrett 2013). Or they "perverted" their femininity to become "manly" fighters, such as the lesbian coded Women's Battalion of Death during World War I and II or sniper Lyudmila Pavlichenko, who was received in America in 1942 as a kind of chunky freak, with reporters marveling that she did not use rouge and nail polish and enjoyed killing Nazis.

During the Soviet period, women from the USSR were generally portrayed as charmless and often bulky drudges, grey asexual analogs of a soulless Communist system. The first Western journalists to report back from the USSR after Stalin's death in 1953 gave eye-witness accounts of Soviet women, who, as René MacColl writes, offer "no pleasure to the eye":

> The women are stocky, thick-waisted and dressed for the most part like a bunch of frights. [...] The women mostly have severe faces, lacking gaiety or charm. Their eyes are hard, their mouths set. Even were I twenty years younger and a bachelor, I would as soon think of trying to kiss a Soviet woman as a thistle. (37)

John Gunther used words like "revolting" and "shabby manginess" to describe Soviet women but noted an acute consciousness of the superiority of Western clothes, and particularly shoes (40). Gunther wrote, "if Marilyn Monroe should walk down the street with nothing on but shoes, people would stare at her feet" (40).

Fictional Russian women, though, were never so outlandish that they could not be redeemed through romance. There was a handful of women who were rescued by the West in popular culture before Romanova: the barrier that had to be overcome in these literary and cinematic tales was always their character. Before the revolution, Americans periodically redeemed beautiful nihilist women with marriage, but only after they had renounced terrorism and distanced themselves from socialism (Barrett 29-33). As Choi Chatterjee explains, "The original model of the Russian revolutionary loses valence and potency as it travels west and becomes a pale, bourgeois version of its former self. Violent and exotic women lose their power to seduce and destroy" (775).

In the twentieth century, many British and American films staged "rescues" of Soviet women who were beautiful, but their loyalties had to be transformed. For example, Elena Moura, Lenin's secretary in *British Agent* (Michael Curtiz 1934), repeatedly informs on Stephen Locke as he tries to prevent the Soviet regime from signing a peace agreement with Germany and organizes white (anti-Bolshevik) resistance; in the end, she acts on her love for him, declaring that she has not the courage to go on being an idealist because she's "too much of a woman." Theodore, the communist streetcar driver in *Comrade X* (King Vidor 1940), starts to change when she and her love interest Mac get tangled up with the secret police; she is gradually won over by her suitor who tells her, "You weren't meant to be a motorman or a pumpkin head. You're a beautiful woman!" In *Jet Pilot* (Josef von Sternberg 1957), Olga Orlief was described by US Air Force pilot Jim Shannon as "a Soviet tootsie roll who made a chump out of me"; she used her good looks to cover her intelligence gathering. When back in Siberia, she rescues her lover and flees with him to Alaska only after she learns that he will be given mind-destroying drugs. In all three cases, Soviet women are transformed through their love of Western men and head for the West.

Other character defects such as hyper-intelligence and martial prowess are intertwined with their suppressed emotions, which rendered them more masculine and less womanly. Almost all of the women boast impressive fighting credentials that exoticize them, usually in a negative way. In *British Agent,* Elena Moura scuffles in the streets of Petrograd during the revolution and shoots a Cossack. In *Ninotchka* (Ernst Lubitsch 1939), Ninotchka fought in the Soviet-Polish War (1919-21) and has a scar from a Polish lancer on the back of her neck. In *Comrade X,* Theodore was in a woman's parachute division. In *Silk Stockings* (Rouben Mamoulian 1957), Nina became a women's tank corps captain at age 18. And both Olga Orlief (*Jet Pilot*) and Vinka Kovelenko (*The Iron Petticoat* [Ralph Thomas 1956]) are air force pilots. The freakish intelligence of Soviet heroines is even more off-putting: Ninotchka masters the hypertrophied French legal code in days, Theodore recites an entire book in hours, and Vinka constantly spouts out Soviet statistics proving the rottenness of capitalism, driving her American companion to comment, "I've never met a woman with a brain like yours."

Although not necessarily Soviet or Russian, the communist women from the US television spy drama *I Led 3 Lives* (1953-56) and the red scare films that immediately preceded *From Russia, with Love* comprised both the manly aggressor and the *femme fatale.* They were either authoritarian and desexualized or highly sexualized, referred to by producers of the television show as the "beautiful Mata Hari-type commie agent" (Kackman 34). In the film *The Red Menace* (R.G. Springsteen 1949), the American dupe Bill Jones gets lured by the sexual gifts of blond Mollie O'Flaherty or yelled at by the tyrannical brunette Yvonne Kraus.

What makes Romanova different from her predecessors, and a marker for the contemporary Russian woman, is that she does not have to be redeemed; she comes ready-made for Bond's conquest and departs from the norm for Bond Girls and earlier Western converts. Although she is a corporal for the State Security apparatus, she barely seems Soviet. There is never a hint of ideology and she is young, 24, "with dreams in the eyes" ("the Soviet machine would not yet have ground the sentiment out of her"), and a name that points to the pre-Soviet past (112). When she is first introduced in the novel, Fleming stresses her non-Soviet normality: she peers at a church, listens to the prelude to the pre-revolutionary opera *Boris Godunov,* delights to "the smell of a good supper cooking" and the beauty of spring, and looks forward with "confidence in the future" (52-3). This description seems to move beyond Soviet stereotypes. She has no fighting skills, no hypertrophied intelligence, and indeed is selected simply because of her talent as "a beautiful lure" (52). She works in the translation section of the MGB and seems to be headed for a "career" as a mistress for one of the senior officers (55). Soon after, it is revealed that Romanova was previously a ballerina with a developed sense of the *kulturnyi* (transliterated in the book as *kulturny*), which in Russian means a combination of cultivated and cultured, and in the novel points Westward. For example, she disdains the orchestra from Turkmenistan that she hears on the radio:

This dreadful oriental stuff they were always putting on to please the kulaks of one of those barbaric outlying states! Why couldn't they play something *kulturny*? Some of that modern jazz music, or something classical. This stuff was hideous. Worse, it was old fashioned. (55)

She also doesn't look like a Soviet spy and wonders if she's "as beautiful as the Western girls" (132). Moreover, she is naïve and remains unaware of her real mission, which is to set Bond up for assassination (134).

If she is a *femme fatale*, she is an unintentional one, which defuses most of the power that comes with that trope. Many have pointed out that Bond Girls usually are fixed into a normative sexuality through conquest (Bennett and Woollacott, *Bond* 118; Funnell, "Negotiating" 201; White 26). But following the pattern of the many previous Russian lures, Romanova turns out to be the conqueror, or at least wins the first battle, since she instigates the sex, first appearing to Bond waiting for him naked in bed. She is not really a spy-courtesan either, which Julie Wheelwright describes as representing "the antithesis of the maternal bond; she is sexually independent, usually childless, and is often estranged from her family—she dabbles on the dangerous periphery of the secret world. This flight from the domestic, however, also represents a deeply-embedded anxiety in contemporary western culture" (294-5). Tatiana has no family and is sexually independent—how could she be a Bond Girl otherwise?—but just barely since she is modest and blushes when asked about her sex life; as Fleming writes, "Russian girls are reticent and prudish about sex. In Russia the sexual climate is mid-Victorian" (61). With Romanova, Bond is able to have his cake and eat it too as she is sexy, willing, *and* traditional, or as one character puts it "unawakened" (65). And any anxiety that might arise because of her "flight from the domestic" is trumped by the advantage that accrues to the awakener (i.e. Bond) who initiates the awe-struck new arrival into the wonders of the West and uninhibited sex, enhancing paternalism and dependency. This is implied by all of the previous redeemed through romance plots too; the rescued always depends on the rescuer. At one point Bond seems like a father watching over a child: "He felt a surge of tenderness and the impulse to gather her up in his arms and strain her tight against him. He wanted to wake her, from a dream perhaps, so that he could kiss her and tell her that everything was all right, and see her settle happily back to sleep" (146). In the film, she receives with delight the suitcase full of clothes and negligees that Bond has provided for her on the train, and asks for his approval ("Do I look right?") when dressed for tea.

Romanova is also marked Western through repeated comparisons to Greta Garbo as she exalts, "a film star—a famous one" (54, 132). One first reads this as a physical comparison, as did the producers of the film, claiming that the Garbo references made casting difficult and forced them to spend as much time on the tests for this one character as the entire cast of *Dr. No* (Terence Young 1962; Rubin 25). Albert R. Broccoli indicated one of their dilemmas: "We don't mind if she looks like Garbo…around the eyes. […] But she has to be a great deal more voluptuous in other departments" (qtd. in Krueger 11). But intertextually, Garbo also points to a number of film heroes who prepared the way for Romanova: the searcher for true love, Anna Karenina in *Love* (Edmund Goulding 1927) and *Anna Karenina* (Clarence Brown 1935), the Russian spy who flees to the west in *The Mysterious Lady* (Fred Niblo 1928), the Russian ballerina Grusinskaya who drives men wild in *Grand Hotel* (Edmund Goulding 1932), the prototype espionage *femme fatale*, Mata Hari in *Mata Hari* (George Fitzmaurice 1931), and the Soviet convert to French hats, evening dresses, and champagne, Ninotchka in *Ninotchka* (1939).

Romanova is also framed Western by the two other Soviet characters: Rosa Klebb and Red Grant. The personality of the lesbian Klebb, Head of SMERSH Department of Torture and Death, harkens back to many Soviet stereotypes, the pre-redeemed Ninotchka type (cold, drab, speaking in monotones) and the manly fighter: "She was a Neuter. […] And this psychological and physiological neutrality of hers at once relieved her of so many human emotions and sentiments and desires. Sexual neutrality was the essence of coldness in an individual" (50). Her physical type was out of central casting for the old Soviet woman. She was short, squat, and dumpy, with thick legs and calves that "were very strong for a woman" and breasts bulging from beneath a uniform that looked "like a badly packed sandbag" (50-1). When Bond sees her for the first time he fixes on her ugly, "toadlike" face and a "nicotine-stained moustache" (187). And just as she has a distorted normative female sexuality with her amorous advance on Romanova, she repurposes a traditional gender marker, knitting needles, as poisoned tipped weapons with which to kill Bond; Klebb is presented as a crab, with deadly claws.

The Red Grant narrative works in inverse to that of Romanova, as he finds his destiny moving East in a downward trajectory of sadism (Cross 320). He is the illegitimate offspring of "a midnight union between a German professional weight-lifter and a Southern Irish waitress […] on the damp grass behind a circus tent outside of Belfast" (15). A strong-arm man for smugglers and Sinn-Fein, boxer, and recreational killer of animals and people, he is ruthless and psychopathic—Fleming labels him "the slaughterer"—as well as the opposite of *kulturnyi* (Cross 320; Fleming 12). Naturally, he becomes attracted to Russians in Berlin: "He liked all he heard about the Russians, their brutality, their carelessness of human life, and their guile, and he decided to go over to them" (17). He finds his true calling in the Soviet Union, becomes Chief Executioner of SMERSH, and is given the code name Granit, which points backward and is reminiscent of the revolutionary names of the previous Soviet generation: Stalin (steel), Molotov (hammer), and "Iron Feliks" Dzerzhinskii, the first head of the Soviet secret police.

Fleming's depiction of Romanova helped to constitute the contemporary reevaluation of the Soviet woman. Although press accounts in the years preceding the novel emphasized their drabness, the period between the publication of the novel and the release of the film was awash with beautiful Russian women. Shel Silverstein began an illustrated travelogue for *Playboy* in 1957, and one of his early stops was Moscow (March 1958) where he reported that "the girls are lovely"; one cartoon has him making love to a young woman with the caption, "Gee, Natasha—you mean you Russians invented *this*?" (49-50).[2] Harrison Salisbury followed him in 1959 and conveyed similarly hopeful news: "Neither puritanism nor emphasis on heavy industry is going to divert the Russian woman much longer from the heritage of her sex, the right and opportunity to look just as pretty as she wants to" (48). According to Salisbury, the evidence was everywhere: mobbed Christian Dior fashion shows, intense demand for nylon stockings, spike heels, and even "a saucy-looking blonde in a cheap blue print dress and cheap red sandals" (46-7). Others reported these changes too: lipstick, wavy hair, jammed beauty shops, Italian hair styles, and window displays of strapless evening dresses and various colored nylon slips (Norton, 88-90; Hindus 13-6). Indicating how quickly the Russian fashion industry had developed, Maurice Hindus referred to John Gunther's comment a few years earlier about a naked Marilyn Monroe: "I can assure John that nowadays the actress' feet would be the only part of her people would *not* stare at" (15).

In this context of the refashioning of the Soviet woman, the film *From Russia with Love* had a much anticipated aspect of sexual titillation. As the Bond Girl featured in the second Bond film, Italian beauty queen Daniela Bianchi was the first to be cast in the full glare of the Hollywood publicity machine. Much anticipatory ink was spilled speculating as to "which beauty will be Bonded" (Krueger 11). Publicity photos featured Romanova as she first appeared to Bond in bed covered by only a sheet and a black ribbon around her neck ("New" 12). But while the sex and her body were evident, transferring the enemy from SMERSH to SPECTRE created a political unintelligibility that often baffled commentators. Many newspaper previews for the film simply got it wrong, reporting that Bond still battled the communists, claiming that the movie is about "an infamous red plot to lure Bond to his destruction" ("James Bond Double" 15). One was way off base, saying that Bond "takes on the whole Russian spy system single-handed" (Case 12). Others sensed something hostile in the title itself. When residents of Duncanville, Texas found handbills "with a picture of a person with a gun and inscribed 'From Russia With Love'" they complained to the police "about communist literature being posted around town" ("Communistic?" 10). Similarly, disk jockeys playing Jane Morgan's recording of the theme song brought anti-communist outrage in New York and Athens, Greece (Wilson 17; "From Greece" 19). For the same reason, the title of the film was changed in India to *From 007 with Love* and the film was banned entirely to Black Africans in South Africa (Lukas 21; "Zulus" 25).

From Russia with Love emerged in a contemporaneous context of hope and fear, Western glamor and political violence. This particular Fleming novel became attached to the excitement of the Kennedys, not just because of the imprimatur that President John F. Kennedy gave it after he declared it to be one of his favorite books (Rubin 35). Its youthful, optimistic, sexy, cosmopolitan tone fit in well with the Camelot glamor; one newspaper columnist even compared the scene in the opening of the book depicting a "naked man [...] splayed out on his face beside the swimming pool" with some recent "swimming pool escapes" of Bobby Kennedy (Miller, "Letter" 6). Fear reemerged when the president was assassinated soon after the film's US release and it was discovered that Lee Harvey Oswald liked this novel too and had checked it out from a New Orleans public library in the summer of 1962 ("Oswald" 1; Powledge 21).

But the self-affirming trope of the beautiful, fashionable, and consumerist (read: Western) Soviet woman proved potent and the phrase "from Russia with love" stuck and tantalized that desire, and not just fears, could emanate from the Soviet Union. This was soon affirmed with a *Playboy* expose, "The Girls of Russia and the Iron Curtain Countries," in March 1964. Not simply a photo spread, the article offered advice on traveling behind the iron curtain to find beautiful women, with tips on where to meet them and how to find prostitutes. The country apparently now brimmed with various "chickniks" who offered "soft, yielding womanliness," with none of the pesky drawbacks of Western women such as "the edgy competitiveness of their American career-girl sisters" ("The Girls" 116). Also, there was no reason to be put off by their occasional manly occupations:

> The image of the husky Stakhanovite lass who could drive a tractor as well as any man is fading fast in the U.S.S.R. Not because girls don't drive tractors anymore, but because today the inroads of make-up, perfume, beauty parlors, and uplift bras can be seen—and—appreciated—everywhere. (ibid. 116)

The work might be "unfeminine" but the women were not; the article stresses the traditional advantages of such women, echoing the paternalism that the films embedded into the discourse: "These girls may handle a rivet or a shovel all day, but when they look up meltingly into a man's eyes, there's no doubt as to who they think is the most" (ibid.). Plus, the country offered free, legal state abortions, letting men off the hook in case sexual contact occurred and pregnancy ensued.

The phrase "from Russia with love" was attached to various campaigns, some by the Soviets, especially surprising given the attack on Bond novels from communist countries (Lenoir BR56). The vodka Stolichnaya was introduced to Americans in 1965 with the advertising slogan, "From Russia with Ice" ("From Russia" 4). The Soviet ambassador to the United Nations, Nikolai Fedorenko, brought love from Russia too by slinging the phrase on the Merv Griffin Show and at a gala reception for the U.N.'s 20th anniversary in San Francisco (Teltsch 8, Grant 172). Many performers recorded the theme song in 1964 and 1965, including Jane Morgan, the Village Stompers, Matt Monroe, Ray Martin and His Orchestra, and the Roland Shaw Orchestra. Christian Dior created a "From Russia with Love" theater coat, "pre-Revolution inspired" ("Fall Fashion" 6) and from Lowell, Massachusetts to Kingsport, Tennessee organizers promoted fashion shows with the phrase: no "shabby manginess" here ("'In' Fashions" 2d; "The Young Generation" 2). Most bizarrely, papers pushed a recipe for a "From Russia with Love" dip— the chili sauce made it red—along with other suggestions for a teen spy party such as "goldfingers" and "Fort Knox punch" ("Teen Spy Party" 11, "This Party" 5).

Although pleasing images of desirable bodies helped to erode Cold War Manichaeism and at the same time buffered patriarchy, they worked on a terrain that still gave great advantage to the West, as the tasty vodka and fashionable coats made clear. By reconstructing the Soviet woman from a mannish drudge to a Western consumerist beauty, fictions like *From Russia, with Love* focused on desires that could best be fulfilled by capitalism. Even the one Russian consumer good that entered the US, vodka, acknowledged this. Back home it was a Russian staple, as common as black bread; in the pull of the rich American market it was transformed into a highly desirable consumer good—a luxury item, "something of a status symbol," priced considerably higher than domestic vodka ("From Russia" 4). In addition, the new Soviet woman was not simply a literary trope; the Soviet Union was changing and devoting more resources to fashion. But Western observers were all too ready to read this as either a nascent Westernization or a creation of a demand that could not be met by the regime. As Susan Reid explains:

> Accounts of "the Russians'" consumption patterns [...] reflected western fascination with this newly rediscovered human species and rendered them less threatening. Assuming that *she*, in particular, was motivated by fundamentally the same needs and desires as American women, reporters predicted that once Russian women's consumerist instincts were aroused their demands would spiral out of control. (223)

Romanova herself feared that she would lose control. While being spirited West, she grotesquely conflates women as sexual objects with women as avatars of consumerism, and reassures male readers that the proper balance between the two will be maintained:

> Since I came out of Russia I am all stomach. [...] You won't let me get too fat James. You won't let me get so fat that I am no use for making love? You will have to be careful, or I shall just eat all day long and sleep. You will beat me if I eat too much? (169)

In this moment she offers an apt and concise summary of her central position in Western fantasies of sex, paternalism, patriarchy, consumerism, and Cold War triumph.

ACKNOWLEDGEMENTS

Thank you to Liisa Franzén for editorial assistance and Sharon Miyagawa for research assistance with this chapter.

NOTES

1   Reference to the Signet publication of the novel.
2   Emphasis is in the original.

CHAPTER 5

"THE OLD WAYS ARE BEST"
The Colonization of Women of Color in Bond Films

Travis L. Wagner

James Bond is privileged. He is granted unprecedented access to the world and his violent actions are sanctioned by his "00" status. More importantly, he is never labeled an outsider in his films; he is not marginalized, stereotyped, and overlooked based on his social locations. As a white, cisgender, heterosexual, upper middle classed, able-bodied, and Western/British man, Bond "operate[s] within a wide comfort zone" that "grants [him] the cultural authority to make judgments about others and to have those judgments stick" (Johnson, "The Social" 19). Constructed to encounter the world through a binary lens, Bond is able to judge Others and create a "reality" in which those who do not share in his privilege hold little significance (ibid. 15-20). Bond shows little remorse for the people he uses to complete his missions and his indifference towards them should render him an unlikeable character. However, Bond is an iconic hero who is featured in the longest running film franchise in history. As a cultural concept, Bond has successfully managed to acclimate to the changing social and political issues of the time, while being presented as the unattainable pinnacle of cool. And yet, it is this very coolness that allows for Bond's oppressive colonizing and patriarchal behaviors to remain unchecked.

In her analysis of *Pulp Fiction* (Quentin Tarantino 1994), bell hooks notes that the film relies on what she terms "white cool"—a high level of suave cynicism that masks various forms of prejudice (*Reel* 47). This concept can be applied to an analysis of the Bond franchise. By stripping away the veneer of the debonair hero, Bond is revealed to be a colonizing agent that invades the space of women of color in order to ensure his own interests. The notion that Bond is an oppressive force is nothing new to the cultural rhetoric surrounding the icon. The franchise has long been criticized for its sexist treatment of women, who are presented as one night stands, damsels in distress, and even human shields. Scholars have also examined how Bond is positioned as a colonizing force in the franchise. What appears to be missing in these critical discussions is a consideration of the ways in which sexism, racism, and colonialism interrelate and how the intersection of these systems of oppression inform Bond's privileged status in the narrative. When Bond asserts his

"Britishness," he often does so as a white man who exercises regional superiority over non-white women. In order to examine the politics of representation at work in the franchise, one must consider the intersectionality of social identities and their corresponding forms of oppression.

Intersectionality is based on the notion that various socially constructed identity categories intersect on multiple levels, and that "the system of representation, and not one category, is responsible for the experience of social inequality" (Funnell, *Warrior* 4). A person is afforded or denied privileges based on interlocking identity categories such as gender, race, and class, among others. For example, a white woman might be marginalized by her gender while still privileged by her race. Her experience of oppression is different than a black woman whose experience of sexism is informed by racism (Hulko 44-5). It is important to consider the intersection of gender and race in the Bond franchise. While some scholars "begrudgingly" acknowledge that Bond is less degrading to women in newer films than in the past (Willman, "The Politics" 351), they fail to account for the manner with which Bond asserts racial privilege over women of color, an aspect that structures the narrative of *Skyfall* (Sam Mendes 2012). For the first time, Moneypenny is portrayed by a woman of color and is featured as an ally agent assisting Bond in the field. The progressive nature of her depiction is quickly undermined when Moneypenny's bullet provides a nearly fatal wound to Bond, suggesting that her place in the field is ill-advised. While *Skyfall* foregrounds the problems that emerge from feminine failings—the competency of an aging M as the head of M16 and the performance of Moneypenny as a field agent—Moneypenny, as a non-white woman, appears to be denied the leniency and mobility that is afforded to M.

It is this problem of intersecting identities and systems of oppression that allows Bond to maintain colonial privilege over women of color. While Bond has been called out on his chauvinism by white women like M, there are no parallel instances in which a woman of color challenges Bond with any credible authority that does not result in her dismissal. Bond moves through the world as a colonizing agent who has learned to appropriate and acknowledge his privilege over the Other on a cursory level, never allowing equal standing to a person who is disadvantaged socially by more than one identity category (e.g. gender *and* race). This essay looks at the relationship between Bond, as a privileged white colonial figure, and the women of color he interacts with in various films from *Dr. No* (Terence Young 1962) to *Skyfall*. While Bond interfaces with various women of color, this chapter focuses on Bond's interaction with black women who range from primary to secondary characters. It explores how racial stereotypes are mobilized in the representation of black women and how their treatment by Bond in the narrative is exemplary of the politics of representation at work in the franchise, with Bond colonizing such cultural assumptions to reaffirm and entrench his privilege.

SILENCING WOMEN OF COLOR IN THE CONNERY ERA

It is fitting that *Dr. No* begins the filmic Bond franchise as it addresses colonization within its Jamaican setting. Jeremy Black suggests that this film is not about the experiences of those living in the newly decolonized space, but one where Bond stifles the attempt of villain Dr. No to "doom" Bond's "decadent civilization" (96). Reading *Dr. No* in such a way allows viewers to see Bond not as a character entering into the recently decolonized space as an aid, but as an agent who assumes innate colonial privilege. The opening moments of *Dr. No* depict a group of blind Jamaican men engaging in the assassination of a British secret agent whose assumption about their blind servility leads to his demise. This moment reaffirms the trope of the colonized subject as animalistic, verified through the song "Three Blind Mice." According to the film, Jamaica is still in great need of colonial authority, leading to Bond's assignment there. His presence is mirrored by his American counterpart, Felix Leiter, who is first shown standing on the second floor of the Jamaican airport watching the locals below and waiting for Bond to arrive. Through the use of doubling, the film presents the impression that Bond, like Leiter, can stand above non-normative bodies and gaze upon them in condemnation. More importantly, it presents the impression that the "binary opposition between colonizer and colonized is not easily reversed" in the Bond franchise (Sharpe 101).

One of Bond's first interactions with a woman of color in *Dr. No* set the tone for future encounters. Early in the film, he asks an older Jamaican woman for directions. Although Bond is known for his ability to seduce every woman he meets, he sheds the charm and politely requests the information. The woman does not speak but simply gestures in the appropriate direction. Her silence can be read as a measured response to Bond and his hyper-colonial privilege. While a person might be wary to speak to someone in a position of social/cultural authority, there is also a danger in silence, which denies the assumption that safety comes from not speaking. Audre Lorde argues that silence "will not protect" persons who are Othered by society, and particularly women of color, whose voices are especially lacking in the "language" of culture (40-2). Silence, though seemingly safe, affirms an Othered identity and internalizes social oppression, which is far more dangerous than speaking out against privileged forces, fearing them to be too powerful to conquer (ibid. 42). Here, the woman remains silent in the presence of Bond, perhaps realizing the immediacy of his request or fearing to speak in the face of authority.

Dr. No exemplifies the oppositional dichotomies of colonial rhetoric in which positive qualities attributed to the (white) self are contrasted with opposite/negative qualities of the (non-white) Other (Goldie 232-3). This is reflected in the casting of a white woman, Honey Ryder played by Ursula Andress, as the loyal helpmate of Bond while a black woman, the unnamed photographer played by Marguerite LeWars, is presented as untrustworthy and villainous. Unlike Ryder, who meets Bond by chance on a beach, the photographer has prior knowledge of Bond's whereabouts and waits for him to leave the airport. She is, however, unsuccessful in getting his picture. Later, while Ryder is invited to accompany Bond on his mission, the photographer proves to be a nuisance as she tracks Bond down to a club where he is having dinner with Leiter and Quarrel. Although she manages to get her shot, she is apprehended and interrogated by Bond. Contrary to the faith Bond has in Ryder, Bond distrusts the photographer and requests that her claim be verified by the club owner. As the first film in the franchise, *Dr. No* establishes problematic politics of representation through its contrasting of the white and black femininity.

Bond's reprimand of the photographer has further implications due to the relational nature of the colonizer, who is often perceived of as a paternal figure, to the colonized subject, who is often infantilized by being viewed as a child. As Jo-Ann Wallace notes, the child trope in colonialism presents an allegory for a subject that needs to be educated or corrected (173). Although Bond condemns the actions of the photographer, he leaves the more physical act of twisting her arm to Quarrel, a black male whose own Otherness as a colonized body suggests that he can act out in a more physical and barbaric way. When the woman yells out in pain, Bond responds with "tell us and he will stop," a statement that clearly indicates that he is in charge of the situation and Quarrel is doing his bidding. Bond's chastising of the photographer is detached from the sexual banter that typically occurs in his relations with white women; here the photographer is Othered as black woman and colonial child.

SUPPRESSING THE SUBALTERN IN THE MOORE ERA

Roger Moore took Bond in a new direction, interpreting the character as a debonair gentleman and wry humorist. According to Chapman, the films starring Moore attempt to transition the franchise post-Connery while remaining in line with "popular tastes" (*Licence*, 123). To write off the Moore films because of their humor is misguided; under the veil of laughter, Bond moves through a new series of colonized spaces, each with new problems for the black women he meets. *Live and Let Die* (Guy Hamilton 1973) finds Bond in the criminal underworld of Harlem, a place not associated with colonization given its American locale. There he meets Solitaire, whose ability to foresee the future using tarot cards is central to Bond's navigation of Harlem. This renders Solitaire, the white British female, a key panoptic figure for a space in which she is wholly privileged and adored.

According to the narrative, Solitaire's power is rooted in her chastity. The film explicitly contrasts her white purity with the moral ambiguity of Rosie Carver, a black American ally agent tasked with aiding Bond on his mission. Carver is, in

160-1). In *GoldenEye* (Martin Campbell 1995), M, played by Judi Dench, criticizes Bond during their first meeting. Calling him a "sexist, misogynist dinosaur," she affirms that Bond has long enjoyed male privilege, providing the film with a guise of reduced sexism. Jim Leach notes that M's "feminist attacks" do not undermine Bond's oppressive nature, but only add irony as M continually encourages Bond to exploit women for personal gain, such as in *Tomorrow Never Dies* (Roger Spottiswoode 1997) when she instructs Bond to sleep with Paris Carver and "pump her for information." Leach suggests that the filmmakers likely included M's criticism in the dialogue to show their awareness of this issue ("Bond" 253) but do little to change Bond's conduct with women. When considering Bond as an oppressive figure, awareness does not equate to criticism or a suggestion that his privilege has been revoked. While Bond may be culturally aware of his misogyny, no one suggests that his colonial authority is a cause for concern. There is no M equivalent to suggest that he is, say, an imperialist caveman.

While the colonial misogyny apparent in *Die Another Day* (Lee Tamahori 2002) is not as blatant, it is certainly as insidious. Viewers are first introduced to Bond Girl Jinx through the male gaze, as Bond views her emerging from the water through binoculars, a homage to the introduction of Honey Ryder in *Dr. No*. Although both women are framed in terms of their attractiveness and Bond's desire for them, they are represented differently in their films. Norma Manatu notes that while white women in film are often presented as delicate and pure, black women are "viewed as symbols of sexual excess" and culturally ascribed with a high degree of "sexual wantonness" (19). After meeting Ryder, Bond spends the remainder of the film getting to know her and even hears about her tragic backstory. In comparison, he quickly jumps into bed with Jinx after minimal conversation and their sexual encounter is quite heated. *Die Another Day* has one of the longest and most graphic sex scenes in the franchise, and although Halle Berry is a multiracial actor her character evokes the sexual excess bemoaned by Manatu. Yet Bond, in his colonizing ways, eventually overpowers Jinx and controls the sexual encounter. Jinx becomes not a point of challenge to Bond as patriarchal colonizer, but another body to exploit, making the final scene of the film, one of the most problematic in the entire franchise.

The film examines the manufacturing and sale of synthetic blood diamonds. Bond is tasked with obtaining the diamonds and suppressing the various villains tied to their production. With the aid of Jinx, he is able to complete his mission and the two hide away in order to share some intimate time. In the final scene, Jinx can be seen laying on her back with Bond hovering over her. Bond then dumps the diamonds onto the semi-naked body of Jinx and her reaction is clearly one of elation. The implications of this scene are troubling, especially in light of the fact that the blood diamond trade in Africa is rooted in colonialism, violence, and genocide. The encounter between Bond and Jinx takes on even greater significance as it reproduces power dynamics that reflect the intersection of gender, race, and sexuality in relation to a clearly problematic context. The fact that the film opens and closes with these sexual encounters detracts from any empowerment her character might seem to have. Jinx's reconstitution of troubling black sexuality affirms the presence of Bond's privilege that remains wildly unchecked. Awareness might be an element in the newer works of Bond, but it extends only to a brief acknowledgement of gender oppression, and as it stands Bond remains a privileged male of colonial means.

CRAIG AND THE FUTURE

Skyfall reintroduces the character Moneypenny in the franchise. Played by Naomie Harris, Moneypenny is revisioned as both a field agent and a black woman. The film opens with Moneypenny accompanying Bond on a mission. Not only does she fail to kill Bond's attacker but she accidently shoots him in the process, believing that she has killed him. From the outset, *Skyfall* presents the impression that Bond is a superior agent to Moneypenny. What is also clear is that this incident helps to reaffirm Bond as a patriarchal, colonial figure whose privilege affords him access to everything, including second chances. Bond is given the opportunity to reaffirm his status as hero. He is privileged with such liberties as a field agent that he can choose to return to the field even if he is discouraged or not sanctioned to do so. In comparison, Moneypenny is denied the chance to prove herself and become a successful MI6 field agent. She is incapable of validation and chooses the post-colonial space of silence in a desk job, serving the narrative and historical advancement of Bond and MI6 at the expense of creating her own identity. In the most telling scene of the film, Moneypenny provides Bond with a "close shave," a figurative reference to the opening moments of her shooting Bond that also acknowledges her literal act of cleaning up the disheveled hero. Moneypenny helps Bond return to his suave, "cool" self, internalizing her own colonization in the face of Bond's privileged body. Through her diminishing position in the narrative, Moneypenny is gradually rendered immobile and reminds viewers, as Manatu does, that cinema is void of "black socio-political heroines" that also happen to be women (42).

Although the character of Bond has evolved over a 50-year period with different actors playing the title role, his position as a colonial oppressor remains unchanged and this defines his encounters with women of color who lack the ability to challenge their oppression (by Bond). Black women, especially those with a clear colonized past, are marginalized by Bond's "coolness." His suave yet cynical worldview, which frames the narratives, works to silence and disempower them because to question such a heroic figure like Bond would be to undermine a sense of hegemony that grows weaker in a post-colonial global framework. It would seem that the more illogical a figure like Bond becomes, the more illogical his colonial sexism becomes, so that by *Skyfall* an unseen force almost wills Moneypenny to fail at her task, while also raising Bond from the dead. Bond claims the non-fictional Sir Thomas Bond's family motto *Orbis non sufficit*, (The World Is Not Enough) because as a white, colonial male he has the entire world, yet quests to consume more, often at the expense of black women and colonized bodies. As evident in *Skyfall*, Bond is more privileged than ever.

ACKNOWLEDGMENTS

The author would like to thank Matthew Buzzell, Ashley Blewer, Mary Baskin-Waters, and Lisa Funnell for their guidance on the writing of this chapter.

CHAPTER 6

BOND'S BIT ON THE SIDE

Race, Exoticism and the Bond "Fluffer" Character

Charles Burnetts

For every woman that shares the final scene, and bed, with James Bond in the erotici-zed denouement of a Bond film, there is always another that didn't get quite as "lucky". She may have had intimate relations with Bond earlier in the film but is nevertheless forgotten by the time he has finished his mission and claimed his "prize"—the Bond Girl. This chapter examines the women that Bond seduces in the middle-portion of the Bond film; the ones he beds but who also conveniently disappear by the end of the film. Like "fluffers" in the porn industry, they keep the male "agent" aroused until the primary sexual object, the Bond Girl, arrives at which point they disappear off-screen. While many of these women work for the villain, they also lack the sociocultural status of their boss in economic, cultural and/or racial terms, and serve as a cosmetic veneer that obscures their boss' nefarious schemes as legitimate business activities. When such characters do disappear, Bond and/or his arch-nemesis appear compli-cit in their situations, having profited from these women as powerful men operating within a patriarchal economy.

This chapter aims to explore how the fluffer character is set up as a commodity in the narrative to be exploited by Bond and/or the villain. Although the pleasures she affords are ephemeral and short-lived, they also signal different, and sometimes unconventional, desires than those represented by the Bond Girl. As a temporary cha-racter, the fluffer must be both eye-catching and invisible, indeterminacies that reveal a more unstable regime of desire in Bond than usually assumed. While the fluffer is more visibly exploited and disposable than the Bond Girl, such secondary characters also make visible certain sexual and racial pleasures that are otherwise repressed by the Bond film, not least in terms of its established adherences to heteronormative sexual pleasure and (neo)colonialist positionings of the foreign Other.

This chapter focuses on the preponderance of black fluffer characters in the fran-chise, in what amounts to a particularly resilient racial exoticism in mainstream cinema. Such exoticism not only demonstrates the Bond film's reification and adapta-tion to post-colonial discourse and contemporary multiculturalism, but also speaks to the intersectional dimensions of the franchise's problematic gender politics. The chapter focuses specifically on the way in which a fluffer typology sits in tension with contemporary mandates for "positive" representation. It shows how the gendered exoticism of various films invite readings that go against the grain, yielding insights with respect to Bond and his pleasures that slip through the matrix of both heteronormative desire and Western hegemony. This is most notable in the casting of Grace Jones as May Day in *A View To a Kill* (John Glen 1985), who embodies aspects of both the "animalistic sexuality" of a colonizing white male fantasy (hooks, *Black* 69) and a hyper-masculinity that threatens to destabilize Bond's sexual politics. I argue that May Day serves as a high-watermark for the fluffer character, and, true to her name, as a kind of emergency distress signal with respect to the Bond film's racial and gender politics. Such problematics persist, despite a marked sophistication in the way race is managed by recent iterations of the franchise, not least in the casting of Halle Berry as Bond Girl Jinx in *Die Another Day* (Lee Tamahori 2002) and, perhaps the ultimate coup, the casting of a black Miss Moneypenny in *Skyfall* (Sam Mendes 2012).

BOND GIRL/BOND FLUFFER

The Bond films work on a definitive contrast between the primary Bond Girl and secondary, or "fluffer", female characters, a division mapped consistently to differentials of class, nationality, and race. The Bond Girl is coded as a good fit for Bond as borne out by the number of times she turns out to share his profession as secret agent (e.g. Tatiana Romanova in *From Russia with Love* [Terence Young 1963], Anya Amasova in *The Spy Who Loved Me* [Lewis Gilbert 1977], Vesper Lynd in *Casino Royale* [Martin Campbell 2006]). In order to serve as Bond's "prize at the end of the dangerous road" (127), as Ian Fleming notes of Solitaire in *Live and Let Die* (1954), she fulfils the criteria of superior physical beauty and the promise of feminine virtue and passivity, just as she effectively learns the lesson of her necessary dependence on a good man to get her out of trouble. This undermining of female agency is, for Christine Bold, particularly pronounced in the Bond films compared to Fleming's novels, specifically in the way they "limit women's initiatives" at the same time as they "represent desirable women as unknowing, helpless dupes" (178). For Lisa Funnell, however, the Bond Girl's significance in the films comes by virtue of her "strong and intimate relationship with Bond" ("I Know" 464). Funnell describes the Bond Girl as the "nonrecurring lead female protagonist" in each film who "functions as the romantic interest and heroic ally of James Bond" (ibid. 464). As such, the particular distinctiveness of the Bond Girl resides in her comparison with other women in the series.

Bond's fluffer characters are marked by a disposability that distinguishes them from the Bond Girl. They also signify alternatives to the Bond Girl's passivity and powerlessness, enjoying a wider spectrum of agency for the limited time they are on screen. While the Bond Girl is usually kept in close physical and emotional proximity to the villain, the fluffer holds her own in the physical world of espionage. In both sexual and spatial terms, the fluffer characters "get around". They are often adept pilots (Helga Brandt in *You Only Live Twice* [Lewis Gilbert 1967]) or highly able combatants (Bambi and Thumper in *Diamonds Are Forever* [Guy Hamilton 1971]). As long as they are not too close to Bond or the villain, such characters appear, according to Bold, as particularly professionalized and "efficient women" (171), in many ways supporting the national structures and institutional matrices that Bond either defends or infiltrates.

While some fluffer characters seem to enjoy greater agency than the Bond Girl, their representation is still undermined by the gender politics at work in the franchise. In her discussion of female villainy in the 1960s, Funnell notes that the "Bad Girls" seem to be accorded a greater level of freedom and movement in their films when compared to the Bond Girls who are positioned in the traditional role of damsel in distress ("Negotiating" 200-2). This agency, however, is somewhat undercut by what Laura Mulvey describes as the "to-be-looked-at-ness" of women on screen ("Visual" 837). The representation of Bad Girls centers on their image and how it plays into Bond's "male gaze." In a similar way, fluffers are set up as objects of desire regardless of whether they are genuinely attracted to Bond and/or have orders to manipulate him. As a result, their agency is undermined by the fact that their identities are derived through their relationships with men in the series.

HENCHWOMEN AND FLUFFERS

The relative agency of fluffer characters is complicated by the fact that many of these women answer to the villain. Such subordination is both class and race-determined, and made particularly apparent with regards to the black women that emerge in the franchise in the beginning of the 1970s. The first black female character in the Bond franchise, Thumper (Trina Parks), in *Diamonds are Forever,* is merely a henchperson for Blofeld, whose sole purpose is to fight Bond alongside her partner Bambi. As young women in an early era Bond film, Bambi and Thumper are certainly sexualized by way of revealing costumes and the suggestion of lesbianism. However, they are positioned differently in the narrative than Bond Girl Tiffany Case and fluffer Plenty O'Toole. Not only are Thumper and her colleague equated with the animal characters from Disney's animated feature *Bambi* (James Algar et al. 1942), but the duo are positioned at the lower end of the social scale—lackeys that serve as physical obstacles that Bond must overcome to achieve his mission goals.

Thumper serves as a template for the representation of black female characters in the franchise. Although Thumper is dark skinned, she is also presented with a more masculine image and gender expression when compared to the white Bond Girl Case and the fluffer O'Toole. Race intersects in powerful ways with gender and appears to signal a different configuration for Bond's black fluffer characters. Thumper shares much in common with Rosie Carver (Gloria Hendry), Bond's first black love-interest who appears in *Live and Let Die* (Guy Hamilton 1973). Carver ostensibly represents a "positive" image of black femininity; she is a CIA agent brought in to assist Bond in his investigation of Dr. Kananga's business affairs in San Monique. Much like the white Bond Girl Solitaire, Carver initially rejects Bond's sexual advances and adheres to the warning issued by her boss, Felix Leiter. Her initial rejection signals a morality that runs counter to neo-colonialist constructions of libidinous black femininity while at the same time indicates the requisite heterosexual desire for their union once the time is right.

As a way of redressing *Live and Let Die*'s problematic appropriation of 1970s Blaxploitation films, Carver serves ostensibly as a Bond Girl in the way she initially signifies deferred pleasure. The film is also troubling in the way that it envisages a black criminal conspiracy to turn America into a nation of heroin addicts by adhering to a combination of black nationalism and Voodoo superstition. With an axis of control coordinated between a fictional Caribbean Island, New Orleans, and Harlem, the story demonizes black identity from the ground up. Aside from a male black CIA agent that comes to Bond's aid, Carver appears as a rare exception in moral terms. It is not surprising when Carver is revealed to be a double agent working for Dr. Kananga. The first clue to this identity comes with her terror at seeing a hat with chicken feathers laid on her bed, moments after she resists Bond's sexual advances. Understanding the symbol as a Voodoo death threat, Carver's professionalism is undermined by her fear and implicit belief in the Other's exoticized culture—recognizing it to be that of her own. Signifying an incomplete conversion to the CIA and Bond's regime of facts, Carver's failure to embody Bond's atheist cynicism reveals a residual black identity that renders her suspect. What is also telling is the timing of the hat's appearance, moments after she rebuffs Bond's sexual advances. Carver is revealed to be a believer of a black ideology (coded criminal) while being threatened for her refusal to act on her heterosexual desire by accepting intimacy with Bond.

Carver adheres to the schemata posed by bell hooks in relation to the Western subject's yearning for the "primitive". Embodied by such figures as Bond, Western subjectivity longs to re-integrate with the Other in the name of a contemporary pluralism that repudiates the white supremacist racism of the past. For hooks, such inclusions are betrayed by residual mechanisms of consumption and fetish, where the "dark Other" remains nostalgically fixed to ideas of "nature" and prelapsarian "harmony". She writes:

> It is precisely that longing for *the* pleasure that has led the white west to sustain a romantic fantasy of the "primitive" and the concrete search for a real

primitive paradise, whether that location be a country or a body, a dark continent or dark flesh, perceived as the perfect embodiment of that possibility. (*Black* 27)

Such longings for the exotic seem to inform much of what is seen in the sequences analyzed above, whereby both a "dark continent" and "dark flesh" retain aspects of a stereotyped primitivism. *Live and Let Die* primitivizes its key locations of black community in America and the Caribbean at the same time as Carver is re-inscribed as a believer of Voodoo; this allows Bond to maintain his difference while being permitted the pleasures of an exotic commodity. Moreover, the film presents a double standard that centers on race and nationality: while Kananga's desire for the white Bond Girl Solitaire is framed in terms of the "oversexualized" black male and his misogynistic abuse of power, Bond's desire for both black and white women becomes naturalized as the right of the white colonial male.

PERFORMING THE PRIMITIVE

The black fluffer's agency is ambiguously split between aspects of racial alterity and classical femininity, both understood in terms of the black female body's positioning within an economy of colonizing male desire. From the short hair of most of the black women analyzed in this chapter to their slender athleticism, the black fluffer character is often presented as being more physically boyish and toned than the Bond Girl. May Day (Grace Jones) in *A View to a Kill* is paradigmatic in such respects, representing an ideal of athleticism, aggression, and strength that dominates not only her child-like employer/lover Max Zorin, but Bond himself throughout the film. May Day also narratively and spatially upstages her conventionally beautiful and white Bond Girl counterpart Stacey Sutton, only to be made scarce and then finally removed like other fluffer characters in the film's latter half.

As if to register her resistance to the fluffer mantle imposed on her by the film's eventual privileging of Sutton, May Day dominates the first half of the film in narrative, sexual, and spatial terms. In at least two sequences, Bond's surveillance of Sutton is disrupted by the entrance of May Day into his field of vision, motioning for him to turn away and mind his own business. Bond's classical (white) male gaze, trained voyeuristically again on a "woman as image", is disrupted here by May Day, a woman of color, who turns the gaze upon Bond himself. Such gender instabilities inevitably extend to the bedroom, where Bond is uncharacteristically dominated by her, a submissiveness on his part that the film struggles to contain. Motivated by Zorin's discovery that he is absent from his bedroom, Bond improvises a seduction of May Day by pretending to have been waiting for her in her bed. Bond *performs* a colonialist desire for the Other, to which May Day responds with an equivalent level of familiarity. Saying nothing to Bond other than "What is there to say?" May Day frames the encounter as an over-determined conquest between historic colonizer and oppressed, an interaction for which nothing needs to be said. Once in bed, however, May Day upturns Bond so that she's on top, her dominance of him redressing its historical corollary; she, with her short hair, muscular frame, and display of masculine strength sits astride a surprised, yet happily resigned, Bond. Such reversal is crudely undermined by the soundtrack as a romantic rendering of the film's main theme switches to a lone trumpet's intoning of a mournful "God Save the Queen" as Bond and May Day kiss. It is here that the spectator must be reminded that Bond is doing this for queen and country only.

A more severe sexual agency is permitted to May Day here, invoking parallels with aspects of "third-wave" feminism that Lisa Funnell writes of in relation to Bond's "Bad Girl" characters of the 1980s ("Negotiating" 204-6). May Day's active, masculinized approach to Bond adheres also to the "wild animalistic sexuality" discussed by bell hooks (*Black* 69), a key corollary to misogynist constructions of the black female body as commodity and "prostitute". In a comparable discussion of Tina Turner's sexual agency, hooks writes: "This tough black woman has no time for woman bonding, she is out to 'catch.' [...] Rather than being a pleasure-based eroticism, it is ruthless, violent; it is about women using sexual power to do violence to the male Other" (ibid. 68-9). Such aspects of "sexual agency," undercut by racist/misogynist constructions of toughness and male unpleasure, clearly demarcate fluffer characters like May Day from her primary, and usually white, counterparts. As a "hunter" (ibid. 68), borne out by her various assassinations of men in the film, May Day signifies the more active black sexuality that is problematically aligned with the black prostitute and the latter's cynical reduction of sex and her body to commodity, for whom "sexual service" is "for money and power" while "pleasure is secondary" (ibid. 69).

May Day is far more predatory than Rosie Carver and possesses a more active form of sexual agency. At the same time, the performance of Grace Jones parodies such constructions, betraying an awareness of the "hunter" typology. While *Live and Let Die* seems content to position its racial inclusivity in terms of a Westerner's taste for the exotic and foreign, *A View to a Kill* is notably self-reflexive about its racial biases, especially in its foregrounding of genetics and the breeding of humans and racehorses. With a sub-plot that revolves around Zorin's engineering of horses through medical tampering, and Zorin's own breeding by a Nazi doctor in a wartime concentration camp, the film relates questions of racial purity closely linked to issues of persecution, commodification, and the global marketplace. Although not much is said of May Day's background, her association with Zorin allow for comparisons with him as a genetically-modified commodity or "perfect" racial Other. Just as Zorin is slurred by a KGB agent as a "biological experiment" and "physiological freak", May Day attacks the agent with a superhuman display of strength as she picks him up and throws him to the ground. If Zorin turns out to be, in all likelihood, a Jew, tampered with to embody the Aryan ideal of Nazi ideology, similar assumptions seem invited here with respect to May Day in her embodiment of an enhanced black masculinity. In both cases, signs of racial purity serve as prized commodities in a volatile global marketplace, with the problematic caveat that such extremes of white and black identity risk going "rogue", compared to the racially normative Bond, or indeed the ideologically homogenous, yet anachronistic, KGB.

MODERN BOND

The enhanced complexity of *A View to a Kill* can be explained, in part, by the fact that it was produced 12 years after *Live and Let Die*, and might reflect key developments in identity politics in the intervening years. The same seems to be true with respect to the Bond films produced in the last 20 years starring Pierce Brosnan and Daniel Craig. The racial dimensions of Bond's fluffer characters has undergone further change, albeit not altogether unproblematically. If the casting of Naomie Harris as Miss Moneypenny in *Skyfall* serves as the ultimate upending of associations in Bond between England and an officious whiteness, its precedent comes with the character of Jinx (Halle Berry) in *Die Another Day*, who survives the film and is bedded by Bond at its finale. As if to underline the use of a woman of color as Bond's primary conquest, the film uses an unprecedentedly big-name actor in the casting of Oscar-winner Berry. The film is quite emphatic as to the saliency of her character as the primary "prize" for Bond. Unlike Carver, Jinx serves as a genuine NSA agent who remains faithful to both her agency and Bond, driven by their shared strategic goals. Promotional materials surrounding the film moreover highlight Jinx's introductory scene, where she emerges from the sea in a bikini, a homage to the now mythical scene in *Dr. No* (Terence Young 1962) where the first Bond Girl, Honey Ryder, made her entrance beheld within Bond's subjective point-of-view. As if acknowledging its own anachronisms with regards to race and the Bond Girl, the franchise deploys a self-conscious imagery of unveiling, or even of birth, as Berry emerges from the water. In this washing away of prejudice, the franchise seems to signal a fresh start to Bond's treatment of race, rhetoric that is imitated almost exactly in *Casino Royale*, where Bond's own body emerges from the sea as an unveiling not only of its new star, Daniel Craig, but also of the franchise's foregrounding of Bond's eroticized body for visual pleasure.

Jinx represents a significant shift in the franchise's racial politics, representing the long-deferred arrival of a black woman as the Bond Girl. Berry's multiracial heritage becomes significant here, being both more light-skinned and curvaceous than her black predecessors, and Jinx aligns more closely to the Bond Girl typology. She adheres also to characteristics of other 1990s Bond Girls who, as Funnell notes, represent shifts from a "sidekick" persona to the more self-sufficient "American Action Hero Bond Girl" figures ("I Know" 485) that seduce Bond as much as he seduces them. Comparisons are invited between Jinx and her key foil, Miranda Frost, a treacherous British spy that turns on MI6 and Bond. In the first half of the film, Frost masquerades as a Bond Girl and when in this mode she is presented as a particularly over-determined candidate for Bond's final girl. Her bedroom scene with Bond, midway through the film, is dominated by an over-stated whiteness in dress, décor, and lighting. Frost is also sexually passive and trusted by Bond, allowing him to take the lead on a bed of ice, their intimacy contrasted sharply with the hot and steamy scene between Bond and Jinx. Frost's "cold" betrayal is made more dramatic at a particularly sophisticated level, with the film's lulling of the spectator into the franchise's more traditional gender politics, only to resolutely undermine those terms.

Jinx successfully escapes the fluffer persona, her sexuality initially contrasted to "whiter" forms of desire and trust, only to be finally repositioned and validated as genuinely "warm" in relation to Bond. Echoes of May Day and Rosie Carver nevertheless complicate such validation. The film foregrounds Jinx's dominance of Bond in bed. Like May Day, Jinx positions herself on top of Bond and when they kiss her silhouetted tongue is clearly visible—this graphic image contrasts with the overly romanticized lovemaking scenes featured in a Bond film. Moreover, like both Carver and May Day, Jinx sleeps with Bond early on in the film and their encounter requires little seduction. She is situated less as an object consonant with the labor of Bond's investigations. Parallels between Jinx and Carver are signaled furthermore by questions levelled at Jinx by Bond with regards to her name and its connotations of "bad luck", echoing the anxieties featured in *Live and Let Die* particularly in regards to the treatment of Voodoo culture and the film's mystifications of black identity. If Bond's distrust of women is officially uninfluenced by race, the playful foregrounding of luck and the supernatural in these comments seem marked again by the possibility of unnatural, demonic powers at play when Bond encounters a black woman.

While the positioning of Jinx as a heroic partner to Bond helps to neutralize the racial stereotypes of black women featured in the franchise, such reminders qualify the sense to which Jinx fully adheres to the Bond Girl typology. These qualifications seem reinforced by a depiction of intimacy between Bond and Moneypenny that precedes the coupling of Bond and Jinx. In a highly unusual turn for the franchise, the audience is treated to a kiss between Bond and Moneypenny, only for it to be revealed as Moneypenny's fantasy envisaged through Q's virtual reality device. As playfully self-conscious and innuendo-laden as the film becomes here, the scene is also tantalizingly excessive in its latent fantasy of return to a topos of white hetero-normativity. In its own cheeky foregrounding of the virtual, the film equivocates here what is expected from a Bond bedroom scene, contrasting the classically passive seduction of Moneypenny with the modern sexual agency, and latent savagery, of Jinx.

BLACK MONEYPENNY

The casting of black actor Naomie Harris as Moneypenny in *Skyfall* can be considered the ultimate renegotiation of the franchise's racial politics, prefigured by the casting of black actor Jeffrey Wright as Felix Leiter from *Casino Royale* onwards. On many levels, *Skyfall* domesticates and nationalizes a black woman to a greater extent than any other Bond film in the franchise's history. Moneypenny represents that which is closest to Bond, his sense of self and nationality, in her embodiment of loyal English femininity that has seemed to always allude/repulse him, or she symbolizes that which must continue to be forever deferred in the economy of Bond's pleasure, a horizon of female Otherness *at home* that must never be fully incorporated. Tara Brabazon argues that Moneypenny is "the bitch, rather than the love, of Bond's life" and "is not only Britain's last line of defence, but feminism's first foothold of attack" (496).

Moneypenny can be read another way, as the crucial secondary character whose exceptionality to the usual conventions of the Bond fluffer character seems very much to prove the rule. Neither yearning for a romantic attachment with Bond nor foreign to the idea of having him sexually, Moneypenny emerges as the woman with the upper hand on Bond, who is always safely ensconced at home, and whose heterosexual desire for him is never in question. Harris and Craig's sensual scene by firelight in *Skyfall*, where she shaves him with a cut-throat razor, comes crucially before her identity as Moneypenny is revealed, where she turns out to be a would-be Bond herself, only to eventually change her mind in heeding Bond's advice that the job's "not for everybody." It is only here, at the point of her assuming the position of "Moneypenny", that another woman of color is integrated into the feminism that is more usually the preserve of her white counterparts.

Harris' casting in such respects expresses a profound ambiguity in regards to how far the franchise has come with regards to gender and race. While the franchise has professed itself flexible in terms of each—with the casting of a female M and a black Felix Leiter—the structures of domination and power defined for Bond and black women remain subject to issues of desire and control. The contours of the fluffer character outlined above allow us to see how gender is divided in the Bond universe between classical forms of femininity and a more fetishized typology of masculinized agency and liberated sexuality. Although these secondary characters "service" Bond in order to distract him from more dangerous or damaging preoccupations, they also reveal the extent to which Bond is willingly manipulated by his own methods of seduction and gameplay. They foreground the ways in which Bond himself is willingly positioned as both consumer and commodity within larger economies of exchange and capital. At the same time, and often in racially codified ways, they signify sexualities that lie outside the mandatory heterosexuality that must be restored by the Bond mission, positions that are nevertheless scrutinized and fetishized by the interrogatory gaze and fantasy of Bond and his loyal audiences. The Bond "fluffer" is at once a commodity and a point of otherness, correlating inevitably with modes of sexual and moral deviance that require regulation within the Bond film's narrative economy. The question remains therefore as to how the Bond film can truly modernize given the constraints inherited by the franchise, or whether its identity politics will eventually require us to live and let it die.

CHAPTER 7

THE POLITICS OF REPRESENTATION

Disciplining and Domesticating Miss Moneypenny in *Skyfall*

Kristen Shaw

In the opening scene of *Skyfall* (Sam Mendes 2012), James Bond, played by Daniel Craig, moves from a dark entryway into the crowded streets of Istanbul. A car pulls up and he steps inside, temporarily a passenger rather than the instigator of the action. Here, audiences are introduced to Eve, played by Naomie Harris, the character who is revealed to be Miss Moneypenny, M's iconic secretary, at the conclusion of the film. With Bond in tow, Moneypenny chases a black car through crowded streets, knocking off one side view mirror in the process, to which Bond casually quips, "It's alright, weren't using it." When the other side view mirror is destroyed moments later, Moneypenny quips back, "I wasn't using that one, either." Moneypenny's playful repartee with Bond is reflected in her ability, throughout the remainder of this scene, to keep up with the action as they navigate cramped Turkish streets. The image of Moneypenny as an action hero eclipses her traditional representation as M's secretary and the doting admirer of Bond. This initial representation of Moneypenny suggests that twenty-first century audiences of the Bond franchise will be provided with a positive representation of a black woman with agency and power to match Bond's own.

The climax of this scene, however, demonstrates that Moneypenny's aggressive agency is out of place and unwelcome within this action narrative. As the chase progresses, Bond ends up engaging in hand-to-hand combat with the mercenary Patrice on top of a moving train with Moneypenny following alongside in her vehicle. Moneypenny remains in contact with M at MI6, reporting the events as they occur. When the road ends, Moneypenny exits her Jeep and prepares to take a shot at Bond's assailant, warning M that "she may have a shot, [but] it's not clean." Despite the risk, M orders Moneypenny to shoot and she accidentally hits Bond, sending him plummeting into the river below.

Moneypenny's bad shot initiates a narrative shift that repositions her as a transgressor of the system rather than a proper agent; the presence of a powerful black woman at the center of the action narrative exceeds the conventions of the genre and poses a threat to its representational codes. The initial depiction of Moneypenny as not only being "in" on the action but also capable of keeping pace with Bond threatens the framework of the action genre, which is predominantly coded as a white, masculine, and heterosexual space. Moneypenny's bad shot literally challenges the prowess of Bond as the idealized white male hero, but this moment also signals her transgression of conventional narrative codes that demand women and racialized "Others" remain on the periphery, rather than at the center, of the action. Throughout *Skyfall*, Moneypenny is made to pay for her "bad shot" by engaging in a series of disciplinary interpellations that (re)articulate her "proper place" and effectively transform her from Bond's equal to a supportive sidekick. Insofar as the film demands that Moneypenny be repositioned and disciplined to understand her "proper place," the film's narrative signals a broader inability on the part of action cinema to renegotiate representations of traditionally marginalized identities and to integrate racial and gendered "Others" into the center of the action.

MONEYPENNY'S "BAD SHOT": PENETRATING BOND'S BODY

Recent analyses of *Casino Royale* (Martin Campbell 2006) and *Quantum of Solace* (Marc Forster 2008) emphasize the specularisation of Bond's body, which becomes a visual guarantee of the ascendency and power of the post-Cold War British nation. Colleen M. Tremonte and Linda Racioppi argue that Bond's body becomes an "object of the gaze" in *Casino Royale* that reverses an objectifying gaze that has focused solely on women (191). This specularisation, according to Lisa Funnell, represents a shift away from the "British lover tradition" and towards a more Hollywood mode of muscular masculinity in which "Bond's body, rather than his libido, [becomes] the new locus of masculinity" ("Negotiating" 208). Where *Skyfall* differs is the extent to which Bond's body is revealed as vulnerable. For as Klaus Dodds notes, *Skyfall* is the first Bond film that visualizes Bond's aging and vulnerable body (121). This is clearly evident in the opening credits, which depict Bond's body being pulled downward through the water by a woman's hand and absorbed into a black pit that emerges from the riverbed. Clouds of blood transform the screen and images of Bond as a shooting target marred with bleeding bullet holes reinforce his vulnerability.

By focusing on the weakness of Bond's body in the title sequence, the film draws a connection between the relative health of Bond and the strength of the British nation. As Dodds notes, it is Bond's vulnerable body that "offers an opportunity to link his eventual rehabilitation to that of the national security state" (122). This focus enables *Skyfall* to establish a narrative of reconstitution, in which Bond must undergo a series of trials that enable him to assert his corporeal superiority. Bond's resurrection as a virile action hero is linked to the ability of Britain to retain its power in an increasingly volatile and uncontrollable geopolitical climate (ibid. 120). If, as Moneypenny notes, Bond can be seen as an "old dog with new tricks," Britain, too, must undergo a similar narrative reconstitution in order to maintain its representation as experienced and strong, its body politic bolstered by the traditional virtues embodied in the British bulldog that sits on M's desk.

In this sense, the focus on the revival of Bond's fit and hypermasculine body throughout the film reiterates the proper gender relations constitutive of a "healthy" British nation. Although women and people of color are not necessarily barred from this sphere, they are fundamentally conceptualized as "out of place" (Woollacott 110) and require a reorientation that resituates them at the margins of a male dominated arena (Tremonte and Racioppi 190). Moneypenny's bad shot challenges the hypermasculinity and strength of Bond's body, quite literally by penetrating the typical sheen of the male action hero. Insofar as one of the underlying themes of *Skyfall* is Bond's bodily rehabilitation and the restoration of his masculinity and heroism, Moneypenny's initial actions interfere with this narrative arc, temporarily stalling this process of rehabilitation. Given Dodds' argument that "'resilience' as with age and gender is something best thought of as being shaped by relations and interactions between different groups" (126), it is notable that the rehabilitation of Bond's white, cisgendered, male body is stalled by his relationship with Moneypenny, whose racial and gendered Otherness is represented as an obstacle to Bond's capacity to reconfirm his own masculinity. Craig's Bond is reproduced as resilient through his interaction with Moneypenny as the racial and gendered Other; an exchange that allows Bond to come out on top but which forecloses the possibility that Moneypenny could achieve the same. Moneypenny's bad shot, and the disciplinary actions she must undergo as a result, reveal the transgressive quality of a strong black woman interfering into and enacting violence within a space defined by gendered and racial parameters.

Moneypenny's reorientation takes place on multiple levels, starting with MI6 the bureaucratic agency that interferes to discipline her as a result of her mistake. In *Skyfall*—and the Craig films more generally—discipline is reframed as a bureaucratic necessity, and disciplinary violence is executed by agencies like MI6. This shift effectively obscures the fact that procedures that marginalize women *are* acts of discipline; instead, these acts are presented as necessary bureaucratic "adjustments" that enable the perpetuation of the normative social order. In this sense, Tremonte and Racciopi's argument that violent women are put into their place by Bond (188) is modified in the Craig-era films; Bond's attempts come second to the activities of the state/MI6 and only reinforce the (ideological) violence that has already repositioned these women.

SKYFALL AND THE BIRACIAL BUDDY

The relationship between Moneypenny and Bond can be conceptualized through the lens of what Ed Guerrero calls the "biracial buddy" narrative, a dynamic that recurs in

Hollywood action films of the 1980s. The biracial buddy formula establishes the white male lead as the hero with the "black buddy" as a supporting figure, invoking the idea of the white hero serving as "cultural and ideological chaperone" (Guerrero 239) to the black buddy. Insofar as they represent simplified versions of biracial homosocial bonding without unsettling the social hierarchy that positions whites as superior to blacks, biracial buddy films "present the audience with escapist fantasy narratives [...] that mediate America's very real and intractable racial problems" (ibid. 240). The first "black buddy" of the Craig era films is Felix Leiter, a recurring character in the series who was recast as a black man played by Jeffrey Wright in *Casino Royale*. Moneypenny effectively replaces Leiter as the "black helper" in *Skyfall* and she, unlike Leiter, is presented as a threat to Bond as she competes with him for heroic status. As a British agent, Moneypenny seeks to occupy the same "field" as Bond, whereas Leiter is an American agent who circulates in the same networks threatening Bond's dominance. Leiter's strength, knowledge, and heroic capacities can be accommodated by the narrative insofar as he uses them to assist Bond in his missions.

While Leiter's masculinity marks him out as an appropriate operator, Moneypenny's competence is constantly called into question. The Craig-era films take for granted the authority and competence of male agents, providing multiple opportunities for these men to recuperate and display their physical and professional superiority. The biracial buddy dynamic is therefore modified by the recalibration of the Craig-era films to reflect Hollywood action film conventions—a shift that inscribes the muscular, hypermasculine body and its physical fitness as the central signifier of heroic competence (Funnell, "I Know" 463). Leiter, who is representative of both male heroism and American interests, is acceptable as a black buddy, while Moneypenny is not. This is best illustrated through a comparison of the relative sacrifices of Leiter and Moneypenny. In *Quantum of Solace*, Leiter puts his career on the line by disobeying his superior in order to save Bond's life and provide him with intelligence. Leiter's "sacrifice" actually works in his favor, resulting in his promotion at the conclusion of the film. Moneypenny, alternatively, sacrifices her position in the field in order to assume the role of informant, and by the conclusion of the film, administrative assistant. The intersection of gender and nationality seems to determine how their respective sacrifices are coded within the narrative. While Leiter's sacrifice proves that he is deserving of a promotion and a more important position in the field, Moneypenny's narrative arc justifies her eventual demotion to a supportive and administrative role.

Moneypenny's transition from autonomous field agent to supportive "buddy" is made clear after Bond returns to MI6 and reassumes his position in the field. During their first exchange after the shooting incident, Moneypenny apologizes to Bond and notes: "I've been reassigned. Temporary suspension from fieldwork. Something to do with killing 007." Bond responds, "Well, you gave it your best shot," only to have Moneypenny snap back with "that was hardly my best shot." Although Bond's comment, framed in a witty and flirtatious exchange, is not intended to be taken seriously, the underlying tension of his statement allows him the opportunity to rearticulate his own competency at the expense of Moneypenny (Dodds 126). Her origin story is minimized and made instrumental to Bond's narrative of resurrection. Bond demonstrates his competence through this relational exchange that ultimately legitimizes Moneypenny's removal from fieldwork by subtly endorsing MI6's decision to reposition her in a supportive role.

The specter of Moneypenny as a threat to the stability of the existing system is foregrounded by Bond's subsequent remark: "I'm not sure I could survive your best." Bond's hesitation is soon mitigated by his insistence that "[Fieldwork's] not for everyone" in response to Moneypenny's enthusiasm for returning to the field. This dialogue represents an indeterminate power relation between Bond and Moneypenny, while also demonstrating Bond's role as ideological disciplinarian who represents and verbally sanctions Moneypenny's repositioning by MI6. By diminishing her capabilities as a field agent, Bond's dialogue acts as a form of disciplinary realignment that suggests Moneypenny does not have the skills or prowess to "hold her own" in the field. Furthermore, Bond's quip implicitly suggests that, while Moneypenny may not be suited for the field, Bond himself will inevitably "bounce back," effectively proving his own resilience and naturalizing his "right" to the field.

RACE, GENDER, AND THE ACT OF "SERVICING" BOND

Moneypenny's acceptance of the buddy role is made visible in China where she and Bond have been sent to investigate Patrice's gambling chip. At the beginning of the scene, Bond is shown topless, shaving in a mirror with a straight razor. Moneypenny arrives at Bond's hotel room, announcing "room service" in a sultry voice. Bond responds, "I didn't order anything. Not even you." This exchange establishes Moneypenny's ability and willingness to "service" Bond, reinforcing the dynamic of "power and subservience" that Yvonne Tasker associates with the biracial buddy narrative (*Spectacular* 36).

The film's positioning of Moneypenny in a servicing role is reminiscent of other Bond films that reinforce this power dynamic between Bond and women who become "helpers," sometimes in more ways than one. In *You Only Live Twice* (Lewis Gilbert 1967), Bond is brought to the home of Tiger Tanaka where he advises Bond to "place himself entirely in [the] hands" of a group of silent Japanese women who bathe and provide him with a massage. During the bath scene, Tanaka boasts about the submissiveness of Japanese women, noting that English women would not be equally willing to service men in this way. Bond responds with "I think I know one or two who may get around to it" to which Tanaka replies, "Miss Moneypenny, perhaps?" This mention of Moneypenny reflects her role as an administrative support but also anticipates her more "physical" role as a helper to Bond in *Skyfall*, where she—like Tanaka's Japanese helpers—aids Bond in the maintenance of his body, and helps facilitate Bond's resurrection as the hypermasculine action hero. The connection between these scenes is emphasized by the use of orientalized settings: Tanaka's Japanese home and Bond's Macau hotel styled to reflect "traditional" Chinese architecture.

The orientalized setting serves to frame Moneypenny as a passive helper, further legitimizing her professional transition. Moneypenny's willingness to acclimate herself to her new position is particularly visible when she announces that she "has some new information," only for Bond to quip back, "aren't you a little overqualified to be delivering messages?" Moneypenny responds, "It's all part of the learning curve." By enthusiastically submitting to her new role, *Skyfall* reasserts that black characters can indeed gain the upper hand by way of their acceptance of white terms (Guerrero 244). The franchise reinforces this idea by frequently representing black women as duplicitous and/or animalistic, and therefore requiring discipline through violence and/or ideological repositioning. Black women are usually revealed to be helpers insofar as it furthers their own goals. Although there are examples in the franchise of Asian women who initially serve as helpers and are later revealed to be double agents—such as the Chinese CSI agent disguised as a masseuse in *Die Another Day* (Lee Tamahori 2002)—representations of Asian women in the franchise alternate between Bond Girl helpers and passive servers. In comparison, black women, up until the casting of Halle Berry as Bond Girl Jinx Johnson in *Die Another Day*, were usually represented as duplicitous, violent, or deviant. Despite the initial introduction of Rosie Carver in *Live and Let Die* (Guy Hamilton 1973) as a CIA ally, she is revealed to be a double-agent who is actually leading Bond into the villain's trap. After being called "a liar and a cheat," Carver is killed by one of her boss' traps. In *A View to a Kill* (John Glen 1985), May Day is represented as a monstrous female: she is unapologetically violent, has superhuman strength, and seduces Bond by jumping on top of him and taking control. Although she switches allegiances at the conclusion of the film, helping Bond and sacrificing her life in the process, she remains coded as animalistic, non-human, and deviant. These black women are reduced to stereotypes; both are hyper-sexualized and represented as duplicitous and violent. Although Moneypenny does find a place in the British secret service, she can only do so by "fully internaliz[ing] the values" of that class (Guerrero 244) whose very power depends on the ongoing marginalization of women and racial Others. By reframing her within the conventions of the orientalized "helper," *Skyfall* effectively differentiates Moneypenny from the "deviant" and self-serving black women previously featured in the franchise.

Moneypenny's ability and willingness to serve Bond is also made visible when she finishes shaving his face with the cut-throat razor. When he hands her the razor, Moneypenny asks, "Are you putting your life in my hands again?" The answer is a resounding "yes" from Bond, who responds by attempting to unbutton her blouse. The scene is appropriately tense, employing the metaphor of the "close shave" to mirror the escalating sexual tension, the culmination of which, notably, remains off-screen, if it happened at all. The danger posed by Moneypenny not only resides in her racial "Otherness" but also in the fact that she is the person who previously shot him, which resulted in Bond's "close shave" with death. The shaving scene effectively demonstrates this reorientation, as Moneypenny transforms from being an impediment to Bond's bouncing back to becoming actively involved in what Dodds' calls his rejuvenation (128).

DISCIPLINING EVE, INTERPELLATING MONEYPENNY

The degree to which Moneypenny is able to successfully integrate herself and indeed internalize the normative values of this society is made visible in her final confrontation with Bond. This is, significantly, also the moment when "Eve" is revealed to be "Moneypenny." This "naming" is an act of interpellation in the Althusserian sense. Althusser writes that "all ideology hails or interpellates concrete individuals as concrete subjects" (173). Moneypenny's official naming signifies her recognition and integration within the dominant social order as a "properly situated" subject. This naming brings her into being as the "proper" Moneypenny, confirming that she has been successfully disciplined and domesticated, and, by extension, has been properly "constituted as a subject" (Althusser 171) by and within the dominant ideology. The moment that audiences "recognize" Moneypenny via her official introduction to Bond is simultaneously the moment that signals her ideological interpellation and ability to be recognized and confirmed within the system.

The success of Moneypenny's disciplining is reinforced by the scene when she passes on M's legacy to Bond. Prior to this moment, audiences see Bond standing on the roof of MI6 headquarters, surveying the streets of London below. In the background, directly above his head, a British flag flies in the wind, demonstrating the longevity and strength of the nation and Bond's role as its representative. Moneypenny greets Bond on the roof of MI6 headquarters after M's death, holding out a box. When Bond opens the box, he finds the vintage British bulldog figurine that M kept on her desk, the item that M left to him in her will. Moneypenny jokes, "Maybe it was her way of telling you to take a desk job." Bond responds, "Just the opposite." Here, Moneypenny literally passes on "good" British virtues in the form of the figurine, which represents—as does Bond himself—the survival and maintenance of traditional British values. These values are embodied in the figurine *and* Bond: both are "old dog[s] with new tricks" capable of surviving even when M herself cannot. The good lines of Britishness survive and live on, as embodied in Bond's fit, white, hypermasculine body, and the tarnished façade of the porcelain bulldog that, inexplicably, survived the earlier terrorist attack on MI6. Bond has demonstrated that he is capable of "bouncing back," and the white male hero has proven himself resilient (Dodds 128). Once again, the narrative positioning of Moneypenny reveals that her value lies in her role as an intermediary between lead (white) characters whose centrality to the narrative and to the action does not challenge the normative system. The bulldog, if we can call it a gift, sharply contrasts Moneypenny's first, initial "gift" to Bond: the transgressive shot itself. What Moneypenny gives to Bond here is precisely the confirmation of her submission to the dominant order. She has receded from view as an action hero in the field; by stepping aside or behind the scenes, Bond's narrative of reconstitution can come to completion. She has learned her place and is now recognizable as the Moneypenny that audiences have come to know and love.

This is not to say that earlier depictions of Moneypenny are all equally problematic, nor are all earlier depictions of Moneypenny equally submissive. As Tara Brabazon writes, "Miss Moneypenny performs a mode of femininity outside of marriage, fidelity and the private sphere [...] she is neither a safely sexual nor predictably patriarchal performer. She remains a bitch, a demanding woman who cannot be trusted" (490). Lois Maxwell's performance as Moneypenny in the earlier Bond films—from *Dr. No* (Terence Young 1962) to *You Only Live Twice*—articulates her role as a "semiotic suffragette: probing and questioning the limits of women's sexual and societal roles" (Brabazon 492). Although she remains "helplessly romantic" and desperate "for a golden wedding ring," she "actively pursues her quarry" (ibid. 491). This ambiguous albeit more equitable flirtation between Bond and Moneypenny begins to change with *Moonraker* (Lewis Gilbert 1979) and *Octopussy* (John Glen 1983). In these films, Moneypenny is represented as a vain and desexualized spinster figure (Brabazon 493). This depiction of Moneypenny as either a desexualized mothering figure or desperate and doting admirer of Bond continues until the refreshing revamping of the character by Samantha Bond in the Brosnan-era Bond films from *GoldenEye* (Martin Campbell 1995) to *Die Another Day*. Samantha Bond's performance of Moneypenny as a strong and attractive yet sexually unattainable woman capable of calling out Bond on his misogynistic antics is, in some ways, a more progressive depiction of Moneypenny than what *Skyfall* provides. Taking *Skyfall* as the chronological precursor to *Dr. No*, *Skyfall*'s disciplining and domestication of Moneypenny is logical insofar as it establishes a smooth transition between the films by demonstrating how "Eve" transforms into the "proper" Moneypenny: the Moneypenny behind the desk.

The representation of Eve Moneypenny in *Skyfall* leaves much to be desired, even if Naomie Harris' performance reveals a Moneypenny who is, at least initially, more active and independent than many of the earlier depictions. Instead of reimagining the character of Moneypenny to the extent that Bond has been reimagined since *Casino Royale*, *Skyfall* reinscribes Moneypenny as a character who must remain behind the scenes. Despite *Skyfall*'s casting of Moneypenny as a black British woman who initially possesses increased agency and professional autonomy, this progressive representation is mitigated by Moneypenny's disciplining and domestication, which acts as a warning to viewers regarding the limited potential of people of color and women to achieve professional and social mobility. Notably, Brabazon writes that it is "when the feminist movement was radical and active in the public domain [that] the representations of Moneypenny were at their most repressive ad disapproving [...] transform[ing] the supersecretary into a warning beacon for ageing women" (493). In the same manner, *Skyfall's* representation of the disciplining and domestication of Moneypenny can be conceptualized as a didactic tool intended to reinforce racial and gendered hierarchies within an increasingly pluralized society in general and in postcolonial Britain more specifically. Moneypenny's disciplining in *Skyfall*, therefore, instructs audiences on how to maintain "proper" racial, sexual, and gendered hierarchies within a contemporary cultural context. *Skyfall's* narrative of discipline and domestication acts as a warning to those who, like Moneypenny herself, may be tempted to transgress. After all, "fieldwork's not for everyone" as some must learn to be content with remaining behind the scenes.

CHAPTER 8

OBJECTS OF WHITE MALE DESIRE

(D)Evolving Representations of Asian Women in Bond Films

Lisa Funnell

The Bond film franchise has been criticized for being sexist and racist (*Licence*, Chapman 12). However, critics and scholars rarely discuss these forms of oppression in tandem; how the sexism is informed by racism and how the racism is influenced by sexism. Gender and race are two dominant forms of social classification that intersect in powerful ways. This interrelation strongly informs the conceptualization and depiction of Asian women on screen. In Hollywood narratives, Asian femininity has historically been defined in relation to white masculinity; the Asian female subject is rarely an autonomous figure and her identity is derived from her relationship to the white male hero. Asian femininity is not only romanticized in physical and sexual terms, but the bodies of Asian women, according to Marina Heung, serve as canvases upon which cultural meanings are projected (90).

This chapter explores the depiction of Asian women across three key phases of the Bond franchise. In the Connery era (1962-71), Asian women are defined solely in relation to the white male hero and the films foreground the distinction between unacceptable and acceptable Asian femininity. In *Dr. No* (Terence Young 1962), Miss Taro is conceptualized as a "Dragon Lady" and vilified for challenging the mission and libido of James Bond. In comparison, Aki and Kissy Suzuki in *You Only Live Twice* (Lewis Gilbert 1967) qualify as Bond Girls for being submissive and eager to please. In the Brosnan era (1995-2002), Asian femininity is re-defined through the star persona of Hong Kong action star Michelle Yeoh. Although her character, Wai Lin, is the most physically empowered Bond Girl of the franchise, *Tomorrow Never Dies* (Roger Spottiswoode 1997) strips away some of her agency by having Bond seduce her at the end of the film. In the Craig era (2006-12), although Severine is initially characterized as a powerful Dragon Lady in *Skyfall* (Sam Mendes 2012), she quickly devolves into a tragic Lotus Blossom; she is presented as a disposable object of pleasure and struggle between two white men. I will argue that as Severine is one of the most disempowered women in the franchise, *Skyfall* is regressive in its representation of Asian femininity.

MISS TARO – THE DRAGON LADY

The first Bond film, *Dr. No*, introduces many key elements that have come to define the franchise. It stars Sean Connery as James Bond, a character adapted from the figure originating in Ian Fleming's novels. The filmic Bond conveys a more "mid-Atlantic" image with a tougher and less overtly British persona in order to better appeal to American filmgoers (Funnell, "I Know" 458). The film features Ursula Andress as Honey Ryder, the preeminent Bond Girl. She was defined by her beauty, compelling backstory, and romantic relationship with Bond. In addition, the film introduces M, Moneypenny, and Q, staple characters who offer institutional support for Bond. Although the Bond franchise continues to develop its generic identity over the next few films, the inaugural *Dr. No* establishes the politics of representation that define the Connery era.

According to Eugene Franklin Wong, Asian actors have historically been limited in Hollywood through the practice of role segregation. While white actors have been cast in a range of ethnic and racial roles, Asian actors are rarely, if ever, cast in white roles (11). Role segregation is apparent in *Dr. No* as all primary characters are played by white actors. Although the villain, Dr. No, is Asian, he is played by Joseph Wiseman, a white actor who performs in "yellowface"—a racist form of theatrical make-up that presents a stereotyped caricature of an Asian person. With the exception of Miss Taro, all other Asian roles in the film are played by Asian actors; these secondary characters are mostly unnamed and have little-to-no dialogue.

Miss Taro is a henchperson and informant of Dr. No. She works undercover as the administrative assistant to Pleydell Smith, the Chief Secretary of the colonial government of Jamaica. Much like Dr. No, Taro is played by a white actor, Zena Marshall, who performs in yellowface. Moreover, she is presented in the film as a Dragon Lady, a racial stereotype of Asian femininity. The Dragon Lady is a figure of the underworld who is cunning, aggressive, and sexually alluring, particularly to white men (Funnell, *Warrior* 10). As noted by Yasmin Jiwani, the Dragon Lady is dangerous because she is capable of seducing the white male hero away from his "civilizing mission and reducing him into naivety" (184). Through costuming, the film emphasizes the sexual appeal of Taro. On the one hand, she appears in various stages of undress—a silk robe, a towel—while wearing a pair of silver heels, a powerful signifier of femininity. On the other hand, she wears form-fitting dresses that highlight her feminine frame. Although she shows minimal skin, the cut and style of the dresses call attention to her body in order to maximize her attractiveness. In addition, she can be seen applying or touching up red lipstick and nail polish in various scenes. As noted by Andrew J. Elliot and Daniela Niesta, "red, relative to other achromatic and chromatic colors, leads men to view women as more attractive and more sexually desirable" (1150). In *Dr. No*, Taro is idealized in physical and sexual terms.

Taro fulfills the role of Dragon Lady through her seduction of Bond. She sets a trap by inviting him to her apartment; she plans to have him run off the road and killed on his drive over. Presented in a single shot, Taro can be seen reclining on her bed while talking on the phone to Bond who does not appear visually in the scene. Instead, the camera focuses on Taro who is positioned as the erotic object of the gaze. According to Laura Mulvey, the gaze in film is male and the female occupies the traditional exhibitionist role. The woman on screen possesses a "to-be-looked-at-ness" and functions as a two-fold object of white male desire: she is an erotic object for the male character(s) in the diegesis as well for the male viewers who share his gaze ("Visual" 837-8). This scene, which is almost 40 seconds in length, emphasizes the sexual desirability of Taro who seduces Bond verbally (by phone) and the audience visually (through her image).

When Bond finally arrives at the apartment, Taro uses her sexuality to distract him while her counterparts organize another attack. Bond, however, anticipates her plan and has her arrested after they have sex. As she is led into the awaiting car, she is dressed in a cheongsam, a traditional Chinese dress, with her hair tied in a bun, and the film uses costuming to (over)emphasize and reiterate the Asian identity of Taro and her connection to Dr. No. When she defiantly spits in Bond's face, it becomes clear that she is still aligned with the villain and her Asian heritage, and has not been swayed by Bond to support white Western society. Given her threat to the mission and libido of Bond, she is quickly escorted out of the scene, presumably to be punished for her transgressions.

AKI AND KISSY SUZUKI – THE LOTUS BLOSSOMS

In *You Only Live Twice*, Bond secretly travels to Japan to investigate the disappearance of a missing spacecraft. He works with Japanese secret service agent Tiger Tanaka (Tetsurô Tanba) and is aided on his mission by two Asian Bond Girls, Aki (Akiko Wakabayashi) and Kissy Suzuki (Mie Hama). As I have argued elsewhere, each Bond film features only one Bond Girl. She is a non-recurring character, the primary female protagonist, and the central love interest of Bond ("From English" 63). However, in *You Only Live Twice*, as well as *Tomorrow Never Dies*, two Bond Girls are introduced but only one survives the film. Bond's relationship with the first Bond Girl (Aki and Paris Carver, respectively) runs its course and he mourns her death before engaging in a relationship with the second Bond Girl (Suzuki and Wai Lin, respectively) who he ends up dating by the end of the film (ibid.). Interestingly, this anomaly only occurs in films featuring Asian Bond Girls, and creates the impression that Asian Bond Girls are not as compelling as their white counterparts. As a result, the films need to provide Bond with two love interests or options.

You Only Live Twice takes liberties with the storyline presented in the original source novel published in 1964. As noted by Jeremy Black, the Chinese play a sinister role in the film and not in the novel, and this adaptation reflects the contemporaneous perception of China as a military threat after their testing of nuclear weapons in the 1960s (95). The film also takes liberties in its representation of Bond Girls. Originally, the script called for one Bond Girl, Kissy Suzuki. The two Japanese actors who were vying for the role were sent to London for six months to learn English. While Akiko Wakabayashi picked up the language quickly, Mie Hama could not learn enough English for the role and was told she would not be in the film. Upset by the decision, Hama told the casting agent that she had lost face and was going to kill herself (Kyriazi ¶ 2-3). As director Lewis Gilbert recalls:

> I didn't want a young woman's death on my conscience nor did the producers want that kind of publicity. So I told Tamba to tell her to stay and that she would be in the movie. Then I came up with the idea to have the two Japanese actresses switch parts because the other part didn't have much English speaking in it, and it worked out okay. (Qtd. in Kyriazi ¶ 4)

Gilbert draws attention to the fact that Aki and Suzuki were initially conceptualized as a single character, and should thus be discussed in tandem. Moreover, this anecdote relies on a romanticized notion of Japanese culture that is arguably transferred onto the Japanese characters, and specifically the Bond Girls, in the film.

Aki and Suzuki, like the other Asian women in the film, are presented through the racial stereotype of the Lotus Blossom. The Lotus Blossom is a submissive and industrious figure who is eager to please the white male hero, and her identity centers on the sexual relationship she develops with him (Funnell, *Warrior* 10). Although Aki is tasked with aiding Bond, she expresses a desire to serve Bond's carnal needs as well. As Tanaka explains to Bond during the infamous bathhouse scene in which they are bathed by a bevy of semi-nude Asian women, "Rule number one: never do anything yourself when someone else can do it for you…Rule number two: in Japan, men come first, women come second." Aki confirms this sentiment when she tells Bond, "I think I will enjoy very much serving under you," a reference to both her sexual and social position.

In order for Aki to win the love of Bond, she must commit herself fully to him, his mission, and his country. As noted by Yen Le Espiritu, Hollywood narratives often feature interracial romances between Anglo American men and Asian women that follow the Pocahontas mythos: the Asian woman commits herself to dominant white culture out of devotion to her lover. She usually dies or ends up leaving her country to go live with her husband (12). Aki is a tragic figure whose love for Bond inevitably leads to her death. She is poisoned by a substance that was meant for Bond while they are sleeping in bed. Through her death, Aki (unknowingly) sacrifices herself so that

Bond can carry on his mission. This narrative, inscribed with the Pocahontas mythos, works to legitimate and naturalize the access of the white West (coded masculine via Bond) to the Asian East (coded feminine via Aki).

Although saddened by the death of Aki, Bond moves forward with his mission by preparing to work undercover as a fisherman in Japan. He undergoes a process in which he "turns Japanese:" he wears yellowface, learns martial arts, and marries a Japanese bride. This sequence of events is grossly problematic as it relays a simplistic and racist interpretation of Japanese culture. Moreover, Bond's greatest fear throughout this process is that his bride will be ugly. Although Suzuki marries Bond, she initially rejects his advances, telling him, "This is business." Her professional approach is reflected in her clothing, as she wears loose-fitting kimonos that cover her body and obscure her frame, and she rejects being positioned as an object of the gaze. Soon after, she begins to develop feelings for Bond and this internal change is signaled externally through a change in costuming. During a reconnaissance mission with Bond, Suzuki wears a white bikini while Bond is fully clothed. As the two lay down to rest on a hill, she leans back placing her body on display for Bond who leans in to kiss her. In a short period of time, Suzuki quickly transitions from ally agent to servile Lotus Blossom and she appears to pick up with Bond where he and Aki had left off.

Racial stereotypes often come in two opposing models defined in terms of their position to white hegemony. According to Frank Chin and Jeffery Paul Chan, the "unacceptable model" is considered undesirable because the person cannot be controlled by whites and threatens the status quo (65). In comparison, the "acceptable model" is permitted because the person is "tractable;" in other words, she/he is easy to control or influence. In the Connery era, Asian femininity is defined in relation to James Bond. On the one hand, Miss Taro is presented as a Dragon Lady who is punished for challenging the mission and libido of Bond. On the other hand, Aki and Kissy Suzuki are presented as Lotus Blossoms who qualify as Bond Girls for desiring domestication.

WAI LIN – THE ACTION HERO BOND GIRL

After nearly 30 years, the Bond franchise cast another Asian Bond Girl. *Tomorrow Never Dies* features Hong Kong action star Michelle Yeoh as Wai Lin, a Chinese secret agent who works with Bond to bring down a media mogul. Lin is one of the strongest Bond Girls in the franchise. Producers relied heavily on the established star persona of Yeoh when crafting her character, much like they did with Grace Jones for May Day in *A View to a Kill* (John Glen 1985; Funnell, "Negotiating" 206). By the 1990s, Yeoh had developed a reputation for being a "real" action star: she performed her own stunts and fought alongside some of Hong Kong's most reputable action men like Jackie Chan, Jet Li, and Donnie Yen (Funnell, *Warrior* 39-42). Given the transnational popularity of Yeoh and her dynamism on screen, Bond producers cast her as an action-oriented Bond Girl in their film.

Skilled in martial arts, Lin outfights and outshines Bond in all of the action sequences in which she appears, regardless of whether she is fighting alone or alongside Bond. Lin is also a skilled investigator as she uncovers similar clues and arrives at the same conclusions as Bond. What differentiates Lin from Bond, however, is her strong sense of purpose. While Bond is easily distracted by beautiful women and even tries to seduce Lin, she remains focused on the job at hand and continually turns him down; she effectively rejects her positioning as a Lotus Blossom in the film. *Tomorrow Never Dies* also presents the impression that Lin might be a superior secret agent. After defending her apartment from attackers, she reveals to Bond that her place doubles as a home base: it has been equipped with technology and gadgets similar to those developed by the Q Branch. As Bond walks through the space, he is presented as the target of a series of gags; he accidentally sets off a number of traps and is almost killed in the process. When Bond insists on sending a message to M16, Lin steps aside and takes pleasure in watching Bond discover that the keyboard has Chinese characters rather than the English alphabet. Although Bond, throughout the franchise, has taken his female allies to task in order to prove that he is a superior agent, the opposite occurs in *Tomorrow Never Dies* and it is Lin who comes out on top.

Lin is not a typical Bond Girl and she is not set up as the love interest of Bond. As previously noted, *Tomorrow Never Dies* is the second film in the franchise to feature two consecutive Bond Girls: Bond has a relationship with Paris Carver (Teri Hatcher) and only begins to work with Lin after Carver has been killed and he has mourned her death. This anomaly arguably aids in strengthening the character of Lin by alleviating her of the burden of appealing to the white male gaze. Since Carver has already fulfilled this expectation, appearing in a cleavage enhancing dress and lingerie, Lin is free to exude a more heroic image. As I have argued elsewhere,

> She is never sexualized or fetishized on-screen, and her body is never placed on erotic display, which would undermine the heroic accomplishments of her character; instead, she is costumed in loose-fitting clothes that offer her practical mobility and provide her with a more masculine image. (*Warrior*, 43)

By rejecting the advances of Bond, Lin is able to distance herself from the narrative and iconographic expectations of the Bond Girl. She is valued as a hero above all else and offers a new image of Asian femininity that centers on her achievements rather than oriental sexuality (ibid.). The film, according to Sheldon Lu, reframes for Western audiences the traditionally libidinous relationship between British masculinity and Chinese femininity by presenting a cooperative rather than parasitic relationship between Bond and Lin (134).

Although Lin is initially depicted as an empowered action woman, the film seems to strip away some of her agency in the final scenes. Captured by Richard Stamper (Götz Otto), Lin is chained to an anchor and tossed overboard. Bond not only rescues a drowning Lin—giving her "mouth-to-mouth" in the process—but he also succeeds in wooing her as this lifesaving act doubles as their first kiss. The sudden romance between Bond and Lin seems forced and contrived. Had the film ended in a non-traditional manner with Bond and Lin simply parting ways, it might convey the impression that Lin, and not Bond, is the superior agent and hero—that Bond needs Lin more than she needs him. Instead, the film neutralizes Lin's threat to the heroic competency of Bond through heterosexual romantic conquest. In an attempt to place Lin within the confines of the Bond Girl archetype, the film concludes with an unconvincing shot of Bond and Lin kissing on a piece of debris in the middle of the ocean.

In spite of its ending, *Tomorrow Never Dies* features one of the strongest and most popular Bond Girls. Not only did the role open up opportunities for Michelle Yeoh in Hollywood, but Bond producers sought her out to reprise her role in *Die Another Day* (Lee Tamahori 2002); Wai Lin would provide Bond with an ally after his escape from the M16 debriefing with M ("Wai" ¶ 1). This was the first time that a Bond Girl had been asked to return to the series in the same role. Yeoh, however, turned down the part in order to shoot a film in Hong Kong with her own production company, and aspects of her character were divided across a number of roles (ibid. ¶ 9). Nonetheless, this request draws attention to the popular appeal of an Asian Bond Girl who has a standalone identity that is defined by her achievements rather than her sexual appeal to the white male hero.

SEVERINE – DISEMPOWERED LOTUS BLOSSOM

The Craig era films constitute a rebooting of the Bond film franchise. They are revisionist in nature: they deconstruct the Bondian genre and refashion key elements in order to appeal to a new generation of filmgoers. This is most notable in the adaptation of the filmic James Bond. As I have argued elsewhere, *Casino Royale* (Martin Campbell 2006) shifts away from the British lover literary tradition and "firmly grounds Craig's Bond in contemporary American ideals of heroic masculinity. Emphasis is placed on Daniel Craig's exposed muscular torso rather than his sexuality, libido and conquest" (Funnell, "I Know" 462). As the reboot trilogy has progressed, additional Bondian elements have been reconceptualized and reintroduced into the series.

Skyfall is notably regressive in its representation of women on screen. For example, the film emphasizes the age and maternal qualities of M (Judi Dench) whose competency as the leader of M16 is constantly called into question. In addition, Eve Moneypenny (Naomie Harris) is presented as a defunct field agent who almost kills Bond and is subsequently demoted to a desk job. In a similar way, the character Severine (Bérénice Marlohe) is presented as one of the most tragic and disempowered women not only in the Craig era, but the franchise at large. Instead of building on the popular appeal of Wai Lin or even continuing the tradition of revisioning characters/ character types, the Bond franchise reverts back to an older, antiquated, and problematic representational mode for the Asian female subject.

Although Marlohe is a multiracial actress—her father is Asian and her mother is white—her character is clearly presented as an Asian "Other" in the film. Initially, Severine is depicted as a mysterious, alluring, and powerful Dragon Lady via iconography. Bond first meets Severine in a casino in Macau. The room is dimly lit and many characters, including Severine, are partially cast in shadow. Severine is wearing a floor-length form-fitting dress. While most of her body is covered, much of the dress is made from a black sheer material, which works to highlight rather than conceal her feminine frame; based on its design, the dress looks more like burlesque lingerie than a formal gown. Severine is also wearing dark make-up and her long nails are painted black, adding to her dangerous yet alluring appeal. Flanked by bodyguards, Severine initially appears to be a powerful and commanding figure.

In a short period of time, a series of events unfold that greatly alter our perception of Severine. She reveals to Bond that Silva (Javier Bardem) saved her from the sex trade in Macau and she is now bound to him. Bond agrees to help her escape in exchange for her assistance in meeting Silva. Following this, Severine and Bond have sex in a steamy shower scene on their way to Dead Island, which houses Silva's base. While Bond is taken prisoner and interrogated by Silva, Severine is beaten and tied to a statue. She then serves as a target when Silva places a shot glass on her head and forces Bond to shoot at her. When Bond misses too far to her left, Silva raises his pistol and shoots her squarely in the forehead. Bond reacts to this event by stating, "What a waste of a good scotch." In the end, neither man shows any remorse for the death of Severine.

Although originally presented as a Dragon Lady, Severine is quickly disempowered and devolves into a tragic Lotus Blossom as the narrative progresses. She is presented as a disposable object of pleasure and struggle between two white men and the identity of Severine is defined solely in terms of her relationships with Bond and Silva. She has limited dialogue, little-to-no personal agency, and, much like Le Chiffre's (Mads Mikkelsen) girlfriend Valenka (Ivana Milićević) in *Casino Royale*, she is paraded around half-naked for the majority of her time on-screen (Funnell, "Negotiating" 209). Her death has little impact on Bond, Silva, or the narrative trajectory. In fact, her role could be entirely eliminated from the film without significantly altering the storyline. As a result, Severine can be considered one of the most disempowered, pitiful, and tragic women in the Bond film franchise.

(D)EVOLVING REPRESENTATIONS

An examination of the intersection of gender and race draws attention to the politics of representation at work in the Bond franchise. While some might argue that the series has evolved in terms of its gender and racial politics, producers continue to rely on racial stereotypes to envisage Asian femininity, defining it in relation to white masculinity. Although *Skyfall* marks the fiftieth anniversary of the series and the conclusion of the reboot trilogy, the film is decidedly regressive in its treatment of Severine and employs antiquated modes of representation that are reductive, sexist, and racist. Given the popular appeal of Wai Lin, an independent and empowered Bond Girl who was valued for her accomplishments rather than oriental sexuality, Bond producers should consider revising their representation of the Asian female subject. Although the Lotus Blossom is considered to be the "acceptable model" of Asian femininity, it is still a racist stereotype and a limited and fixated form of representation. While seemingly positive traits are romanticized and exoticized, this generalization continues to define Asian femininity in relation to the white male status quo, that being James Bond.

Section 3

FEMINIST CRITIQUES AND MOVEMENTS

CHAPTER 9

"NEVER TRUST A RICH SPY"

Ursula Andress, Vesper Lynd, and Mythic Power in *Casino Royale* 1967

Robert von Dassanowsky

The concept of the female spy permanently ruptured the polarized good/bad images of women in Anglo-American dominant cinema and television. *Film noir* had much to do with this, as did Hitchcock, and the short-lived sub-genre of the caper comedy provides a unique conflation of postwar cinematic influences and 1960s sexuality, further destabilizing traditional female imagery on screen. Ursula Andress' Vesper Lynd in the multidirectional Bond spoof, *Casino Royale* (Val Guest et al. 1967), is no ordinary *femme fatale*, but arguably the most remarkable female character of the entire decade's espionage genre, for her vast independent power and wealth. The 1967 Vesper Lynd also echoes Andress' role in the first Bond film *Dr. No* (Terence Young 1962) as it intertexts with the "real" Bond series and conflates the other sexually domineering characters she previously portrayed.

Much has been written about the unfinished qualities of the 1967 *Casino Royale*. While it is true that Peter Sellers dropped out of the project leaving his role incomplete, and that segments from three credited screenwriters and five credited directors provided such varied narrative arcs that director Val Guest was asked by producer Charles K. Feldman to ensure continuity in the editing room, the film should be considered a classic because it embraced the feel of the era's "Happening." Although a spy spoof, the film's actual sub-genre might be called "psychedelic mainstream cinema," which was first attempted with *The Loved One* (Tony Richardson 1965) and *What's New Pussycat?* (Clive Donner and Richard Talmadge 1965). As the response to the demise of studio-based cinema, these destabilizing and self-subversive social satires dared to take on aspects of life, death, identity, capitalism, the American middle class, and the British upper class in a way that was anathema to Hollywood censorship. Nevertheless, the screwball comedy-as-hallucination did not just appear but had been birthed by pushing the envelope even further on social and political farces of the late 1950s and early 1960s. The more brazen independent films of Billy Wilder such as *One, Two, Three* (1961) are seminal to the mix, but so are John Boulting's comedies with Peter Sellers, such as *Carlton-Browne of the F.O.* (1959), and Stanley Kubrick's *Lolita* (1962) and *Dr. Strangelove* (1964), which literally took the proverbial gloves off as to what could be shown and how. With the birth of the James Bond films in 1962, which re-visioned Hitchcock—particularly *North By Northwest* (1959)—and the sub-genre of the caper films in which traditional morality was questioned, iconoclastic satire needed only a dose of "mod" cool and the visual emulation of hallucinogens to reach the zenith of *Casino Royale* in 1967.

In the glut of the spy films and spoofs of the 1960s, mainstream international cinema offered only three true attempts at creating a female James Bond with all the power and sexuality that the concept entailed. Joseph Losey's Felliniesque *Modesty Blaise* (1966), based on the popular French comic strip, offered a talented female spy, but unlike her morally superior male counterparts, she was a master thief and associated with the underworld. Her independence, rejection of the intelligence establishment, and nontraditional sexual mores might have developed into a strong proto-feminist series, but traditional critics and audiences rejected a liberated female as hero because of the moral ambiguity. Frank Tashlin's slapdash *Caprice* (1967), with Doris Day in a title role she despised, pretends to be a female version of the male spy spoof, but is actually about corporate espionage. Day's Caprice is a thin reworking of her career-women characters of the late 1950s, and even her flirtation with casual sex is so convoluted as to slip by without any ramifications to character or plot development (Dassanowsky, "Caper" 108).

It is Andress' Vesper Lynd in *Casino Royale* that attains a memorable quality of power, wealth, and an independent lifestyle that have little to do with patriarchy. Andress' Lynd, along with David Niven's Sir James Bond, Joanna Pettet's Mata Bond, and Woody Allen's Jimmy Bond/Dr. Noah, are the only fully developed characters in the 1967 *Casino Royale* that provide a through-line for the episodic, fragmented narrative. Andress and Niven also returned to the film to shoot additional scenes to provide linkages for new (sub-)plot directions, and despite the intentional cameo feel to the cast, the film is anchored by their personalities and roles. It was a particular coup of the filmmakers to employ Andress as the lead female role, given her Bond film pedigree, and to some extent her character is linked with Honey Ryder in such a way as to suggest they might actually be the same person.

THE B(L)OND GIRL: TRADITION AND EXCEPTION

Andress was a difficult fit for Hollywood's imported glamour girl phase of the late 1950s and early 1960s. Her German-Swiss accent was too heavy and she was re-voiced in her first films, including *Dr. No*. Her classic, statuesque look would often connect her with Greco-Roman imagery, but her intelligent, often purposive expressiveness made her an unsuccessful match for Elvis Presley, who normally dominated his blander female co-stars on screen, in *Fun in Acapulco* (Richard Thorpe 1963). In *4 For Texas* (Robert Aldrich 1963), an all-star western that vacillated between cliché and spoof, Andress and her female co-star, Anita Ekberg, who became an international icon with *La Dolce Vita* (Federico Fellini 1960), were obviously cast to exploit their fashionable exotic starlet status. But Andress' more enigmatic and larger than life roles in *She* (Robert Day 1965), *What's New Pussycat?*, and *The Blue Max* (John Guillermin 1966) revealed her to be a talented and self-aware performer especially adept in playing the icy *femme fatale*. This made her somewhat of an acquired taste and certainly limited her roles. Even in period costume, or in more dramatic parts as the adulterous wife of General Count von Klugermann, who chafes at the limitations of her freedom in the World War I German flying ace saga, *The Blue Max*, Andress was encouraged to exploit an inscrutable domineering quality that had quickly become her trademark. The year before, she had mocked her goddess image by descending from the sky with a parachute and demanding that a befuddled Peter O'Toole join her in bed in *What's New Pussycat?*. In the same film, Peter Sellers' character defends himself from his wife's accusations of infidelity with Andress in an obviously improvised response when he points out that she "is a close personal friend of James Bond!"

In the original Fleming novel *Casino Royale* (1953),[1] Vesper Lynd was Bond's passive love interest who betrays him, and in the 2006 film directed by Martin Campbell she was presented as a sensitive and conflicted double agent. In the 1967 *Casino Royale*, however, the character was tailored to the Amazonian-like quality that Andress had first suggested in *Dr. No* and since developed in such roles as *She*. In this historical fantasy, Andress delivers a commanding interpretation of Ayesha, the immortal high-priestess queen known as "She-Who-Must-Be-Obeyed." The blend of seduction and cruel manipulation seems like an audition for *Casino Royale*, where she adapts the type to slightly more human parameters in her mythic Lynd. More than a decade and a half later, her role as Aphrodite opposite Laurence Olivier's Zeus in *Clash of the Titans* (Desmond Davis 1981) revisited the super-woman qualities she projected in *She* and it became one of her notable international film appearances.

Lisa Funnell argues that the early "Bond Girls" were vulnerable sexual objects, and those with any agency were the "enemy", unless converted by Bond like Pussy Galore in *Goldfinger* (Guy Hamilton 1964). Females with true authority were masculinized and middle-aged, having no sexual attraction for Bond: Rosa Klebb in *From Russia with Love* (Terence Young 1963) and Irma Bunt in Peter Hunt's 1969 film *On Her Majesty's Secret Service* ("From English" 64-6; "Negotiating" 203-4). This makes Andress' Lynd a major rupture in the conception of the Bond myth as it applies to women and sexuality, even though the 1967 *Casino Royale* is not part of the official Eon series. The central subplot in the film involving Lynd, Bond, and the casino game with Le Chiffre is nevertheless rooted in Fleming's novel. Lynd's betrayal of Bond in that novel would have given the cinematic Bond no "good" girl to play with or convert, but Lynd, as Fleming wrote her, would also fit with the "bad" girls of the early series since their limited power is manipulated by a male authority and leads to their demise. While Andress' Lynd does betray the Sellers' Bond-for-a-day by killing him, she admits her motivation as she points a gun at her "boss" Sir James Bond (David Niven):

> Sir James (on the phone): I want London, Whitehall double O – O7
>
> Lynd: (pushing down the receiver hook and pointing gun at him): Too bad you won't get it Sir James. I went through a lot of trouble to bring you here.
>
> Sir James: Dear Vesper, the things you do for money.
>
> Lynd: This time it's for *love*, Sir James (indicating with the gun)… back to the office!

The film's new Connery-style Bond, Cooper (Terence Cooper), interrupts her by announcing that American aid has arrived. Lynd runs for cover, but makes it to heaven with the other "good" characters after the casino explodes, because of her confession that she was motivated by love.

Sellers had taken the role in an attempt to refashion his strongly character-oriented comic image into a more romantic-comedy hero. He envisaged the transformation of the easily intimidated baccarat expert, Evelyn Tremble, into a surface imitation of a serious James Bond, albeit with an underlying comedic wit that would be more screwball Cary Grant than the grotesques he played for Kubrick (*Lolita, Dr. Strangelove*). But it was his success in playing the eccentric sex-mad Austrian psychoanalyst in *What's New Pussycat?* opposite Andress, Capucine, and O'Toole that gave the 1967 *Casino Royale* producer Charles K. Feldman the ultimate concept for presenting a Bond film without Sean Connery—another mod "event" film reuniting many of the stars from *Pussycat*. Sellers' dissatisfaction with his segment director Joseph McGrath, whom he had campaigned to get onto the film, and the intimidation Sellers felt from the grandstanding of Orson Welles, resulted in his departure. But in leaving, Lynd's relationship with his character had to change as well. Sellers' Bond had to be killed off and Feldman would bring in the other directors to build a new multidirectional film around the Sellers and Andress footage.

The experience had nevertheless changed Sellers' idea of his own star persona and following his pairing with Andress, most of his subsequent films placed him in the role of a lover with an attractive "leading lady." What survives of the original expanded relationship scenes between Andress' Lynd and Seller's Bond surfaces in a brief druggy-dream sequence and still photos. It is clear that the characters had a deeper relationship than the one-night-stand that makes up the center of the finished film, which Lynd uses to seduce him into being Bond and according to Sir James' orders, to destroy Le Chiffre at a baccarat game at the Casino Royale. As in the novel, Lynd is kidnapped following the victory over Le Chiffre, and Sellers' Bond goes after her and ends up being tortured by Le Chiffre. It is not the scrotum beating of the novel or the 2006 film, although as a nod to the novel Seller's Bond discovers a chair with a hole in the seat and questions it. Instead, Le Chiffre subjects him to an LSD-influenced and electronic "torture of the mind." Bond hallucinates his imprisonment in a Scottish castle, and a perilous collision with a battalion of threatening Scottish pipers and Lynd's appearance to save him, which breaks through the hallucination but also takes on its qualities as well. Dressed as a Scottish piper, Lynd uses her bagpipe machine gun to eradicate the threat. Had Sellers remained with the film, Andress' Lynd *might* have been the first Bond Girl to have true agency and be on the side of "good" decades before what Funnell describes as the Action Hero Bond Girl stage of the series, where particularly "Jinx" Johnson (Halle Berry) in *Die Another Day* (Lee Tamahori 2002) displays professional prowess, sexuality, and an independence equal to Bond ("From English" 77). Lynd, however, gives a final statement on the amoral nature of espionage and her own immense success in it before she also guns him down and out of the film: "Mr. Tremble...never trust a rich spy."

PUTTING ON AND PLAYING (WITH) THE (GENDER) ROLE

Dual representations of mythic superiority essentially subvert traditional gender roles in the 1967 film. Sir James is the elite aesthete in lordly retirement, whereas Lynd is the consummate international business tycoon. Bargaining over the quantity of nuclear warheads to offer France for purchase of the Eiffel Tower, she changes her mind about buying Rockefeller Center, and moves the statue of Lord Nelson from its Trafalgar Square column to outside her living room terrace. "Isn't he beautiful?" she comments, appreciating the idealized male figure in the way men gaze at women. Although she "saves all her energies for business," Sir James manages to persuade her to take on the mission of creating a baccarat playing Bond by appealing to that sensibility and suggests the possibility of leniency in her case of "just over five million pounds tax arrears." The process of Lynd's seduction of Evelyn Tremble in order to fashion an imitation Bond is now the most appreciated aspect of a film that has never been favored by critics. "The Look of Love," sung by Dusty Springfield, underscores Lynd's sexual-psychological refashioning of Tremble's shyness into confidence by showing him, beyond his belief, that he *can* have her. But it is also here that symbolism and cinematic intertext allows insight into what Lynd represents in her time and in film in general—as a woman who "creates" Bond. The year 1967 is known for other transgressive flips on traditional morality and the dominant male/passive female binary in international cinema: the tragic frustrations and sexual diversion of Mrs. Robinson in *The Graduate* (Mike Nichols 1967); the cannibalization of an abusive man by his bourgeois wife in Jean-Luc Godard's *Weekend* (1967); and the relative gender equality of desire and violence in *Bonnie and Clyde* (Arthur Penn 1967).

Michael Stringer's immense and lavish set designs for *Casino Royale* not only outdo previous Eon Bond series films and influence those to come, but they specifically associate Lynd with empowering symbolic imagery throughout the film. Most notably, her entry door bears the large golden bas relief of a goddess face wearing a sunburst crown. Two monumental Grecian goddess caryatids, suggesting those from the Erechtheion temple dedicated to Athena (goddess of wisdom, courage, inspiration, and skill) at the Acropolis in Greece, are visible in her immense office earlier in the film, and there is a long Grecian frieze resembling a portion of the Elgin Marbles (from the Parthenon, also dedicated to Athena) that hangs over the elevator conversation pit in her apartment. She is able to dispatch the bodies of her victims via an interior shaft exposed by a sliding fake oven panel, a wry twist on the woman's traditional role association with the kitchen and the concept of housekeeping. It is a male servant she calls on her intercom phone to remind him to empty "the deep freeze first thing in the morning." There are also clues that she may be a version of Ryder from *Dr. No*, the highly independent beachcomber, perhaps converted through her adventure with Connery's Bond to become a spy. Ryder's capitalist impulses in selling her shells along with her physical self-awareness and instinctive mistrust of men (i.e. brandishing a dagger on Bond and relating how she killed a man that raped her) are amplified and transformed in Lynd. When Sir James claims "the whole world believes that you were eaten by a shark, Miss Lynd" she replies with ennui, "That was no shark, that was my personal submarine."

Lynd is associated with water—the female element—which is also the "home" of Ryder who emerges from the sea foam like a modern-day Botticelli "Venus" in the iconic scene in *Dr. No*. In a striking tracking shot in *Casino Royale*, the camera shoots in slow motion through and across a wall-length aquarium in Lynd's apartment, as she leads Tremble across the room, seemingly floating to her lair. There are elements of skin diving equipment, particularly a spear gun, displayed on a wall in her kitchen. She shoves Tremble into a shower and douses him with cold water when he is drugged by Miss Goodthighs and loses confidence in himself prior to the casino game. Lynd is "just about getting into the bath" as Sir James attempts to warn her about Tremble on Q's "two-way television and radio wristwatch." Above her tub hangs a large pop-art painting of a female eye peering out of blades of grass and flower petals. Whether meant to be the eye of the goddess, an emblem of the female in nature, or a symbol of spying, it is a telling visual element that signals a shift in power dynamics. With Lynd, women can also occupy the gaze that Bond has.

Vesper Lynd circa 1967 is the subject of voyeuristic pleasure for both genders in the audience that oscillates between baiting male desire as an erotic object and empowering the female gaze. Postcoitally, she films Tremble posing on a revolving bed and captures him "in a ridiculous striped outfit of no discernable category—a one-piece affair with shorts and a revealing V-neck (in the back), a sort of Matelot pajama" (Sikov 253). But as he playfully looks at her upside down from a prone position that mocks Golden Age Hollywood female sex symbol poses, the film's wide shot of this tableau is suddenly edited upside down for several frames. Lynd's "home movies" allow her symbolic control of the visual for a brief moment and foreshadow her ultimate control of this character, but the edit suggests it is nevertheless Tremble's male-dominant view (upside-down) that controls the film's simulacrum of reality. Lynd is also a still photographer with a fully stocked dark room in her mirror-lined fuchsia bedroom. The viewer becomes aware of the male performativity of dominance and its absurdity when overlaid on the Bond manqué of Tremble through her eyes and again through her lens, as she costumes him as hyper-power icons Hitler and Napoleon, but also as Toulouse-Lautrec, with Sellers on his knees and Andress towering over him with her light meter. This sequence is a metaphoric framework for her creation of a Bond imitation as it simultaneously subverts the historical myths of male superiority as a "putting on." She destabilizes and reverses the traditional heterosexual dyad by being his educator, guide, and protector but ultimately kills him (she is in male drag at the time as a Scottish piper) when he becomes problematic to her own agenda. Along with her ambiguous amorality, Lynd's photographing of Tremble as Hitler is evocative of Leni Riefenstahl in her visual creation of the "heroic" image of the physically unimpressive leader in *Triumph of the Will* (1935).

Throughout the film, Lynd's self-conscious exhibitionism and her own empowering female gaze that objectifies men must undermine John Berger's limiting concept that in classic cinema "men look at women. Women watch themselves being looked at" (47) for the audience of the era. Mary Ann Doane's solution to Laura Mulvey's insistence that women must identify with the masculine gaze given the patriarchal construction of society and dominant cinema, is that a woman must "masquerade as spectator" (not as a theoretical transvestite as Mulvey would have it) to distance herself from her own male-objectified image (*Femmes* 26). Indeed, this is the most important aspect of the 1967 Vesper Lynd character—she is a metaphor for a gender/spectator masquerade that allows the gaze without the loss of being gazed upon. She is a mythic *feminine* leader in the male world of hyper-finance, a *female* James Bond, and mirrors her status in the masking of Tremble, a passive man (with a feminine name) as an iconic, dominant one. There is, however, a proto-feminist impulse at work in Joseph McGrath's empowerment of Andress' Lynd to balance out the excess of Sellers' self-depreciating improvisational comedy. Unlike all other Bond Girls of the era who are basically Bond's sexual *projections*, Lynd interrupts the Bond mythos and the masculine gaze with a gaze wholly her own, albeit as a "superior woman" fantasy. She indicates this with her own cameras, through which she also blatantly deconstructs the very thing she is charged with "creating"—and which the audience has come to fantasize about—a powerful alpha male.

The 1967 Lynd hides from the world as her evolved female cannot co-exist in a traditionally male dominated space, but only in her own esoteric economy. At the same time, however, she mocks traditional female roles and spaces. Her character stands alone among the short-lived power-villain roles in the genre of 1960s spy film, which were actually reactionary responses to growing female liberation consciousness and manufactured to validate male guidance and authority. Yet Lynd's sharp intellect is replaced with ill-fitting emotionalism during her last minutes on screen—it is not clear who or what she loved—and the response, which only emulates a formulaic narrative twist of betrayal, is a cinematic slap in the spectator's face for believing that Lynd might be more than a tease.

CONCLUSION: FORGETTING THE GODDESS

In her article "'I Know Where You Keep Your Gun': Daniel Craig as the Bond–Bond Girl Hybrid in *Casino Royale*" Funnell argues that:

> Bond and the Bond Girl have been merged into a single figure. The evolutionary nature of both characters renders them suitable for hybridization. The Bond–Bond Girl composite maintains the British identity and male sex of the title character. Aligned with Hollywood models of masculinity, the conflation of Craig's contradictory body presents him as physical, heroic and thus masculine while engaged in action, and feminized through youth, spectacle and passivity to the gaze when disengaged from physical activity. (466)

Ironically, it is Craig's re-presentation of the first significant erotic gaze in Bond film history, by emerging from the sea in the same way that Andress did in *Dr. No*, which is essential in the ontology of this hybrid of Bond-Bond Girl. In the 1967 *Casino Royale*, Andress is first seen in her office, wearing her exotic elephant boy outfit, followed by obedient male assistants and secretaries, who hang on the nuances of every order she gives. While Connery's Bond sees Andress from the beach, in a subjective, voyeuristic gaze the audience shares, Andress' Lynd is spied on by Sir James, in a self-conscious statement on voyeurism and on Andress as an actress whose career is positioned as spectacle. He has gained access to her office and spies at her from behind a potted tree, parting the leaves with his fingers so that his eye gains access and becomes the central aspect of the medium close-up shot. It is a reference, of course, to Connery's Bond seeing Andress for the first time in *Dr. No*. However, the actual *erotic* gaze of the "celibate" and highly moral Sir James on Lynd comes later in this film, as he attempts to sneak a peak of her getting into the bath on his television wristwatch. Lynd covers the watch face screen with her hand to block his view, and with the painting of the large female eye hanging over her bathtub and seemingly staring at the audience, the scene symbolically flips the gender control of the cinematic gaze from male to female.

Lynd manipulates Tremble and the audience by moving between a hypersexual Bond Girl image and that of the power female. She first lures Tremble to her home by telling him she is reading his baccarat study but that there are "several passes in your book that I don't fully understand" while he is dumbstruck by her very presence. She continues by telling him she cannot remember the specific chapter, and so she would need to consult the book, which is in her bed. Her intelligence and underlying calculation adds the frisson of a slight dominatrix quality to the initial meetings with Tremble. She begins their conversation by recalling the playful disbelief James Bond exhibits upon learning a Bond Girl's sexually suggestive name: Lynd: "I thought Evelyn was a girl's name?" / Tremble: "No…its mine…actually." The conversation is ended with Lynd's challenging stare at Tremble while her gloved hand firmly grasps and strongly pulls the phallic slot machine handle (she fondled one with a bright red knob earlier) to a clattering release of coins. The message of Lynd's sexual domination is not lost on Tremble or the audience. Even after he has been trained to be "Bond" this dynamic remains. At a moment of insecurity in the casino manager's office prior to the game, the normally icy Lynd gives a performance of sensitive female reassurance complete with whispered voice and tender smile as she tells him, "don't worry, I'll take care of you." And in the parlance of a hitwoman, she eventually does.

It is clear that the Bond-Bond Girl hybridization apparent in Craig's characterization of the millennial Bond was attempted in reverse by the creation of Andress' hybrid Bond Girl-Bond blend in 1967, and it fed on the tropes and clichés that began with Connery and Andress in *Dr. No*. Interestingly, that first meeting is recontextualized as a tribute with Pierce Brosnan and Halle Berry in *Die Another Day*, and revisited with the gender role flip with Craig in the 2006 *Casino Royale*. Either as parody or as action/drama, the mix of Bond and Lynd causes some gender role destabilization in its reflection of the original Connery-Andress relationship in 1962.

Eva Green's Vesper Lynd of 2006 recalls a bit of Andress in her initial dominant quality and the Grecian cut of her casino gowns, but the film ultimately reframes the 1967 pseudo-goddess fantasy as an officious bureaucratic figure. The impossible super-fe/male has become a politically correct authority image. Unlike the arrogant, self-assured, mythically powerful 1967 incarnation, the new Lynd is aware of her loaned power, is openly but not fetishistically sexual, and yet is obviously sophisticated beyond the neophyte Bond whom she also educates. While Fleming's postwar Bond novel reasserts male dominance and the danger of female agency with the betrayal of Lynd, the 1967 version is a prismatic translation of the original relationship. True to the intended kaleidoscopic and necessitated patchwork quality of the film, the emphasis is on questioning perception, bending reflection, and creating destabilization. Andress' Lynd began as reference to her previous Bond Girl in what would become a sprawling

Bond satire, and was inventively swayed into a bold exercise on female authority by the production disruptions of Sellers and the need to re-anchor the narrative(s). The post-Cold War Lynd of 2006 is only nominally aligned to the values of espionage, and although she expects agency and mentors to desires that ultimately destroy her, she does so on a very human scale.

NOTE

1   Reference to the Thomas & Mercer publication of the novel.

CHAPTER 10

"THIS NEVER HAPPENED TO THE OTHER FELLOW"

On Her Majesty's Secret Service as Bond Woman's Film

Marlisa Santos

Peter Hunt's *On Her Majesty's Secret Service* (*OHMSS*, 1969) has been considered an outlier in the James Bond canon for many reasons, but particularly for being the "experiment" after Sean Connery took a hiatus from the franchise and George Lazenby was cast in his first and only Bond role. The other feature that draws *OHMSS* into sharp relief from the other Bond films is the fact that this is the only one in which James Bond gets married. The "Bond Girl" who features as his love interest and eventual wife, Contessa Teresa di Vicenzo (a.k.a. Tracy), displays the kind of female wholeness that is not seen in even the most autonomous women in other Bond movies. It is no accident that this relationship lends a certain vulnerability to the Bond character, not seen again until Daniel Craig's reinvention of him in *Casino Royale* (Martin Campbell 2006). Although some features of bravado notable in Connery's interpretation of Bond are still present in *OHMSS*, Lazenby's Bond seems less of a caricature and more of a human being, and this is in large part due to the role of women in the film. *OHMSS* arguably fits the formula of the Hollywood Golden Age "woman's film" that disappeared at the end of the classic studio cinema in the 1960s.

Critical views of the "woman's film" have ranged over time from the disparaging treatments of Mary Ann Doane (1987) and Molly Haskell (1987) to the more complex considerations by Jeanine Basinger (1995) and Pam Cook (1998). The films often presented contradictory images of women in plots, showing them performing powerful actions and having independent thoughts, but ultimately succumbing to the traditional societal mores of domesticity. Where Doane sees this contradiction as performing "a vital function in society's ordering of sexual difference" (*The Desire* 3), Basinger calls the woman's film "the slyboots of genre," arguing "how strange and ambivalent they really are. Stereotypes are presented, then undermined, and then reinforced" (7). One could argue that the woman's film operated in much the same way as *film noir*, presenting characters and narratives that undermine social mores, only to present a conventional outcome in the end. But one of the most important characteristics of the woman's film is, as Basinger argues, "to place a woman at the center of the story universe" (13). It is this feature that sets *OHMSS* apart from other Bond films.

Because of Connery's departure, *OHMSS* was in an unusual position to break new ground and take risks beyond what had previously worked for the franchise. Albert R. Broccoli and Harry Saltzman knew that *OHMSS* could not simply move in the direction that the other films had taken. Because of its differences, the film has been both derided and praised, and much myth has surrounded it, from the rumored garlic breath wars between Rigg and Lazenby to the supposed status of the film as a box office failure (Sterling and Morecambe 187-90). Critics could not decide whether the film was a lukewarm imitation of the Connery invention or a calculated failure. *Variety* characterized Lazenby as "pleasant, capable and attractive" in the role of Bond, but paling in comparison to Connery's "physique, voice and saturnine, virile looks" (¶2). In her discussion about the "public ownership" of the Bond character on film, Katharine Cox points out the challenges of "the baggage that actors bring to the part of Bond," adding that Lazenby was the only Bond actor not "heralded for the part through the suitability of previous roles" (2). What seemed to bother critics and perhaps Bond-following filmgoers was what they perceived as his shortcomings in "virility." The action of the film does not really bear this criticism out, as Lazenby's Bond beds three women over the course of the film, a respectable number by Bond film standards. But his heart is not really in it—neither in the sex nor in his identity as an MI6 agent.

The unfavorable perception of Bond's masculinity in *OHMSS* is arguably reinforced by his identity crisis in the film, one that calls into question basic assumptions of the Bond character. Martin Sterling and Gary Morecambe argue that Connery's "insouciant invincibility" may have spoiled the "essential humanity" of *OHMSS*: "This is the one film where James Bond could not—and should not—be a superman" (191). While Connery's Bond is confident and fearless, Lazenby's Bond is adrift; he is frustrated with M for not wanting to pursue Blofeld and his removal from the assignment leads him to attempt to resign. It is the intervention of Moneypenny that arrests this drastic step; instead of drafting a resignation letter to M, she composes a request of leave letter, an act for which Bond later thanks her. The interaction between Bond and Moneypenny is also somewhat unusual in this film. True, there is the customary office flirting: after she responds to his drink invitation by musing, "If only I could trust myself," he counters with, "Same old Moneypenny. Britain's last line of defence." This response hearkens back to Connery's Bond referring to the threat of his lovemaking to Moneypenny in *Dr. No* (Terence Young 1962) as "illegal use of government property." But Tara Brabazon points out that Lazenby's "new" Bond "claimed both a similarity and difference with the past by maintaining the Moneypenny moment.

Significantly, on this occasion it was Moneypenny who rejected Bond's advances." (492). The body of Moneypenny represents a bulwark of protection for the realm, as her actions insure that Bond is not irrevocably separated from the service. There is a separation though—one that creates a rift in Bond's professional identity and allows the entrance of emotion and the prospect of monogamous romantic love into his life.

It is significant that *OHMSS*, with the exception of the opening scene of Roger Moore's Bond at Tracy di Vicenzo's grave in *Live and Let Die* (Guy Hamilton 1973), is the only pre-Craig era Bond film with a memory. The longevity of the Bond franchise may be attributed to this lack of linear narrative—Bond persists through the decades, not only played by different actors, but without any past or progression from one mission to the next. This convention allowed Broccoli and Saltzman to continually reinvent the character as times and casting changed, but it does lend a peculiarity to the series, especially as certain actors portraying consistent characters (notably Moneypenny, Q, and M) did persist through a long period of Bond films. At the end of the opening sequence of *OHMSS*, Lazenby's Bond breaks the fourth wall by facing the camera and quipping, "this never happened to the other fellow," a move that immediately sets this Bond apart from all others. This is only one of many indications that this Bond story and character will be different, because he has a past to answer to—he does not simply appear in the action as if the story were being told for the first time. And of course these references were deliberate: to attach continuity with the persona of Bond even as the actor with which he was identified had changed, a concern that did not persist in later films once this initial acting change had occurred.

The film's title sequence cues the viewer for such a significant shift. Shots of previous Bond films in hourglass graphics remind the viewer that this is one more in the series of Bond, while signifying the temporality of both the character and the actor portraying him. There is also an unprecedented use of British Empire imagery in the title sequence, including naked silhouettes of women facing each other under an imperial crown and the image of the Union Jack superimposed inside a martini glass. James Chapman notes that the titles of *OHMSS* reinforce it as one of the most patriotic of the Bond films, replacing the cheeky mockery of the service with a more earnest sense of duty (*Licence* 140-1). The emphasis on the words "her majesty" provides the mood that establishes Bond's conflict early on in the film. If one wants to consider the role of the female in Bond films, the presence of the ultimate woman monarch in *OHMSS* deserves mention, since Bond continually faces the gap between his own wishes and his obligation to her service. When Bond is essentially kidnapped to meet Draco, Tracy di Vicenzo's father, this issue comes to light, as Draco, who wants Bond to marry his daughter, reveals that he does not know where Blofeld is, but if he did, he would not tell "her majesty's secret service…but [he] might tell [his] future son-in-law." This kind of familial interjection is quite foreign to the narrative of the Bond character, and it signals a shift into a more personal and vulnerable sphere for the character; will he be a human being who has family members to whom he would owe fidelity, or will he remain an orphan servant to his country, devoting his life to the eradication of national threats? Bond continues to consider this question after he believes he has resigned, when he enters his office. This is the only Bond film in which viewers will see his office, even though his office work is regularly shown in the Fleming novels. In the films, it is better suited to show Bond as essentially rootless, with no strong ties to the home or office of MI6, aside from the moments in which he is obliged to check in to M or to try out the newest gadgets with Q. In *OHMSS*, not only is his office shown, but it is the locale of his thoughtfulness about his past and future.

The idea of *OHMSS* having a memory is demonstrated in the scene when Bond cleans out his desk. As he re-discovers various artifacts from past missions (Honey Ryder's dagger from *Dr. No*, the garrote-watch from *From Russia With Love* [Terence Young 1963], the re-breather from *Thunderball* [Terence Young 1965]), the theme music from those films plays, to provide the viewer with a connection to the previous Bond chronology. This was a deliberate reinforcement of the Bond character history to aid in the transition to a new actor, but the effect provides an unintended depth to this incarnation of Bond: a sense of the past, to link to his duty and obligation to the future. During this scene, Bond drinks from a flask and directs his gaze toward a picture of Elizabeth II, commenting, "Sorry, Mum." His face is reflected in the glass of her portrait, and the threat of his direct abdication of his allegiance is strikingly clear, along with his ambivalence toward this abandonment. Therefore, this Bond does not simply continue the solipsistic tradition of the previous Bond but instead he is subsumed with the weight of his past actions and how they will impact his present and future. The Bond of *OHMSS* leans toward Fleming's Bond who, in each novel, looks back to the past, which informs his present. A significant example of this is *Casino Royale* (1953), in which the trauma of losing Vesper Lynd haunts Bond in successive novels, and had that story been filmed earlier on, the impact of *OHMSS* might have been lessened. Regardless, the fact that this past has emotional baggage aligns Lazenby's Bond more toward the female characters in traditional women's films, who must always contend with the gains and mistakes of previous time.

The other part of the "anti-Bond" equation is the character Tracy di Vicenzo. She is a headstrong, spoiled, and troubled woman who has no investment in plots against Bond, nor is she a henchwoman serving villains who are pursuing him. She and Bond meet by accident when he is undergoing the aforementioned struggle with his identity, and she is the locus of the realignment of his life and priorities. Initially resistant to any long-term attachment to her, particularly when he is propositioned by her father Draco, Bond finds himself inexorably drawn to her compelling combination of fearlessness, sexuality, and loyalty. Tracy di Vicenzo drives recklessly, gambles indiscriminately, and loves unabashedly. Her father's best efforts to provide her with a structured boarding school upbringing backfired and led her down a path of rash love affairs, which culminated in a disastrous marriage to an Italian playboy count and the tragic death of her child to meningitis. As Draco puts it, his daughter is one of those people who "burn the heart out of themselves by living too greedily." Bond meets her when she is desperately trying to destroy herself, and despite what should have been a one-night stand, Bond is attracted by a desire to save her and be enveloped by her energy. When di Vicenzo shows up in Bond's room on the night they meet, she turns his own gun on him and dares, "Suppose I were to kill you for a thrill." Though he does overpower her and gets his gun back, one never senses that Bond truly has the upper hand in their initial encounters: she outdrives him on the road to the sea, eludes him after he rescues her from drowning, manipulates him into paying her gambling debt, and leaves him alone in bed the next morning. The empty robe di Vicenzo leaves on the bed signifies both her destructive emptiness and search for meaning, as well as her elusiveness in response to Bond's pursuit.

Tracy di Vicenzo's desire for independence and her struggle to find her own identity parallels Bond's and also recalls the typical predicament of a woman's film heroine. Bond is continually intrigued by her mixture of strength and vulnerability. When he meets her again at Draco's birthday party, she boldly gives Draco the ultimatum that he release Bond from his obligation or sever his connection with her. She defiantly states, "Now Mr. Bond need have no further interest in me." At every turn in which she dares him, he becomes increasingly attracted to her, just as at every turn in which she displays her confrontational boldness, she equally displays her fragility, evident from the tears she sheds when Bond catches up to her after the above exchange with her father.

Later in the film, she will prove indispensable to Bond and perfectly able to take care of herself. Following his daring escape from Piz Gloria down the mountain and after eluding Irma Bunt and her henchmen, Bond finds himself at a Swiss Christmas carnival, looking exhausted and unsure of where to turn. This is a curious image of Bond as he sits on a bench, dazed and uncertain, watching ice skaters, and trying to blend in with the crowd. There is a cut to a shot of ice skates at his feet, the camera panning up to reveal a dazzling di Vicenzo; she says, "Stay close to me," and her car provides the means of escape. It is not unusual for Bond to gain the aid of women, especially his sexual partners, but this usually occurs when the woman has held past allegiance to the villain or has a stake in the outcome of whatever mission Bond is pursuing. This is different, as di Vicenzo has her own agenda that has nothing to do with Bond's mission goals. She is the one who has rescued him, and this action carries particular weight. When she is later captured by Blofeld, Bond is intent on rescuing her but this attempt does not go the way that things usually do in Bond films. For one, when she realizes, through radio transmissions, that Draco and Bond are on their way to rescue her, she slyly keeps Blofeld at arm's length to distract him, in order to buy time for the escape. And once the raid is under way, she does not hide or passively wait to be liberated; rather, she throws a bottle at one of Blofeld's henchmen, and breaks another bottle to use as a weapon against the other. When he catches her, she struggles and breaks free, ultimately pulling his head through a screen, after which he falls down a flight of stairs. He comes to, but she finishes him off by impaling him on decorative spikes that are anchored on a wall. Tracy di Vicenzo is neither a soldier nor a spy, unlike henchwomen in other Bond films; these actions are simply displays of her fierce independence and her refusal to be bested.

For the viewer, Tracy di Vicenzo has taken center stage in the narrative, with her story infinitely more interesting than Bond's, whose vacillation between his own conflicting feelings matches her own. These conflicting feelings are another area in which Bond is a foreigner; it is only his separation from MI6 that justifies such contradiction and his orientation into the world of the feminine. It is not as though contradiction and ambivalence are the sole realm of the female, but in the world of Bond, to be anything less than arrogantly sure of self, in all its masculine glory, is to have breasts and a vagina. One of the characterizations of the woman's film, according to Basinger, is the ever-present conflict regarding the proper role in life:

> Should she have children or not have children? [...] Should she kill the rat who ruined her life or just grin and bear it? By asking these questions, the film prepared an audience to find its own answers [...] When morality has to dramatize its own opposite to make its point, the opposite takes on a life of its own. (11)

When Bond enters into his relationship with di Vicenzo, he is in such a position, freed through leave of absence from the formal constraints of the service, yet haunted by the unfinished business of the past and his enduring loyalty in the future. Tony W. Garland argues that "desire and duty are closely connected in the character of Bond. His ability to keep sex and violence separate and to take pleasure in sex but also to keep his mission objectives in perspective facilitate his consistent triumphs against repeated adversity" (180). It is this separation that becomes blurred in *OHMSS*, primarily because love, and not merely sex, enters the equation, at a time when his mission objectives also reside in a gray area. Bond's attachment to various women in previous and later films ranges from frivolous to tender, but never displays the depth of commitment that he found with di Vicenzo.

One of the filmic signals of this commitment is the "courtship montage," cut scenes of di Vicenzo and Bond engaging in various romantic activities paired with the film's theme, "All the Time in the World," crooned by Louis Armstrong. This technique is a singular convention of the woman's film called the "Happy Interlude" or "Bliss Montage." Basinger notes that this kind of sequence is "presented as visual action, but it is actually a static piece of information for the audience […] further-more, they also grasp a secondary level of information: 'And it isn't going to last'" (8). Such montages condense the passage of time to evoke the quicker conclusion of the falling-in-love process, but can feel ominous, almost like a portent of doom. And if the blissful courtship can be reduced to mere seconds of screen time, one can be sure that the disaster to follow will be stretched out to long minutes of agony. In *OHMSS*, it is no different, as is visible at the close of the film when tragedy strikes. The appea-rance of such a segment, especially with the presence of the wistfully romantic theme song, is shocking for a Bond film. Other Bond songs tend toward either a brash evo-cation of the power of Bond himself or his adversary (Shirley Bassey's "Goldfinger," Tom Jones' "Thunderball") or a sultry celebration of Bond's sexuality (Carly Simon's "Nobody Does It Better," Rita Coolidge's "All-Time High"). However, "All the Time in the World" is drastically different from any of these theme songs—the lyrics are unabashedly romantic ("We have all the love in the world/If that's all we have you will find/We need nothing more"), which almost belie the melancholy melody. The song corresponds to the intent of the bliss montage—pleasure in the present, pain in the future—and seems very out of place in a Bond film. Bond's sexual encounters with the hypnotized, would-be-assassin women at Piz Gloria almost serve as an antidote to all this romance, as Bond appears in more familiar territory, bedding multiple women in one night to serve the ends of the mission to destroy Blofeld. But just as the woman's film often presents contradictory messages regarding the protagonist's conflic-ting obligations and desires, so too does the romantic relationship with di Vicenzo counteracted with Bond's limited romantic escapades, serve as the barometer that undermines the heretofore image of Bond as a static, single-minded, adventurer.

The most critical defining factor of *OHMSS* as a "woman's film" is Bond's marria-ge. Following di Vicenzo's rescue of him at the carnival, as they take refuge in a barn in a snowstorm, Bond proposes to her. Her car has run out of gas, and so they have reached the end of the line literally, as well as symbolically—their deep affection for one another is clear and they could very well meet an unpleasant fate together as they hide out in this elemental place. It is telling that she asks him what had happened up on the Piz Gloria mountain, and his response is reticent: "I can't tell you; her majesty's secret service is still my job." However, he seems to reconsider, countering that "a man shouldn't be concerned with anything but himself" and further concluding, "I'll have to find something else to do." This "something else" is apparently not something that would interfere with his being a husband, as his proposal follows, and he calls her, "Mrs. James Bond." His vow to separate himself from his identity as an MI6 agent would have been rather surprising for a viewer, and perhaps a signal that this could have been the final Bond film. There is no future in a married James Bond, and it is not as if Lazenby's Bond is attempting to unite these two worlds; marriage means the end of service. Haskell argues that, in contrast to the woman's film, in the "man's film," "[m]arriage becomes the heavy. The implication is clear: All the excitement of life—the passion, the risk—occurs outside marriage rather than within it. Marriage is a deadly bore, made to play the role of the spoilsport, the ugly cousin one has to dance with at the ball" (156). Here, though, marriage is presented as Bond's salvation, an antidote to his frustrating, unsatisfying, and deadly avocation.

Bond's ambivalence, however, lingers—at the wedding he tosses his hat to Moneypenny, his final hat toss, which finds its resting place in her own hands—and there is a subtle and meaningful melancholic understanding shown between his face and hers. His ultimate fulfillment is signaled to reside with Tracy Bond, who, even though she rejoices in the prospect of domestic life and her future children, it is clear that she will maintain her independence: in response to Draco's entreaty that she obey her husband "in all things," she retorts, "Of course—as I've always obeyed you." And in a final gesture of respect, Bond returns Draco's "dowry" money, stating, "As the proverb said, her price is far above rubies... or even your million pounds." It would be worth mentioning that Proverbs 31:11 goes on to say, "The heart of her husband doth safely trust in her, so that he shall have no need of spoil." This is her value to Bond: a refuge of love and trust that he not only has never known, but that also positions him as an almost feminine hero, who forsakes the active ventures in life for the rewards of a home and family.

As is suggested by the "bliss montage," the happiness of the married couple is doomed to tragedy. As Bond and his wife depart on their honeymoon, Tracy is shot and killed by Bunt, riding in a car driven by Blofeld. One might comment on the irony of the lesbian-coded Bunt assassinating the wife, and presumably potential last lover of the hyper-masculine figure of James Bond, but the more important issue is the pathos involved in this last segment of the film. Funnell calls the tragic ending "devastating" ("I Know" 457), and indeed it is—although viewers might have been trying to wrap their heads around how there could be any future Bond films, with Bond married and resigned from the service, the murder of Tracy Bond is still a shocking turn of events. Moments after Tracy tells Bond that he has given her the best wedding present she could have—"a future"—she is ruthlessly gunned down and that future cancelled out. But beyond the fact of the murder itself, it is Bond's reaction to it that makes *OHMSS* more aligned with a "woman's picture" and less with the usual Bond formula. Stunned, he cradles Tracy in his arms, responding to the attending police officer with "It's all right...she's just having a rest. We'll be going on soon. There's no hurry, you see; we have all the time in the world." He then kisses her ring finger, buries his head in her limp body, and cries. Of this uncharacteristic display of emotion, Garland argues that "the death of Tracy immediately after her marriage to Bond establishes an emotional vulnerability similar to the loss and despondency experienced by noir protagonists" (183). This seems an accurate interpretation, as Lazenby's Bond has been forced entirely out of his prior element—cut loose from both the power and the restrictions of his

007 status, he is left adrift and particularly susceptible to emotional loss. And viewers are also forced out of their element—used to feeling afraid for Bond, but not sorry for him. Contemplating the overwhelming sorrow facing Bond, we almost feel as though we are watching Bette Davis in *Jezebel* (William Wyler 1938) facing uncertain days ahead in a yellow fever quarantine colony, or in *Dark Victory* (Edmund Goulding 1939) climbing the stairs to her brain-tumor death.

More than any other Bond film, *OHMSS* centralizes the role of the woman, defining Bond through the main female character of Tracy di Vicenzo/Bond, as well as the symbolic female influence of country, the locus of Bond's professional and personal identities with which he struggles throughout the film. This definition stands in direct contrast to the other 007 films, in which women are defined by and through Bond. Robert Castle calls *OHMSS* "revolutionary," and bemoans that "the counter-revolution then commenced and reclaimed the old Bond dominion" (¶15). Connery's return and the roles of the several Bond actors that followed brought the character back to its relatively static and male-dominated origins. Although this wistful and melancholy film reveals that Bond's genealogical heraldic motto is *"Orbis non sufficit,"* or "The world is not enough," Lazenby's Bond discovers that his world is both too small and too big, and ultimately not enough to contain his desires. From the courtship montage to the tearjerker ending, *OHMSS* temporarily breaks the androcentric mold of Bond movies, positioning itself as a curious anomaly and hesitant interloper into the world of the female.

CHAPTER 11

"WHAT REALLY WENT ON UP THERE JAMES?"

Bond's Wife, Blofeld's Patients, and Empowered Bond Women

Dan Mills

Published in 1963, *On Her Majesty's Secret Service* (forthwith referred to as *OHMSS*)[1] was Ian Fleming's tenth James Bond novel and the second part of his "Blofeld Trilogy," which is bookended by *Thunderball* (1961) and *You Only Live Twice* (1964). With *OHMSS*, Fleming sought to overcome the negative reviews of his preceding novel, *The Spy Who Loved Me* (1962), in which Bond plays a small role in the narrative. Bond marries in *OHMSS*, only to see his wife murdered on their wedding day by villain Ernst Stavro Blofeld and his aide Irma Bunt in the final pages of the novel. Fleming "took as much trouble as ever" in writing *OHMSS* (Pearson 308) and believed the novel to be "his best yet" (Lycett 409).

In 1969, the novel was adapted into a film directed by Peter Hunt. *OHMSS* starred George Lazenby in his only outing as James Bond. Early in the film, Bond becomes betrothed to his future wife, Contessa Teresa "Tracy" di Vicenzo, played by *Avengers* (1965-68) star Diana Rigg. He must first complete his mission, which requires him to travel to a mountain retreat where Blofeld is conducting experimental treatments to cure allergies of female "patients." Bond works undercover as a genealogist in order to access the retreat and in the process has sex with three women in one night. Michael Rogers writes that *OHMSS* helped bring Bond "into the Swingin' Sixties" (123). Indeed, the free sex depicted in Bond's visit to Blofeld's retreat incorporates the 1960s culture of unrestrained sexuality, and it serves as Bond's de facto bachelor party before his marriage to di Vicenzo. Although the film was a close adaptation of Fleming's novel, it received poor critical reviews and is considered a box-office failure. However, scholars like Jeremy Black contend that *OHMSS* "is one of the richest and most interesting Bond films" (140).

This chapter will examine *OHMSS*, a film that is considered an outlier in the Bond canon. Both the film and its source novel offer a significant departure from the typical treatment of women in the franchise. This has arguably impacted the reading and reception, particularly of the film. This chapter aims to explore the representation of women in the film, who play vital roles in the narrative and demonstrate considerable autonomy, which, at times, works to emasculate their male counterparts. For, as Lisa Funnell notes, di Vicenzo herself represents a "threat to Bond's heroism through the 'domestication' of Bond and his libido" ("From English" 70). I will argue that both the novel and film versions of *OHMSS* break generic conventions by depicting strong female characters (di Vicenzo, Bunt, and Moneypenny) who are more interesting and actively involved in the development of the narrative than their male counterparts (Bond, Blofeld, and M). The depiction of di Vicenzo and Bunt radically reverses gender roles in the Bond canon in a way that makes *OHMSS* an aberration in the series.

BOND GIRLS, BAD GIRLS, AND SECONDARY GIRLS

Tracy di Vicenzo is not a typical "Bond Girl," a term that is itself problematic as it has conventionally been used to describe every woman appearing in the Bond franchise, including "Bad Girls" (i.e. villains) and "Secondary Girls" (i.e. relatively unimportant characters in the narrative). In early discussions, the Bond Girl is largely defined in relation to Bond. Eleanor and Dennis Pelrine argue that Bond's women "are not true sexual objects" but rather "a series of love 'em and leave 'em episodes," going so far as to describe the "Bond Girls" in *Goldfinger* (Guy Hamilton 1964) as "contestants" vying for Bond's affection (152, 89). The Pelrines describe Bond Girls as being "passionate, when [Bond] wants them to be [...] regardless of the unfortunate backgrounds which might have made them a might frigid" (59). Kingsley Amis notes that Bond is never unkind to women since he does not physically and verbally abuse them (41). However, Bond does not necessarily respect women either as he "collects almost exactly one girl per excursion abroad" (36). Amis claims that Bond is "protective, not dominating or combative" to women (42), and he seeks "not to break down Bond-girl's defenses, but to induce her to lower them voluntarily" (49). Through his defense of Bond, Amis draws attention to some problematic notions of gender, sexuality, and power in the franchise that work to build up Bond at the expense of the women around him.

Recent criticism has offered more definitive assessments of the Bond Girls. Christine Bold argues that the early films "limit women's initiatives" by "playing down the threat of alternative sexualities" so that "they represent desirable women as unknowing, helpless dupes" (214). Robert A. Caplen claims that Bond Girls "present neither strong nor capable female characters" because they merely constitute "sexual stereotypes" (61). Michael Denning connects the Bond Girl figure to a similar "enabling mechanism," and argues that in Herbert Marcuse's sense of "desublimation," the objectified sexuality of Bond Girls "becomes the master code into which all discourses—commercial, political, philosophical, even religious—are translated" ("Licensed" 73). To fulfill their role as an "enabling mechanism," Bond Girls, according to James Chapman, must be sexually and ideologically "out of place" (*Licence* 26). Tony Bennett and Janet Woollacott contend that Bond Girls serve as objects against which Fleming constructs Bond's sexuality, arguing that their image constitutes a "model of adjustment, a condensation of the attributes of femininity" needed to accommodate Bond's "new norms of male sexuality" ("Moments" 24). These critics see the "Bond Girls" as less important and integral to the narratives in which they appear.

Some scholars have argued that Bond Girls actually have agency and do not merely serve as companions for Bond. Lisa Funnell writes that the Bond franchise has "registered and interrogated…feminist gains" since the release of *Dr. No* (Terence Young 1962) through the depiction of strong and capable female villains ("Negotiating" 200). In addition, Daniel Ferreras Savoye claims that Tracy di Vicenzo "signifies the end of Bond's career as a secret agent" (169). This signification, for Savoye, results from Bond's "irresistible appetite for sex [as] a statement of individualism as well as freedom" (Ibid.). *OHMSS* seems to be an exception to the rule that Bond quickly loses interest in a Bond Girl once they have had sex.

The first Bond film was released just one year after Betty Friedan published her highly influential book, *The Feminine Mystique*, which is widely credited with sparking the second wave of feminism. Other texts such as Simon de Beauvoir's *The Second Sex* and The Kinsey Reports *Sexual Behavior in the Human Male* and *Sexual Behavior of the Human Female*, reacted against Freud's phallocentricism in his famous "repressive hypothesis." Freudian psychology remained prevalent, however, and, as Friedan demonstrates, many women turned to psychotherapy to cope with a lack of identity beyond their roles as mothers and wives (220-5). Bennett and Woollacott argue that the early Bond films responded to the Women's Liberation Movement by attempting to counteract feminist progress in order to maintain a "phallocentric conception of gender relations" ("Moments" 28). *OHMSS* appears to be the exception to this rule as the film emasculates Bond and empowers female characters.

BOND'S (HYPER)SEXUALITY

Criticism has shown some consistency in describing Bond's sexuality in psychological terms. Lycurgus Starkey argues that "Bond's primary concern is the passion of an animal function" (17). The Pelrines similarly refer to the Bond narratives as "primitive, id level material, buried deep in the unconscious" (154), and Sue Matheson describes Bond as a "master animal" (66). But this seems fitting in light of M's labeling of Bond as a "blunt instrument" in the novel *OHMSS*, or rather, a flat and undeveloped character, much like the typical Bond Girl, most of whom James Chapman has argued "are fairly two-dimensional" (*Licence* 95).

Bond's "animalistic" sexuality permeates every aspect of the Bond universe. Jaime Hovey argues that the hyperbolic nature of Bond's sexuality actually places Bond closer to the queer end of the gender spectrum, as Bond's sexuality falls outside of heternormative sexual behavior (48). Bennett and Woollacott argue that the 1960s Bond films depicted women "freed from domesticity and allowed sexual desire without either marriage or punishment but only in terms of the compulsions of a 'liberated' male sexuality" (*Bond and Beyond* 228). Jeremy Black notes that Bond "represent[s] the values and self-image of manly courage" (xi), but Bond's cover identity in *OHMSS* undermines the typically hyper-masculine image of Bond.

To prepare for this cover, Bond visits genealogist Sir Hilary Bray, whom he later impersonates wearing a kilt and glasses. This costuming works to symbolically emasculate Bond and serves as an important component of his cover as Bray, ostensibly sent to verify Blofeld's claim to the title of Comte Balthazar de Bleuchamp. Bond's attire and demeanor, as well as his feminized name, assisted in the film by a voice-over by actor George Baker, contrasts significantly with the heteronormative masculinity Bond normally exhibits. Fleming suggests that Bond's exaggerated heterosexual activity is merely a "subconscious protest against the current fashion of sexual confusion" (qtd. in Zeiger 112). Bond's impersonation of Bray in the film, however, comes off as very effeminate, especially for the typically hyper-masculine Bond. As Mary Ann Doane notes, "[m]ale transvestism is an occasion for laughter" ("Film" 138).

Bond's effeminate cover story and ultimate vulnerability undermine what Bennett and Woollacott call "phallocentric conception of gender relations" ("Moments" 39). Once he has reached Blofeld's compound, Bond finds himself surrounded by beautiful, sexually liberated women deprived of the company of men. Bond learns that the women have severe allergies for which they are receiving treatment. Various women of color are among the allergy suffers and the Pelrines note that Bond, like Fleming, enjoyed the company of "gorgeous and exotic females" (43). Caplen labels this collection of women in the clinic a "harem" (218). In reaction to Bond's effeminate mannerisms, one of the women says "I know what he's allergic to," implying he is allergic to women. At dinner Bond lectures on genealogy as the women stare at him lustily, and Bond tells them that part of his own coat of arms refers to "gold balls," that is to say, better than brass balls. All of the patients appear to be attracted to Bond and Ruby makes the first pass at him by writing her room number in lipstick on this inner thigh.

Blofeld's compound is tightly guarded, and this security serves to highlight how issues of nation and nationhood are "transposed on to those of sexuality" (Bennett and Woollacott, "Moments" 19). The female patients have virtually no freedom to move about or communicate in private with anyone inside or outside the compound. Bond breaks out of his electronically locked room and puts his self-made skeleton key in his "purse." Bond enters Ruby's room and she says, "You are funny pretending not to like girls." When Bond drops his kilt, Ruby giggles and says, "It's true," apparently referring to his "gold balls." After they have sex, Bond returns to his room, looks into a mirror and says "Hilly you old devil" before he quickly finds another woman, who used a nail file to break out of her room, waiting for him. Bond employs the same line he had used with Ruby: "Usually I don't, but you're not usual. Coming here was an inspiration and so are you." Bond attempts to get the second woman to talk about herself, but she replies, "I'll tell you all about myself later in the morning," reversing Bond generic conventions as well as societal gender roles. This precisely demonstrates Bennett and Woollacott's observation that Bond represents a "reformed model of male sexuality" that "supplies the point of reference in relation to which female sexuality is to be adjusted" (*Bond* 127). In this "adjusted" sexual encounter, Bond is out-sexualized by a woman who refuses to provide her name, much like di Vicenzo in the novel, who during their first sexual encounter says she is "not interested in conversation" (30). Ruby and the other women in the clinic demonstrate Jane Gerhard's claim that "[p]art of the revolutionary aspect of the 'sexual revolution' of the 1960s was the greater acceptance of women as agents with sexual desires" (81).

The following morning Bond arranges for two more sexual encounters, after which he says to one of the guards, "Well, back to work. You have no idea how it is piling up." Such sexual behavior by Bond once led spy novelist John le Carré to refer to Bond as the "ultimate prostitute" (qtd. in Zeiger 123). That night, however, Bond visits one of the women's rooms but finds in bed the asexual Irma Bunt, one of the administrators of the clinic and Blofeld's henchwomen. Bond is taken prisoner and his ruse has ended. Umberto Eco reads this section of the narrative in almost Foucauldian terms, contrasting the "hypnotic control of Blofeld" with "the virginal surveillance of Irma Bunt" ("Narrative" 44), both of which serve to repress the sexuality of the female patients in addition to "curing" the patients' allergies.

Bunt's jarring appearance into what Bond, the reader, and the audience assume will be merely another sexual conquest highlights the asexuality of Bond villains. Eco notes that Bond villains are frequently sexually impotent or aberrant ("Narrative" 38, 40). Bennett and Woollacott similarly note that female villains were "characterised by extreme ugliness and sexual deviance" ("Moments" 30). When he finds Bunt in the bed, Bond confronts abject horror made worse by his expectation of another sexual liaison, and Bunt's appearance performs another moment of Bond's castration. Bunt's sexually perverse appearance brings Bond into the Lacanian Real, an impossible and unthinkable rupture in the Symbolic order. Bond was expecting to have sex and to exert his masculine phallus or Law, and Bunt's appearance and the physical revulsion Bond surely experienced results in him losing consciousness in the film. Lisa Funnell notes that, like Rosa Klebb in *From Russia with Love* (Terence Young 1963), Bunt challenges Bond's heterosexuality through an "aberrant" homosexuality that "destabilize[s] the status quo" ("Negotiating" 203). Klebb and Bunt, according to Funnell, are "sexually unavailable" because of "age and orientation" and play the role of deviants by serving as "unbridled challenges to his phallic masculinity" (ibid.).

FROM SECONDARY GIRL TO BOND GIRL

OHMSS relies heavily on the female lead, Tracy di Vicenzo, but she initially appears as a "Secondary Girl" early in the film and novel. Both texts open with Bond observing di Vicenzo as she walks into the ocean followed by Bond's "rescue" of her. The opening scene of *OHMSS* leaves the audience wondering what made Bond think di Vicenzo was committing suicide, and the image calls to mind the conclusion of Kate Chopin's 1899 novel *The Awakening*, in which the female protagonist commits suicide by walking into the ocean instead of continuing to live within a stifling patriarchy. The audience also sees Bond voyeuristically watching di Vicenzo through a rifle scope, which calls to mind Freud's examination of scopophilia in his *Three Essays on Sexuality*; Laura Mulvey has famously connected scopophilia to the unconscious perpetuation of patriarchal submission as an "erotic basis for pleasure in looking" ("Visual" 835).

The title sequence follows, conspicuously using the Union Jack image to establish one of the film's central motifs of the conflict between duty to country and duty to self. It also shows images of the Bond Girls who appeared in the preceding films. Perhaps this serves to depict di Vicenzo as the best of the Bond Girls, or at the very least the last of them, the one who marries the lifelong bachelor Bond. The end of his single life also signals the end of the 1960s film versions of Bond, as the 1970s would take the film franchise in vastly new directions.

Wearing a somewhat flamboyant ruffled tuxedo shirt instead of the plain-front point collar style worn by Connery, Bond first encounters di Vicenzo at a casino table. Pretending to know her, Bond pays her gambling debt and di Vicenzo dutifully repays the debt with her body. Fleming's description of this transaction is business-like: "She rose abruptly. So did Bond, confused. 'No. I will go alone. You can come later. The number is 45. There, if you wish, you can make the most expensive piece of love of your life. It will have cost you forty million francs. I hope it will be worth it'" (30). As Bennett and Woollacott note, *OHMSS* is atypical because this Bond Girl appears in the middle of the narrative's action instead of being only Bond's "phallic fodder" (*Bond* 197). Bond is eventually saved by di Vicenzo after his escape from Blofeld's compound, so it seems that Bond's "investment" does pay off. In the film, the sexual encounter begins with a kiss, and then a cut to an image of flowers for the implied sexual act, and finally to a shot of Bond alone in bed the following morning. Bond puts on the short robe di Vicenzo wore the night before. In the novel, di Vicenzo propositions Bond in the following passage:

I said "no conversation." Take off those clothes. Make love to me. You are handsome and strong. I want to remember what it can be like. Do anything you like. And tell me what you like and what you would like from me. Be rough with me. Treat me like the lowest whore in creation. Forget everything else. No questions. Take me. (30)

This sexual encounter serves as the beginning of a more traditional courtship and marriage, as Bond agrees to marry di Vicenzo to get information from her father.

Bond's fake marriage in the preceding film, *You Only Live Twice* (Lewis Gilbert 1967), differs significantly from his marriage to di Vicenzo, as Bond's Japanese "wife" exhibits the Western stereotype that Asian women are submissive to men while di Vicenzo represents a much more independent post-Women's Liberation, Western woman. Tony Garland writes that although di Vicenzo is initially "antagonistic," Bond ultimately "subordinates her to sexual consummation [in] the patriarchal system" (183). Garland's assessment does not take into consideration di Vicenzo's heroics when Bond breaks out of Blofeld's compound.

After escaping, Bond skis down the mountain with Blofeld and his men in pursuit. At the bottom, di Vicenzo suddenly appears and rescues Bond by out-running Blofeld's men in a car chase. When she first appears to Bond in the novel, Bond says to her, "Tracy. Hold on to me. I'm in bad shape" (129). Her actions in this sequence demonstrate what Funnell writes as a strengthening of "notions of the Bond Girl heroic competency" ("From English" 66). As di Vicenzo drives, Bond kisses her on the cheek and at one point even says "good girl." In the novel we learn that Bond prefers "private girls, girls he could discover himself and make his own" (20), and this precisely describes the melancholy of di Vicenzo. Henry Zeiger notes that Fleming preferred "undemanding, helpful women" (84). Once safe they take shelter in a barn where Bond proposes to di Vicenzo, who asks, "What really went on up there James?" Like Bunt, di Vicenzo serves as a rupture in the Symbolic domain, but di Vicenzo constitutes a Lacanian Imaginary figure, a non-hostile messianic crack in the Symbolic order.

FATHERS, LITERAL AND SYMBOLIC

Tracy di Vicenzo's father, Marc-Ange Draco, is positioned in narrative contrast with M, Bond's boss, whom many critics have labeled as Bond's surrogate father. These two patriarchs play vital roles in forwarding the narrative's central motif of duty to country versus self. Bennett and Woollacott describe the portrayal of M in the films as a "fuddy-duddy Establishment figure" ("Moments" 23), while Eco notes that M represents "Duty, Country, and Method" and always leads Bond "on the road to Duty (at all costs)" ("Narrative" 37). Bennett and Woollacott astutely comment that M is a Lacanian Symbolic father (*Bond* 131). Lacan's other domains, the "Imaginary" and the "Real," serve as lapses in the Symbolic domain, in essence symptoms that lead to neurosis. Lacan's Symbolic domain is associated with Law-of-the-father and serves as the site of the symbolic phallus and the power associated with it (Evans 82-4, 159-61). M to Bond is literally "the law," as he has professional control over Bond.

When Bond returns to England, Bond learns that M has taken from him the operation to find Blofeld during the obligatory briefing scene in M's office; this amounts to a symbolic castration of Bond. After the meeting, Bond speaks with Moneypenny, a kind of surrogate "Mother" to complete the Oedipal triad with M and Bond. In response to his removal from the operation, Bond refers to M as a "monument." Tara Brabazon writes that Lazenby's replacement of Connery in *OHMSS* allows Moneypenny to be "even more pivotal to the survival of Bond" (493) because she prevents Bond from retiring. Brabazon also labels Moneypenny both "Britain's last line of defense" and "feminisms first foothold for attack" (496). The message here is clear: Bond needs Moneypenny, his surrogate mother, to keep him from doing anything self-destructive and to mediate between Bond and the stern "monument" father-figure, M. In the Lacanian notion of the Imaginary, Moneypenny emasculates Bond, and, as the Pelrines note, Fleming as a child "had been pushed and pulled and pummeled by a domineering mother" and as an adult "fell victim to the vicious circle" in his marriage (33).

Bond is again propositioned with di Vicenzo's body when her father kidnaps Bond to offer him one million pounds to marry his daughter: Draco says she needs a "man to dominate her." In exchange Bond barters for the location of Blofeld, whose whereabouts he has sought for two years, a sexual transaction that reflects what Denning calls "new organisation of sexuality in consumer capitalism" ("Licensed" 73). For the film version of this transaction, Bond meets Draco and di Vicenzo in a Hemingwayesque scene at a bullfight. Bond again wears a ruffled, very courtier-like shirt, highlighting the change in Bond's treatment of women from frequent, casual encounters to the more "formal" courtship of di Vicenzo. Near the end of the film Bond must appeal to Draco to help rescue his daughter from Blofeld's compound, and in doing so appeals to his future father-in-law because his symbolic father, M, has become impotent and unable to mount the rescue operation. Draco, the head of a large criminal organization, constitutes not only the literal father, but also the big Other, the confessor, that to whom Bond needs to appeal for help despite the fact that this help falls outside of the law, the Law-of-the-father, or rather, M's wishes and admonitions. In other words, Bond again chooses one patriarch over another.

There is something appropriate about Lazenby playing Bond only once, in the film where the title character gets married. Lazenby's Bond differs from that of Connery and Moore primarily in his relative helplessness and vulnerability, professionally as well as personally and romantically. Not until the official reboot of the 007 franchise does Bond again fall in love, but Daniel Craig's Bond soon returns to his characteristic icy coldness near the end of *Casino Royale* (novel, 1953; film, Martin Campbell

2006) when he says of Vesper Lynd, "The bitch is dead." But as Fleming tells us, Bond has "come a long way" since *Casino Royale*, and he visits Lynd's grave in the early pages of *OHMSS* (19). Lazenby, however, cries at the end of *OHMSS* and this is the only time this occurs across a franchise that spans 23 films and 50 years. Lazenby's Bond proposes to di Vicenzo precisely because she rescues him: this is the gesture that makes him fall in love. This reverses the typical Bond trope in which women fall in love with Bond when he rescues them. Bond also considers resigning from MI6 and finding a new profession, as does Craig's Bond in *Casino Royale*. Black argues that Lazenby's Bond is "vulnerable and consequently more human" (115). This means that di Vicenzo simply had to die, if for no other reason than to allow Bond to remain, as George Grella notes, "chaste" to fight "evil" (20). The film's final shot of a bullet hole in the car's windshield suggests a crack in Bond's armor and a rupture in the Symbolic organization of the Bond canon. Perhaps Bond's marriage represents "little more than a momentary desire to be ordinary" (White 30), but nevertheless, Bond's marriage and di Vicenzo's death lurk in the background of future Bond films: in *The Spy Who Loved Me* (Lewis Gilbert 1977) Bond changes the subject when Agent XXX asks him about his wife, and *For Your Eyes Only* (John Glen 1981) begins with Bond visiting di Vicenzo's gravestone.

For Your Eyes Only also marks the final film appearance of Blofeld, now confined to a wheelchair and wearing a neck brace. Blofeld's plot in *OHMSS*—to render all plant and animal life infertile—is arguably the most terroristic plot in the Bond canon. In an essay response to the September 11 attack, Slavoj Žižek likens the world's most famous terrorist to Blofeld, calling Osama bin Laden "the real-life counterpart of Ernst Stavro Blofeld" against whom "Bond's intervention, of course, is to explode in firecraks (sic) this site of production, allowing us to return to the daily semblance of our existence" (¶ 6). But in *OHMSS*, Blofeld's asexual second in command Irma Bunt plays a larger role in the narrative as she is the one who kills di Vicenzo and not Blofeld. As Funnell notes, Bond never kills Bunt, and Bunt thus represents "the only villain in the history of the film series to escape the violent retribution of James Bond" ("From English" 204). As with Bond's marriage, the survival of the asexual Bunt problematizes many of the gendered positions held by female Bond villains, and *OHMSS* thus stands as a significant generic rupture in a film series that largely meets audiences' expectations. With the success of the most recent Bond film, *Skyfall* (Sam Mendes 2012), it appears as if we will be able to return to the "daily semblance" of Bond's existence for some time to come.

NOTE

1 Reference to the Signet publication of the novel.

CHAPTER 12

SISTERHOOD AS RESISTANCE IN *FOR YOUR EYES ONLY* AND *OCTOPUSSY*

Fernando Gabriel Pagnoni Berns

In *The Spy Who Loved Me* (Lewis Gilbert 1977), James Bond (Roger Moore) works alongside Major Anya Amasova (Barbara Bach). The film centers on the idea that Bond has finally met his match with his new counterpart, who was marketed as a "female Bond." Unlike previous Bond Girls, Amasova remains fully clothed and the film, according to Jeremy Black, "can be seen as a reaction to claims that the early Bond films were sexist and also to the growing feminist current from the 1960s" (137). And yet, Amasova is always presented as being two steps behind Bond and her positioning in the narrative draws into question the progressive nature of her characterization.

It is not until the 1980s that Bond finally meets women who are on his level. Melina Havelock (Carole Bouquet) in *For Your Eyes Only* (John Glen 1981) is one of the few Bond Girls that do not jeopardize Bond's mission by making mistakes. With her deadly crossbow and intelligence, Havelock takes the lead on occasions and helps to ensure the success of Bond's mission. The following film, *Octopussy* (John Glen 1983), might initially be perceived as one of the most misogynistic based on title alone. Even though Bond ventures to an island occupied by women only, the film foregrounds Bond's interactions with two strong and highly proficient women—Octopussy (Maud Adams) and Magda (Kristina Wayborn). These characters seem almost interchangeable in the narrative given their close connection that causes them to act more like sisters who protect each other rather than romantic rivals who compete for the affections of Bond.

This opens up an important line of inquiry: why in the 1980s, a decade defined by the presidency of Ronald Reagan (1981-89) and the "neoconservatizing of feminism" (Palmer 254), do Bond films feature strong women who function more like allies to Bond and companions to each rather than enemies and competitors? In this chapter, I will argue that the representation of Bond women in the early 1980s is influenced by the radical feminist movement of the second wave and especially the emergence of female-only communities that offered women a place to live beyond the reach of patriarchy. Although this experiment did not last long, ending around 1984, it was important enough to be reflected in various facets of popular culture including the Bond franchise. This chapter will explore how *For Your Eyes Only* and *Octopussy* register the impact of second-wave feminism through a consideration of the Sisterhood communities that emerged in places like the United States and India.

FOR YOUR EYES ONLY AND THE FEMINISM IN THE EIGHTIES. SISTERHOOD IS HERE.

Second-wave feminism refers to a collection of feminist movements that emerged in the 1960s. The second wave was "primarily concerned with eliminating gender inequality and the systematic oppression of women" (Funnell, *Warrior* 3) and focused on a range of issues including equal pay in the workplace, reproductive rights, and the ability for women to define their own sexuality (Hollows 3-4). The two most significant branches of the second wave were radical feminism and liberal feminism.

Radical feminism was the first branch of the second wave to emerge. Radical feminists viewed patriarchy as the most fundamental form of oppression after which all others have been modelled (Wood 74). They were deeply suspicious of the social hierarchy; they "opposed liberalism [and] pursued social transformations through the creation of alternative non-hierarchical institutions and forms of organization intended to prefigure a utopian feminist society" (Taylor and Whittier 173). Moreover, radical feminists championed the idea of sisterhood, which Renate Klein and Susan Hawthorne describe as "the recognition of a sense of political commitment to women as a social group" (57). The concept of sisterhood, however, proved to be problematic; by universalizing womanhood, it effectively eliminated differences of identity between women (Kamitsuka 96).

By the 1970s, radical feminists among other second wavers were subjected to a backlashing at the hands of media, which distrusted the revolutionary radicalization of the movement. Feminists were depicted in popular media as lonely and depressed women due to the shortage of men in their lives (Faludi 1). As noted by Bonnie Dow, "the issue was no longer whether or not women could succeed but how they would handle the consequences of that success" (83). As a result, the social advances of women were put under a media microscope and various popular cultural texts, such as the Bond franchise, "register[ed] the political impact of the women's movement and reflect[ed] popular attitudes to the evolving feminist agenda" (Funnell, "Negotiating" 199).

Traditional gender roles are notable in the representation of women in promotional posters for the films. For instance, Amasova is conceptualized as a female Bond and poses beside the title character in the center of the poster for *The Spy Who Loved Me*. While both Bond and Amasova are fully clothed in formal wear, Amasova's body is placed on display through the design of her evening gown: her cleavage and bare outstretched leg are emphasized by the cut of the dress and her posture. The explicit display in the Bond Girl's body is even more overt in the poster for *For Your Eyes Only*, which displays Bond at the center framed by a pair of female legs of an anonymous woman; this woman is presumably Havelock since she is carrying a crossbow, the weapon that the character uses in the film. Here, the Bond Girl is depicted from the waist down in a bikini bottom, which highlights her bare legs and buttocks. In both cases, the Bond Girl occupies the traditional exhibitionist role and the strength of her character is downplayed through her overt sexualization. Moreover, these images shape viewer expectations regarding the representation of traditional gender roles in the films.

In spite of the poster, *For Your Eyes Only* presents a noticeably different representation of the Bond Girl. Havelock is introduced in an airplane on route to visit her parents who work as marine archaeologists on a yacht. In these first moments, Havelock is shown touching up her makeup, an image that reinforces the notion that aesthetic femininity is a primary concern of Bond's women. However, the sequence ends with an extreme close-up shot of Havelock's eyes after her parents are killed by an airplane flying over the area. With this final shot, the film stresses that Havelock's desire for revenge will be her primary motivation. From this moment forward, Havelock is presented as one of the strongest Bond Girls in the franchise, who is actually on par with Bond.

One of the recurring scenes in the Bond franchise features Bond saving the female lead who is in grave danger. In *For Your Eyes Only*, however, it is Havelock who saves Bond twice. In the first instance, Bond is monitoring the criminal activities at a pool party in Madrid when he is caught spying. Bond is able to escape from two armed guards when Havelock shoots one with an arrow. However, Bond continues to be pursued by henchmen and again it is Havelock who saves Bond by flirting with one of his pursuers. To compensate for these female heroic acts, Bond is the one who guides them through the deep vegetation surrounding the area. Bond's recovery of his heroic status is brief: when Bond discovers that his car is unusable, it is Havelock who conducts him through the wild landscape to some other spot, reversing the role of guide. She is not leading him randomly, but to her own car. Bond stops to observe the precarious vehicle, which is clearly different from the high technological gadgets he has access to as the male hero; this scene contrast Bond's silver sports car, the technologically enhanced Lotus Esprit (which is coded masculine), with Havelock's older yellow economy car, the Citröen 2 CV (which is coded feminine). In order for Bond to return to the traditionally male heroic role Havelock is occupying, Bond steps in to drive midway through the scene to bring the chase and the narration to more familiar ground.

Once they are out of danger, Havelock is positioned as an Other in the film. She tells Bond: "I don't expect you to understand. You're English, but I'm half Greek. And

Greek women, like Electra, always avenge their loved ones." This statement marks the difference between hegemony (i.e. Great Britain as a central country and colonizer that is, through Bond, coded masculine) and difference (i.e. Greece as a subordinate country that is, through Havelock, coded feminine). On the one hand, this exchange between Havelock and Bond works to reestablish traditional gender roles in the film. Bond, as the British hero, is motivated by a sense of moral duty to England and the collective good. In comparison, Havelock does not share his patriotism and is motivated instead by a personal vendetta. While Bond's mission is acceptable, Havelock's quest for vengeance is less so. On the other hand, this exchange opens up space in the narrative for Havelock. Since she is operating outside of the system, she does not need to abide by traditional social norms. She can possess traditionally masculine qualities without any repercussions.

The capacity of Havelock to drive the narration appears again when she and Bond are captured by Kristatos (Julian Glover) and tied to a boat that will drag them into the Aegean Sea. While Bond manages to cut the bonds that tie them to the boat, it is Havelock who conducts Bond to a safe spot under the waters she knows so well, thus saving them both. From this moment onwards, Havelock plays an integral role in the film's climax whereby Bond leads an assault on Kristatos' fortress. Unlike other Bond Girls, Havelock does not play a damsel in distress since she is never captured or held hostage by the villain. In fact, Havelock and her crossbow save Bond again from imminent death when one of Kristatos' men tries to shoot him in the back. Bond's heroic and virile masculinity are restored in the end when Bond and Havelock engage in lovemaking, a perquisite scene that closes the canonical Bond films. Interestingly, before this moment, Havelock has never shown sexual interest in Bond, so their interaction comes across as being somewhat forced.

In spite of this final encounter, Havelock can be considered a strong character. Lisa Funnell argues that the level of equality between Bond and the Bond Girl can be measured through five categories: physical, emotional, intellectual, courage, and sexual prowess ("From English" 68). On the one hand, Havelock is not equal to Bond physically, emotionally or sexually, but she still demonstrates strength in these areas— Havelock does not match Bond physically but has an unmatched proficiency with the crossbow; she is not as stable in terms of her emotions but presents an unwavering sense of purpose; she is not as dominant sexually but is still able to attract the attention of Bond and other men. On the other hand, Havelock is equal, if not superior, to Bond in the areas of courage and intelligence—this is impressive given the fact that she is not a trained agent! While Havelock is not Bond's strongest partner—Funnell argues that Pussy Galore is the most equitable partner before the 1990s (ibid. 67)—she certainly holds her own in the film. An often overlooked heroine, Havelock represents the values of radical feminism and is able to subvert some of the gendered codes of the series.

OCTOPUSSY AND THE SEPARATIST FEMINIST GROUPS

By the late 1970s and early 1980s, some feminists including those that self-identified as lesbian feminists or Radicalesbians, desired greater social autonomy. They became a part of another branch of second-wave feminism, separatism, and sought to build communities in which women could be separated from patriarchal society and live independently in female-only communities. According to Julia T. Wood, "separatists believe it is impossible [...] to reform America's patriarchal, homophobic culture. Instead they choose to exit mainstream society and form communities that value women and strive to live in harmony with people, animals and the earth" (78).

Although not all separatists were lesbians, many of them were and these separatist communities concentrated especially on lesbian culture. Wood notes that Radicalesbians "took the radical feminist idea of putting women first a few steps further by asserting that only women who loved and lived with women were really putting women first" (77). They argued that women who orient their lives around men could never truly be free (ibid. 77). As a result, lesbian feminism became "the most assertive arm of the feminist movement, espousing a politic that encouraged feminists to turn their energies toward women in every aspect of their lives" (Boyd 213). For some feminists, lesbianism became a way to dedicate oneself more fully to feminism (ibid. 213).

Kathy Rudy notes that working and living in these communities fostered female independence in a world dominated by men. She contends that "lesbianism was the most legitimate way to act out our politics. In the process of developing feminist theories rooted in the unique, caring nature of women, many theorists suggested that the best way to demonstrate such female sensitivity is by caring exclusively for other women" (195). In other words, by avoiding contact with men and their rules, these communities were trying to change the world (ibid. 195-6).

It is this discourse of sisterhood in which women, lesbian or not, share everything in "quasifamilial relations" (Weiss 12) that structures *Octopussy*. The first moment of sisterhood appears after the opening credits. Before receiving instructions for a new mission from M, Bond goes first through his secretary Monypenny (Lois Maxwell) who is split into two—for the first time, Moneypenny has an assistant, Penelope Smallbone (Michaela Clavell). The film is unprecedented in presenting two "Moneypennys" falling for Bond. Although Bond gives more attention to Smallbone, offering her a bouquet while reserving only a single flower for Moneypenny, Moneypenny does not appear jealous or angry. To the contrary, she advises her young assistant to accept the gift: "Take it, dear. That's all you'll ever get from him." Her advice, like that of an older sister to her younger sibling, is a cautionary tale about the dangers of caring too much for a man like Bond.

This division of Moneypenny into two characters is replicated in the film, on a much larger scale, through the characterization of the Bond Girl. As noted by Funnell, each Bond film contains only one Bond Girl: she is Bond's primary girlfriend and the woman with whom Bond connects emotionally ("From English" 63). In *Octopussy*, however, there are two women who interact with Bond and share similar traits. The primary Bond Girl is Octopussy. She is a classic Bond heroine who, while being strong and independent, requires saving from Bond in the end. Magda, however, is a far more interesting and anomalous character. She is not a criminal despite her association with the film's main villain, Kamal Khan (Louis Jourdan). According to Bond tradition, this partnership might not render her a villain but it would, at the very least, cast her as a tragic figure who must die midway through the film at the hands of the villain for switching sides after experiencing Bond's irresistible charm. As expected, Magda sleeps with Bond; this is part of Khan's plan to steal the original Faberge egg Bond has in his possession. Naturally, Bond anticipated Magda's actions and placed a tracker on the egg. When Bond tracks it down, Magda is not punished by the villain for her mistake. Later, when Bond is imprisoned by Khan at his estate, Magda quietly observes him breaking out of his room and roaming throughout the manor. She does not raise the alarm and simply smiles, showing her approval of Bond's actions. Again, Magda is not punished by the villain for her complicity in Bond's escape.

The narrative treatment of Magda is extraordinary when considered in relation to the Bond franchise at large. Her exceptional status is the product of her deep loyalty to Octopussy and not with a male faction (i.e. Bond, Khan, or any other male character). Moreover, the bond of sisterhood she shares with Octopussy is cast in a positive light and presented as a redeeming/saving quality. As a result, she is able to circumvent the gender politics at work in the Bond franchise. This renders Magda an anomaly in the film as she does not clearly fit into any character category. Moreover, when Octopussy is introduced into the film, Magda is relocated to the periphery of the narrative and becomes part of the background.

Octopussy replaces Magda in the film as Bond's primary love interest. What is striking is that both women, beyond their hierarchical relationship in which Octopussy is the owner of the island and Magda her henchwoman, have traits that are not all that different. Both women are smart, strong, and independent; they are capable of handling themselves in a range of situations. In fact, one could argue that either character is expendable: Octopussy could well fill the role of Magda or vice versa. Both women seem interchangeable, which is strange in a franchise that has always been careful in differentiating Bond's women. This is one reason why Magda has to fade into the background; if she did not, the audience might be confused as to which woman is the Bond Girl.

It is my argument that, much like the doubling of Moneypenny with Smallbone, the Bond Girl is reconstituted into two characters that are not antagonistic, but rather presented as sisters. This is not surprising considering the fact that most of the action occurs on the island of Octopussy, which is populated by a separatist community of women who are loyal to their female leader. The island is clearly a nod to the emergence of separatist communities in the United States and abroad. Each woman has been branded with an "octopussy" tattoo somewhere on her body. Moreover, the film suggests that these women are lesbians via the root word "pussy." The use of this term recalls the representation of Bond Girl Pussy Galore, who is overtly presented as a lesbian in Ian Fleming's 1959 novel *Goldfinger*, while her sexual orientation and conversion to heterosexuality is more subtly suggested in Guy Hamilton's 1964 film adaptation. Thus, Octopussy replicates, within popular culture, contemporaneous anxieties regarding the emergence of militant feminist separatist groups like Cell 16 and lesbian communities like The Furies Collective in America (Buchanan 28, 38). Moreover, India also saw the rise of radicalized feminist groups during this time including the first women's publishing house "Kali for Women", along with women's centers that "try to put feminist concepts of sisterhood into practice" (Singh 33-4). Interestingly, the film works to quell these fears of lesbian separatism by having both Magda and Octopussy sleep with Bond in order to demonstrate their conversion back to heterosexuality; in the same problematic way, *Goldfinger* suggests that Galore is "converted" through her sexual encounter with Bond. In addition, the film ends with Bond (along with an aged Q) saving the women on the island from Khan and his goons, thus reasserting the superiority of Bond, the importance of patriarchy to civil society, and the traditional notion that women need men to love and protect them.

A VIEW TO A KILL AND THE LAST TRAITS OF FEMINISM

In her article "The Ideal of Community and the Politics of Difference," Iris Marion Young argues that community "privileges unity over difference" and this idea, while interesting, is "politically problematic" (300). While separatist communities were considered, by some participants, to be a feminist triumph, they were highly idealized and problematic. These communities were based on the idea that the differences between the participants could be ignored (Young 302) in favor of qualities that unite them. Differences between women such as race, class, religion, sexual orientation, and so on were not being addressed. Thus, "putting women first" was not enough to sustain these communities, which fractured and dissolved soon after. Much like other second-wave feminist movements, these separatists fell into the trap of universalizing the experiences of some women as being the experiences of all women (Funnell, *Warrior* 3).

    A View to a Kill (John Glen 1985) is the last Bond film of the 1980s to include traces of the concept of sisterhood, an ideal that was losing steam as the decade progressed. In the film, Bond is tasked with stopping the villain, Max Zorin (Christopher Walken), from destroying Silicon Valley in order to monopolize the electronic market. Zorin plans to detonate a bomb that will trigger a cataclysmic earthquake burying Silicon Valley. Sisterhood is embodied in the character of May Day (Grace Jones), Zorin's primary henchwoman, a tough woman of few words who is masculinized by her aggression, physical prowess, and stoicism. As noted by Antonia Castañeda, women of color are presented in two stereotypical ways: the light-skinned are presented as civilized and the darker-skinned are depicted as being savage (517). Although May Day is presented as being wild, unpredictable, and animalistic, her characterization also appears to be informed by contemporaneous feminist sentiments.

First, May Day does not fall for the charms of Bond. Although she sleeps with him, she does so in order to determine his agenda; she is not attracted to Bond and her loyalty to Zorin does not waver. Bond may have finally found "his match" in May Day as the posters for the film announce. In fact, May Day only acts out against Zorin after he initiates an explosion in the mine; this act not only puts the life of May Day in danger but he also kills her close confident, Jenny Flex (Alison Doody), in the process. May Day is visibly emotional upon discovering the body of Flex and Bond has to physically pull her away from her friend. It is at this moment that May Day decides to work against Zorin in order to thwart his plan. While motivated by personal betrayal, May Day is also seeking vengeance for the death of her friend. One could argue that the bond of sisterhood she shared with Flex supersedes any allegiance that May Day had to Zorin.

It is important to note that Flex along with Zorin's other female assistants do not play a central role in the film. It is clearly through the sorrow experienced and expressed by May Day that the feminist idea of sisterhood is introduced into the film, even if the interactions of these women have not been of vital importance in the narrative. In addition, May Day commits suicide without engaging in an anticipated physical confrontation with Bond. May Day would clearly defeat Bond in physical combat and the film skirts the issue in order to maintain Bond's honor and heroic masculinity. Nonetheless, May Day is presented as being equal to Bond and loyal to her sisters, qualities that connect her character with second-wave feminist notions that were already in retreat.

CONCLUSIONS

Grace Jones was the first black woman to be cast in a lead role in a Bond film. While Funnell argues that May Day represents the emerging third wave feminist impulse ("Negotiating" 205), I would argue that her character shares more in common with the Bond Girls of the early 1980s who are reflective of second-wave. *For Your Eyes Only* features one of the strongest Bond Girls in the franchise who acts on her own accord and is never presented as a damsel in distress. *Octopussy* centers on two women who live in a separatist community and share a strong bond of sisterhood with each other and other women. The character May Day seems to pull from both of these films as she is presented as a strong and independent woman who is supremely loyal to her female friends.

The first three Bond films of the 1980s show how far the ideas of second-wave feminism were embedded in popular culture, even if the subversive potential of these women is undermined by having each of them sleep with Bond and/or require saving, thus reaffirming patriarchy. But it is important to note that despite all this, the legacy of feminism is present in these women that are on par with Bond, at least for a good part of the film—women who seem to care more about their personal goals and female friendships than they do about Bond and his mission. In a franchise that has been accused of sexism, the representation of women in the 1980s stands out against the homogeneity of the series.

CHAPTER 13

BOND IS NOT ENOUGH

Elektra King and the Desiring Bond Girl

Alexander Sergeant

Over the past half century, the James Bond franchise has demonstrated a remarkable ability to adapt to the various cultural, social, and political paradigms surrounding its production. This polymorphous feature of the franchise also applies to its treatment of women. Bond has pursued relationships with women as brief as a momentary flirtatious glance through to his marriage to Tracy di Vicenzo in *On Her Majesty's Secret Service* (Peter Hunt 1969). Yet, the diverse relationship between Bond and the Bond Girl is often summarized by commentators as an objectifying one in which female characters are only valuable to the hero "to the extent that they are capable of bringing him sexual pleasure" (Arp and Decker 202). According to traditional arguments, the Bond Girl functions as a "reaffirmation of male supremacy" by playing a passive role to a virile seducer, her identity controlled, manipulated, and dominated by the larger meaning of Bond himself (Bold 169). Such analyses not only fail to give female characters throughout the franchise enough scope to exist in a theoretical space outside of the eponymous hero, but they also risk obfuscating a fundamental paradox buried at the heart of Bond's masculinity that, like all phallocentric discourses, is "dependent on the image of the castrated woman to give order and meaning to its world" (Mulvey, "Visual" 833). This chapter aims to understand the gender politics of the franchise free from the simplistic binary assumptions of active/passive or seducer/seduced by discussing the Bond Girl not as a concept subservient to Bond but instead as an autonomous character with as much potential to challenge traditional phallocentric notions of masculinity embedded within the franchise as she does to conform and perpetuate such discourses. Utilizing a case study of Elektra King in *The World is Not Enough* (Michael Apted 1999), I will discuss the franchise's portrayal of the Bond Girl's desire and sexuality as a way of understanding the manner in which phallocentrism permeates throughout the Bond film, as well as serving as a key device that disrupts the embedded ideologies of patriarchal society. Discussions of the Bond franchise's perpetuation of patriarchal ideology often focus solely on the character of Bond and the problematic masculinity he embodies. Yet, as Jeremy Black argues,

Bond's masculinity is not a force of itself but is instead something that is intrinsically tied to his position as a "successful seducer" of the female characters he encounters throughout the franchise (108). Whether this be a character significant to the plot like Pussy Galore in *Goldfinger* (Guy Hamilton 1964) or a character like Jill Masterson who Bond meets and seduces in the opening moments of that film, Bond is defined by his ability to attract women in order to service his own means. By overtly sexualizing the gender dynamics in this manner, the Bond franchise makes explicit what is very often left implicit within other portrayals of masculinity in mainstream cinema. Rather than relying on symbols of sexuality, the reality of sex is frequently presented on screen in the Bond film, albeit in a censored and stylized manner. Bond's position as an affirmation of patriarchal ideology is far less certain than it might seem to be. His function as a typical figure of phallocentric masculinity is to dominate agency and control the discourses of sexuality. He must define gender difference through male-orientated terms that place him as the controller of desire. Yet, in order to achieve this, he is dependent on the desire of female characters. It is this central paradox that is buried at the heart of the franchise's varied representations of women.

Scholarly accounts of Bond's sexuality have explored Bond as an embodiment of *the phallus*: a recurrent symbol of masculinity discussed prominently amongst psychoanalytic theories of patriarchy. However, they have often done so through male-orientated terms, using psychoanalysis as a "preferred system of inscribing ethical incompleteness" onto Bond rather than as a device to inscribe ethical incompleteness onto the franchise (Miller, "Cultural" 295). Bennett and Woollacott's discussion of sexuality in Fleming's source novels draws attention to the importance of phallic discourses in the Bond story's perpetuation of patriarchy. Yet, their work focuses only on the use of "phallic imagery" in the form of the quasi-Oedipal relationship between M as father, and the role of the gun as the definer of Bond's masculine prowess as "signifying devices which add an extra dimension to the tensions that are set up and resolved in the course of the narrative" (*Bond* 128). While Bond may not give the women he meets little more than a passing thought, analyses of his relationship with women must not to fall victim to the same kind of phallocentrism that Bond himself is guilty of exhibiting. It is important that we refuse the obfuscation of the Bond Girl that the franchise encourages through many of its formal and stylistic devices, and to see her desire as an expression of her own identity. In this manner, female sexuality and desire become devices that can serve to confuse and complicate Bond's function as a viral embodiment of a patriarchal form of masculinity.

In George Stevens' classic western *Shane* (1953), the hero's status as a stand-in for the phallus is achieved through the film's valorization of the cowboy's precision with his pistols. As Shane grips his gun to demonstrate his unmatched skill, he grips his own sexual agency—homogenizing and masculinizing the erotics of gender and, in the process, denying women access to a similar form of vitality. Bond, however, has no such luxury. By the very fact that his phallic prowess is explicitly sexualized, he is utterly dependent on the unapologetic force of femininity that the desiring Bond Girl represents. Bond is a character heavy with the weight of his own phallocentric burden and his relationship to his own masculinity is, in comparison with his Hollywood contemporaries, racked with anxiety, hysteria, and a deep-seated suppression of the possibilities of female desire. Critics examining *The Searchers* (John Ford 1956) find Martha's longing for Ethan in the occasional gesture within a *mise–en–scène* otherwise preoccupied by the anxieties of men. In the Bond film, the desiring Bond Girl is invoked on screen for all to see, to know, and to feel. I contend that an important function of feminist critiques of the franchise should be to expose the moments where the franchise's often frenzied portrayal of masculinity is brought to the surface, and to use these moments in which female desire is articulated on screen as the road mark for a progressive future for the Bond film.

MR. KISS KISS BANG BANG: THE DOMESTICATION OF FEMALE DESIRE IN THE BOND FRANCHISE

The phallus emerges in psychoanalytic theory as a pervasive idea that manages to articulate the unconscious gender dynamics surrounding the construction of patriarchal society. The concept first appears in Sigmund Freud's writings on infant sexuality as a relationship between the male subject and his developing libido. As the child emerges out of the latency period, the penis becomes the primary focus of his fascination as the organ that comes to define his status as male in contrast with the absence of a penis the child notices in his mother. Misunderstood by the male subject, this observed difference gives rise to the idea of the castration complex, in which the child associates his sense of having a penis with a recognition of its possible absence. The emergent sexuality of the male subject channels the castration anxiety into a focus on "the primacy of the phallus", a more elusive concept that is somewhat separated from the biological reality of sexuality (*On Sexuality* 308).

It is in Jacques Lacan's reinterpretation of Freudian psychoanalysis in which the phallus emerges as a key concept to understand the tendency amongst various societies towards patriarchal structures and phallocentric discourses. For Lacan, the phallus is not simply a relationship between the male subject and his penis but a wider symbolic attachment that shapes his sense of identity. It "functions as a knot" by which the subject establishes a sense of *I* in contrast to others while simultaneously functioning as a force by which the subject must measure himself up against ("Signification" 575). As Elizabeth Grosz argues, "the phallus functions to enable the penis to define all (socially recognized) forms of human sexuality" (116-7). It expresses the difference between the two sexes in terms of presence and absence, and soothes the male ego by defining desire in male-orientated terms and defining the woman "for what she is not" (Lacan,

"Signification" 581). Possessing a penis, the heterosexual male subject is dependent on the vagina. Possessing the phallus, the male subject controls sexual agency, and the vagina becomes an empty vessel of meaning subjugated to his own desire.

Both Freudian and Lacanian notions of the phallus have been utilized by feminist theorists to articulate the manner by which individuals may fall victim to the phallocentric mind-set often perpetuated by patriarchal society, and the manner in which the phallus is based upon a fundamental insecurity embedded within the male subject. In the case of the Bond franchise, for Bond to function as a phallic symbol, he must perform this same colonization of desire. He cannot simply express a sexualized form of masculinity, but rather one that is reliant upon negating the role of the female. To be deliberately crude, Bond's function as a manifestation of the phallus is not achieved simply by fucking the Bond Girl, but by fucking the desire out of her. In that symbolic act, Bond obliterates the concept of a female-orientated desire, and stands as a signifier for a dominating form of male sexuality that valorizes the penis to mask the unknown enigma of the vagina. The various films in the franchise are therefore tasked with the job of expressing the Bond Girl's desire for Bond and then silencing it—enacting it temporarily, only to remove its possibility altogether. It is this that gives the Bond film its patriarchal ideology.

A standard way the symbolic force of the phallus is felt within the guise of mainstream cinema is through a misogynist fantasy built around the male subject's anxieties over castration. Within the Bond franchise, this anxiety largely expresses itself through female villains such as Fiona Volpe in *Thunderball* (Terence Young 1965) right through to a more recent incarnation such as Xenia Onatopp in *Goldeneye* (Martin Campbell 1995) who each display an aggressive form of sexuality as part of their character construction. Another manner in which the franchise projects a phallocentric discourse of desire is through the recurring characterization of the Bond Girl as a submissive daughter. Notably, it is the term "Bond Girl" and not "Bond Woman" that has come to define the lead female protagonists, and this infantilization works to alleviate Bond to the position of a controlling patriarch. Examples of this character type range from Solitaire in *Live and Let Die* (Guy Hamilton 1973), who is seduced and made powerless by Bond (as she loses her ability of foresight after sleeping with him), through to Stacey Sutton in *A View to a Kill* (John Glen 1985), who not only physically resembles Roger Moore's daughter given the age gap between the two actors, but also spends the majority of the film being escorted by the hand through dangerous situations. The Bond Girl is not allowed to be equal to Bond for fear of challenging the autonomy of the phallus, and so she must be positioned as physically and intellectually inferior to the male hero.

The infantilization of the Bond Girl demonstrates a key aspect of phallocentrism exemplified by Lacan's concept of the paternal metaphor, a theory he develops from Freud's oedipal conflict between the male subject's latent desire for his mother and the competition for her affection posed by the father. Lacan posits that through this conflict, the male subject comes to identify the father as a symbolic stand-in for society itself. In the eyes of the male subject, the father represents not only an obstacle for the affection of the mother but the ideal of masculinity to which he must live up. In symbolic terms, the father comes to "represent the vehicle, the holder, of the phallus", and the male subject must adopt his mantle to become the phallus and be capable of satisfying desire (*Psychoses* 319). Between these two recurring characterizations of the Bond Girl and the female villain, the franchise has served patriarchal ideology by continually suppressing the concept of a female sexuality equal to Bond's masculine prowess. Yet, while it is true that most Bond films fall victim to a form of phallocentrism, there are moments throughout the franchise where the Bond Girl's sexuality is articulated outside of Bond's complex role as seducer. Elektra King in *The World is Not Enough* is a key example of just such a paradigm. She is a character that, while contained within the patriarchal structure of the typical Bond film, is nevertheless able to present a version of female sexuality unmediated through the eyes of Bond. It is by highlighting such moments that feminist film theory might negotiate and subvert the established politics of desire within the Bond franchise.

"THERE'S NO POINT IN LIVING IF YOU CAN'T FEEL ALIVE": THE UNTAMED SEXUALITY OF ELEKTRA KING

Within the promotional materials for *The World is Not Enough*, King emerges as a prominent figure that the film's producers, director, and star would be keen to discuss. In an interview, director Michael Apted expressed his desire—shared by producers Barbara Broccoli and Michael G. Wilson—to adjust the gender politics of the franchise and include a female character that would more than just "sexual decoration" (qtd. in Jones 36). The dynamic between Bond and King would take center stage as the key relationship in the film as reflected in various marketing campaigns. This worked to obscure more traditional character types such as the cold, calculating Bond villain epitomized by Robert Carlyle's Renard and the Bond Girl, nuclear physicist Dr. Christmas Jones played by Denise Richards. In creating this atypical dynamic, King becomes one of the few characters to radically challenge the franchise's varied discourses on patriarchy. Her very name seems to be a deliberate play on Jung's concept of the Electra complex, his equivalent term for Freud's oedipal struggle within the developing female subject, and through her performance Marceau seems fully aware of King's position as both an independent character in the franchise and as a character riding on a wave of self-conscious fandom. The knowingness Marceau brings to the role becomes King's greatest virtue, allowing the character to adopt a form of self-conscious masquerade that simultaneously performs the various roles established for the Bond Girl and yet acknowledges the falsity of such discourses.

The reason that King serves as such a fascinating case study is due to her ability to enact and yet hold at bay the problematic legacies of representation established by her predecessors. She plays on the various female character types established by the franchise as a key plot device. Bond is assigned to protect King, the daughter of a wealthy oil baron, after her father is assassinated within the walls of MI6. After an initial glimpse of her at the funeral, Bond's first encounter with King comes through his research within the MI6 archives. Looking over news footage of her kidnapping, King is introduced as a frightened, physically frail woman who was abused by a physically stronger man. Bond is seemingly tasked with his traditional role as the dominant patriarch while King is infantilized by his gaze. When Bond meets her face to face, this dynamic of protection is further established. Although King initially insists that she does not need the protection of MI6, she requires Bond's rescue from Renard's henchman during a spectacular ski chase. Bond assumes the role as protector, and she is left with the perennial choice of the Bond Girl to either sleep with this surrogate father and give up her capacity for independence or doom herself to be killed at the hands of Renard. King chooses the former, and she and Bond quickly engage in a sexual relationship.

In a sequence of short dialogue exchanges, Bond and King are seen naked in bed together. As if aware of the function of this scene in the traditional Bond film, King confesses to Bond that she "knew" from the moment she first saw him that they would end up in bed together, a comment that exemplifies the standard archetype of submissive Bond Girl as she suggests to Bond that her desire for him was overwhelming and all-consuming. Much like Solitaire, she was able to see her fate in front of her and yet was powerless or unwilling to prevent it. Such a statement, however, is inaccurate and speaks of the masquerade being perpetrated by King. Prior to this scene, King had attempted to sleep with Bond only to have him refuse her advances in the line of duty. Now in her bed, it is not that King has been seduced by Bond but that Bond has finally given into his desire for King. Rather than presenting a male-oriented fantasy of desire being satisfied, her comment that she "knew" speaks of a determination on her part far more in keeping with the vamp-like Bond villain than the traditional submissive character of the Bond Girl that King is supposed to embody. She is not being desired, but is instead desiring in this moment. While they make love, King reaches across the bed and grabs at a container of ice used to chill a bottle of champagne. So often a symbol of Bond's phallic prowess, King rejects the unopened bottle, which in previous movies Bond has been so keen to uncork and pop, in favor of the ice itself. She places the blocks in her mouth, and enjoys the sensation of them melting. King has transferred Bond's traditionally phallic display of male sexuality into a metaphor for her own desire: replacing the bottle with the ice and the popping with a sense of wetness.

In perhaps his most misogynist piece of analysis, Freud's brief essay on female sexuality discusses the complications that female arousal has on his developing theory of the phallus. Freud's notion of the phallus is based around the supposedly primordial expression of sexuality: the erect penis. Yet, as Freud acknowledges, the erect penis is one of two crucial expressions of sexual excitement, the other being the "lubrication of the vagina," which forms a far more hysteric notion in his theory of sexuality (*On Sexuality* 129). For Freud, the unseen, wet vagina represents mystery, perhaps even danger, and his discussions center around the elusiveness of female sexuality as lacking an overt symbol in the manner of the phallus. In *The World is Not Enough*, King provides a vivid counter-argument to Freud's mistaken notions. King holds Bond at bay—allowing him the fantasy of domination but refusing him the actual dominance to which he has grown so accustomed. She expresses desire clearly and articulately, and does not succumb to the dominance of the phallus but rather holds it at a distance as she performs her role as the Bond Girl. This sense of distance in these scenes is compounded later when King reveals the true nature of her character. Midway through the film, King is revealed to be the true mastermind behind a scheme to steal a nuclear submarine. She is not the Bond Girl but in fact the Bond villain, and these bedroom scenes are given a greater symbolic charge as her masquerade is exposed. Bond has not managed to enact the phallus' ultimate fantasy and satisfy King's desire. Instead, he has been used by King just as he uses the various women he meets in his life. Like Volpe, King has used Bond for sexual gratification and to acquire information. But unlike Volpe, her seduction has succeeded, duping Bond into an unsuspecting encounter with Renard, who is revealed to be little more than a hired henchman that King utilizes for her own gain.

Rather than being kidnapped by Renard, King has seduced Renard and the two lovers are revealed to be plotting together to exact revenge on both MI6 and King's father for the treatment and subjugation she suffered earlier in life. In a brief bedroom scene between the two, what is notable is the lack of authority expressed by the male villain. In contrast to Bond, Renard is vulnerable and exposed, unable to feel the ice that Bond so expertly manipulated. Renard is incapable of embodying the kind of masculinity Bond exhumed in those previous scenes, and yet it is those very qualities that seem to excite King. She chooses Renard as a partner precisely because he does not have the phallus. Without it, her sexuality—her desire, want, and arousal—can be dominant. She embraces the complexity of her own desire and its independence from the phallus, accepting the desiring "cunt" over her desired body. This acceptance of the cunt as a figure of symbolic equivalency of the phallus—as something forceful, self-reliant, and without the need for Bond or Renard to be made whole—expresses a feminist goal to represent, articulate, and celebrate female sexuality as female sexuality. King embodies these notions on screen by daring to articulate her unsatisfied desire.

The most explicit confrontation with discourses surrounding the phallus comes during a sequence in which Bond is tortured by King for information. Bond is captured and brought to *her* lair by *her* henchman and the scene has a familiar feel to Bond fans. It is akin to Goldfinger's laser torture device: a huge phallic symbol is placed between Bond's legs that exposes the vulnerability of his penis as the two characters engage in a game of one-upmanship. This time, however, Bond's male rival has been replaced by a woman. Revealing a torture contraption hidden by a dustsheet, King proceeds to explain to Bond that by cranking a leaver behind his head, she will slowly insert a brass rod into his windpipe that will choke him to death. Strapping him to the device, King begins to turn the handle and suffocate Bond playfully. Bond is literally being choked to death by a phallic substitution manipulated by King. In a vaguely misogynist exercise, King has claimed the phallus as her own and uses it against Bond for her own sadistic pleasure.

Yet, King mocks this discourse with a continued sense of masquerade. She simulates the sex act on Bond, jumping onto his crotch in a manner that invokes desire and highlights both the physical and emotional distance between the former lovers. She playfully asks Bond if he knows what happens "when a man is strangled", and invokes the idea of the post-mortem erection. In this image of the lifeless but nevertheless erect penis, the complexity by which King reacts to Bond's phallic mastery is revealed. King desires Bond, but that desire is not enough to define her. She is not dominated by her desire, but is still able to express it. In that act of simulation, she straddles literally and metaphorically two prominent characterizations of Bond women: the Bond Girl, who is beholden to the phallus, and the female villain who desires the phallus for her own means. She is neither and yet both at the same time, refusing the "abstraction of women" as a collective concept that mainstream cinema and indeed the Bond film often presents through its focus on exteriority, and instead insists on being *a woman that desires* (Bolton 3). The phallus is presented, but the cunt is still enforced. She can desire, and yet not be the victim of that desire.

CONCLUSION

The lackluster finale of *The World is Not Enough* is a by-product of the franchise's larger politics of desire. As King steps deeper into her role as villain, Bond's function as a phallic symbol soon becomes clear as he is presented with the choice between killing her or risk being obscured by her. Her death brings an end to any disruption she might have brought to the franchise's traditional discourses of masculinity, and a far more mundane action climax plays out in which two inadequate men do battle on a submarine which, as if haunted by the specter of the desiring King, is slowly filling up with water, drenching and drowning them in equal measure. As Mary Anne Doane argues, desire is linked closely to narrative, and the standard Hollywood film positions it as inherently masculine due to its persistent formal and stylistic eroticization of the female form (*Desire* 9). This has never been the exclusive case with the Bond franchise. Its ability to present Bond as a seducer of women leads to multiple occasions where Bond is invited to be a figure of desire as well as a figure who desires. This stretches back to the opening scenes of *Dr. No* (Terence Young 1962) where Bond is first introduced through the character of Sylvia Trench, but has perhaps reached a far more overt level in recent Bond films as the visual spectacle of Daniel Craig as Bond has been positioned as the key erotic symbol of the franchise. Yet, in dislocating and arguably removing the position of the Bond Girl, the franchise risks retreating into a more dangerous form of phallocentrism. Rather than confront its own infamy, the contemporary Bond film shies away from it. Rather than dealing with female desire as a concept that should be represented on screen without repercussion, the contemporary franchise instead removes it altogether.

In articulating the role of desire in the gender politics of the Bond franchise, this chapter has aimed to deliberately shift the discourses surrounding the Bond film away from a focus on its central protagonist. I have insisted on comparing Bond with his female counterpart, and have done so in order to suggest movement towards a future in which a Bond film might indulge in all its well-documented tropes and conventions while at the same time ridding itself of its more problematic agendas. Ultimately, my desire is to save Bond from himself. As has been well documented, the victims of patriarchy are not simply women, but all those who dwell within its oppressive symbolic power. In making such a statement, I do not wish to demean or dismiss the very real economic, political, social, and physical oppression that has been suffered by women at the hands of men. Women are the ostracized members of a patriarchal society, but the society it leaves in its wake becomes poisoned by that same ideology, as both men and women are forced to homogenize themselves against phallocentric notions of masculinity and femininity. Bond is forced to be the patriarch, and as such he is stuck embodying a pernicious and ultimately misguided portrayal of gendered identity. By (re)addressing the representation of desire, Bond can, will, and does provide hope that future films will be invested in a world of gender equality. As always, James Bond will return. In what manner of adventure remains to be seen.

Section 4

GENDERED CONVENTIONS

CHAPTER 14

FEMALE BODIES IN THE JAMES BOND TITLE SEQUENCES

Sabine Planka

James Bond, as a character, is virtually inconceivable without women. They serve as his enemies, allies, and lovers, and their characters are defined almost exclusively by their relationships with him. While scholars have explored the representation of Bond Girls, female villains, M, and Miss Moneypenny, little critical attention has been directed towards examining the women and, more specifically, the female bodies, featured in the opening title sequences. This chapter will redress this critical oversight by examining the form and function of these title sequences, as this element has helped producers to integrate more women and especially female sexuality into the Bond franchise. Using the work of Laura Mulvey and particularly her gaze theory, I will argue that the (semi-)nude female body is served up as an appetizer to a presumed male audience in order to peak their interest in the forthcoming film.

HISTORY AND TYPOLOGY OF THE TITLE SEQUENCE

The term "title sequence" denotes the part of the film that preludes the main narrative. It serves three key purposes: first, it provides detailed information about the cast and crew (Stanitzek 12); second, it helps to draw the audience into the film (ibid. 8); and third, it prepares the viewer by integrating relevant information from the film, announcing how it is to be read and providing clues about the genres they will be confronting (Gardies 25). The title sequence can be presented in a variety of forms including live-action, animation, or even a mixture of the two. It also features writing and, in some cases, a title song. As Georg Stanitzek notes, this diversity renders the title sequence a small work of art or even a "little auteur film" (9, 13, 17).

The history of the title sequence dates back to 1897, when Thomas Edison inserted cards with the title, company name, and copyright information before the start of his films to indicate ownership. Over the next 50 years, title sequences expanded to include more content such as the cast and the scriptwriter (Stanitzek 12). In the 1950s, the design and production of title sequences evolved as companies began to produce them. Title sequences created in the 1950s and 1960s were characterized by "a single metaphor into which the film seems to be concentrated in its title sequence" (ibid. 16), and are related stylistically to contemporary poster art (ibid.). Title sequences of the 1980s and 1990s began to reduce the credits, and it is becoming more common to name only the title, lead actors, and key creative personnel such as director, producer, and screenwriter, and to move all other credits to the end titles (Hediger 112).

Given the diverse range of title sequences, numerous attempts have been made to create a typology. This has not always proven to be easy since title sequences contain mixtures of different elements, both graphic and live-action, which make it difficult to assign them to distinct categories. The following typology is based on Deborah Allison's categorization, but also takes into account André Gardies' observations about the embedding of writing in the title sequence. Unlike the film, the title sequence always has to contend with writing, which is both a characteristic and obligatory part of it (Gardies 23), and which is always meant to be emphasized (especially if there is next to no film material, and the title sequence consists almost solely of writing).

1. Title Sequences that have No Direct Connection to the Diegetic Space

The first category described by Allison includes title sequences that show no connection, or only a potential connection, to the diegetic space ("Innovative" 93-5). Here she works on the assumption that the credits are written on objects that are not always presented as part of the diegesis. André Gardies' classification of writing in title sequences seems to be relevant here, and especially his remark that the writing can also be superimposed on an abstract background (24). This renders the title sequence even more separate from the film and serves the sole purpose, according to Stanitzek, of naming the people responsible for the film and drawing attention to production processes, for economic and legal reasons (12). One example of a title sequence completely separate from the film is *The Terminator* (James Cameron 1984).

2. Title Sequences with a Connection to the Diegetic Space

Allison's second category includes films that "inscribe their titles into the diegetic space by positioning the text as part of the scenery in which the action occurs, occasionally proceeding without even a cut at the end of the title sequence" ("Novelty" ¶ 20). A good example is the title sequence of *The Birdcage* (Mike Nichols 1996). The film opens with an aerial shot moving across the Atlantic Ocean towards the Birdcage drag club located on the coast of South Beach, Florida. In a long single-take shot, the mobile camera enters the establishment, slowly drawing viewers into the narrative and the diegesis. As observed by Allison, the title sequence merges into the body of the film without any visible boundary (ibid.).

3. Interaction between Credits/Titles and Actors or Crew Members

In her third category, Allison describes title sequences that are created by the actors of the film, or in which the protagonists of the film play a part independently. One prominent example is *The Pink Panther* (Blake Edwards 1964): here, "The Pink Panther" manifests in the form of a pink panther that happily hops and skips its way through the title sequence. The sequence is animated, in the tradition of most title sequences of the 1950s and 1960s, and shows the panther moving between the letters and playing with them. The letters also respond to him: for example, when he wolf-whistles at the credits for Claudia Cardinale, the 'E' turns into a hand that slaps him. This title sequence is an early reference to gender theory discourses; the sequence hints that Cardinale is emancipated and can defend herself against shameless "flirtation".

FEMININITY IN TITLE SEQUENCES

Since the 1960s, title sequences have presented femininity and female bodies in an erotically charged and appetizing manner. When examining gendered verbal communication, Julia T. Wood notes that "language reflects cultural values and is a powerful influence on our perceptions [...] our language continues to devalue females and femininity by trivializing, deprecating, and diminishing women and anything associated with femininity" (123). Women are often labelled as immature or juvenile (e.g. baby, girlie), equated with food (e.g. sugar, sweet thing), discussed as animals (e.g. chick, bitch), and called derogatory terms (e.g. slut, whore). And so, the representation of women as appetizers—small dishes of food served before the main course of a meal in order to stimulate one's appetite—through non-verbal means has the same effect of deprecating femininity. The seduction taking place on screen is often achieved through disguising, defamiliarizing, and, importantly, fragmenting the female body. Title sequences rely on the principle that "sex sells," which requires the overt sexualization and exploitation of the female body and a clear ascription of gender as defined by Simone de Beauvoir (295) and Judith Butler (25). In these schematic representations, feminine contours of the body are emphasized to an extreme degree. As noted by Jean Baudrillard "eroticisation always consists in the erectility of a fragment of the barred body" (102), a statement that draws attention to the essence of a fetish. In the title sequence for *Last Woman on Earth* (Roger Corman 1960), for example, the camera pans across a photo in a close up shot and fragments the body of the subject. This body becomes a puzzle that viewers have to put together themselves. At the same time, this title sequence eroticizes the individual fragments of her body and presents the woman in a de-individualized manner.

The title sequence for Michelangelo Antonioni's 1966 film *Blow-Up* also presents the eroticization of female body fragments. Cut-out letters of the credits reside in the foreground while female body parts appear in the background and offer the viewer mere glimpses of the dancing body; the viewer senses the body rather than really seeing it. This is exactly what makes the title sequence appealing—it stimulates the viewer's interest in the film much like an appetizer does for a meal. While the dancing woman plays a critical role in helping to draw the viewer into the film and diegesis, she remains anonymous and is not granted an identity in the film.

In comparison, the title sequence in *Barbarella* (Roger Vadim 1968) not only presents femininity but also celebrates it in the form of a strip-tease performed by a space woman while the whole body can be seen. As noted by Alain Bernardin, the woman is "dancing in the void. Because the more slowly a woman dies, the more erotic it is. So I believe that this would reach its apex with a woman in a state of weightlessness" (qtd. in Baudrillard 107). Jean Baudrillard expands on this point when he writes:

> The whole erotic secret (and labour) of the strip lies in this evocation and revocation of the other, through gestures so slow as to be poetic, as is slow motion film of explosions or falls, because something in this, before being completed, has *time to pass you by*, which, if such a thing exists, constitutes the perfection of desire. (108)

This kind of representation of femininity—as lascivious, physical, and erotic—is designed to attract the gaze of the male viewer and peak his interest in seeing the rest of the film. The female body thus becomes part of a commodity of aesthetics that foregrounds consumption, and turns sex into a consumer product.

This overt sexualisation of women has long been a concern of feminists. Virginia Woolf was one of the first to note that "[w]omen have served all these centuries as looking-glasses possessing the magical and delicious power of reflecting the figure of man at twice its natural size" (43). Simone de Beauvoir further contents that women are what men turn them into (qtd. in Schößler 54). This is exactly what is taking place in the title sequences: directors and/or title designers are turning women into objects that are used to hook viewers and draw them into the diegesis. In the James Bond films, which rose to worldwide popularity in the 1960s, women are similarly featured in the title sequences as appetizers whose sole function is to attract and hold the attention of the assumed male spectator.

JAMES BOND TITLE SEQUENCES

The Bond title sequences rely on the de-individualization, objectification, and overt sexualization of women. The female body is deployed as a defamiliarized or veiled enticement in order to stimulate the desire for femininity and female sexuality, and to prefigure the action to come. The mobilization of women as objects of seduction was established within the first four Bond films.

Although the title sequence for *Dr. No* (Terence Young 1962) is atypical for the series, it provides some insights into the initial conceptualization of gender. The title sequence is composed of three parts. First, it opens with a series of animated dots and squares that flash across the screen; the credits are positioned between these shapes. Second, these dots are replaced by the silhouettes of one man and two women dancing, their images superimposed on top of one another; this image is then doubled so that there are two images of the same man and two images of each woman. Finally, the title sequence ends with the silhouette of three (blind) men walking across the screen and this leads directly into the film. The middle section is of particular importance as it prefigures the interplay between Bond (the one man dancing) and his girls (the two women who arguably represent Sylvia Trench and Honey Ryder) in the film. Interestingly, the male body moves more actively and dynamically than the female bodies and this arguably reflects the physical dominance of Bond as the hero of the film and by comparison the relative passivity of the women who are saved by him.

The title sequence in *From Russia with Love* (Terence Young 1963) offers a different representation of a dancing woman. Although no longer animated, the woman is still presented in shadow and her body functions as a de-individualized object on which the credits are literally projected. The woman is further dehumanized through her representation in fragments. Similar to the title sequence in *Last Woman on Earth*, the audience is provided with close up and medium shots of body parts but never the full image of the woman. This creates a desire in the viewer to see the whole image, which may happen if they continue watching the film.

The title sequence of *Goldfinger* (Guy Hamilton 1964) expands on the technique of projection by casting images of the main characters (Bond, Auric Goldfinger, Pussy Galore) onto the body of a motionless woman painted in gold. The gold body is a direct reference to Jill Masterson, a companion of Goldfinger who is seduced by Bond and killed by Goldfinger via epidermal suffocation. The motionlessness of the gold woman featured in the title sequence prefigures the moment when Masterson shifts from an active to permanently immobile object. At the same time, the gold color stylizes the body into a luxurious object that one can possess or collect. The title sequence both foreshadows and commemorates the violence that is to come through the symbolic and aesthetic rendering of the golden female body. And it is this element—a female body marked symbolically and aesthetically by violence—that draws viewers into the diegesis.

The title sequence for *Thunderball* (Terence Young 1965) shows a further variation through the representation of the female body in black (and non-animated) silhouette. Here, the viewer is faced with the aestheticization of women in silhouette who show no individual features. Instead of dancing, women are swimming underwater and being hunted by men with harpoons. The title sequence prefigures the plot: not only does Bond participate in a spectacular underwater fight scene but he also meets his Bond Girl, Domino Derval, underwater. Although their bodies are fully presented (rather than in fragments), these women still lack coherent identities by being envisaged in shadow. The feminine frame is being used to tantalize the audience into watching the film with the promise that these or other women will subsequently appear on screen (and in color) for their viewing pleasure. More importantly, the sequence foregrounds the impression that the women featured in the sequence as well as the forthcoming film are not self-determined but rather are the trappings of men, and especially Bond and his male adversary.

The Bond title sequences therefore envisage women in two key ways. First, they present women as two-dimensional figures. They might be depicted as black or white silhouettes positioned in front of a monochromatic and varicolored background (as seen in *Thunderball*) or as colored silhouettes in front of a monochromic and typically dark background (as shown in *Dr. No*). Second, they present women as three-dimensional objects. They might appear in fragments (as seen in *From Russia with Love*) or be recognizable as individuals (as in *A View to a Kill* [John Glen 1985]). Bond title sequences in the 1970s, 1980s, and 1990s continue to present the female body in eroticized and sexualized ways. This is most striking in *A View to a Kill* when the woman unzips her jacket and the numbers "007" appear in neon red between her breasts. This sexualization is further intensified by presenting various women holding pistols while dancing slowly in front of the camera. While the gun is certainly one of Bond's trademarks, symbolizing the life and death that he can inflict, it becomes sexually charged (Greiner 174) when placed in the hands of semi-naked women.

Subsequent title sequences go even further by presenting the gun as part of the woman, thus transforming her into a dangerous factor that must be eliminated. A good example of this appears in *GoldenEye* (Martin Campbell 1995). The title sequence no longer shows the penetration of a female body by a phallic gun, but the emergence of the gun from the female body. On a visual level, the woman has appropriated the gun, a phallic object, and is thus presented as a hermaphroditic, Janus-like creature beginning to resist male attempts at sexualization. This image signals a shift in female representation in the franchise during the 1990s in which women claim phallic power and pose a new threat to Bond.

In the 1990s, female representation in the Bond film is strongly informed by post-feminism. As noted by Lisa Funnell, these "new" women are threatening to Bond because they use his sexuality against him: "By retaining his old-fashioned notions of masculinity and conquest, Bond becomes a target for 'empowered' 1990s women, who systematically use their bodies to seduce him, render him vulnerable, and then attack him" ("Negotiating" 208). Even though these women demonstrate an awareness of their sexual power, they are still brought under patriarchal control by the end of the film. As noted by Funnell, "Bond's old-fashioned masculinity is presented as once again triumphing over dangerous women with liberal sexual identities" (ibid.). These dynamics (i.e. superficial empowerment and inevitable subordination) are reflected in the title sequences for the films. Although women are presented in three dimensions and in color, and are clearly recognizable as individuals, they are still being escorted, hunted, and subsequently oppressed by men in the title sequences. The work of Pierre Bourdieu offers insights into the gender dynamics in these sequences. He writes:

> If the sexual relation appears as a social relation of domination, this is because it is constructed through the fundamental principle of division between the active male and the passive female and because this principle creates, organizes, expresses and directs desire—male desire as the desire for possession, eroticized domination, and female desire as the desire for masculine domination, as eroticized subordination or even, in the limiting case, as the eroticized recognition of domination. (21)

It is this relationship that is revealed in the title sequences: Bond appears as an individual, actively directing the sexualized woman at his side through the sequence.

Although the women in the title sequences are given more material definition, they are still pushed into a passive role. Women remain objects of sexualization in the title sequences. As noted by Laura Mulvey, "people [can be taken] as objects [by] subjecting them to a controlling and curious gaze [...] Hence the look, pleasurable in form, can be threatening in content, and it is woman as representation/image that crystallises this paradox" ("Visual" 835-7). *GoldenEye* visualizes this paradox in its title sequence through the image of a woman with a gun emerging from her mouth. The sequence relays the impression that men/Bond need to contain, control, and repress this 'new' and dangerous woman. Mulvey explains that in psychoanalytic terms, the female figure

> connotes something that the look continually circles around but disavows: her lack of a penis, implying a threat of castration and hence unpleasure. Ultimately, the meaning of woman is sexual difference, the absence of the penis as visually ascertainable, the material evidence on which is based the castration complex essential for the organization of entrance to the symbolic order and the law of the father. (840)

In *GoldenEye*, women claim a different gender role—they possess the weapon/the phallic symbol—and become a risk to the "law of the father". They no longer function as symbols of sexual difference and threaten the position of Bond/men as potential voyeurs. The only way for Bond, who functions as a screen surrogate for the male viewer, to maintain his narrative/social privilege is to (re)assert control over the women in the film.

NEW DIRECTIONS

The Bond title sequences can be allocated to the first category of Allison's typology: they contain elements from the films, but are not usually part of the diegetic space. The purpose of their film-related elements is to prepare viewers for the coming action, and to draw them into the diegesis. An exception is the title sequence to *Die Another Day* (Lee Tamahori 2002), which can be located in Allison's second category. Here, the imprisonment of Bond, which takes place at the end of the opening action sequence, is continued into the title sequence, which centers on his torture. Moreover, the title sequence ends with Bond's release, which begins the narrative of the film. In spite of this continuity, the title sequence still features the silhouettes of dancing women—in this case animated with ice and fire—superimposed onto shots of Bond being tortured.

Bond title sequences are thus designed to attract the attention of the viewer through the overt display of female sexuality. As a result, these anonymous women have evolved into a kind of trademark for the franchise, allowing the viewer to explicitly identify the Bond title sequence as such. Although there are different variations of the title sequence, what they share in common is their reduction of women to their physical frames and emphasis on erotic movements. These women are objectified rather than being individualized, positioned in the title sequences as schematic objects, and used for projection in two key ways:

1. The male viewer can look at the women without inhibition, take pleasure in their aestheticized physicality, and project his fantasies onto their bodies.

2. The title designers use the women as a surface onto which the credits are projected; this also gives them the status of an object, or more specifically a screen, inviting close examination.

The treatment of women in the title sequences foreshadows the way in which women are degraded as objects of desire in the film; they exist for the sexual gratification of men and specifically Bond, who serves as a screen surrogate for the presumed male viewer. Even when women are positioned as his adversaries, like in *GoldenEye*, Bond always seems to react accordingly and is the source of their downfall. The title sequences have responded to the ways in which women have changed in the films, and have adapted their depiction of female bodies accordingly. In the title sequences, women are conceptualized and presented as appetizers that not only guide the viewer into the diegesis, but also prepare them for the action to come.

The title sequence in *Casino Royale* (Martin Campbell 2006), the first Bond film starring Daniel Craig, is an outlier to this tradition. It is an animated sequence that features multiple male silhouettes—black representing Bond, and red and yellow for his opponents—fighting with one another and being struck down by card suits that function as weapons (Funnell, "I Know" 463). Female silhouettes are strikingly absent from this sequence; only a single image of Eva Green who plays Vesper Lynd appears on one card. The title sequence prefigures a key aspect of the film, a poker game that is presented as "an allegorical battlefield" in which Bond defeats an array of opponents; Craig is positioned as a new Bond who is able to "defeat [his] enemies through exercisable physical control" in a new atmosphere of muscular masculinity (ibid.).

As a prequel, *Casino Royale* revisions various elements of the Bond film franchise including the title sequences. Interestingly, this change was only temporary and in the following film, *Quantum of Solace* (Marc Foster 2008), the title sequence reverts back to tradition by showcasing female body parts in a desert and dancing women in a terrestrial globe reduced to latitudes and longitudes. Women are reintroduced as objects, devoid of autonomy, serving as surfaces for the projection of the male gaze, and contributing to the characterization of Bond, whose control over women—both in the title sequence and the film—casts him as a lady-killer (romantically and otherwise).

Skyfall (Sam Mendes 2012), in comparison, offers a new variation. Before the title sequence starts, Bond is shot by a female agent and falls into the river below. While descending into the water, the title sequence begins with Bond being pulled down by a hand (which I presume is female). The majority of the sequence takes place along the bed of the river; it combines various elements from the forthcoming film with images of sexualized and lascivious dancing women. What strikes me as most interesting is the fact that Bond is positioned at the center of the title sequence. Craig is clearly recognizable here as Bond. The sequence features multiple images of Bond—identical pictures, shadows on walls, reflections in mirrors—that foreshadow the identity crisis that Bond experiences through the film. Moreover, each element is destroyed—the pictures are burning, the shadows disappear, and the mirrors are split into pieces— suggesting that Bond will likely sort things out by the end of the film.

In *Skyfall*, Bond is presented as the subject of the title sequence, which foreshadows the narrative that is to come. The women, in comparison, remain anonymous and are not integrated into the storyline. They are still presented as trivial and sexualized objects, but in this sequence they are not being escorted, hunted, or marginalized. While one might be tempted to read this as an indicator of female empowerment or progress in the Bond film, it might signal the very opposite. *Skyfall* arguably develops the legacy of Bond—who works to overcome mental, physical, and emotional trials—at the expense of women in the film; Bond is not presented with a competent female ally or a formidable female opponent. Thus, the limited role of women in the title sequence arguably reflects their reduced role in *Skyfall* and could signal a new trend in female representation in forthcoming films.

NOTES

1 My translation.
2 My translation.
3 Emphasis in original.

CHAPTER 15

RANDOM ACCESS MYSTERIES

James Bond and the Matter of the Unknown Woman

Eileen Rositzka

The first scene of the first Bond film, *Dr. No* (Terence Young 1962), opens with a forma-
tive introduction: "I admire your courage, Miss...?" – "Trench. Sylvia Trench. I admire
your luck, Mr...?" – "Bond. James Bond". 007 has just won a game of baccarat and
learns the name of his next sexual conquest. But this is not another case of "boy meets
girl." It is this brief situation that sets the framework for the Bond formula: rather
than generating new stories, the film series constitutes a game world in which the
characters merely act and react, and in which courage and luck are elementary. Seen
in this way, all the components within that game function as instruments that Bond
uses in order to win. We can therefore assume that Bond's encounters with women are
as inevitable as they are constitutive. But these encounters are always ephemeral, with
women of a certain type, and individually rather meaningless. Although women are
woven into the narrative, there is never enough time to fully develop their characters
and, as a result, there is no time for Bond to get to know them either. He seems to
pick his girls at random, or, one could argue, that they are randomly picked for him
as much as the game system allows for coincidence. These factors contribute to the
impression that Bond's women are mysterious sphinxes, which cannot be fathomed
on every level. This is the case for the main "Bond Girls" and minor female characters
in the series—be they good or evil. In fact, these minor characters, which I will refer
to as "Secondary Girls", encompass and problematize the basic traits of Bond Girls
and Bond Girl Villains without being one or the other. Instead, they build on the
mythical quality of the female body rooted in the opening credits of the films. This
chapter will explore this argument by bringing into focus the narrative structures and
aesthetic strategies of the Bond films, shifting the emphasis from Bond to the women
surrounding him and inspiring him into action.

SECONDARY GIRLS

As many scholars have noted, the Bond films are structured around their plot and
repertoire of characters. For instance, John Cawelti's concept of "formula" has

been used to define the seriality of Bond films in a cultural context (Moniot 25, 33). According to Cawelti, formula "represents the way in which a culture has embodied both mythical archetypes and its own preoccupations in narrative form" (387). In the franchise, Bond does not merely follow in the footsteps of traditional heroes, but rather serves as a mythical archetype himself, representing the phantasmagoric male imago of the 1960s in a transnational shape. Primarily being a servant of the British Empire, Bond's cultural contexts and geopolitical interests involve both Britain and America. The character, originally depicted in Ian Fleming's novels, has been remodeled in order to present a more "mid-Atlantic" image suitable for the American film market. Due to the influence of producer Albert R. Broccoli, Bond was envisioned "to appeal to American filmgoers as a man of action without putting them off with jarring British mannerisms" (Black 113). His character arguably corresponds with what Charles A. Reich describes as the "new man" of the technological age: "He is an artificially streamlined man, from whom irrationality, unpredictability, and complexity have been removed as far as possible" (161). Bond as an "artificially streamlined man" is a highly technical figure, surrounded by commercial goods and values being consumed within the framework of tourism. This is what constitutes his game plan and renders him a "man of action" in the world in which he operates. The superficial exoticism of the Bond films can be seen as a mechanism to provide them with a certain mythic metalanguage. It connects 007 to a world that is both accessible and enigmatic, where he is just as secret as he is an agent.

Bond's various mythic journeys circulate around key settings, situations, and figures that have to be "unlocked" in order for him to progress. All of these factors revolve around the films' female characters and their positioning in the narratives, the pattern of which originates in Fleming's novels. In his summary of Umberto Eco's patterning of the typical Bond narrative scheme, Toby Miller writes:

> M assigns a task to Bond; the villain or his agents appear to Bond; the villain and Bond do battle; the woman appears to Bond, who seduces her; the villain captures Bond and sometimes the woman, then tortures his captives; Bond kills the villain and/or his perversely proportioned assistant; and Bond escapes to temporary happiness with the woman, who is then taken from him. (130)

As foundational texts, the Bond novels provide a narrative pattern that has been played out in the Bond films. It is the villain who serves as the male counterweight to Bond's agency. The woman, however, functions as a seductive device to overbalance this constellation—working for one side or the other, but never motivated by her personal ambition. As a result, the woman functions as a "tipping point" that helps to ensure the success of Bond's mission (Black 109).

The film *Octopussy* (John Glen 1983) provides one of the best examples of the functionality of the Secondary Girl. At a hotel casino in India, Bond makes the acquaintance of Magda, a mysterious blonde woman he had noticed at an auction. As he speaks to her, she replies, "You have a very good memory for faces", with Bond responding, "And figures." Bond peaks Magda's interest when he reveals that he is in possession of the Fabergé egg she thought she had acquired at the auction. Although she initially declines his offer for a drink, she later meets him in his hotel room where their materialistic game is transformed into a love story. John Barry's romantic score sets the scene: the camera pans from clothing scattered across the floor to the bed where Bond and Magda have just made love. As she leans over, an octopus tattoo on her lower back becomes visible. When asked about it, she replies, "That's my little octopussy." Not only is this statement an allusion to Magda's sexual attractiveness, but the word "octopussy" is also a reference to the film's title and Bond Girl. An enigmatic figure, Octopussy commands a squadron of Amazonian beauties living and training on an island, where men are excluded. Magda belongs to this mysterious cult of women withdrawing from patriarchal society. Bond's intimate encounter with her is thereby labeled as an exquisite achievement. Moreover, it relays the impression that sleeping with Magda will bring Bond one step closer to meeting and bedding her female leader. Thus, it is Octopussy, symbolically marking Magda as one of her subordinates, who represents Bond's sexual goal.

As exemplified by Magda, Bond's Secondary Girls are "unknown women" whose potential, once revealed, is turned into effectiveness again. They have to stay unknown to be means of attraction and keep the story going. Their myth is not only constituted on mystery and fascination, but draws on reproducibility, randomness, and a systematic affirmation of anonymity. In this regard the apparent demystification, that is, the undressing and instrumentalization, of the Secondary Girl is part of her "remystification"—it pushes her back into randomness, so that the game can start over again—in another Bond movie, with other women.

MOVING IN MYSTERIOUS WAYS: THE FEMALE BODY IN THE BOND OPENING TITLES

While the positioning of the Secondary Girl serves a narrative function, it also helps to structure the visual aesthetics of each film. The image of the mysterious but reproducible woman is set up and reinforced by the title sequences. The female body serves as a projection site for erotic fantasies, ideas of power, and danger. Maurice Binder's opening titles set the precedent for the depiction of Bond's unknown women. His first title sequence in *From Russia with Love* (Terence Young 1963) projects credits onto the body of a belly dancer. The movement of dimly lit arms, legs, and veils makes the neon letters dance with/on them. A fragmented body, divided into several close-ups, moves within the frame. In terms of ancient legends, this depiction is reminiscent of Salome's dance of the seven veils. But in regards to the cinematic apparatus itself, Mary Ann Doane argues that the veil "acts as a trope that allows one to evade the superficial, to complicate the surface by disallowing its self-sufficiency. But what the veil in the cinema makes appear to be profound is, in fact, a surface" (*Femmes* 55). Consequently, the dancer's face is revealed once early in the sequence, but is then concealed in shadow and later three neon numbers, "007", are superimposed onto it. In the following film, *Goldfinger* (Guy Hamilton 1964), the title sequence not only shows production-related text merging with the female body, but also displays a woman painted in gold, with actual scenes from the film projected onto her body. This image is a reference to Secondary Girl Jill Masterson who is found dead on a hotel bed, suffocated by gold paint.

It is my argument that the title sequences both anticipate and illustrate the treatment of Secondary Girls within the Bond narrative. These female silhouettes are just as anonymous as the Secondary Girls featured in the films, and similarly reduced to their physical appearance. This exploitative strategy reflects a symbiotic relationship: the female body is the foundation on which the narrative and imagery of the Bond films is structured. It is the underlining framework for the secret agent's actions. As such, the unknown woman is consequently framed in terms of visual aesthetics.

The title sequences link the female body with objects of power, violence, and nature. The living body is reduced to a surface onto which different textures are projected. In the title sequence for *Thunderball* (Terence Young 1965) plain black silhouettes of naked women are set against an underwater background, while in *Diamonds Are Forever* (Guy Hamilton 1971), a woman's body is decorated with jewelry, and even becomes a diamond textured silhouette. In other films, female figures are linked to gun barrels, as in *Licence to Kill* (John Glen 1989), or even oil drills in *The World is Not Enough* (Michael Apted 1999). In some cases, their faces might be shown, but this only underscores their lack of relevance in the film; these women never appear in the movie and are merely positioned as models of idealized beauty.

The motif of the shadow-figure is highly significant for the Bond title sequences. It represents a thoroughly stylized body that is a product of and driving force for these visual dynamics. While the female body is presented as an object of desire, it is also reduced to a surface with a somewhat mechanical quality. The most elaborate example can be found in *Tomorrow Never Dies* (Roger Spottiswoode 1997). The title sequence starts with a shattering screen and an inward movement through a digital matrix with bits and bytes, and twitching electric impulses. Then tiny female bodies emerge while floating next to each other like small organisms observed through a microscope. Radiographic images of a watch, bullets, and guns contrast with smoothly winding figures of women. In this collage, all objects are somehow connected to female figures and these bodies become deadly weapons, gaining control over time and violence. Following this, the image dissolves to a computer chip, with a female face emerging from within. Shortly after, a full body rises from the bottom of the screen, being partially radiographed again. This time, the X-ray fragments superimposing the technological physical structure are presented as deceptions. They conceal the woman's true mechanical nature. Technology is treated as a manipulative threat to human existence, which is a familiar topic of the Bond narrative. In *Tomorrow Never Dies*, this threat becomes more subversive, infiltrating civil society, and maneuvering the fallible minds of everyday people. As a product of the 1990s, the film is critiquing the political power of media. The seductive woman can therefore be seen as a metaphor for the media's persuasiveness.

Tomorrow Never Dies only accentuates what has always been constitutive for the Bond formula: the notion of the woman as an automaton. Of course, thinking about female characters as self-operating machines falls short in terms of their representation. Nevertheless, it is precisely the juxtaposition of natural beauty and mechanical superficiality that lies at the heart of the title sequences and is affirmed throughout the plot. This equation of girls with guns and gadgets, I would argue, seems consistent with Christine Buci-Glucksmann's idea of "the feminine as allegory of the modern" (qtd. in Doane, *Femmes* 1). As a consequence of urbanity and industrialization, the woman comes to over-represent the body to which the male loses access (ibid. 1).

E.T.A. Hoffmann's short story *The Sandman* (1816) offers a good illustration of this idea. The protagonist, Nathanael, falls in love with Olimpia, his professor's daughter. From an objective point of view, she is nothing but beautiful, only reacting to Nathanael's expressions of love. But ignoring his friend's advice to let go of her, he becomes deeply obsessed with the girl, only to find that she is a mechanical doll. The story emphasizes Nathanael's constant oscillation between desire and fear, and his passion results in rejection when Olimpia is destroyed. It is this ambivalence of desire and deception that Laura Mulvey defines as the crucial ambiguity of cinema.[1] Examining the work of Alfred Hitchcock, she notes the recurrence of a blond woman who serves as a metaphor for the male obsession of looking at and fetishizing women. Seen in this way, the woman is an enigma, which the man tries to investigate and deconstruct. The fascination with artificial femininity illustrates the beauty of cinema itself, which enhances the sense of surface regarding the female body. As Mulvey highlights, the rear projections frequently used by Hitchcock double the effect of exaggerated flatness.

Applied to Bond title sequences, this interpretation sheds some light on the representation of women. The female silhouette can serve both as a projection site and a projected fantasy itself—the enigmatic quality assigned to the body can explain why these women are often associated with mythical characters/creatures and connected to the element of water. Whether hunted by harpoons in *Thunderball* or appearing ghostly underwater while the camera sinks to the ground in *Skyfall* (Sam Mendes

2012), these sequences conjure up images of the nymphs in Greek or Latin mytho-logy—beautiful maidens filling nature with life. A nymph is also regarded as a siren who lures a man—to his death. As such, the "sirens" featured in the title sequence (and by extension the secondary female characters in the film) can be considered threats to Bond if he allows himself to be drawn into their beauty and away from his mission. This is most evident in *For Your Eyes Only* (John Glen 1981), whereby singer Sheena Easton is featured in the sequence singing the title track, and her image is framed by women in silhouette dancing in an underwater setting. It is this impression of the woman as a mysterious being, encompassing fear and desire, life and death, power and disempowerment, which is taken to another level in the narrative characteriza-tion of both Bond Girls and Secondary Women.

YOU KNOW HER NAME: WOMEN OF (NO) MYSTERY

In each film, Bond interacts with a variety of women. While some of them are named, others are not, which puts them into a position of being anonymous objects of desire. If they are in fact introduced, their names are often sexually connoted, since the combi-nation of first name and surname creates a double entendre. This naming convention can be traced back to Fleming's source novels. Toby Miller notes that in *Dr. No* (1958), the name of Honeychile Rider helps to define and position her character in the narra-tive: "Her name symbolizes sexual lubrication and exchange [...] She is open-hearted and positive [...] she emerges from the sea like an innocent aqua-goddess" (131). Indeed, this combination of qualities is a continuous thread throughout the Bond films. On the one hand, the Bond Girl is unreachable and enigmatic (a goddess, in that way), and on the other hand, she is alluring and inviting—an objectification that determines Bond's first encounter with Honey Ryder in the film. As she emerges from the sea, she meets Bond and asks him if he is looking for shells. He responds with, "No, I'm just looking." While the phrase "just looking" might imply that Bond is gazing at Ryder without a specific purpose in mind (much like a shopper browses casually), it also relays the impression that his looking is "just" or legitimate. He thereby claims the visual right, his "license to look," from the outset. In order to possess the Bond Girl and solve her mystery, Bond first needs to look at her. In many instances, it then becomes imperative for him to know her full name in order to determine who he is dealing with and if he can work (with) her. In fact, 007's insistent curiosity regarding the names of Bond Girls is very peculiar in the Bond films starring Sean Connery such as *Dr. No* ("What's your name?" "Ryder." "Rider what?" "Honey Ryder.") and *Goldfinger* ("Who are you?" "My name is Pussy Galore." "I must be dreaming..."). The suggestive names at first create the impression that these Bond Girls might be all too easy pushovers. But they are, by contrast, intended to pose sexual challenges for Bond. It is Honey Ryder whose first name "promises sexual lubrication" whereas her surname points to the fact that she is likely to take a superior position in this exchange. The name Pussy Galore almost guarantees erotic overabundance, but she is presented as a sexual challenge due to her presumably lesbian orientation.

While this is the naming convention for Bond Girls, it should be noted that, in contrast, Secondary Women play to their names (if they are even named at all). Once Bond gets to know their names, mostly bearing a double entendre, he immediately pegs these women as sexual toys by confirming the verbal ambiguity of their names and, at the same time, negating it. This is most evident in his introductions to Plenty O'Toole (*Diamonds are Forever*), Jenny Flex (*A View to a Kill* [John Glen 1985]), and Strawberry Fields *(Quantum of Solace* [Marc Forster 2008]). In each instance, Bond replies: "But of course you are". Although all three women are of different narrative importance, they seem to be self-fulfilling prophesies as a tool, a flex (to the villain), and a field to explore, respectively. Other names like Dink and Countess Lisl von Schlaf (the German word for "sleep") are just as ironic, and the corresponding women perfectly fulfill their promise without posing a challenge. With these Secondary Girls, what Bond sees is what he gets, and so does the spectator. What is confirmed is the basic expectation set up from the beginning of each Bond film—the image of the female body as an ever replaceable and reducible object of desire.

Occasionally, a few minor characters do not meet this expectation, such as Bambi and Thumper who are unwilling to surrender to Bond's charm in *Diamonds Are Forever*. Bond eventually drowns Bambi and Thumper in a swimming pool and literally pushes them back into their mythical place of origin. This scene can be read as the rejection of the sirens, which is conducted by humiliating them as a punishment for their resistance. The fact that most of Bond's Secondary Girls affirm the cliché of "being easy" (to get) distinguishes them from the Bond Girls. Both minor and major female characters share the potential of being reduced to the apparent promiscuity suggested by their names. The difference between Bond Girls and Secondary Girls is that it takes Bond much longer—if not the entire film— to seduce/control the Bond Girl. In this sense, both female types have to be named in order to be distinguishable in terms of their resistance to 007. Thus, the Bond Girl offers a greater challenge to Bond and is presented with a higher degree of personal autonomy, which is required for this resistance.

This mode of female characterization allows for some surprising variations. For example, in *Goldfinger*, the symbolic function of the female naming scheme is taken to an extreme. With Pussy Galore being "too much of a woman" for Bond to handle, Dink literally lies at the opposite end of the resistance scale. While Jill Masterson is killed by Goldfinger for her liaison with Bond, her sister Tilly is disinterested in Bond and committed to avenging Jill's death. It is therefore important for Bond (and by extension the audience) to know the name of Tilly in order to understand her role as a mirror figure to Jill: While Jill has to pay, Tilly initiates "payback"—the root word of her name, "till," references a cash drawer found in stores and banks in which payments are collected and stored. Seen in this way, every woman in a Bond film is designed to fulfill a certain purpose within the narrative. Her positioning in the narrative as a major (e.g. Bond Girl) or minor (e.g. Secondary Girl) character depends on her ability to increase narrative tension—that is, the tension between Bond and herself.

The Bond Girl Villain complicates the discussion of major and minor female characters in the franchise. In each Bond film, various women are presented in a hierarchy according to their narrative importance, and the Bond Girl Villain usually resides between the Bond Girl and Secondary Girl(s) on this scale. A consideration of the Bond Girl Villain provides some important insights into the Secondary Girl as the two character types share some common traits. The Bond Girl Villain is also seductive and has a double entendre for a name—e.g. Fiona Volpe (*Thunderball*), May Day (*A View to a Kill*), and Xenia Onatopp (*GoldenEye* [Martin Campbell 1995]). However, she is strictly opposed to 007 and becomes threatening both because of her physical skillfulness and loyalty to the villain. Therefore, when encountering Bond, her cold-blooded intention makes her not a key for him to "unlock," but rather an obstacle to overcome. As Tony Garland puts it, the Bond Girl Villain "was established in continuity with and deviation from a cultural understanding of the cinematic depiction of dangerous women" (181), which primarily points to the classic (*film noir*) *femme fatale*. The *femme fatale* can be regarded as the prototype of the cinematic woman of mystery, hiding "something which must be aggressively revealed, unmasked, discovered" (Doane, *Femmes* 1). Her sexuality becomes the site of both epistemophilia and scopophilia, while she "inevitably comes to recognize that her radical insistence on independence is a delusion" (Bronfen 106). Such tragic sensibility is not established in depth for the Bond Girl Villain. Depending on the arch villain, she is reduced to her aggressive and violent sexuality, or to her condemnable dirty work, for which she usually has to pay with her life. Since the fate of the Bond Girl Villain is sealed from the very beginning, it is in fact the Secondary Girl that is the tragic figure in the Bond films. Whether she is a pawn sent out by 007's opponent to turn him over, or an ally to help him, her sympathy with Bond results in her punishment. The real tragedy lies in the very fact that the Secondary Girl is discarded and erased from the film. Because her presence does not exceed a limited purpose, there is no need for her to be further developed within the narrative. Despite her potential to become either a Bond Girl or Bond Girl Villain, her narrative "upgrade" is denied in the end.

CYCLE OF MYSTIQUE

A consideration of the Secondary Girl, especially in tandem with the Bond Girl and Bond Girl Villain, draws attention to the importance of mystique to female characterization in the Bond franchise. For example, in *Live and Let Die* (Guy Hamilton

1973), the Bond Girl oscillates between the narrative treatment of Secondary Girls and the self-consciousness of a typical female lead in trying to break the circle of being a pawn. As her name already points out, Solitaire is an isolated figure, devoted to the power of Tarot cards, and a psychic who can maintain her visionary skills only by preserving her virginity. Working for the villainous Dr. Kananga, she also functions as the key for Bond to foil his opponent's plans. Since Solitaire believes that her fate can be predicted by her Tarot cards, she is deceived by Bond who manipulates her deck: the card entitled "The Lovers" suggests that it is her destiny to sleep with him. In losing her virginity she also loses her psychic abilities and this is the moment when Kananga loses control over her. Through this rouse, Bond "demystifies" Solitaire by stripping her of her powers (and virginity) and tipping the scales in his favor. Once the new couple escapes San Monique, Solitaire is pushed back into anonymity, having lost her mystique, and becomes a disposable character like other women in a Bond film. As soon as her individual mystic aura vanishes, no individual personality is revealed. More likely, her submission to the rules of the game makes her even more anonymous—enigmatic, again, but in terms of being reconstructed to a "perfected surface."

This typical ending of a (love relationship in a) Bond film makes way for a new beginning—another opening sequence featuring anonymous women in silhouette, a familiar jumping-off point from which the narrative can start and repeat itself over again. In the end, even the Bond Girl is subjected to what the Secondary Girl realizes right away—that her role in Bond's life is temporary and her position in the narrative is exchangeable. Once the (female) enigma is solved, she is rendered unremarkable and new enigmas are produced to take her place. Every now and then a mystery is revealed, but randomly, and superficially, only to reinforce the drive of the game.

NOTE

1   Here I draw on Laura Mulvey's talk "Hitchcock's Blondes and Feminist Film Theory" (2013).

CHAPTER 16

PUSSY GALORE
Women and Music in *Goldfinger*

Catherine Haworth

Music is a core component of any James Bond film. In addition to providing a vital tool for synergic marketing and cross-promotion, the soundtrack highlights and extends the various strands of the Bond narrative "formula"—those elements of plot and packaging that remain pleasurably familiar throughout the series, but also offer enough scope for variation to keep new films feeling fresh. Music not only forms a core part of the Bond "brand," but is also used within the narrative to articulate and exaggerate the series' exotic locations, romance, suspense, and action, and the traits of both new and recurring characters (Mera 7-8; Smith, "Unheard" 100-2). These strong links between the sound of the series and its characterization, style, and story mean that music is also implicated in the Bond films' problematic identity politics (Haworth 117-9). Bond stories tend to employ difference as a reductive tool for characterization; a tendency to which the sexually, ethnically, racially, and/or ability-coded deviance of villains, and the feminine charms of the passive, disposable "Bond Girl" bear frequent witness.

My focus here is on the interplay of music with the representation of women in *Goldfinger* (Guy Hamilton 1964), the first film in which the combined elements of the Bond formula appear in their definitive form. As well as the girls, guns, and gadgets we expect from the typical Bond storyline, the film also includes the first fully-realized example of the series' title sequences, where the credits appear after Maurice Binder's gun barrel sequence and an action-heavy teaser segment, and are accompanied by spectacular visuals and a tailor-made title song sung by a well-known and suitably glamorous artist. *Goldfinger*'s title sequence is significant: its musical and visual motifs spill over into the film's narrative proper and have the potential to create spaces within which female desire and agency might be articulated. The extent to which these musically-marked spaces disrupt the prevailing order becomes clear when considering the overall scoring of the franchise: a sound representative of, and belonging to, Bond himself.

THE MEN WITH THE MIDAS TOUCH: SCORING BOND

Bond soundtracks typically sit at the intersection of two cinematic traditions, combining the extensive orchestral scoring established during the studio era with original popular music that keeps pace with changing tastes. Behind this signature sound was British composer John Barry, who assisted Monty Norman in scoring *Dr. No* (Terence Young 1962) and went on to provide incidental music and title songs for a further 11 Bond films. Barry's Bond scores combine jazz-inflected big band brass and sweeping, romantic string lines with classic song writing skills that continue to provide a template for contemporary musicians working on the series.

The Bond sound is dominated by music that centers on the title character. Jeff Smith describes Barry's musical Bond formula as comprising of four discrete (though musically linked) and flexible elements: the famous "James Bond Theme" (henceforth "Theme"); "007," a march often heard during action sequences; a title song that also provides the basis for cues within the orchestral score; and a recurring motif associated with Bond's primary adversary (101-2). Barry's musical universe is designed primarily to reinforce Bond's own supremacy. Cues most commonly act as a means of highlighting Bond's presence, his positioning within exotic locations or tense situations, or his own perspective on events or characters, which work to align the experiences of the audience with the hero. This includes aspects of the soundtrack associated with female characters, which, regardless of their thematic basis, most commonly align themselves with Bond's view of women as potential conquests or adversaries. An obvious example can be found in *On Her Majesty's Secret Service* (Peter Hunt 1969), where Bond is disguised as the chaste, bookish Sir Hilary Bray, but a florid and seductive saxophone cue reveals his underlying interest in a bevy of Blofeld's beautiful "Angels of Death." Music like this is typically part of the film's—or Bond's—discourse about these women, and therefore acts to curtail, rather than create, female agency.

Within this overarching musical formula, the "Theme" acts as both a stylistic anchor and a basis for musical development. Its tightly constructed set of memorable "hooks" provide the stimulus behind many other motifs, as well as material that features explicitly in several title songs. It is also a highly effective and quickly established aural signifier of the Bond persona—an "ownership" of musical material that is immediately established in Bond's first scene in *Dr. No*, where his "Bond. James Bond." introduction is synchronized with the "Theme's" appearance on the soundtrack. The "Theme's" particular combination of catchy musical features and contextual associations mean it can function both as a distinctive, flexible marketing tool, and as an easily referenced element within the narrative fabric and standardized "packaging" of the Bond film: it represents the sound of Bond himself, and is a crucial tool in promoting his particular brand of masculinity.

Goldfinger is no exception to this franchise-wide use of the "Theme," or indeed to a reading of Barry's scores that emphasizes their primary correlation with the eyes and ears of Bond. The film's pre-credits sequence is typical in this regard. Bond swims ashore in an unnamed coastal location, destroys a heroin processing plant, canoodles with a double-crossing dancer, and fights off the thug who ambushes him in her dressing room. As Bond leaves, the slam of the door ushers in the start of *Goldfinger*'s title sequence. Music is used to emphasize Bond's position at the heart of this compressed dramatic arc. The sequence is dominated by material from the "Theme," appearing in a variety of guises to accompany and create tension (its chromatic bass line cycles throughout suspenseful sections), mimic action (brass stabs play during fights, the pace increases as Bond starts to run), reinforce location (an "exotic" guitar variation plays inside the bar), and underline humor (high, sustained strings highlight the reveal of Bond's under-wetsuit dinner jacket). Bond's experience is stressed throughout this sequence, reassuring the viewer that the film offers more of the same hero who featured in *Dr. No* and *From Russia with Love* (Terence Young 1963). It would therefore seem to set the scene for a title sequence that continues this brand reinforcement—but while *Goldfinger*'s titles do conform partially with this model of masculinized Bond-centricity, they also start to disturb it, setting up a complex series of interrelated audiovisual signifiers that have far-reaching implications.

"BEWARE OF THIS HEART OF GOLD": FEMALE VOCALITY IN THE TITLE SEQUENCE

Robert Brownjohn's celebrated title sequence for *Goldfinger* projects scenes from *Dr. No, From Russia with Love,* and *Goldfinger* across the human canvas of a bikini-clad, gold-painted woman. Like many Bond titles, *Goldfinger* reinforces the idea of women as conquerable and fetishized signifiers of difference, giving its golden girl anonymity via her painted body and expressionless face that turns her into a literal trophy. However, this analysis of the titles is heavily biased towards the visual, ignoring not only the music and lyrics of "Goldfinger," but also the powerful, distinctive sound of the woman who gives voice to them—an audio-visual reading of the sequence that mirrors elements within its creation, where Barry and Brownjohn viewed each other's partially-completed work during production (Fiegal 136-7).

The foregrounding of music and sound within a reading of *Goldfinger*'s titles undermines a straightforward understanding of the sequence as reductively misogynist: it draws out significant similarities between the film's construction of both Bond and the villain; it has the potential to give voice to the silent, passive woman of the visual track; and it introduces the star persona of Shirley Bassey. Whenever "Goldfinger" material is heard in Barry's orchestral score it articulates a complex series of connections between Bond and Auric Goldfinger, and also conjures the specter of the woman who sings about them. This overtly polysemic aspect of Barry's "Goldfinger" theme is relatively atypical of classical film scoring models, as Smith notes (115-7). Explaining this lack of musical integration and "unity," via a discussion of the blockbuster structures of Bond films and their position as part of a self-referential franchise, Smith also draws attention to the ways in which these overlap in the signification and "ownership" of material from the title song that complicate the film's approach to characterization and identity.

The first of these "complications"—the similarities between Bond and his primary adversary—is one that applies to many of the films, and a majority of Fleming's source novels. A tense, suspenseful Bond story requires a villain (almost always male) who is a convincing match to the hero's own prowess, and the narrative becomes a battle for supremacy waged not only along the axis of "good" and "evil," but also along the lines of sex, violence, intelligence, class, money, and power. Both Bond and Goldfinger are dangerous, persuasive, greedy, and egocentric. Bond's Queen-and-country motivation is therefore key in distinguishing his violent masculinity from that of Goldfinger; a pragmatic justification of attitude and behavior that is further reinforced through the construction of the protagonist's (hetero)sexuality.

Both Bond and Goldfinger "consume" women in a way that serves to highlight their characterization as strong, powerful, and selfish men. But while Bond's voracious sexual appetite is used (not unproblematically) to valorize his masculinity as a virile and irresistibly attractive "ladies man," Goldfinger's attitude towards women is seen as a perverse extension of his warped personality, thematizing his gold-lust and desire for wealth. Thus he "likes to be seen with" the beautiful Jill Masterson but has no sexual interest in her, until he avenges her dalliance with Bond by painting her with gold, skin-suffocating paint and displaying her corpse as both a trophy and warning. Fleming's novel is even clearer about Goldfinger's deviant consumption of women, as Jill's sister Tilly describes to Bond: "He has a woman once a month [...] He hypnotizes them... he paints them gold [...] Jill told me he's mad about gold. I suppose he sort of thinks he's—that he's sort of possessing gold. You know—marrying it" (230).[1]

Goldfinger's title sequence takes its inspiration from the striking image of Jill's golden corpse, reinforcing the idea of a woman being a submissive and spectacular trophy. In opening with projections of Goldfinger and then Bond's face over the girl's body, it also reinforces the connections between these two men, and especially their relationships with women. It thereby highlights Bond's own attitude towards the seduction of women as often aggressive, emotionally detached, and with little thought for anyone but himself; a point of comparison between Bond and Goldfinger also highlighted in Anthony Newley and Leslie Bricusse's lyrics, which warn any "golden girl" to beware the "cold" heart and "web of sin" of the "man with the Midas touch."

In addition to these visual and lyrical comparisons, "Goldfinger" also heavily references music associated specifically with Bond, both in the construction of its melodic motifs and through direct quotations from the "Theme." Its opening four-note chromatic bass line loop acts as "Goldfinger's" section bridge and plays throughout the lengthy and dramatic outro, where high trumpets also quote the melody from the big band-style swing break section of the "Theme"—Bond's music is also at least partially Goldfinger's, and vice versa. This provides *Goldfinger*'s score with an element of structural unity and "Bond-ness," and means that the title song can be used flexibly in scenes featuring Bond and/or Goldfinger to highlight their positioning as closely matched adversaries. But complicating matters here is the sound and implied presence of the vocalist: not just a physically absent singer who balances out the mute figure of the visual track, but a strong, identifiable woman who gives voice to Newley and Bricusse's words of warning.

The aural presence of this singing body both intensifies and challenges the visual and lyrical elements of the "Goldfinger" sequence. The singing voice represents a physicality and self-produced "excess" that transcends the tightly policed (if spectacular) visual boundaries in place, where the woman's body is rendered mute and static by her gold paint, fragmented by the tight camerawork, and overlaid with Brownjohn's projections. As demonstrated by the film musical, song has affective potential, powerful emotional resonance, and strong links with the persona of the onscreen singer (Laing 7). "Goldfinger" implicates no single character as the source of its lyrics, therefore this emotional resonance is instead transferred to the film's women more broadly. This intensifies the meaning of the words, casting the storyteller-vocalist in the additional roles of victim and survivor (of Goldfinger and, by implication, Bond). Although she sings of suffering and of the power of men, the vocalist retains the agency of the survivor: she is a woman who desires to tell *her* story and vocalize *her* experience, which suggests a possibility of reading the imagery of the sequence against the grain.

However, it is also possible to argue that the female voice of "Goldfinger" becomes just another vehicle for misogynist fetishization. Scholars like Kaja Silverman have argued that commercial cinema has a tendency to confine significant, authorial episodes of female vocality to closely defined and guarded "textual space" (56-7) where its effects can be easily exploited but also contained; a maxim that would seem to apply in a textbook-fashion to the closed-off audio-visual spectacle of a Bond title sequence. But the containment of vocality is only partially present here, given the way in which *Goldfinger*'s titles are used to introduce the primary themes (in both a general and specifically musical sense) throughout the film's narrative proper: the "Goldfinger" sequence *is* the narrative and characterization of much of the film itself, and the echoes of its female voice reverberate throughout. While the woman's warning cannot prevent the deaths of Jill or Tilly Masterson—which of course, are pre-ordained by the demands of the Bond narrative for sacrificial victims, additional motivation for the hero, and multiple conquests—it does lend those deaths additional poignancy and resonance, with "Goldfinger" acting not just to articulate the presence of the men who cause them, but also the female subjectivity of their victims.

Further intensifying the signification and disruptive potential of the female voice in "Goldfinger" is the performance of Shirley Bassey, the vocalist most closely associated with the franchise. "Goldfinger" was the first of several Bond songs recorded by Bassey, who also provided vocals for "Diamonds are Forever," "Moonraker," and a version of "Mr. Kiss Kiss Bang Bang" (originally intended as the theme for *Thunderball* [Terence Young 1965]). As became common practice, Bassey brought a distinctive star presence to the Bond soundtrack that provided additional marketing potential, as well as fitting Barry's own musical vision: "Shirley was great casting for 'Goldfinger.' Nobody could have sung it like her. She had that great dramatic sense" (Barry qtd. in Fiegal 136). Bassey's exacting enunciation and clipped consonants, carefully controlled but ever-present and expressive vibrato, and dramatic performance style ensures her voice is instantly recognizable, challenging the gold-painted anonymity of her visual counterpart in *Goldfinger*'s titles. Her thoroughly-trained voice and technically precise singing is emotionally communicative and highly personal, but is also atypical of the broad stylistic conventions of lighter "pop" recording, bringing a sense of the operatic, or at least the theatrical, into much of her work. This not only makes her an appropriate choice for the full orchestral sound and dramatic musical styling of "Goldfinger" (Fiegal 143), but also enables her to fit vocally as well as socially into the cultural space occupied by the prima donna, and more particularly into the exaggeratedly dramatic and fiery stereotype of the diva (Cowgill and Poriss xxxiv-xxxv).

As Ros Jennings notes, Bassey's life and career have followed a well-trodden path to divahood (37-8). Celebrated now as a powerfully voiced, occasionally tempestuous, and always fabulously glamorous establishment figure, Bassey's emergence into 1950s British cultural life was a rags to riches story that pitted burgeoning talent and tenacity against the hardships of life as a mixed-race teenage mother from Cardiff's docklands. She was a regular feature in the UK charts and gossip columns by the early 1960s, and her Bond performances bring into play the diva's complex, feminized (and sexualized) mix of despair, tragedy, celebration, and survival (Koestenbaum 133). Bassey's star persona therefore extends and reinforces the complex series of gendered relationships already present in the title sequence, her celebrated difference and resistant divahood making her powerful vocal contribution to "Goldfinger" one that resists any conventional understanding of the boundaries between soundtrack and story (an overlapping of texts and identities that can also be seen in Bassey's adoption of elements of the "Bond Girl" archetype within her own star image).

Bassey adds more than a "voice" to "Goldfinger's" anonymous golden girl; she brings her own identifiable stardom to bear on the sequence and thereby adds weight and emphasis to the title song's tale of female experience, solidarity, and warning. This striking female voice undermines any reading of *Goldfinger* as a score purely about Bond, or even Bond and Goldfinger. *Goldfinger* also offers numerous moments of resistance to the all-encompassing dominance of the hero and villain; moments where textual spaces for female agency are opened up and exploited by the soundtrack.

"YOU'RE A WOMAN OF MANY PARTS, PUSSY": MUSIC AND FEMALE CHARACTERIZATION

The rest of *Goldfinger*'s soundtrack also conforms to and challenges the expectations of a typical Bond film. Three women occupy significant roles in the plot: Jill Masterson (Goldfinger's secretary, and the gold-painted victim discussed above), her sister, Tilly (killed by Oddjob whilst trying to avenge Jill's death), and Pussy Galore (a talented pilot, who plays a key role in Operation Grand Slam—first in Goldfinger's employ, and then as a double agent who switches loyalties to Bond). "Goldfinger's" frame of reference encompasses both the male leads and the three primary women of the story, and aside from a motif specifically associated with Oddjob and some geographically-flavored linking pieces, almost every cue in the score is built around material from the title song (whether used alone, or in conjunction with elements from the "Theme" and "007").

"Goldfinger's" use as a love theme, or at least a signifier of some kind of sexual desire, is therefore highly appropriate, if not always unproblematic. In lush string or jazz-inflected lounge-style arrangements, this music accompanies Bond's early dalliance with an enthusiastic Jill Masterson; his quickening pulse as her sister, Tilly, drives past in her convertible; and his eventual romantic clinches with Pussy Galore. These instances, which can be considered representative of many other moments of "Goldfinger"-accompanied romance or desire, demonstrate the varying ways in which Bond retains the agency of soundtrack ownership in his interaction with women.

Although Jill Masterson's engaging confidence and obvious attraction to Bond allows her to share ownership of the sultry "Goldfinger" material that accompanies their canoodling, Bond's musical dominance is asserted in the snippet of the "Theme" that accompanies his trademark introduction. The aftermath of the scene makes clear the devastating punishment for Jill's transgressively guiltless and positive sexuality, as Bond's discovery of her corpse is accompanied by the metallic dissonance of Oddjob's motif. Jill's attempt to step outside her role as objectified possession is, predictably, doomed to failure; instead, all that occurs here is effectively a temporary transfer of ownership, underlined by the soundtrack, which bookends her joint ownership of music with the themes of her male aggressors.

Tilly Masterson is distinguished from her sister through a notable absence of thematic material on the soundtrack in the majority of her scenes with Bond. This absence of music only occurs after Bond meets Tilly face to face: prior to this we see his interest piqued as she zips past him in her convertible, with the "Theme" section of a jazzed-up "Goldfinger" instrumental used to highlight Bond's sudden excitement.

But Tilly's clipped manner and lack of interest in Bond (Fleming's novel is clear about Tilly's homosexuality) forbids any further musical support or expansion of their relationship, and even Bond's trademark introduction line is left unscored. Although there is some dramatic underscoring in scenes featuring Tilly, especially those leading up to her death, there is no hint of anything more personal and certainly nothing that can be identified as either "Goldfinger" or "Theme"-based romance. This might seem a minor point—after all, Tilly is a secondary character—but it demonstrates her refusal to conform to stereotype and act as a mirror for Bond's own narcissism. Bond's masculinity is symbolized musically by his control of the soundtrack and the presence of "his" music, and that masculinity is at least partially dependent on the validation provided by female approval; therefore, Tilly's disinterested musical silence presents a significant challenge to Bond's agency.

Tilly, like Jill, steps outside the boundaries of acceptable female behavior and is punished for it. Whilst Jill's "Goldfinger"-accompanied celebratory sexuality is tamed through death and the (re)imposition of music that is not "hers," Tilly's disinterest in Bond is signified through silence—a withholding of musical accompaniment that, while providing little in the way of "support" to her character, also articulates the challenge that her closeted lesbianism presents to Bond's self-assured masculinity.

While Pussy Galore is the most significant of *Goldfinger*'s women, she does not appear until well into the film, and initially mirrors Tilly's lack of interest in Bond and the corresponding absence of "Goldfinger" on the soundtrack. In Galore's case, however, this contextually subversive relationship between sexuality and music is brutally "corrected." Galore's prominence and power within the narrative is much greater than that of Tilly Masterson: she is witty and charismatic rather than withdrawn and surly; a powerful and favored employee of Goldfinger instead of a lone wolf intent on revenge; and she enjoys exerting control over Bond as her prisoner, reversing his prior attempts to restrain Masterson. Bond tries to flirt his way out of trouble, but Galore archly informs him she is "immune" to his charms—the first of several relatively obvious references to her homosexuality, and an element of assured and open identity proclamation that is a significant factor in Galore's pleasurable agency (Ladenson 193).

This unusual degree of self-sufficiency is cemented in the sequence that introduces the glamorous female pilots of Galore's "Flying Circus" returning from a successful rehearsal of Operation Grand Slam. The camera cuts alternately between shots of the pilots, a back view of Galore watching them run towards her, and a close up reaction shot of Galore's face. Florid, jazz-style scoring accompanies these shots, articulating an almost comic musical stereotype of the attractive woman that not only highlights the appealing nature of the pilots, but also clearly signals Galore's sexual appreciation of them. This short but unusual scene grants Galore control of the soundtrack and demonstrates its importance in the articulation of desire—something more commonly associated with Bond. Galore's agency, together with the sexual rejection of Bond symbolized aurally by the absence of "Goldfinger," therefore poses a serious threat that results in her moral, sexual, and musical repositioning as Bond's love interest.

Pussy Galore's sonic and sexual independence is brutally removed inside one of Goldfinger's barns, where, after a wrestling match that results in a literal roll in the hay, she capitulates to Bond's (forceful) advances. Despite the best efforts of the soundtrack to remain light-hearted in the first half of this sequence, mirroring Bond and Galore's scrimmage with wind and string flourishes, music can do little to obfuscate the clarity of Galore's repeated refusals to let Bond kiss her. But, as her strength gives out, she is shown to relax and seemingly to enjoy Bond's embrace: perhaps not unexpectedly, "Goldfinger" strings enter languorously at this point, and music becomes complicit in positioning this sequence as one of willing, rather than forced, submission.

This scene marks a turning point in the narrative, where Bond is once more "on top." Once again secure in his virility and attractiveness, Bond's relationship with Galore provides his salvation: Bond has "won" Goldfinger's previously unattainable woman, and his possession of her also thwarts Operation Grand Slam. Bond's return to sexual agency is marked musically by a reinvigoration of the romantic signification of "Goldfinger" on the film's soundtrack, both over the end of the barn scene and during the film's closing shots of Bond and Galore embracing. "Goldfinger" signifies not only Bond's presence and power, but also breaks Galore's silence where Bond is concerned, replacing it with the mixture of female desire and fear that the song articulates—a combination that rings especially true given the problematic nature of the barn sequence. Galore is at once the objectified, silenced possession of Brownjohn's visuals, and the enigmatic, individualized survivor of Bassey's vocals.

It is this multi-layered engagement of "Goldfinger" with the film's women that is facilitated by the film's title sequence. Music is not always subordinate to Bond's high degree of control, and while these moments are sometimes fleeting, and often subtle (especially given their bells-and-whistles action film context), the fact that they are there at all is striking in a franchise that has often been criticized for its two-dimensional, formulaic portrayal of female characters. In particular, they allow Tilly Masterson and Pussy Galore moments of resistance to Bond's dominating worldview, allowing them effectively to queer the hero's pitch through their rejection of his masculinity as desirable or necessary. Their latent lesbianism is symbolized through control of the (sometimes absent) soundtrack, as well as through more frequently-noted coded references within dialogue, costuming, and plot.

"I THINK YOU'VE MADE YOUR POINT, GOLDFINGER. THANK YOU FOR THE DEMONSTRATION."

While exploiting the connections between "Goldfinger" and the "Theme" to create a Bond-saturated soundscape where the hero triumphs eventually, *Goldfinger*'s soundtrack is also used to tie the film's female characters together through their shared experience of the cruelty and opportunities afforded by both male leads. Barry's score also individualizes these women: Jill Masterson's confidently willing compliance is highlighted musically; the stony silence of Tilly Masterson and Pussy Galore demonstrates their "immunity" to Bond's charms; and Galore's unusual degree of narrative agency—and her "deviant" sexuality—is symbolized in her aural appreciation of the Flying Circus pilots. This flexibility is set up in the title sequence, where lyrics, music, voice, and visuals act together to both reinforce and destabilize the dominance of the Bond persona.

Bond songs provide additional revenue streams, crossover marketing potential, and are an important and iconic structural device. But they also have the potential to affect audience engagement with the narrative. "Goldfinger" goes beyond its obvious dual references to Bond and the villain to facilitate moments of resistance to the image of the static, silenced woman of the opening titles who returns, along with Bassey's "Goldfinger," as the brief end credits roll. Bassey provides a powerful voice borne of experience, articulating the warnings that Jill and Tilly Masterson might formulate were they still alive, and reminding us of Galore's former agency. Although the golden trophy woman might be *Goldfinger*'s most enduring image, her appearance also evokes the musical message of warning, solidarity, and survival that accompanies it: none of the film's principal female characters survive with both their life *and* their identity intact, but their musical presence (and that of the supposedly vanquished Goldfinger) echoes almost as loudly as Bond's. Music reinforces and extends both the pleasurable and the problematic within the Bond formula, and the series' often unpalatable politics of identity and representation are no exception to this. But within *Goldfinger*—often cited as the archetypal Bond film, and therefore raising the possibility that these patterns can be found more widely across the franchise—the soundtrack also provides opportunities to subvert these politics and put women's desires and agency center-stage. The presence of these moments, which co-exist in an uneasy, but correspondingly flexible relationship with music about and for the hero, acts as a powerful reminder that there is potential for resistance for both characters and audiences, even to Bond's all-encompassing lure.

NOTE

1   Reference to the Vintage publication of the book.

CHAPTER 17

FEMALE VOICE AND THE BOND FILMS

Anna G. Piotrowska

The soundtrack for James Bond films is one of the most characteristic features of the series. The key components of the Bond musical formula include the famous James Bond theme, often called a signature motif reserved for the male protagonist; the so-called 007 theme, based on marching rhythms; a motif for the opponent, usually a male villain; and a title song (Smith, *Sounds* 104). All of these elements relate to certain male characters and the musical template does not include space for a motif characterizing the Bond Girl. And yet, the title songs featured in the opening credits most often feature female voices. While the list of female performers is long—from Shirley Bassey to Adele—male voices are heard less frequently. Considering the importance of the title song as an imminent part of the Bond (musical) formula, the preference given to female performers seems striking. Hence, it is not only the persona of the female singer that requires consideration, but also the specific quality introduced in these title songs, which I will call the "feminine quality." Even the majority of male performers of Bond songs possess either a delicate timbre of voice (e.g. Paul McCartney) or a high vocal range (e.g. Morten Harket from A-ha known for his falsetto), qualities traditionally associated with female performers. I would argue that the "feminine quality" introduced in the title songs can be interpreted as aural compensation for the insufficient portrayal of women on screen, as well as a musical counterpoint for the male main themes.

The composition of a signature theme in film is a way of acknowledging the existence of a hero. Musical themes are specific pointers that fulfill an important referential function within the musical score (London 87) and highlight the narrative importance of certain characters. If, as noted by Drew Moniot, "the purely technical aspects of the Bond films such as the cinematography, editing, musical scoring, etc., were executed with an air of true professionalism" (26), this opens up an important line of inquiry: why is there no musical theme for the Bond Girl? Is the Bond Girl represented differently in the sphere of music? And is it appropriate to perceive the title songs in direct relation with the Bond Girls?

LEITMOTIFS AND SONGS

MALE MUSICAL REPRESENTATION: LEITMOTIFS

Cinema has been adjusting the relationship between dialogue, music, and sound effects since the start of the sound era (Altman et al. 351). The audio layer corresponds with visuals by closely illustrating what is happening on screen, or the opposite, by remaining indifferent towards the portrayed images and actions, providing a sonic counterpoint. Most scholars agree that it was John Barry, the composer who scored 11 Bond films between 1963 and 1987, who established the formula in which music closely follows the action. This technique, known as "Mickey Mousing," is considered a kind of musical mimicry (Paulin 69). The Bond film themes connected with the main protagonist betray the traits associated with his personality. Active, decisive, and focused, Bond is presented as a man on an important and time-sensitive mission. His ubiquitous signature theme by Norman Monty centers on the sharp, energetic sound of rock style guitar riff. Various arrangements of the theme appear in the Bond films, performed by a full orchestra in *Thunderball* (Terence Young 1965) and a Moog synthesizer in *On Her Majesty's Secret Service* (Peter Hunt 1969). The theme might appear fragmented or rescored, often departing from its original jazzy version as introduced in *Dr. No* (Terence Young 1962). Just like Bond serves as a mobile signifier denoting various values at different moments (Bennett and Woollacott, *Bond* 42), so too does his musical theme. However its prevailing trait, the agitated quality that inspires feelings of suspense and anticipation, is sustained. The Bond theme not only underlines the character of the hero, but also enhances the atmosphere of certain scenes, for instance when stylized as a funeral march in *You Only Live Twice* (Lewis Gilbert 1967). Although Bond films resist a firm location in time (Citron 321), the arrangements of the Bond theme may sometimes help viewers to relate to a specific period, such as in *The Spy who Loved Me* (Lewis Gilbert 1977), where it is presented in a disco version.

The Bond persona is also characterized by another motif—the 007 theme composed by Barry for *From Russia with Love* (Terence Young 1963)—which can be described as his "adventure" motif. As Mark Richards explains, it is the "buoyant and active sound of the theme that provides the action with some levity" (18). Due to the upbeat syncopated rhythms and staccato performance and the choice of major keys, this theme introduces a breath of freshness into the score. The primacy of Bond in the narrative is emphasized by having two themes for his character. Music is also a fundamental component of Bond's representation and his themes are expected in his films, despite the fact they may be transformed in some way.

Various male villains are provided with their own musical motifs, although many are in close melodic relation to Bond's. For example Goldfinger is ascribed a theme that "has the basic shape of the Bond theme's [...] central motive, the famous four-note trumpet blast" (Smith, *Sounds* 123). Not only does this theme privilege the villain in the narrative and signal his influence even in scenes where he does not appear, but it also undergoes the process of "masculinization" by its direct relation to Bond's theme. Through music, Goldfinger is presented as a significant obstacle that Bond needs to overcome.

FEMALE MUSICAL REPRESENTATION: SONGS

While literature on "Bond music" has yet to identify a musical theme for the Bond Girl, I would argue that the music associated with the figure is located not in the score but in the Bond songs. Although scholars have discussed these title tracks in relation to film marketing and their partial incorporation into musical scores (see Smith 1998, Burlingame 2012, Richards 2013), I would like to draw attention to the performative aspect of these songs. It seems striking that title songs have been predominantly recorded by women, or, alternatively, by men with lyrical and nostalgic qualities. These traits constitute a specific "feminine quality" in Bond music whose appearance I see connected with two factors: the first is allied with the role of women in the development of pop music and the second refers to the intertextual function of the Bond song within the series.

Although many theorists discuss classical scores in the context of their "inaudibility" (Gorbman 31), it has been noted that musical unobtrusiveness seems overestimated (Smith, "Unheard" 232). Film music can exercise power "as a subjective, non-discursive, non-representational discourse" due to its "ability to appeal to the emotions, and through them, to memory" (Everett 100). Bond songs may refer viewers to meanders of pop music history and the position of female performers in that realm. Although women were actively involved in pop music in the 1960s, the following decade was when dominant patriarchal ideals were questioned and feminist activism revaluated the pop music scene (Walser 369). While Helen Reddy composed the 1972 hit "I am Woman," which became the anthem of second-wave feminism, Bonnie Raitt demonstrated that women could be both talented singers *and* skillful instrumentalists. Women no longer had to choose between being feminine and powerful in popular music (Walser 369). In the 1980s, the MTV era saw a rise in the popularity of artists like Madonna, Cyndi Lauper, and Tina Turner, which continues on today. However, the increasing visibility of women in the industry often stemmed from compromises they had to make in regards to their image, which was defined in terms of their sexuality and patriarchal relations.

But already in 1964 Shirley Bassey sparked interest in female vocalists for Bond songs when she was asked to sing the title track for *Goldfinger* (Guy Hamilton 1964). Her performance led to her recording subsequent songs for *Diamonds Are Forever*

(Guy Hamilton 1971) and *Moonraker* (Lewis Gilbert 1979), and opened the door for other female vocalists on title tracks. Female vocalists were hired to recreate Bassey's achievement by invoking the memory of her (Britton 96). For example, Carly Simon's style of singing on "Nobody Does It Better" for *The Spy Who Loved Me* emulates "the Shirley Bassey standard" (McDermot 109). There were also attempts aimed at recreating the musical material associated with Bassey's success. In the song "Licence to Kill" performed by Gladys Knight, whole phrases are directly borrowed from *Goldfinger*'s score.

This predilection for female singers has become an important element of the Bond formula. The choice of vocal performer, especially as the Bond films gained popularity, became widely publicized (Britton 92). Much like the casting of the Bond Girl, the inclusion of a singer on title tracks became another female-oriented mechanism mobilized by the Bond franchise to market its films. She became the Bond Girl in popular music and her image became a primary factor in her selection as a vocalist. For instance, Nancy Sinatra was asked to perform "You Only Live Twice" despite her weak vocal dispositions; producers believed that her image would resonate well with younger audiences and attract them to the film (ibid. 88).

In recent years, the role of women performing title songs has expanded. They are not only hired as vocalists but also serve as co-writers of the title tracks: Sheryl Crow for "Tomorrow Never Dies" (1997), Madonna for "Die Another Day" (2002), Alicia Keys for "Another Way To Die" (2008), and Adele for "Skyfall" (2012). Moreover, Adele won an Oscar (2013) and a Grammy (2014) for her composition of and vocal performance on the song. Notably, all of these songwriters grew up watching Bond films and were familiar with their formula (McDermot 111). Hence their success as songwriters and performers may be connected to their understanding of the nuances affecting the position of women in the Bond films.

HER VOICE ...

... IN THE CULTURAL CONTEXT

The connection between female voice and sexuality dates back to ancient times. In Homer's work, *The Odyssey*, sirens seduced men more with their singing than they did with their looks; these dangerous creatures were known for leading sailors to shipwreck by luring them with their enchanting voices. This connection between female voice and sexuality persists into the modern era. In the nineteenth century, well educated women were expected to sing in the privacy of their homes and perform for visitors. Popular parlor songs conveyed a message in their lyrics by praising female fidelity and helped to reinforce the subjugated social status of women in the patriarchal world (Cook, *Music* 133).

The image of the singing woman is reinforced by the introduction of Bond Girl Honey Ryder in *Dr. No* as a sexual object of the male gaze (Hines 169). She is presented as emerging from the sea while singing "Underneath the Mango Tree" composed by Monty Norman. The lyrics confirm Ryder's sexual availability by positioning her as a prospective bride dreaming of getting married, making "boolooloop" and having children. Interestingly, the song was performed by Norman's then wife, Betty Diana Coupland, rather than Ursula Andress. This vocal detachment highlights the fact that the link between female voice and sexuality in *Dr. No* is being artificially constructed; in order to make Ryder more attractive to Bond, her voice is replaced in postproduction by Coupland for the song and, as Lisa Funnell notes, by Monica van der Zyl for the dialogue ("From English" 64).

The perception of the female voice in Bond songs has evolved. This change can be observed in the title track for *Die Another Day* (Lee Tamahori 2002). Although Madonna is a high-profile artist, her voice was altered via Auto-Tune and produced an overall effect comparable to a "discordant techno theme" (McDermot 113). The machine-like quality of Madonna's voice can be interpreted as a deconstruction of the female voice. At the same time, it can also be read as a response to the technological advances of the modern era and an immediate, female answer to the series' fascination with technology. While Bond is portrayed as a technician capable of mastering an array of advanced gadgets, women, according the series, can exercise power by utilizing their bodies *and* their voices.

... AS A COUNTERBALANCE FOR BOND WAGNERIAN SCORES

Heavy instrumentation plays an important role in the late romantic musical idiom (Prendergast 39-40). The hegemonic sound of the full orchestra can provoke parallels with male domination. In one of the most controversial statements in modern musicology, Susan McClary described listening to romantic symphonic music as the "most horrifyingly violent episodes in the history of music" (128). Using metaphoric language, she linked this type of music to the rage accumulated by "a rapist incapable of attaining release," associating the symphonic arrangement with patriarchal culture (ibid. 129). Bond musical scores are based in the romantic idiom, which "heightens film pathos by drawing the audience into personal involvement" (Madden 118). These scores also partially draw from Russian late romantic music. Scholars usually write about the lush orchestration anchored in strings, the jazzy mix of saxophones, and muted trumpets as well as the use of the electric guitar that immediately—by recalling rock music—connects Bond films with a new generation of viewers (Britton 89). The brassy musical layer of the Bond franchise hinges on dramatic melodic lines—either sinister or melancholic—and exploits strong contrasts involving shifts between major and minor keys. The harmony follows the pattern of tension versus relief (the relation of Dominant, often with the diminished seventh, followed by Tonic).

This type of music is not only interpreted as the reflection of patriarchal order but also discussed in relation to the figure of the composer—the great man, as established by the tradition of such masters as Bach and Beethoven, among others. Many view John Barry as a "great composer" and this public perception was important to the producers (Smith, *Sounds* 128) who viewed him much in the same way they did Bond: Barry was both an English gentleman and a modern man, given his membership in a rock and roll band, ownership of a sports car, and his multiple marriages. While Barry was a great composer, he could also be presented as Bond's "twin" in the world of music. While both the music and the composers of Bond scores may be easily associated with the "masculine quality," it is the introduction of the female composers and performers in the songs that offers—to a certain degree—its counterbalance. Once Bond's male counterpart in the musical world is no longer part of the series, women are able to come to fore as composers and writers in their own right.

GENDER BALANCE IN BOND MUSIC?

THE FEMALE PERSPECTIVE IN THE LYRICS

The role of the title song as a commercial tool in helping to advertise films has been widely discussed. However, the producers of Bond series have taken steps to incorporate the title song into the standardized process of production (Smith, *Sounds* 103). The "feminine quality" of these songs—referring to the choice of female performers, preference for feminized voices, and lyrical content—was introduced as an aural compensation for the visual portrayal of women on screen as well as a musical counterpoint for the male themes (e.g. Bond, 007, villain). Thus the female aural presence constitutes one of the axes for the Bond series. Although McDermot states that the title song exists "almost completely outside the [Bond] narrative" (102), I would argue that the lyrics of the song as well as its musical material are always somehow incorporated into the score and the diegesis. Title songs play a crucial role in sustaining the gender balance in Bond films.

In most cases, the lyrics establish the female perspective as a main male character (either Bond or his opponent) is being scrutinized by the female gaze. For example, Mark McDermot describes the song "Goldfinger," as a "paean to the movie's villain" (106). Most songs make reference to male sexual abilities, although these allusions are more camouflaged in earlier films. Recalling the recording session for "Diamonds Are Forever," Bassey notes that Barry suggested that she think of male gems in order to come across as more convincing (Britton 92). In addition, the title song "The Man with a Golden Gun" performed by Lulu is full of sexual innuendos and the golden gun is presented as a phallic object. Such lyrics can be interpreted as a warning of Bond's fatal attraction to women (Madden 124) but also the other way around as the women's fatal attraction to Bond. Moreover, these lyrics draw attention to the female desire for Bond and his multiple admirers. For example, "GoldenEye" is written from the perspective of a woman stalking Bond (McDermot 112). Although the song was actually composed by men—Bono and the Edge from the band U2—it is performed by Tina Turner, an iconic figure of popular music, who authorizes female fantasizing about Bond, as if permitting other women to be mesmerized by him as well. Turner, who has had a long career with a string of hits about sex and love with songs like "What's Love Got to Do With It" and "Private Dancer" legitimizes female attraction to Bond, his adventures, and even his libido.

LISTENING BETWEEN THE LINES

The Bond song—which functions as a substitute for the Bond Girl's theme—plays an intertextual role within the series. Many of these songs are merged, to varying degrees, with musical scores. Hubai suggests that the level of incorporation often depends on whether or not the title song was (co-)written by the composer of the score (138). Usually tunes of songs are tightly integrated into the musical tissue of the film and serve as the basis for instrumental arrangements or a kernel motif for further melodic development. They either counterbalance or (in)directly refer to the melody, harmony, rhythms, etc. of other themes.

While discussing the musical score for *Goldfinger*, most authors suggest that the arrangement of the James Bond theme is influenced by the jazzy title song. Moreover, the song corresponds with the theme by the means of the four-note opening figure. Mark Richards says that

> with *Goldfinger*, Barry established the technique of beginning each song with a distinctive figure or two. [...] this technique [...] had a functional aspect in that Barry generally employed these figures as recurring motives in the film. Notably, his title songs often open with the interval of a fourth or fifth, making them easy to identify when they return. (12)

These motifs—often heard in the title songs during the beginning of films—assure the cohesion of the musical layer. Thus the melodic material of "Goldfinger" is used as a basis for musical sub-themes appearing in the film. It also affects the theme associated with the villain. Although the assimilation of the song into the score of *Goldfinger* has been compared to a "close-knit relationship" (Hubai 131), the score itself has also been critiqued for its lack of musical development and accused of being an assembly of tunes without a clearly developed concept responsible for internal integration (Darby and Du Bois 391-2). It has been discussed in reference to the concept of fragmentation as a collection of "seemingly interchangeable parts" (Smith, *Sounds* 117). In contrast, I would argue that it is the title song that remains the ultimate point of reference since viewers/listeners can easily identify melodic motifs of instrumental arrangements with which they became familiarized during the opening sequence.

The scores for other Bond films also include references to the title track. "Diamonds Are Forever" is the glue that holds together the musical components of the films' soundtrack. The score for *The Man with the Golden Gun* (Guy Hamilton 1974) is monothematic as the title track serves as the basis for the main motif. Moreover, the title tracks for *Octopussy* (John Glen 1983) and *A View to a Kill* (John Glen 1985) are craftily incorporated into the score, usually linked with love scenes. There are, however, Bond films in which the title song is featured only during the opening sequence and does not reappear over the course of the film. While talking about musical linkages between these songs and film scores, Hubai says that they "have absolutely no impact on the score itself" (130). However, even these songs seem essential in establishing the equilibrium between female and male components of films. For example, the title track for *Die Another Day*, although never thoroughly adapted into the main score, is heard in the scene when Bond is tortured in a prison camp in Korea. Not only is the immediate reference to the lyrics established, but more crucially what appears is the question of female power/ability to control—not only her own voice but also men. Strikingly, Madonna appears in the film in the fencing scene, so while her song is not woven into the score, her presence, persona and voice certainly do suggest her controlling position.

TOWARDS CONCLUSION

The Bond formula—"a conventional system for structuring cultural products" (Cawelti 386)—includes more than just sex, gadgets, and violence (Moniot 26). Part of the success of this formula resides in the consistent musical template operating in the framework of certain procedural and stylistic expectations (Smith, *Sounds* 117). They affect both the "inside" as well as the "outside" of the film, stimulated by various commercial needs. In other words, anticipating a new Bond Girl (within the diegesis) is as exciting as awaiting a new Bond song (broadcast even before the release of the film). The very treatment of songs stays in line with the presentation of other components of the Bond formula; much like the famous gun-barrel opening, it is extremely similar across the Bond films even though it is slightly different each time.

The Bond musical formula has, obviously, evolved (Hubai 129) forcing stylistic changes that affect title songs. However, the function of the Bond song has remained consistent. Despite various revisions to musical formula, its relationship with the series' narratives has remained stable with respect to gender representation. While analyzing the gender roles portrayed in Bond films, scholars tend to focus on the narrative and visual elements. They utilize the concept of the "male look" (Hines 173) drawing on the work of Laura Mulvey who describes the "silent image of woman" ("Visual" 838). In this chapter, however, I suggest a slightly different approach to the study of gender representation in Bond films by drawing attention to the aural, and more specifically musical, elements constituting the series formula.

While I agree that the plot and visual depiction of Bond films structure and reproduce gender conventions, I would argue that—at the same time—the fragile balance between men and women is negotiated, in part, by the "feminine quality" hidden in the title songs. As they have become an integral part of countermelody, harmony, and other elements of every Bond score (Smith, *Sounds* 102), their narrative and dramatic role cannot be overlooked for at least two reasons. First, a female perspective is forwarded in the lyrics. Second, female voices—understood here as voices characterized by certain sonic qualities—usually, but not unconditionally, remain in close relation to the performer's sex. Although Bond films were rightly accused of not exactly being "paragons of gender equality" (Amacker and Moore 144), this inequality does not immediately transfer to the musical sphere. Surely, visually the main protagonist "exhibits an identity with hyper-masculine signals that construct male behavior and values as dominant" (Dutz 198), and the title songs are indeed first heard during opening sequences featuring silhouettes of naked women. It could be then assumed that both the female body and female voice are fetishized. However, it seems that Bond films defy the onscreen misogyny: while the stories develop Bond at the expense of his "girls" in the film, these women remain immortalized in the form of disembodied voices and their eternal presence is asserted as voices of consciousness. Their position is revealed by the lyrics in which they display omniscient predispositions and knowledge of Bond. Furthermore, both musical themes connected with the figure of Bond—despite their different arrangements in various films—remain predictable and self-reflective, almost becoming a parody of themselves. In comparison, the title songs—which are associated with women—are versatile and changeable, always offering a new form of excitement while influencing the film score. As a result, the musical representation of the feminine element in the Bond series offers more than meets the eye.

CHAPTER 18

DESIGNING CHARACTER

Costume, Bond Girls, and Negotiating Representation

Andrea J. Severson

In *Dr. No* (Terence Young 1962), the preeminent "Bond Girl," Honey Ryder (Ursula Andress), was first glimpsed by James Bond stepping out of the ocean in a white bikini with a dagger strapped to her thigh. This iconic scene was recreated 40 years later in *Die Another Day* (Lee Tamahori 2002) to introduce Bond Girl Jinx Johnson (Halle Berry). In *Casino Royale* (Martin Campbell 2006), this scene is referenced again, only this time it is Bond (Daniel Craig) who emerges from the ocean in a swimsuit. These three variations of the same scene reflect changes in gender representation in the Bond franchise. Over its 50-year history, the films have shifted from portraying Bond Girls as damsels in distress and sexualized objects to strong and independent women. Moreover, these films present a change in the depiction of Bond from the subject of the gaze (i.e. active gazer) to the object of the gaze (i.e. passive object); in *Casino Royale* he takes over the traditionally exhibitionist role of the Bond Girl.

The relationship between Hollywood costume design and the Bond films, especially in regards to the changing perspective of the Bond Girl, has received little critical attention. This chapter aims to redress this oversight by utilizing costume theory to explore how the rhetoric of the franchise's costume design constructs femininity and power in regards to the Bond Girls. Two films will serve as case studies for this analysis: *Dr. No*, the first Bond film, which marks the beginning of the series, and *Casino Royale*, the prequel, which marks the re-conceptualization of the franchise, and I will explore how costume design provides deeper insights into the ways in which Bond Girls (are fashioned to) operate in their narratives.

COSTUME DESIGN AND FILM

Costume design is an integral part of the production process and costumes say much about the character and their role within the film. Despite the long history of costume design, there are many misunderstandings about the nature of film costuming and its narrative function. As Deborah Nadoolman Landis explains, "Fashion and costume are not synonymous. They have directly opposing and contradictory purposes. Costumes are never clothes. This is a problematic concept [...] a real stumbling block to being able to understand costume design" (7). Jane Gaines similarly notes that feminist scholars frequently mistake costuming for fashion, viewing it in opposition to feminist thought for the way in which it "enslaved" women and put them on display ("Costume" 3). Likewise, the fact that costume design has largely been a female dominated field may have led to an assumption that costume design is "women's work," thus resulting in its marginalization both in the industry and academia. Only recently has the study of costume design become recognized as a legitimate field in film studies.

Costume design is important on several levels. First, it is one of the foundational elements of film production and the designer is a core member of the production team. Second, a greater understanding of costume design helps scholars better understand character development within the narrative. Finally, costume studies help scholars to recognize the connection between character, costume, and audience, and more specifically, the ways in which the audience interacts with both the character and the costume on screen. This has particular implications towards the use of brand name designers and labels in the costumes and the relation between costumes and consumer behaviors.

While there are certainly connections between fashion and costume design, there is a notable difference in the ways in which clothing is conceptualized and deployed. The costume designer employs elements of costume theory into their design for each role, taking into consideration the psychology and motivations of the character, as well as key points in the narrative that may affect the costume design. As noted by Jane Gaines, "costumes are fitted to the characters as a second skin, working in this capacity of the cause of narrative by relaying information to the view about a 'person'" ("Introduction" 181). They provide information about gender, age, socioeconomic status, and motivations. Costumes also serve as external indicators for broader internal changes; as a character develops over the course of the narrative, these changes are often signaled, if not partially embodied, through costuming. The costume designer must also be mindful of the audience viewing the film. According to Sarah Street, "[if] the audience has 'suspended disbelief,' then it is possible that there might be an 'imagined embodiment' in process whereby the audience imagines that the character has exercised a degree of individual agency when deciding what to wear, just as they experience in their own lives" (*Costume* 7). This relationship between designer, costume, and audience is a complex one that requires careful navigation.

Given the popularity of the Bond franchise and its history as a trendsetter (for fashion, watches, cars, and drinks), it is surprising that little academic attention has been directed towards costume design. Most scholarly works focus on the lead hero while the women featured in the films, and especially Bond Girls, have received less critical attention. This chapter explores costume design in relation to the Bond Girl and examines the rhetorical statements designers are making through particular costumes.

DR. NO: THE BEGINNING

Dr. No was released in October of 1962. The film introduces Sean Connery in the iconic role of James Bond, a British secret agent who attempts to solve the murder of a fellow agent. He uncovers and takes down a criminal mastermind, Dr. No. Along the way, Bond meets a number of characters, including several gorgeous women like Sylvia Trench and Miss Taro. However, none compare to Honey Ryder, the Bond Girl of the film, who not only attracts but holds Bond's attention long enough to become his girlfriend by the end of the film.

Tessa Prendergast was commissioned to design the costumes for *Dr. No*. After studying and living in New York, Paris, and Italy, she returned to her native Jamaica to work as a clothing designer in the late 1950s. When the production company for *Dr. No* arrived, the filmmakers approached Prendergast to design the costumes. With an estimated budget of just over $1 million USD, there was little money in the budget for costumes, and this might be one reason why they hired a relatively unknown designer to make them. Prendergast not only designed the costumes for the film, playing a key role in developing the signature look and brand of Bond, but she also created one of the most iconic costumes in cinema history—the ivory bikini, which helped to establish Ryder as the quintessential Bond Girl.

Ryder is introduced midway through the film. Asleep on the beach of a mysterious island, Bond is awakened by Ryder who is singing "Underneath the Mango Tree" as she exits the ocean wearing a small, ivory bikini. The details of the gathered fabric and bow on the upper portion of the bikini give it a feminine appearance while the wide belt and dagger hanging on her hip immediately identify Ryder as a woman who has the ability to defend herself. The designer could have mitigated this effect by presenting her unarmed or having the dagger positioned behind her back where it could be hidden from sight. Instead, the dagger is positioned in close proximity to her hand and she quickly draws it when she is surprised by Bond. The creative team made an intentional decision to give a threatening edge to a feminine bikini.

It might be tempting to argue that this scene exemplifies the male gaze. Laura Mulvey argues that in film, men are presented as active gazers while women are positioned as objects of their gaze. Moreover, she notes that the female body on display functions on two levels: "as erotic object for the characters within the screen story, and as erotic object for the spectator within the auditorium, with a shifting tension between the looks on either side of the screen" ("Visual" 838). At times, the costuming of Ryder seems to deflect the gaze. Unlike previous women in the film, Ryder is not taken in by Bond's flattery and charm. Although some women in the film, like Miss Taro, have malicious intentions and are working for the villain, Ryder is the first to pose an immediate physical threat due to the fact that she is armed. Her apparent strength and confidence render her more than just a sexual object. Yet, there is evidence of Bond's male dominance as he gazes objectively at Ryder despite her attempt to appear threatening while dressed in the revealing costume. While it would seem as though the knife would give someone pause to approach her, Bond's continuing gaze implies that he is attracted to dangerous women and/or that he intuitively knows that she is a "good" girl and means him no harm, as reflected in the white color of her bikini which signals her innocence.

Bond and Ryder soon come under fire from Dr. No's security team, and as they flee Ryder grabs a shirt from her boat. This attempt at modesty soon fails as she gets the white shirt wet and it becomes transparent. In a later scene, Ryder relays to Bond her traumatic past—the murder of her beloved father, subsequent rape, and the revenge she took by killing her rapist. Throughout this scene, Ryder is wearing the shirt, which is now dry, opaque, and covering her body, thus allowing the focus to be on the details she is sharing with Bond rather than her body. The audience along with Bond learns that Ryder is a woman of substance and not just an object of desire. In this scene, the white shirt works in opposition to the male gaze and allows for deeper character development. While the knife and dry white shirt help to relay the impression that Ryder is a strong woman emotionally, the bikini and her costuming later in the film keep her positioned as an object of desire for Bond.

Eventually Bond and Ryder are captured by Dr. No and held as "guests" in his lair. After a decontamination process in which their clothes are taken and destroyed, Bond and Ryder are dressed in the clothing that is available in their room. Ryder emerges wearing a pink floral cheongsam top with bright pink pants, an Asian-inspired outfit that reflects the Chinese roots of Dr. No. The shift in color, from white to pink, seems to suggest an attempt by Prendergast to emphasize Ryder's femininity and offers a contrast to the previous costume, which implied strength and self-sufficiency through the belt and dagger. The costume change also signifies a change in behavior. The filmmakers suggest that she now needs a man to protect her and this is highlighted by dressing her in pink, the color commonly associated with femininity. As they are led out of their room, Ryder reaches for Bond's hand and presses against his body for reassurance. This vulnerability continues during dinner with Dr. No, where the men participate in conversation while Ryder remains silent. Separated from Bond, she becomes a stereotypical damsel in distress as signified by the exaggerated femininity of her costume. Later, Bond returns to rescue Ryder, who is now wearing the same top but no pants, save for a pair of matching pink underwear.

Ryder's costumes indicate the duality of her character and the ways in which the costume designer and filmmakers manipulate that duality. On the one hand, she is a loner or "tough girl" who can take care of herself, and on the other hand, she is psychologically damaged, naïve, and in need of a strong male figure in her life. She is allowed to be independent only to a point. Each time an attempt at modesty is made—putting a shirt over the bikini and changing into a shirt and pants ensemble—something happens to make the costume suggestive again; the white shirt becomes transparent in the water and somehow Ryder has lost her pants by the time she reconnects with Bond. The audience is never given an explanation, and so the end effect is that Ryder once again comes across as a sexualized object who is in need of rescue.

Through costume design, Prendergast regulated the male gaze of Bond, and the audience, in relation to Ryder. Although she is initially set up as an erotic object of desire, there are disruptions via costuming that provide her character with more depth than the other women featured in *Dr. No*. When she is captured, her position as an erotic figure of the male gaze returns. Overall, the costumes in *Dr. No* helped to construct the image of the quintessential Bond Girl and created a character template (i.e. a woman who is emotionally strong but needs Bond to save her) that future Bond films would continue to build on.

CASINO ROYALE: THE NEW ERA

Casino Royale was released in November 2006 and introduced Daniel Craig in the role of Bond. As a prequel, the film reboots the Bond franchise and presents Bond's origin story. It begins with the moment Bond earns his "00" status and license to kill. His first mission is to capture the villain Le Chiffre after defeating him during a poker game. He works with Vesper Lynd, played by Eva Green, who is an officer for the Treasury and controls the money that Bond uses to buy into the tournament. Although Bond interacts with various beautiful women like Solange and Valenka, he falls in love with Lynd and wants to marry her.

Lindy Hemming, an experienced costume designer, was hired for the film. In the years since *Dr. No* was released, the field of costume design has grown more detailed and nuanced. As a result, Hemming's designs for *Casino Royale* are more intricate and meticulous than the designs in *Dr. No*, or even in her previous collaboration with director Martin Campbell on *GoldenEye* (1995). Hemming's work evokes the history and glamor of the Bond films and creates a timeless effect for *Casino Royale* that connects it to the earlier films in the franchise. Hemming was also able to collaborate with major fashion labels, such as Roberto Cavalli, Versace, and Jenny Packham, who provided gowns for several of the women in *Casino Royale*. As costume designer, Hemming is responsible for developing each character through their clothing and, by extension, helping to reframe the dynamics of gender and sexuality in the prequel.

Her designs for Bond and his Bond Girl uphold—and sometimes challenge—previous constructions of these archetypes. With *Casino Royale*, Bond producers not only rebooted the franchise but they also renegotiated the generic conventions and gendered codes of the Bond films.

This renegotiation is seen most clearly with Bond, who is now presented as the object of the gaze. In *Casino Royale*, Bond spends more time semi-nude or naked than any of the female characters, including Lynd who is always covered in some way. In two prominent scenes Bond is seen emerging from the ocean and the camera (and thus the audience's gaze) is focused on his body. In the second of these scenes Bond is on the beach with Lynd; while she is wearing a white cover-up, Bond's body is visible and becomes the focus of the shot. Similar to the way in which the white shirt deflected the gaze from Ryder in *Dr. No*, the cover-up worn by Lynd helps to shift the focus away from her and onto Bond. Commenting on the change in representational codes, Lisa Funnell writes, "through intertextual referencing of renowned Bond Girl iconography [...] Craig's Bond is positioned as a visual spectacle and aligned with the Bond Girl character type rather than with his Bond predecessors in the filmic franchise" ("I Know" 456). Funnell argues that throughout *Casino Royale* intentional emphasis is placed on Bond's body in a manner that had always been applied to the Bond Girls (ibid. 463). The Craig era of Bond films has adjusted, if not inverted, some of the previously established codes and conventions. While the Bond Girls have long been positioned for the visual consumption of the heterosexual male moviegoer, Craig's Bond can been seen as the equivalent for contemporary heterosexual female viewers.

Similar to Ryder, Lynd is not introduced until midway through the film. Up to this point, Bond has had the chance to flirt with several women although he does not sleep with any of them. During their initial conversation on the train to Montenegro and on route to the hotel, Lynd resists the gaze commonly associated with the Bond Girl. Her initial costuming consists of a structured black suit with a high collar. Her second look continues this coverage as she is dressed in a black Alexander McQueen trench coat, dress, and black stockings; the only skin visible in both scenes is her neck. In addition, she also distances herself from other typical Bond Girl characteristics—she refuses to use the double entendre "Stephanie Broadchest" as an alias and she maintains a romantic distance from Bond when she demands separate rooms. Hemming's costuming reinforces the formal, rigid demeanor of Lynd's character.

That evening, while preparing for the poker game, Bond brings Lynd a dark purple Roberto Cavalli evening gown to wear. He says that she needs to look amazing when she comes down so that all of the players will be thinking of her and "not their cards." He asks, "Can you do that for me?" to which she replies with a smirk, "I'll try." True to his character, Bond is attempting to objectify Lynd and use her for his own gain. Shortly after, he finds that his move is being used against him when he returns to his room and finds a tuxedo lying on the bed, purchased by Lynd. A well-fitted tuxedo requires tailoring, which Lynd claims she was able to do by "sizing" Bond up visually, suggestively letting her eyes slide from his head to toes. A moment later, Lynd watches Bond primp in the mirror, oblivious that he is being watched until Lynd laughs. Lynd takes these opportunities to turn the gaze and the process of objectification around to Bond. As a result, the clothing, for both of them, becomes part of the metaphorical game of poker they play with each other throughout the film.

Lynd dramatically arrives at the game in the gown chosen for her. Bias cut, it clings to her body as she moves and features a plunging neckline in front with crystal and beaded detail and a low open back. While the dress is very alluring, there is sarcasm in the way she goes up to kiss Bond at the table that tells the audience that although she is going along with his plan, she refuses to let herself be objectified. She enters from the opposite direction that Bond had instructed. Rather than coming in from behind Bond so that the other players would see her first, she comes into the room so Bond is the first to see her and the other players don't notice her until she enters the playing area. In the next scene these costumes magnify the situation for each character when they are forced into a grueling fight in the stairwell. Bond is still able to be active in his tuxedo, going so far as to use his jacket in defense against a machete. Lynd races down the stairs, trying to stay ahead of the action, dropping her chiffon wrap that floats delicately to the ground in stark contrast to the fighting. Unlike Ryder, who stood back and allowed Bond to do the fighting, Lynd rushes in and wrestles the gun away from their attacker, Obanno, while Bond grips him around the neck. Although Bond is getting used to killing as a part of his job, Lynd's participation in Obanno's death takes a toll on her. After finishing the game for the evening, Bond finds Lynd sitting in the running shower in her dress, clutching her knees to her chest, visibly shaken. Bond joins her, fully dressed as well. Though not particularly sexual, the shower scene is arguably the most intimate of the film and establishes a shift in relations between the two characters. Interestingly, Bond is the one who is wearing the white shirt, which becomes transparent when wet, and it is the body of Bond and *not* Lynd that is being put on display in this emotional moment.

Throughout these scenes the Cavalli gown serves a number of different functions. Hemming's choice of a dress with a silhouette and color that enhances Lynd's attractiveness is a focal point when she enters the playing room, while during the fight scene it illustrates her fragility. The silk chiffon fabric billows and floats behind her as she flees the fight and is a visual representation of Lynd's own breakability. Finally, in the shower scene, the color plays an important role. While the dark purple was a striking feature of the dress in the casino, when wet the color is muted and allows the dress to fade from the audience's attention, enhancing the emotional performance as the walls between Lynd and Bond begin to come down. This dress illustrates the challenges designers face when one costume must serve several narrative functions. The use of color, mass, and silhouette are all integral parts of the final look.

The next evening, when the poker game resumes, Lynd is dressed in a black Versace evening gown with a low sweetheart neckline (the only truly feminine detail of the gown) and wide straps that go into an intricate crossing pattern in the open back. The severity of her hairstyle makes her come across as businesslike. She is no longer vulnerable or in need of Bond's sympathy and comfort. This look suggests that Lynd is reverting back to her personal style. Hemming's choice of costume demonstrates that Lynd is determined to be in control—she is professional, methodical, and conservative. After Bond loses the game, he tries to convince Lynd, as the Treasury representative, to release more money so he can remain in the game. She holds this power over Bond and her function is visually represented by the severity of her costume. Hemming has added a black lace and beaded jacket covering her shoulders and upper arms, which provides coverage like virtual armor. When Bond's charm changes to bullying tactics, Lynd remains defiant, refusing to transfer the money. Where the Cavalli gown was chosen to attract attention to Lynd, the Versace gown enhances Lynd's power and authority in this scene. Soon after Bond is poisoned and races out to his Aston Martin, equipped with combi-pen and defibrillator, to try to save himself. Lynd arrives in time to find an unconscious Bond, with his shirt ripped open and defibrillator pads stuck onto his chest, on the brink of cardiac arrest. Unlike *Dr. No,* which features Bond rescuing Ryder, *Casino Royale* has Lynd rescue Bond, keeping her composure and dressed in the formal black gown, while Bond is positioned as the semi-naked "damsel in distress." The result is a representation of Lynd as a Bond Girl for a new era.

Throughout the film, Lynd's costumes go through a complete character arc demonstrating visually the path she is taking emotionally. With finesse and attention to detail, the costumes work in tandem with the script, cast, and production team, helping to create a complete *mise-en-scène* that allows the audience to be immersed in the world of Bond. The perfect example of strong costume design is when the audience barely notices the designs and focuses on the characters instead.

CONCLUSION

This paper has explored the rhetoric of costumes in the Bond franchise and the ways that they help to negotiate issues of gender and power in the films. While key elements of the franchise have stayed consistent over its 50-year history, the characters have become more complex and have evolved with the ever-changing society they represent. These differences are especially evident in the costuming of the Bond Girls. Ryder's costumes alternate between various stages of dress and undress, illustrating how her character shifts from being independent from Bond to being dependent on him throughout the second half of the film. Lynd's costumes illustrate her professional savvy and intelligence as well as reflecting her underlying mystique that draws in both Bond and the audience.

The field of costume design underwent many changes during the latter part of the twentieth century and the Bond franchise has been a witness to, and an example of, many of those developments. These changes are especially evident in *Casino Royale*, which stands out as a more powerful example of effective costume design than *Dr. No*. Shifts in the field have allowed the costumes to have greater rhetorical effectiveness and the designer to make more specific statements with the costumes for the Bond Girl. Although this chapter has focused on *Dr. No* and *Casino Royale*, further studies are needed to explore where specific shifts have occurred in order to gain a better understanding of the representational codes of the Bond franchise as well as the history of costume design and changing gender roles in society.

Section 5

FEMALE AGENCY AND GENDER ROLES

CHAPTER 19

SECRET AGENT NUPTIALS

Marriage, Gender Roles, and the "Different Bond Woman" in *On Her Majesty's Secret Service*

Stephen Nepa

In *Licence to Kill* (John Glen 1989), James Bond visits Key West for the wedding of Felix Leiter. After capturing a drug kingpin in mid-air, Bond and Leiter parachute down to the church where Della, the future Mrs. Leiter, is waiting. A reception follows at Leiter's home and as the party winds down, Della removes her garter and playfully tosses it to Bond. Responding with a sorrowful smile, Bond declines it and replies, "no thanks, Della, it's time I left." Thinking she has offended him, Della asks Leiter if something is wrong. Leiter, having known Bond for 27 years, responds "he was married once, but it was a long time ago."

Since Bond's first appearance in *Dr. No* (Terence Young 1962), few could have imagined that the British spy, known for his serial seduction of women, would fall in love and get married. In the franchise, marriage is presented as part of Bond's cover story, masking his working relationship with a female spy. This is certainly the case in *You Only Live Twice* (Lewis Gilbert 1967), in which Bond pretends to marry Kissy Suzuki in order to keep his cover as a Japanese man intact. Besides *Licence to Kill*, *For Your Eyes Only* (John Glen 1981) is one of the few films to reference Bond's previous legitimate marriage by depicting him placing flowers on his wife's grave before he defeats Blofeld, the arch-villain and head of SPECTRE, who is responsible for her death.

Between the Sean Connery (1962-71) and Roger Moore (1973-85) eras, George Lazenby assumed the title role for only one film, *On Her Majesty's Secret Service* (*OHMSS*, Peter Hunt 1969). An unknown actor, Lazenby offered an alternate version of the brash, hyper-masculine spy. Panned by critics for lacking the élan of its predecessors and described by James Chapman as "deviating furthest from convention," *OHMSS* is an atypical Bond narrative by virtue of its characters' gender roles (*Licence* 95). The film's trailer promoted Lazenby as a "different Bond" and the female lead, played Diana Rigg, as a "different Bond woman." This chapter explores what exactly is different about Bond and this woman, focusing on the messages being relayed about femininity and masculinity through their secret agent nuptials. Moreover, I will examine how shifting gender roles in *OHMSS* influence the representation of future Bond women and 007's relationships with them.

CULTIVATING A "DIFFERENT BOND"

Ian Fleming's novel, *On Her Majesty's Secret Service*, was published in 1963. In his review for the *New York Times*, Anthony Boucher remarked "incidentally, Bond gets married. Since the girls with whom he beds even casually died in previous novels, you may imagine the fate of his bride" (BR4). In addition, the *Manchester Guardian* noted Bond was "callous and brutal in his ways, with strong undertones of sadism, and an unspeakable cad in his relations with women, towards whom sexual appetite represents the only approach" (qtd. in Lycett 447-8). Long before the filmic release of *OHMSS*, Bond's sexist playboy paradigm was firmly established. The staples of the first five films (sleek cars, ingenious gadgetry, cunning villains, and beautiful women) revolved around 007's missions and his inflexible allegiance to Queen and Country. Framed by a pre-détente Cold War, many Connery era films contained a nuclear-related threat; whether preventing Auric Goldfinger's irradiation of the bullion at Fort Knox or thwarting SPECTRE's ransoming of the West with stolen warheads, 007 was never far removed from contemporary geopolitics.

When *OHMSS* opened in theaters, *détente* had commenced while Britain's "world role" was on the wane (Westad 194). Sheared of many long-standing colonies and burdened by a sagging domestic economy, the incumbent Labour Party under Harold Wilson and "disarmers" in Parliament scaled back military expenditures and minimized their nation's role in conflicts such as Vietnam, Nigeria, and Rhodesia (Sked and Cook 233-8). Given Britain's domestic and foreign entanglements and the resiliency of decolonization movements, *OHMSS* was the first Bond film removed from the vertices of the Cold War. Producers Albert R. Broccoli and Harry Saltzman and screenwriter Richard Maibaum narrowed 007's mission solely for the purposes of bringing a "non-aligned" Blofeld to justice.

There were other reasons for cultivating a "different Bond." Critics pointed to the fact that from *Dr. No* through *You Only Live Twice*, Bond had devolved into caricature while the films were "dominated by hardware, empty spectacle, and comedic gadgets" (McKay 115). Even Broccoli and Saltzman noted these Bond films were "pure entertainment. We emphasize all the way that it is completely unreal" (qtd. in Watts X13). As such, *OHMSS* omitted Bond's reliance on Q Branch gadgetry, allowing for greater narrative development; however, the requisite action sequences remained. From a financial standpoint, Connery, by 1967, was comfortably embedded in the role and demanded £1 million GBP (or $1.7 million USD) for a sixth appearance. In comparison, Lazenby, a car salesman turned TV commercial actor, was retained for far less money. Lazenby was chosen after impressing producers with a Jermyn Street suit and his hand-to-hand combat skills. While he looked the part, critics were divided about his performance. A.H. Weiler termed him "a spurious Bond, a casual, pleasant, satisfactory replacement" (¶ 2) while Pauline Kael lamented that the film "was the best of them except for the substitution of George Lazenby for Connery" (359).

CULTIVATING A "DIFFERENT WOMAN"

Critical response to Rigg's performance of Contessa Teresa ("Tracy") di Vicenzo was overwhelmingly positive. Vincent Canby remarked "the thing that ruins the film however is Diana Rigg, who is such a beautiful, intelligent, responsive, mysterious actress that her presence makes everything around her look even more dull and foolish than is absolutely necessary" (81). Unlike Lazenby, Rigg had considerable acting experience. Director Peter Hunt recalls telling her "if you don't like this boy, then we won't go with him" (qtd. in Giammarco 108). A stage veteran with Shakespearean training, Rigg had risen to fame as Emma Peel in Britain's popular series *The Avengers* (1961-69). In 1965, she replaced Honor Blackman who left the show to play one of the most infamous Bond Girls, Pussy Galore in *Goldfinger* (Guy Hamilton 1964).

When *The Avengers* debuted in 1961, Blackman initially read for a man's part. Brian Clemens, a writer for the show later called her "the first emancipated woman on television" (Soter 81). Armed with a PhD in anthropology, a black belt in judo, and clad in tight black leather, Dr. Cathy Gale played by Blackman gave post-war feminism a televised role model. Prior to the 1960s, women on British television comprised just 22 percent of all characters (Ryan and Macey 192). Moreover, gender roles in post-war Britain reflected their American counterparts as women, whose work outside the home was valued in wartime, relinquished their jobs to men and returned to domesticity and child-rearing. Beyond occupational spheres, women in post-war Britain were expected to be "modest, reserved, passive, and chaste" (Montgomery 229). Gale inverted such traditional stereotypes. As Blackman notes "women had always taken a back seat [...] everything was male [...Women] smelt liberty, I think, and freedom, and confidence from it" (qtd. in Soter 88).

The producers decided that Blackman's replacement in *The Avengers* needed softer edges in order to exude "man appeal" for male viewers. In writers' memos, "man appeal" was shortened to "M. Appeal," which is how Rigg's nomenclature (i.e. Emma Peel) developed. Peel offered more balanced qualities, appearing softer and more playful in terms of sexuality, and "could be motherly or sexy, domestic or night-club-by" as opposed to Blackman's Gale, whom many male viewers found overpowering (Soter 96). As Blackman's husband Maurice Kaufmann recalled, "men seem to resent the way Cathy can take care of herself. It takes away their male ego" (Wright 200). Yet Peel was not without confidence. Commenting on her character, Rigg notes that

Peel "was a woman who had the capacity for doing everything that a man can do, and that's what makes the character so extraordinary" (Soter 80). Rigg continued in the role until she too was cast as a Bond Girl in *OHMSS*. Ultimately, Rigg's "heroic competency" displayed in the *Avengers* allowed for di Vicenzo's parity with Bond in terms of intellectual and physical prowess (Funnell, "From English" 66).

With the exception of Blackman, few Bond Girls have exhibited a high degree of confidence and competence. Typically they provide Bond with a woman to rescue, to affirm his sexual prowess, and/or to recruit for access to the villain. Bond keeps his "girls" fixed in a particular sexual order regardless of whether or not they would be killed as a consequence of him doing so. Rigg's character, however, does not fit any of these molds, as di Vicenzo remains cloaked in mystery. She first appears driving a Cougar Eliminator, a popular muscle car of the era, passing Bond at high speed on a coastal road. This echoes Bond's rally with Tilly Masterson in *Goldfinger*, in which Bond's Aston Martin shreds Masterson's tires, forcing her off the road. The chase between Bond and di Vicenzo is less aggravated until she attempts suicide; Bond then intervenes, trying to understand her motives. Her stunt driving skills emerge later in the film, when she barrels through a stock car race held on a frozen lake with an impressed Bond in the passenger seat. Her first words to Bond, after he assumes her gambling debt of 20,000 francs, are "why do you persist in rescuing me?" Insisting that she repay her debt, she drops her room key in front of him, saying "come later, partner." When Bond awakens, he finds her gone though not without leaving two 10,000 franc chits in a drawer, provoking his comment "paid in full." The sexual behavior of di Vicenzo licensed for future women the possibility of sex without commitment.

THE ROLE OF MARRIAGE

The assertiveness of di Vicenzo and Bond's corresponding deference reflect the seismic changes in post-war gender roles. In the 1960s, female activists revolted against a host of constrictions including "marriage, the vaginal orgasm, and housework, along with the fight for the legalization of abortion and for sexual harassment laws" (Hesford 2). Influential texts by Simone de Beauvoir (1949), Helen Gurley Brown (1962), and Betty Friedan (1963) challenged women's acceptance of their Otherness by stressing that their cultural passivity and limited career options shackled them to a male-dictated Cold War social order that existed on both sides of the Atlantic. Throughout Western Europe, a desire for women to uphold "political quiescence, family stability, and domesticity" not only reaffirmed patriarchy but also allowed a soft, pro-Western femininity to discredit "tough Communist female factory workers" (Mazower 295). American post-war feminism sought greater parity with men and a dismantling of the nation's patriarchal rigidity, while in England post-war feminism championed women's survival skills (Hartmann 288). Yet not all women subscribed to these changes. The more conservative among them in the United States viewed liberation activists as aggressive progenitors of the country's moral decline. In Europe, women working outside the home were exceptional, pitied for living "empty lives," and undermining the consensus that paid employment was a "*man's* natural right" (Shapira 93). From *Dr. No* through *You Only Live Twice*, Bond not only protected a threatened masculine ideal but through sexual conquest allowed "regular dads" to fantasize about being "unapologetic bad boys" (Lynch 18). *OHMSS*, however, condemns Bond's irresponsible playboy nature and di Vicenzo's casual sexual escapades through the stability of marriage.

OHMSS employs meta-fictitious elements, including Lazenby speaking to the audience and odes to previous Bond films. Even his dialogue with Moneypenny goes beyond flirtation; for the first time, 007 makes a pass at her: "cocktails at my place... just the two of us." Surprisingly, she turns *him* down: "I'd adore that if only I could trust myself." When he kisses her lips lightly, viewers who were uninitiated with the Bond saga might have imagined they once were intimately involved. After 007 receives two weeks leave from MI6, he meets di Vicenzo's father Draco to hear a proposal; if Bond agrees to marry his daughter, Draco will reveal Blofeld's whereabouts. Bond refuses at first, replying "I have a bachelor's taste for freedom." Yet after bonding with di Vicenzo (in a montage set to Louis Armstrong's "We Have All the Time in the World"), his guard lowers as their mutual attraction and future nuptials seem more assured.

The marriage functions as more than a storyline stand-in for Cold War diplomacy and nuclear threats. By 1969, filmgoers in Britain and America had been exposed to New Hollywood cinema, led by auteur directors schooled in French New Wave techniques and eager to bring realism to the big screen. Though *noir* movies had appeared as early as the 1940s, by the close of the 1960s, films with anti-heroes, social malaise, racial and class tensions, and unhappy endings were the norm; John Schlesinger's *Midnight Cowboy* (1969) won the 1969 Best Picture Academy Award. For the *Easy Rider* (Dennis Hopper 1969) generation, the politics of the decade demanded a tearing down of the old order of which Bond's chauvinistic, conservative attributes were a part. A second possibility for having 007 wed was to distance the series from the icy, calculating persona of Connery and develop through Lazenby a Bond who would be defined by his compassion and ability to grieve while detaching from his unyielding loyalty to Britain. Lazenby's Bond, who supplants his duty for the mission with love for di Vicenzo, is humanized, a quality that is almost non-existent in Connery's Bond, whose cocksure arrogance by the close of the 1960s felt anachronistic with shifting ideals of masculinity and femininity. As the film's conclusion confirms, morbid endings without resolution were fashionable devices in British and American cinema (Biskind 22).

The marriage also mirrored Fleming's personal life, for whom Bond was a literary alter ego. *OHMSS* was his most successful novel, which explains its faithful film adaptation (Parker 9). Fleming possessed a ravenous appetite for vice, from gambling and liquor to illicit sexual affairs. It was not until his forties that he committed to marrying Ann Rothermere, wife of his close friend Esmond and his mistress of 14 years, after learning she was pregnant with his child. Though his love for Ann never seemed in doubt, marriage was a harder commitment. Many who knew Fleming felt that he "was not the marrying type" and that he showed "nonchalance about discarding women in the past" (Lycett 324). In *The Man with the Golden Gun* (published in 1965), Fleming wrote that Bond "knew, deep down, that love from Mary Goodnight, or from any other woman, was not enough for him. It would be like taking 'a room with a view'. For James Bond, the same view would always pall" (qtd. in Black 87). Ann had equal reservations about legitimating their romance, but as close friends later reported, she exerted a powerful influence over him. In a correspondence to Fleming when her marriage to Esmond unraveled, she boldly announced "I could be in your bed with a raw cowhide whip in my hand so as I can keep you well behaved for forty years" (qtd. in Lycett 198). Similarly in the film, di Vicenzo exerts a unique power over the normally domineering Bond. As her father explains, di Vicenzo was "part of the fast international set," an indication that she enjoyed sexual liberation without consequence. While Bond at Piz Gloria was surrounded by women who gravitated to him in hormonal desperation, following his rescue by di Vicenzo he states "I'll never find another girl like you," suggesting that his days as a bachelor will soon be past him. His gentleness towards di Vicenzo, who challenges him sexually and otherwise, reverses the 007 tradition of keeping women in their place, sexually or violently. With genuine feelings for one another, their nuptials are legitimized to a degree far greater than the "cover marriage" featured in *You Only Live Twice*, which dissolves without future mentioning.

Yet to suggest Lazenby jettisoned all traditional Bond qualities on the basis of settling down is misleading; critics and audiences would not have accepted a complete abandonment of the agent's loutish behavior or the endurance of his marriage. For much of the film, di Vicenzo is absent as Bond infiltrates Blofeld's mountain retreat. Disguised as a genealogist charged with confirming Blofeld's royal lineage, Bond finds himself in alpine exclusion with "patients" who happen to be young, attractive, sexually repressed females lorded over by Irma Bunt, Blofeld's brutishly asexual aide-de-camp. Bond engages with multiple partners in secret in order to discover Blofeld's plans while enjoying a libidinal last hurrah before taming his sexual appetite for domesticity. The wedding sequence suggests a finality to not only Bond's ravenousness and di Vicenzo's carelessness but to Bond's career as well. MI6's human apparatus emerges from its secretive confines and participates in the joyous fetes; children dance around Bond's flower-draped Aston Martin, M cavorts pleasantly with Draco, and Q, seeing Bond off, announces "I must confess that I sometimes thought you irresponsible. This time, my boy, I can't complain." As the newlyweds pull over after leaving the reception, Tracy Bond notes her wedding present "is the best I could have, a future." Seconds later, Blofeld and Bunt speed by, spray the car with gunfire, and kill the new Mrs. Bond through the windshield. The film's final shot, with Bond quietly crying over the body of his wife seen through bullet-riddled glass, reveals the eerie termination of their nuptials, which easily allow for 007's subsequent return to form.

THE CONTEXT OF MARRIAGE

OHMSS, despite its action sequences, capable performances, and anomalous plot twists, does not rest in the pantheon of memorable Bond films. Unlike *Goldfinger* or *Thunderball* (Terence Young 1965), it was not a box office hit (a mere $22.8 million USD in North America versus *Thunderball*'s $63.6 million USD), audience favorite, or critical success (Giammarco 80). While Lazenby's Bond ordered Dom Pérignon '57 and caviar convincingly, and held his own in the action sequences, he resembled a sensitive everyman when weighed against Connery's suave Bond. Connery returned to the role in 1971 while Rigg, after turning down the lead alongside Clint Eastwood in *Paint Your Wagon* (Joshua Logan 1969), never appeared again in an action film. In fleshing out how Bond and di Vicenzo's marriage influenced gender roles in future 007 films, *OHMSS* must be bookended with Connery's performance in *You Only Live Twice*, his final role as Bond in *Diamonds are Forever* (Guy Hamilton 1971), and selected films from the Roger Moore era (1973-85).

Aside from Bond's first trip to East Asia after faking his death, *You Only Live Twice* contains few surprises. Typical of Connery's Bond, upon learning from Tiger Tanaka, his Japanese counterpart, that "in Japan, men come first, women come second," he replies "I just may retire to here." Part of Bond's disguise is to blend in with local customs; he trains with ninjas, wears artificial eyelids to hide his Westerness, and marries Kissy Suzuki, a woman from a local fishing village who is actually a Japanese secret agent. When Bond makes repeated advances towards Suzuki after their fake wedding ceremony, she reflexively replies "this is business." Glancing at a plate of oysters, he cheekily states "I won't need these, then." As the film proceeds, Bond charms Suzuki into submission, perhaps nostalgically pining for Britain's then-disappearing global authority.

With Connery's return in *Diamonds are Forever*, it becomes clear that Lazenby's "different Bond," transitioning from caddish womanizer to grieving widower, was a briefly visited way station. The film not only reverts 007 back to his derrière-slapping ways but explicitly lacks female characters with the self-assurance so integral to Rigg's di Vicenzo. Bond Girl Tiffany Case first appears unfazed by Bond's overtures though her resolve withers by the middle of the film. Plenty O'Toole, whom Bond picks up at a craps game, is thrown out of a window by thugs only to land in the hotel pool; Bond rotely replies "exceptionally fine shot." Moneypenny returns to waiting-in-the-wings by asking Bond to bring her a diamond ring from Amsterdam. The film's exceptions are Bambi and Thumper, nimble martial arts experts who guard the reclusive Willard Whyte. When Bond's sexual charms fail to persuade them, he bests them in combat, nearly drowning them in Whyte's pool. Reviewing the film for the *New York Times*, Peter Schjeldahl noted "if Bond actually ever ceased to be a sexist bully, he would simply no longer be Bond" (Schjeldahl D15).

After *OHMSS*, the Bond Girl underwent a paradigmatic shift rather than a reversion. While di Vicenzo is one of the most competent Bond Girls, she also is the last to exude the independence and liberation of post-war feminism. Beginning with *Diamonds are Forever* and continuing through the Moore era, the Bond Girls are presented as "American sidekicks" who are less assertive and require the rescue from the hero (Funnell, "From English" 74). According to Tony Bennett and Janet Woollacott, "this shift in narrative reorganization clearly constituted a response [...] to the Women's Liberation movement [by] fictitiously rolling-back the advances of feminism in order to restore an imaginarily more secure phallocentric conception of gender relations" (*Bond* 28). As a result, Bond Girls like Solitaire from *Live and Let Die* (Guy Hamilton 1973), Dr. Holly Goodhead from *Moonraker* (Lewis Gilbert 1979), and Stacy Sutton from *A View to a Kill* (John Glen 1985) assist Bond but do not overshadow him as the primary hero. Even in the Dalton era, Pam Bouvier in *Licence to Kill*, who has "flown through the toughest hellholes in South America," sheds her commando persona and adopts a sexy secretarial look in deference to "the man's world" in Panama. While these Bond Girls possess intelligence or a skill set that aids Bond on his missions, they also serve as easy targets who put up little fuss in sharing Bond's bed, only to be forgotten by the start of the next film.

DEATH OF THE BRIDE

Casino Royale (Martin Campbell 2006) is a prequel and presents a rebooting of the Bond franchise. In an early scene, Bond, played by Daniel Craig, is asked to describe the type of women he likes. He responds with "married," indicating his desire to maintain little emotional attachment to the women that he beds. Midway through the film he meets Vesper Lynd and falls in love. He plans to run away with her; he submits his resignation to M and hopes to build a new life outside the service with her. However, much like Tracy di Vicenzo/Bond and Della Leiter, Lynd is killed, leaving Bond (like his American counterpart Felix Leiter) free to continue on as a secret agent.

The novel for *Casino Royale* was published in 1953 and appears 10 years before *OHMSS*. In terms of the novel series, Lynd is the first love that Bond has tragically lost and this event arguably influences our reading of the fate of Tracy di Vicenzo; the impact of her death is somehow lessened by the fact that a similar situation (Bond falls in love, resigns from M16, suffers the loss of his love, and returns to the service) has previously occurred and that in some respects Bond should have known better. Conversely, in the film series Bond's marriage to di Vicenzo occurs 37 years before his courting of Lynd, granted *Casino Royale* is conceptualized as a prequel and the events are assumed to have taken place first. Nevertheless, the film *OHMSS* contains the first instance of love and loss in the Bond film series, and the death of di Vicenzo arguably influences our reading of Lynd. While di Vicenzo's death is referenced in a few subsequent Bond films, an element that is remarkable given the episodic nature of the series, Lynd's death has a lasting impact on Bond and appears to be a strong motivational force in the next film *Quantum of Solace* (Marc Forster 2008). In light of the serial nature of the Craig era films, the impact of Bond's loss is carried through successive films, which more strongly reiterate the notion that marriage is unsustainable in the Bond franchise. Secret agent nuptials put at risk not only the Bond Girl but all of M16; Bond simply cannot divide his attention between his responsibilities to the Queen (his first and primary love/wife) and his potential domestic responsibilities to the Bond Girl.

CHAPTER 20

THE SPY WHO FOOLED ME

The Early Bond Girl and the Magician's Assistant

Ross Karlan

James Bond is more than just a fictional superspy; he is an iconic figure in global popular culture and his name has become synonymous with various elements featured in his films. Agent 007 is known for his espionage skills, dashing good looks, smooth personality, refined taste, inventive gadgets, slick cars, extensive travel to exotic locations, unrivalled ability to defeat deadly villains, and perhaps most importantly, his relationship with the Bond Girl. From novel to film series, the Bond Girl has become one of the most memorable and marketable elements of the franchise. While most women featured in the films are generally referred to by the colloquial descriptor of "Bond Girl," Lisa Funnell argues that the term should be reserved for the non-recurring lead female protagonist featured in each film. She notes that while "Bond engages with numerous women" the Bond Girl is defined by "the strong and intimate relationship she builds with Bond by the end of the film" ("I Know" 465). In essence, she functions as Bond's primary girlfriend/lover and her (sexual) role in helping to confirm Bond's masculinity and heterosexuality is often signaled through the use of a double entendre for her name (e.g. Honey Ryder, Pussy Galore, Dr. Holly Goodhead, etc.).

However, it is my contention that the Bond Girl functions as more than just Bond's sexual partner in the film. The Bond Girl, in many ways, operates like a magician's assistant, as her performance is largely defined by her relationships with both Bond and the audience of the films. In this chapter, I will first explore how the Bond Girl, like the magician's assistant, acts as an object of desire. Using Laura Mulvey's gaze theory, I will argue for a scopophilic relationship between the assistant and the audience—i.e. that the Bond Girl is there to be looked at and distract the audience from the trick that is taking place, a principle in magic known as misdirection. Second, I will examine how the Bond Girl, like the magician's assistant, must also be extremely skilled in magic as she is the one who actually does the majority of the work in an illusion. While Bond, like a magician, is the one who takes the bow and receives the credit through applause, it is the Bond Girl, like the girl in the box, who has done most of the hard work. When viewed through the lens of magic, the Bond Girl is "more than meets the eye" as she takes on a more active role in the Bond universe.

JAMES BOND AS MAGICIAN

In the literary and film franchise, Bond functions much like a headlining magician in Western magic. On the most basic level, Bond is the headliner of the novels and the films, which focus on the amazing feats he performs. However, Bond's "magician-ness" is also defined by the similarities that can be seen between his Cold War appearance and the somewhat stereotypical image of the Victorian-Age magician. According to Francesca Coppa, the traditional attire worn by a magician is white tie or "a top hat and tails"—a black evening tailcoat and trousers, a white dress shirt and bow tie, and a black silk top hat. First worn in the Victorian era, this style of formal evening dress was a way of "asserting the superiority of the British gentleman over the Eastern 'other'" (Coppa 85). In her book *Vanishing Women*, Karen Beckman traces the influx of magic into Great Britain. During the second half of the nineteenth century, as British imperialism flourished in India, tales of mystics and magicians came back to England and caught the attention of the British public. In response to the relocation of these exotic performers to Great Britain, local magicians began to develop a more professional and polished approach to their art. During this time, "the Victorian conjuror begins to dress in evening suits rather than mystical magician's robes, and his assistants are almost invariably either Indian males or English females" (Beckman 42). Thus the British magician was perceived as being a "Western capitalist rather than an Eastern mystic" (Coppa 86). Through costuming, the magician was able to convey powerful messages about his identity, and particularly his nationality, ethnicity, and class.

Much like the magician emerging in the British colonial system, Bond was defined by his image and especially his costuming. In the midst of the Cold War (1947-91), Bond is set up as a British gentleman and model of Western civility, a figure, in the words of Jeremy Black, "designed to resist the threat to empire" (4). Beyond the larger image of Bond as the manifestation of the "skill, brains, and professionalism" necessary to express the political threat to Great Britain that existed during this period (ibid. 4), Bond is, in many cases, explicitly defined in contrast with the Eastern Other both politically as well as aesthetically. *From Russia with Love* (Terence Young 1963), for example, is concerned with the portrayal of the Eastern Other, from the opening credit sequence focusing on the body of a belly dancer to the exotic Turkish setting of the narrative. Istanbul exemplifies the conflict of "East-West intelligence operations and confrontation and offered the opportunity of describing a place that could be at once gritty and exotic" (Black 29). It is this exoticism that forms the basis of establishing Otherness (ibid. 29). In one memorable scene, Bond watches a belly-dancing performance by Turkish gypsies during his stay in Istanbul—a performance that eventually turns into a fistfight between two women who are in love with the same man. Like the Western magician whose clothing separates him from the Eastern mystic, Bond sticks out in his charcoal suit against more traditionally dressed Turkish people, adorned with bright colors, flowing skirts, and tan suits. It is also important to note the contrast between Bond and the Russian Other. While not necessarily analogous with the eastern mystic, within the context of the Cold War, one cannot help but notice the costuming differences that exist: Bond in his neutral business suits versus the Russians portrayed in green military uniforms.

From a geopolitical perspective, costuming has played a key role in helping to define the identities of both Bond and the Western magician, and Bond offers a contemporary manifestation of the Victorian self/Other dichotomy. The parallels that exist between the colonial and Cold War periods in Great Britain in terms of the distinction between British high culture and the Eastern Other allows for comparisons to be drawn between Bond and the Victorian magician.

OBJECT OF THE GAZE

Historically, most great Western magicians have been accompanied onstage by a female assistant who played two important roles in their act. First, she was positioned as an object of desire and framed through the traditional male gaze. The magician's assistant was not only beautiful but she was often scantily dressed and provided "eye candy" for the audience. Secondly, the magician's assistant was also extremely skilled in magic, for she is the one that actually does the majority of the work in an illusion. Whether an assistant is a contortionist or very agile, she must perform the majority of the painful physical labor for an illusion to work with a smile on her face. It is my argument that the Bond Girl functions as a magician's assistant to Bond and plays an active role in helping him to sell his act.

Much like the magician's assistant, the Bond Girl is presented as the object of the gaze. Laura Mulvey describes the relationship between the (assumed) male spectator and female characters on screen, explaining that "in their traditional exhibitionist role women are simultaneously looked at and displayed, with their appearance coded for strong visual and erotic impact so that they can be said to connote *to-be-looked-at-ness*" ("Visual" 837).[1] According to Mulvey, women on screen function as a twofold object of desire: they are placed on display for male characters to look at while being positioned as an object of desire for the (presumed male) audience (838). Both groups of men—within and outside of the film's diegesis—experience a scopophilic relationship with the women on screen, succumbing to the imbalance that exists between the active male gazer and the passive female recipient of the gaze.

Although Mulvey's essay explores women in film, her gaze theory can be applied to female representation in other types of media and performance styles, including magic. When a magician's assistant first appears on stage and makes her grand entrance, she is scantily clad and her presence is designed to increase the audience's visual pleasure. From her sexy strut to her revealing sequined costumes, the sex appeal of the female assistant increases the interest in and excitement for the magic show. The assistant also functions as an object of desire for the magician himself. In most magic shows, there is sexual tension between the magician and his assistant, and in some narrative magic acts—ones in which a story is told—the vanishing assistant is portrayed as the loss of a great love. The sexual chase between the magician and assistant also works in favor of the magician as it reaffirms his power and sexuality. He has the ability to summon beautiful women out of thin air and he proceeds to sexualize them as objects of desire, confirming a sense of machismo masculinity.

The Bond Girl is presented in a similar way in the Bond novels and films. In the world of 007, she functions as a twofold object of desire for Bond, the primary male protagonist who gazes at her, and the audience, who shares his spectatorial position. According to Christine Bold, "one great prowess" of the Bond Girls as "insisted on by narrative voice and Bond's own comments […] resides in their bodies" (172). The female body is positioned as the object of the male gaze throughout Fleming's works. One of the most direct examples takes place in the short story, "The Living Daylights" (1966), from Fleming's final Bond collection. In it, Bond acts as a sniper, tasked with killing a Russian assassin code-named "Trigger," who also happens to be a cellist in an orchestra. While much of the story consists of Bond waiting in an empty apartment for the sniper to appear, he finds pleasure in watching a woman—who turns out to be the cellist sniper, as well as the Bond Girl of the story—through his sniper scope. Fleming writes,

> The woman's orchestra came trooping down the pavement toward the entrance. Twenty laughing, talking girls carrying their instruments—violin and wind instrument cases, satchels with their scores—and four of them with the drums. A gay, happy little crocodile. Bond was reflecting that some people still seemed to find life fun in the Soviet Sector, when his glasses picked out and stayed on the girl carrying the cello. Bond's masticating jaws stopped still, and then reflectively went on with their chewing as he twisted the screw to depress the sniper scope and keep her in its center. (97)

Through Fleming's narrative, the reader is placed in the position of Bond, noting both the mundane nature of waiting alone, which forces Bond to notice even the most intricate details of the world below the apartment, as well as finding relief and excitement in spotting a beautiful woman, who is explicitly the object of the gaze for the duration of the story.

In the film series, the Bond Girl also exhibits the "to-be-looked-at-ness" of a magician's assistant, and this is most notable in the introduction of Bond Girl Honey Ryder in the first Bond film *Dr. No* (Terence Young 1962). Midway through the film, Bond, who is napping on a beach, awakens to the sound of Ryder singing. As Bond looks out into the water, the camera cuts to show his point-of-view and captures the image of Ryder emerging out of the sea. Her grand entrance from seemingly out of nowhere is markedly similar to the opening of a magician's stage show. Furthermore, her costuming in a white bikini—one of the most iconic images of the Bond Girl in the film franchise—positions her as the object of the male gaze and draws attention directly to her body. As noted by Lisa Funnell, "the image of a bikini-clad Honey Ryder coming out of the water effectively positioned the first Bond Girl as an erotic object of the gaze; the arresting image of Ryder not only attracts and holds the attention of Bond but also distracts him from his colonizing mission on the island" ("I Know" 466-7). Finally, Bond explicitly points out Ryder's "to-be-looked-at-ness" in their first conversation. Frightened, Ryder asks Bond, "What are you doing here? Looking for shells?" to which Bond responds, "No, just looking!" In his response, Bond both confirms his role as the male gazer and positions Ryder in the role of erotic object. More importantly, as a screen surrogate, Bond's admission to gazing reflects directly onto the audience who suddenly realize that they too are participating in the same act.

This iconic scene was reinvented in *Die Another Day* (Lee Tamahori 2002) through the introduction of Bond Girl Jinx. In a similar way, Jinx seems to magically appear out of water in a bright orange bikini reminiscent of the bathing suit worn by Ryder. This time, Bond, who peers at Jinx through a pair of binoculars, opens up conversation with the Bond Girl by stating, "What a view!" His comment, which references the words of Bond 40 years prior, not only reaffirms his own male gaze at the objectified Bond Girl but also draws attention to the longevity of this particular act. As noted by Claire Hines, Ryder "set the standard for the characteristic look of the Bond girls who followed her on screen over the last fifty years" (170), giving her objectified physical appearance a long-lasting legacy.

The iconic and arresting images of Ryder and Jinx emerging from the sea, as well as the beauty of Bond Girls as a collective unit, can arguably be interpreted as acts of misdirection. In the world of magic, misdirection is one of the most important tools for an illusionist. It is premised on the idea that the magician can force someone to look one way, often with the help of a beautiful assistant, while the actual magic takes place elsewhere. Tracy di Vicenzo in *On Her Majesty's Secret Service* (Peter Hunt 1969) is a perfect example of the Bond Girl-Magician's Assistant hybrid who uses misdirection for Bond. She acts like a magician's assistant towards the end of the film when she is being held hostage in Ernst Blofeld's headquarters in the Alps. While Bond and her father prepare to attack Blofeld's headquarters, di Vicenzo provides the all-important misdirection. As Bond and his gang approach in their planes and helicopters, di

Vicenzo asks Blofeld to show her the views from his headquarters, and seduces him with her charm and beauty. As an assistant to Bond the magician, di Vincenzo uses her femininity to entice Blofeld to look the other way while Bond and Draco mount their attack and places Blofeld in the position of the magician's audience. He is misdirected and consequently fooled. Although di Vicenzo does all of the hard work, Bond takes credit for her actions as the hero.

The use of misdirection does not always work in Bond's favor, as he is often the victim of misdirection on behalf of a "bad" Bond Girl. Shifting the role of the magician from Bond to the villain in these situations, the "bad" Bond Girls cause Bond to take his attention off of his work, potentially putting him in danger. Rosie Carver from *Live and Let Die* (Guy Hamilton 1973) is a great example. She is able to lure Bond into trusting her with her sexuality, until she finally reveals that she is a double agent working for Dr. Kananga, the arch villain of the film. Again, Bond's trusting nature and lack of attention leads him right into the "magician's" trap. While the audience of a magic show is not necessarily put in danger at any time like Bond is, the idea of misdirection as a means of control still applies. As a magician, the villain can deploy a "bad" Bond Girl in order to control the gaze of Bond (and by extension the audience) in order to achieve his task.

THE GIRL IN THE BOX

For the magician, part of the illusion of magic is forwarding the idea that *he* is doing the majority, if not all, of the work. In many cases, it is the assistant who actually performs the labor of the illusion, all the while giving the impression that she is merely a passive participant that submits to the magician's conjuring. For instance, with the infamous "sawing in half" illusion, a woman lies down in a box and then appears to be cut at the waist into two pieces. As Francesca Coppa explains:

> The true illusion of the Sawing is, of course, female passivity: all versions of the trick rely on the spectator's continuing afterimage of a woman stretched out, tied down, and immobile. But in fact, the woman inside the box is always actively laboring. [...] All these tricks depend on the assistant's speed, dexterity and flexibility: if there is a secret to these illusions, it's female skill and labor. (93)

The assistant is not only physically responsible on stage, she also possesses all of the secrets that the magician possesses; she must know the inner workings of each prop and contraption, and be familiar with all of the cues that go along with her every move. However, magic relies on traditional gender roles and in order for the illusion to work the audience must perceive her to be unknowing of these secrets. The magician's assistant appears to engage in a masquerade of femininity, which is defined by Mary Ann Doane as the process by which women (in film) "hide the possession of masculinity [...] to avert the reprisals expected if she was found to possess it" (*Femmes* 25). The goal of this masquerade, according to David Roger Coon, is to present the impression that she is "excessively feminine (read: weak, passive, helpless, and most importantly non-threatening)" to conceal her possession of stereotypically masculine traits like intelligence and physical strength (5-6). For an illusion to be convincing, the audience must believe that the female assistant is a passive participant rather than an active and intelligent magician herself.

Much like the magician's assistant, the Bond Girl is also privy to the inner workings of the international spy world. As noted by Christine Bold, Fleming's novels present the impression that "the British Secret Service depends upon its female infrastructure: women carry the files, operate the decoders, oversee the paperwork, screen the appointments, and supply the canteen services which keep the institution running" (171). While these responsibilities may appear administrative on the surface, it is important to acknowledge the access granted to these women in the Secret Service in the 1950s. By working with decoders and top secret files, they have not only gained an understanding as to how the spy network operates, but they also have access to sensitive information that may put Bond's life in danger. The access to secret knowledge arguably connects the magician's assistant and the Bond Girls in the novels. Much like the assistant who performs all the tasks that keep the show going, many of the Bond Girls are responsible for the continuous success of Bond and MI6. As Bold explains, Bond would be lost in the field without the Bond Girl's knowledge of exotic lands. In the novel *Dr. No* (1958), Bond would not be able to navigate his way through the Jamaican jungle and waters without Honeychile Rider who is a native of the island. In *You Only Live Twice* (1964), Kissy Suzuki helps Bond transition into his Japanese life and is responsible for leading him to the Garden of Death (in the book) and Blofeld's headquarters in the volcano (in the 1967 film directed by Lewis Gilbert). Without this specialized knowledge, Bond may not have been able to complete his missions, or worse, he could have been killed.

In many instances, the Bond Girl actually performs much of the dirty work for which Bond gets the credit. That is to say, while these women are presented as objects of sexual desire, they are also responsible for saving the day. Bond Girl Pussy Galore, featured in *Goldfinger* (Guy Hamilton 1964), is perhaps the best example of the Bond Girl-Magician's Assistant hybrid. Galore is introduced as the personal pilot for Auric Goldfinger, the arch villain who plans to rob the US gold reserve at Fort Knox. In Fleming's original novel (1959), Galore is a lesbian who falls in love with Bond after he forces himself upon her. While the film never explicitly relays Galore's sexual orientation, it does provide some visual cues that suggest homosexuality, if not bisexuality. As noted by Tom McNeely, Galore is "always wearing pants, usually with a blazer" and "shows no sexual interest in Bond until he forces himself on her" ("Somebody" 179). Much like the novel, Galore expresses an attraction to Bond after their sexual encounter in the film. Regardless of her sexual orientation, Galore is still presented as an object of sexual desire for Bond and by extension the audience.

In spite of this representation, Galore is one of the most powerful Bond Girls of the first three decades of the franchise. Like a great magician's assistant, Galore does the majority of the work allowing Bond to swoop in as the hero. Galore, unlike other Bond Girls, is not merely an accessory; her role is crucial because she allows Bond and the CIA to counterattack Goldfinger's Operation Grand Slam (Ladenson 188). She is the leader of an all-female flight team, aptly named Pussy Galore's Flying Circus, which Goldfinger has hired to spray gas over the area surrounding Fort Knox, killing everyone who is exposed to it. After sleeping with Bond, Galore decides to turn against Goldfinger, switches the poisonous Delta 9 nerve gas on the planes to a harmless gas—a sleep agent, hence the name of the new mission "Rock-a-bye Baby"—and warns the CIA of Goldfinger's plan. The audience, however, is unaware of Galore's actions—she is not shown in the film calling the CIA or switching the canisters of gas on the planes. Much like the magician's assistant, her actions take place off-screen and away from the view of the audience; she is the woman behind the curtain who manipulates the outcome of the trick. It is unlikely that Bond, without her help, would have had enough time to disarm the bomb and his mission would have failed.

Pam Bouvier, featured in *Licence to Kill* (John Glen 1989), is another highly competent Bond Girl. While Tom McNeely argues that the strength of Bouvier's character stems from her personality, romantic inclinations, and preparedness, I would argue that it resides in her willingness to perform the labor required to prepare for and operate in the space of action. Midway through the film, Bond meets Bouvier at a dive bar near the docks. Unlike Bond, who is armed with only his pistol, Bouvier is wearing a bulletproof vest and hiding a shotgun under the table, anticipating a more volatile situation. Like a magician's assistant, Bouvier is not only prepared, she actually takes the laboring role as the female sidekick. When a fight breaks out, Bouvier is instrumental is expediting their escape: she blows a hole in the wall and they drive away on Bond's boat. In the process, Bouvier is shot in the back and the audience, unaware that she is wearing a bulletproof vest, is under the impression that she is dead. At this point, Bond steps in and gets credit for their escape. It is not until Bouvier gets up and exclaims, "Look! I just saved your life back there! If it wasn't for me, your ass would have been nailed to the wall," that the audience realizes the instrumental role she played in their escape.

CONCLUSION

Viewing the Bond Girl through the lens of magic offers some important insights into female representation in the Bond novels and early films. The Bond Girl, much like the magician's assistant, represents a very small, specific, and independent group of women in popular culture. More importantly, this comparison draws attention to the fact that the Bond Girl plays a more important role than some may have previously thought. Too often, Bond Girls are seen simply as beautiful objects for the audience to watch and for Bond to sleep with. However, just as the magician's assistant is in charge of the inner workings of an illusion, the Bond Girl actually takes on much more responsibility within the Bond novels and the early films of the franchise. These women are often in charge of forwarding the narrative through their use of misdirection, knowledge of espionage, and their underrated skills. While their beauty plays a role in the success of the trick/mission, the passivity of these Bond Girls, much like the magician's assistants, is merely part of the illusion and these women play a very active and important role in the success of their film/show.

NOTE

1   Emphasis in original.

CHAPTER 21

"WOMEN DRIVERS"

The Changing Role of the Bond Girl in Vehicle Chases

Stephanie Jones

"Continuity and change" James Chapman notes "perfectly describes the nature of the Bond series which constantly strives to maintain a balance between familiarity and tradition on the one hand and variation and innovation on the other" (*Licence* 196). This explains the process by which the Bond series traverses cultural, social, and technological developments. This chapter will examine how the car in Bond films serves as an object that reflects changing ideas about the role of women and technology. I will examine three similar scenes in which Bond receives a new car from Q—in *Goldfinger* (Guy Hamilton 1964), *The Spy Who Loved Me* (Lewis Gilbert 1977), and *Tomorrow Never Dies* (Roger Spottiswoode 1997)—and trace the change in gender ideologies within them as the series registers broader social transformations in technology and gender. In addition, I will examine the role of women in a number of car chase scenes. I will argue that this strategy of balancing tradition with innovation is necessarily conservative in nature—while change is allowed, it facilitates a limitation of more substantial transformations in gender representation (ibid. 39).

The car is a compelling case study as it is bound up in a broader gendered ideology of technology, particularly in the earlier part of the twentieth century. According to Sean O'Connell, the car arrived "at a time of great controversy over the issue of women's role in society, with the debate over women's suffrage raging" (45). As a result, the woman driver emerged as "a powerful symbol of potential equality" given that "the driver's seat was seen as a naturally male position" (ibid. 45). Sarah Redshaw notes that cars are not only gendered "but the relationship between the car and the gender of the driver has important cultural and social implications" (9). Car cultures tend to exclude women, even though women have historically played a role in inventing cars and automotive technology (ibid. 19). Redshaw argues that male dominance is even evident in the design of cars: "Men have [...] generated technology which suits male ideas of power, use and form, and these ideas have in turn been 'baked' into the technology" (35). This sentiment is echoed by Deborah Clarke who notes that women often feel patronized and/or intimidated by dealers when purchasing their cars or by mechanics when servicing their vehicles. More importantly, she contends that automobile advertising commonly links the car with the female body. This further genders car culture by "promising men control over speed and women" (1). Despite the fact that women buy more than half of the cars in the US, there are relatively few female race car drivers or mechanics, and female sales associates at car dealerships remain a distinct minority (ibid. 2).

The interior of the car has been a site of struggle for female equality. Yet, as O'Connell notes, "the car's association with the engineering industry implanted the car in a world of masculine language of engineers and entrepreneurs" (45). The car is coded masculine, especially when technical knowledge is involved. The passenger seat was typically reserved for the woman and the driver's seat for the man with a vast amount of rhetorical work expended on making these roles seem natural and incontestable (ibid. 46-51). It is into a fictionalized version of this male dominated space that the Bond car chase appears first in the novels and then, from 1962, in the series of films.

However, the gender/car axis should not only be read in terms of its technical aspects. Deborah Lupton has gone so far as to describe a car's interior as being womb-like (60), leading Jim Conley to note that cars are labeled as an ambiguous gendered space: "cars have sometimes been seen as androgynous with an external masculine side counterpoised to have an internal feminine one" (40). Cars are often given female names and referred to with feminine pronouns. The car is also a symbol of consumerism. As Daniel Miller argues, "clear gender divisions in car use might be viewed as much as an unusual foray by males into an otherwise female-dominated world of consumption as a struggle by females to prevent their exclusion from an arena of consumption associated with male technological issues" (29). The car, then, is a complex cultural phenomenon. At once, the car is an artefact, a space, and a consumer product. A variety of cultural discourses envision the interior of the car as feminine, masculine, or neuter. The car's exterior absorbs multiple social and cultural meanings relating to gender, many of them contradictory, at any given time or place. These meanings also change over time. By employing cars in a central position for 50 years, Bond films navigate this complicated field and, at crucial times, use the multiple meanings of cars to negotiate broader changes in gender ideologies.

1962-71: CONNERY, LAZENBY, AND THE "PROGRESSIVE/CONSERVATIVE" ERA OF GENDER IDEOLOGY

Bond's car functions as a work-place object, especially before the Roger Moore era. Unlike the overtones of connoisseurship in the way that Bond selects food and drink, the car is presented to Bond as an object for work by the narration of the scenes in Q Branch. This has the effect of shutting down the overtly consumerist aspects of the car and emphasizing instead the technological ones.

The Bond films emerged during a decade of great social upheaval in relation to technology. As noted by Chapman, "It was a decade in which technology and technological progress came to the fore" (*Licence* 94). The early Bond films reflect and comment on this growth, weaving technology into the emerging formula for the Bond films. *Goldfinger*, in particular, does two important things for the discourse on gender and technology. First, it loads the car that Bond drives, the Aston Martin DB5, with hi-tech modifications, which allow him to easily out-drive his competition. Second, it makes a star of the car as the Aston Martin became a transcendental symbol of the Bond franchise. This car also appears in the pre-credit sequence of the next film, *Thunderball* (Terence Young 1965). It went on tour across Europe and North America to promote both films at premiers, motor shows, and on television. Lavish descriptions of the modifications made to the car filled reviews, newspaper features, and television spots. In fact, the fame of the DB5 outlived its usefulness as a promotional tool for *Goldfinger* and *Thunderball* as specific films, contributing instead to a trend in which Bond's car becomes a major part of the Bond film formula. Aston Martins have appeared in 10 films to date and continue to appear in the series, often to surround a new and untested actor in the Bond role with familiarity and tradition—Lazenby, Brosnan, Dalton and Craig all drove Aston Martins in their inaugural outings as Bond. Moreover, the Aston Martin DB5 reappears in *Skyfall* (Sam Mendes 2012) to celebrate the fiftieth anniversary of the series just as the Aston Martin Vanquish helped to commemorate the fortieth anniversary in *Die Another Day* (Lee Tamahori 2002).

Given the range of modifications to the car, the film presents the impression that it will take about an hour for Q to brief Bond on how all the components work. The scene fades into the next, suggesting that we only hear the first part of his lecture. This narrative strategy builds expectation for when the modifications—oil slick, machine guns, smoke screen, and ejector seat—will be used and works against the idea that Bond has a natural or intuitive relationship with the car. Instead, seeing Bond learn how to use the DB5 with its modifications plays into the idea that Bond's relationship with technology falls within the sphere of work and merit rather than the world of leisure. In this context, driving the car and using its modifications is something that must be learned and not something for which Bond has a natural talent.

By linking Bond's car so closely to the discourse on technology, however, it becomes bound up in a related press debate about gadgets. While Chapman notes that technology becomes a focus for Bond critics from *Goldfinger* onwards (Chapman, *Licence* 94), what has been overlooked is the way in which the use of gadgets was often read (by those same critics) as a *reliance on* technology, something that undermined Bond's self-sufficiency. As Dilys Powell puts it, "Bond himself is faintly diminished by an excess of contraptions which never leave him at a loss. Mechanical ingenuity undermines human resource" (33). Human, in this patriarchal context, denotes men and male experience stands in for all human experience through a process Dale Spender calls "male as norm" (2). Anxieties surrounding technology at this time fundamentally challenge what it meant to be a man.

From *Goldfinger* on, sports cars become part of the iconography of the Bond film. Moreover, cars are used to anchor meanings associated with Bond Girls. Muscle cars (such as Ford Mustangs and Mercury Cougars), which tend to be the most "openly phallic" (Roof 81), are often owned and driven by women in this era. Indeed, one of the most proficient pieces of driving by any Bond Girl, in any era, appears in *On Her Majesty's Secret Service* (Peter Hunt 1969). This film sees Tracy di Vicenzo rescue Bond from the SPECTRE abettors who are pursing him. She is played by Diana Rigg, who starred as Emma Peel in the British action TV series *The Avengers* from 1965 to 1968 and who, according to Marc O'Day, encapsulated "the paradigm of the independent action heroine" (225). The chase takes place with Bond in the passenger seat and di Vicenzo at the wheel of her Mercury Cougar. She outdrives two others cars on snow-covered roads and outmaneuvers several others taking part in an ice track derby. Bennett argues that, in this period, Bond:

> facilitated an ideological shift from [...] one set of gender identities to another
> whilst preserving a degree of continuity between the two. An ideal popular
> hero, he was both 'progressive', a sounding-board for change, yet also conser-
> vative, limiting change within clearly defined boundaries. (39)

This display, while somewhat progressive in its representations, is carefully limited in terms of its gender ideologies to avoid wider change. Tracy di Vicenzo is the only character to marry Bond and so the driving spectacle is partly an audition for her worthiness for that role. While the spectacle of di Vicenzo's driving skill does progress the narrative, it ultimately ends with her being shot in the head in the passenger seat of 007's Aston Martin DBS. If di Vicenzo had been driving the car things may have turned out differently.

1973-85: ROGER MOORE AND THE "REACTIONARY" ERA

The next time Q instructs Bond on how to use his gadget-laden car is in *The Spy Who Loved Me*. In this film, however, the car has been actively reconfigured to align an affinity for machines and technology with the basic requirements of heroic masculinity. Femininity is positioned to take on the role formerly occupied by Bond—that of the professional who, while unable to operate on pure talent and intuition alone, achieves results through hard work. Bennett describes this process of representing women as "more straightforwardly reactionary" than earlier Bond films where women were less prominent and less directly in competition with Bond in professional terms. For Bennett "the main ideological work accomplished in the films of this period is that of a 'putting-back-into-place' of women who carry their independence and liberation 'too far'" (39). Bennett argues that, by giving more emphasis to certain female characters but still showing them to be insufficient in matching Bond's talents in the end, the adjustment masks a reactionary step that seems progressive on the surface, by giving particular Bond Girls larger roles in their narratives, but ultimately subordinates them as the films conclude.

Major Amasova (codenamed agent XXX to echo agent 007 but with extra sexualized and almost pornographic connotations) is a Soviet/Eastern female counterpart to the British/Western male Bond. The East and West are repeatedly mirrored throughout the film, for instance through a corresponding chain of command with matching red telephones. By adopting and adapting the trope of the way a Bondian hero is introduced (particularly by mimicking the leisure-bound and sexually-active way Moore's Bond was first introduced in *Live and Let Die* [Guy Hamilton 1973]), Amasova is shown to be Bond's counterpart, the USSR's best agent using the same measures.

These mirrored characters, however, are clearly gendered—the UK's best agent is a man (007) and the USSR's best agent is a woman (XXX)—and the characteristics associated with Bond in the film seem to be privileged over those associated with Amasova. Technology, and in particular the gadget-laden car, plays a pivotal role assigning these gendered roles. By showing that men and women use machines differently, *The Spy Who Loved Me* aligns the intuitive use of technology with Bond as a basic requirement of heroic masculinity. For example, midway through the film Q arrives in Sardinia with a new Lotus sports car for Bond. Much like the Q Branch initiation scene in *Goldfinger*, Q tries to explain the special modifications he had made to the car but, after parking Amasova in the passenger seat, Bond simply drives off without listening to any of the guidance. He is still able to use the car and all its modifications perfectly, even as it transitions into a submersible. This is markedly different from the lengthy tutorial Q gives Bond in *Goldfinger* where the scene fades out as Q explains the range of modifications his department has made to the Aston Martin.

In comparison, Amasova does not possess this natural ability and her attempts at mastering technology render her an inferior agent. At the pyramids in Egypt, for example, Amasova is in the driver's seat as she tries to start a van so the pair can escape from Jaws. Bond, who is in the passenger seat, comments wryly upon "women drivers" as she struggles to find the right key to put in the ignition and to get the vehicle in gear. Amasova does, however, get the hang of driving the van in time and uses it to pin Jaws against a wall. Over the course of the film, Bond and Amasova develop an almost adversarial relationship by trying to constantly one-up each other. This ultimately works to Bond's advantage since most of these challenges entail the use of technology and Bond appears to be superior to Amasova in this respect. Their respective abilities with cars and technology are vital to the way in which their relationship becomes hierarchical.

The Spy Who Loved Me presents a remarkable shift in the meanings associated with technology and gadgetry compared to previous Bond films. Chapman argues that the film changes the emphasis in the franchise from adventure and espionage, with an emphasis on Bond's relationship with the villain, to spectacle and romance with a focus on Bond's connection with the Bond Girl (*Licence* 158). The presence of agent XXX as a romantic lead gives a new emphasis to women in the way that Bond's masculinity is adjusted. The implication is that understanding how high-technology works takes time, effort, and learning. Towards the end of the underwater scene, it turns out that Amasova can work the car too but, as she explains, she can only do so because she studied the blueprints of it. XXX can work the modified car but without intuition and flair. This repositions Amasova into a professional role, much more in keeping with meritocratic discourse that distinguished Connery's Bond from the character's origins in the talented amateur gentleman era of Edwardian adventure fiction (Spicer 65-79; Chapman, "Bond" 130-1). At this time, however, the professional role is marked as second best to Bond's more leisure-bound, intuitive approach to heroism.

1995-2002: PIERCE BROSNAN AS "TECHNOLOGICAL MAESTRO"

The Brosnan era further repositions the connotations of masculinity and femininity in relation to technology so that the feminine Other bolsters the naturalness of Bond's instinctive way with machines. *Tomorrow Never Dies* is a film that exemplifies the ways in which Bond's relationship with motor vehicles has been reframed. Early in the film, Bond arrives in Hamburg to pick up his new BMW 750iL. Q steps into the frame dressed as a car hire rep replete with a bright red jacket. Another tutorial takes place, but one quite unlike *Goldfinger* or *The Spy Who Loved Me*. Bond is able to operate the car remotely with spontaneous skill much more precisely than its inventor, Q. This contrast is achieved, in part, by gendering the way in which Bond interacts with the car. During the briefing, it is revealed that the car's onboard computer has a female voice, which not only humanizes the way in which Bond interfaces with the technology but feminizes it as well. The voice, perhaps fitting of a BMW, has a German accent and Brosnan's reaction indicates that the commanding tone is sexy too. Q instructs Bond on how to use the car's mobile phone remote control but is able only to elicit jerky movements from the vehicle. Bond takes the control and, referring to the car with feminine pronouns, says "let's see how she responds to my touch eh Q?" Bond is not only able to bring forth much smoother movements in the car, but manages to perform quite complicated maneuvers instinctively.

Martin Willis has argued that Brosnan's tenure "illuminates a fascinating reinvention of James Bond as a technological maestro" (152). While this also happened with some success 20 years earlier in *The Spy Who Loved Me*, the Brosnan era films seem to make a virtue of reinventing technology as a place for the display of Bond's instinct for machines— but with a different set of comic and sexual inflections. According to Willis, "Bond's role is to uphold the central position of the capitalist nation-state in the face of a technoculture that threatens to dismantle it [...] Bond's aptitude reconfigures the relationship between the technological object and the 'user' of that object" because it is clear that Bond has mastery over it (153). Expanding on this, I would argue that there is an important gendered aspect to the way technology is presented where Bond, instead of standing in for the nation state as Willis has it, stands as a symbol of masculinity, in part through the way he interacts with technology given a feminine interface. In addition, the scene intervenes to change the connotations of gadgets compared to previous set pieces of this type.

While Willis is correct that Bond is shown to be a maestro in his use of machines, the film also conveys the impression that Bond's expertise with technology has been repositioned through contrast with a feminine Other. When performing a complex maneuver with the car, Bond sends it hurtling towards the place where he and Q are standing. He hits the brakes and the car's front bumper comes to a stop only inches away from them at crotch level, marking another way in which the technology is coded as feminine (here as a blatant, and comically knowing, threat to Bond's phallic power). The feminine is folded into the technology itself and rendered part of how Bond masters it. As Willis puts it: "Brosnan's Bond is not simply extending his sexuality through technology, he is transferring that sexuality from his own body onto the hardware itself" (156). In order to wrestle the connotations of the gadget from the fundamental meaning-making power of the distinction between man and machine, the feminine must be conjured up to complicate the axis allowing Bond to seduce the machine into his power as he would a woman. The BMW, as with many Bond women, ends up paying the price for Bond's seduction with its life—it is destroyed when Bond sends it through a storefront window.

Bond's relationship with motor vehicles is complicated by the fact that he is paired with a strong female agent in *Tomorrow Never Dies*. Wai Lin is played by Hong Kong action star Michelle Yeoh who, according to Lisa Funnell, "offers a new image of Asian femininity that is based on physical abilities and achievements" (*Warrior* 43). Much like Amasova, Lin develops a competitive relationship with Bond that is played out during their mission together. Where they differ, however, is in the way in which their effectiveness as agents is measured in relation to technology. *Tomorrow Never Dies* features a daring motor cycle chase through the streets of Saigon. Bond and Lin ride the motorcycle while handcuffed together, and their success in this endeavor depends on their ability to work together (rather than one-upmanship). Interestingly, this is their only collective encounter with motor vehicles, leaving Bond's relationship with car culture relatively intact.

Much like *The Spy Who Loved Me*, Bond and his counterpart are representative of wider oppositions in terms of geography (Britain and China), ideology (capitalism and communism), and gender (man and woman). In the motorcycle chase and the scenes that follow, Bond is shown to have a markedly less intuitive talent for technology than with the remote controlled car. For example, Bond follows Lin to her home only to discover that it is her secret spy den and the Chinese equivalent of Q Branch. In a light-hearted scene, Bond is the butt of several sight gags in which technologically enhanced objects act as booby-traps and threaten his life. Bond then tells Lin that he will send a message to his government, only to discover the keyboards is labeled with Chinese characters rather than the English alphabet. This moment offers a contradiction to a scene in *You Only Live Twice* (Lewis Gilbert 1967) where Bond tells Moneypenny that he has a first class degree in "Oriental Languages." In *Tomorrow Never Dies*, however, Bond is presented as a fish out of water in East Asia. In 1997, the year the film was released, Britain had returned Hong Kong to Chinese rule, signaling a familiar Bondian theme of loss-of-Empire. In this new geopolitical context, Bond requires help in navigating his way through East Asia. Through the motorcycle sequence, Bond and Lin learn how to cooperate with each other and pool their resources.

Tomorrow Never Dies offers a reasonably progressive view on women and technology through the character of Lin. As Funnell argues, Lin provides an image of the Bond Girl that is less sexualized and more masculinized (*Warrior* 42); even though romance and spectacle are still foregrounded, Lin is not used as a foil for displaying Bond's almost superhuman talent with technology in the way that Amasova was. Rather, this film heralds a return to the conservatism of the 1960s, progressive on the surface, sounding out new representations within carefully limited boundaries. Lin embodies the world of professionalism in spying, much as Amasova did 20 years earlier, but this approach is not positioned as second best through the use of automotive technology.

This adjustment in the late 1990s—i.e. letting the Bond Girl competently control a vehicle—might have signaled progress if subsequent Bond films had kept technology at the forefront of the Bond myth. Instead, following the infamous invisible car in *Die Another Day*, the car enhanced with gadgets beyond day-to-day technology has been largely absent from the Bond series from *Casino Royale* (Martin Campbell 2006) onwards. Gender identities have been played out in relation to Bond's muscular body that returned the franchise "back to basics" and marked a "reboot" for the series (Chapman, *Licence* 241). There has been a shift in masculinity from a libido-based heroism (prominent in Bond films from 1962 to 2002) to muscular masculinity (Funnell, "I Know" 462). If the heroic model has changed from the reboot onwards, then so too have the ways in which Bond's masculinity is inscribed through his interaction with women and technology.

The role of gadgets in the reboot is heavily reduced. Q is missing from *Casino Royale* and *Quantum of Solace* (Marc Forster 2008) but appears in *Skyfall* to make jokes about the expectation of hi-tech gadgets. The cars of this era are not modified with special technology and there is no corresponding Q tutorial. Yet motor vehicles continue to reflect discourses on gender, sometimes excluding Bond women, and emphasizing differences between men. In *Casino Royale*, Bond is mistaken for a valet by a hotel patron and entrusted with his Range Rover. Bond uses this opportunity to distract hotel security by ramming the car into a barrier and setting off several car alarms, but not before demonstrating his mastery of the vehicle by parking it using a complex steering maneuver.

While Bond still interacts with women in his films, the Bond Girl has also been transformed in the Craig era. Women tend to impede Bond's goals or endanger his life with their negligence in this period. *Casino Royale's* crashing motif is repeated when Bond flips his car in order to avoid hitting Vesper Lynd who is tied up and lying down on the road; she functions as an obstacle to Bond who is trying to capture the villain in his newly acquired Aston Martin. In *Skyfall*, Moneypenny conducts fieldwork with Bond and is positioned in the driver's seat of a Land Rover. She accidentally shoots Bond during their mission and her mistake leads to her demotion to a desk job. In addition, M is positioned as a Bond Girl in the film (Krainitzki 38). Like di Vicenzo, M takes the perilous passenger seat in Bond's enhanced Aston Martin DB5 from *Goldfinger*; in the final scenes, M is killed, the car is destroyed, and Bond mourns his loss.

With the destruction of *Goldfinger's* iconic car, the franchise leaves open the question as to how women and cars will be mobilized in configuring Bond's masculinity in the future. Cars function as a reminder that human beings want to exceed the limits of their humanity—to travel further and faster than the body allows. Technology could play a role in helping to level the playing field between men and women as agents in the Bond franchise, opening up an opportunity for highly progressive representations. As Craig ages, will Bond's rebooted brand of muscular heroism be enhanced by technology? Will women return to mitigate this process by making the affinity between boys and their toys seem natural? Only time will tell.

CHAPTER 22

"IT'S NOT FOR EVERYONE"

James Bond and Miss Moneypenny in *Skyfall*

Klaus Dodds

In *Skyfall* (Sam Mendes 2012), James Bond's remark to Miss Moneypenny that field-work is "not for everyone" is a calculated retort in the midst of Bond's greatest physical and professional crisis. While his competence has been questioned (e.g. *The Man with the Golden Gun* [Guy Hamilton 1974]), and his health subject to vital intervention (e.g. *Thunderball* [Terence Young 1965]), Bond's superiors usually trusted in his pro-ficiencies. In the pre-Daniel Craig era, the secrets of his enduring success involved a combination of physical resilience, risk management, heterosexual romance, tech-nological competence, and a capacity for extreme violence. There was a great deal of labor, experiential knowledge, and luck at play in his fieldwork-based missions.

In *Casino Royale* (Martin Campbell 2006), however, scholars such as Lisa Funnell have argued that a new model of heroic masculinity is presented. Instead of romantic conquests, Bond's hard body serves as the locus of his heroism, and specifically his capacity to act, react, and endure pain ("I Know" 461-4). In the film, he is poisoned, beaten, tortured, and shot at while operating in Italy and Montenegro. He might not have been able to save his lover Vesper Lynd, but his anger is channeled in *Quantum of Solace* (Marc Forster 2008) as he violently pursues those responsible for her death (Dittmer and Dodds 77). Bond's body endures further punishment but again pre-vails despite attempts to burn, blow up, and batter him. In the following film, *Skyfall*, focus remains on Bond's body. Accidentally shot by Moneypenny while pursuing an adversary, his physical recovery and return to active service is not straightforward. Embittered towards M who ordered Moneypenny to shoot, patronized by a new intel-ligence leader Mallory, and forced to undertake a series of physical and psychological tests, he is only cleared to return because M lies about his test scores. Throughout this process, Bond's body is shown to be aging (Dodds 121-3).

Skyfall is the first to present the impression that *both* Bond and M might be too old to continue in their professional roles. In previous films, actors playing Bond have been replaced if they are considered too old for the role (e.g. Roger Moore) or if they prove to be less popular with audiences (e.g. Timothy Dalton). Other recurring characters, such as Q and Moneypenny, are allowed to age because their roles center on the value of their technical and administrative skills respectively, and when they do venture into the field their function is largely advisory. Q played by Desmond Llewelyn (1963-99) accompanies Bond into the field on numerous occasions from *Thunderball* to *Licence to Kill* (John Glen 1989). Q's role varies from being a brusque colleague to a fatherly confidante, and the continuity of Llewelyn's presence allowed for the exchange of paternal advice in *The World is Not Enough* (Michael Apted 1999). Likewise, when Moneypenny played by Lois Maxwell (1962-85) accompanied Bond into the field, she served in an administrative capacity. The aging of both actors was tempered by the casting of young colleagues in their films. For example, Q is paired with an assistant, Sharon, in *For Your Eyes Only* (John Glen 1981) and another, R, in *The World is Not Enough*. Furthermore, in *Octopussy* (John Glen 1983), Moneypenny introduces Penelope Smallbone as her new assistant in the office.

What is significant here is the different trajectory of Q and Moneypenny. Llewelyn played the role of Q until he died in December 1999 after the release of *The World is Not Enough*. In comparison, Maxwell was replaced as Moneypenny after *A View to a Kill* (John Glen 1985) even though she was far younger than Llewelyn. Caroline Bliss took over the role in *The Living Daylights* (John Glen 1987) and *Licence to Kill*; she was 26 years old when she first appeared as Moneypenny and remains the youngest actor to be cast for the part. When Bond reappeared in 1995, Samantha Bond was featured in the role and Moneypenny is presented as a professional and independent woman in her thirties; Samantha Bond's Moneypenny shares more in common with the iterations offered by Maxwell and Naomie Harris than Bliss. With the casting of Judi Dench in the role of M in *GoldenEye* (Martin Campbell 1995), the Bond franchise has attempted to reshape its gender politics by featuring the title character now working within a professional network of women.

Gender and age intersect in powerful ways in the Bond franchise. The character M is a good case in point. Actor Bernard Lee occupied the role between 1962 and 1979, and only missed the next film, *For Your Eyes Only*, because of a serious illness that led to his death. Much like Llewelyn, he was able to age in the role until his death and the character was recast. In the Bond franchise, there seems to be a pattern in which recurring male characters like Q and M are permitted to age (signifying wisdom and experience) while recurring female characters like Moneypenny are replaced when they are no longer considered a creditable source of flirtation for Bond. It is not enough for Moneypenny to be a competent administrator or, as Bond describes her in *On Her Majesty's Secret Service* (Peter Hunt 1969), as "Britain's last line of defence." As Samantha Bond's depiction of Moneypenny illustrates, she still needs to be young and beautiful in order to be considered sexually viable for Bond to flirt with. She can be career-driven and have relationships with other men, but if she continues to age then the sexual politics of the office are subject to intervention. Samantha Bond's

Moneypenny was replaced after four films when she was 41.

Significantly, Moneypenny is not present in *Casino Royale* and *Quantum of Solace*, the films that restart the Bond series. One reason for this is that the films are fixated on Bond—his emergence as a field agent, tragic love affair with Lynd, and changing relationship with M. In *Skyfall*, Moneypenny is re-introduced after a 10-year hiatus but the character is vastly different from earlier incarnations; she is depicted as a field agent rather than office worker. Subsequently, when Bond tells Moneypenny that field-work is "not for everyone," he draws attention to the intersection of age and gender that underscores the narrative of the film and, in many ways, the franchise at large. *Skyfall* puts forward the impression that (older/experienced) male agents belong in the field over (younger/less experienced) female ones who serve better as accomplices or sidekicks rather than professional colleagues.

While Bond has worked with competent female agents from other intelligence agencies (e.g. Jinx in *Die Another Day* [Lee Tamahori 2002] and Camille Montes in *Quantum of Solace*), his British female counterparts have been ridiculed and seduced by him in the field. Egregious examples include Mary Goodnight in *The Man with the Golden Gun*, Caroline in *GoldenEye*, and Strawberry Fields in *Quantum of Solace*. While Fields appears to have greater agency than the other two, she is killed by the Quantum group for her association with Bond. Besides Dench's M, who develops a strong maternal connection with Bond, Moneypenny has served as Bond's most pro-tracted British female ally in the franchise. With the exception of *Casino Royale* and *Quantum of Solace* her presence has been constant, albeit modest in terms of actual screen time. She has left the London-based office, but in the main only to recreate an office-like environment in a submarine (*You Only Live Twice* [Lewis Gilbert 1967]), an abandoned ship (*The Man with the Golden Gun*) and a pyramid (*The Spy Who Loved Me* [Lewis Gilbert 1977]). In order to better understand the politics of representation surrounding fieldwork in *Skyfall*, I will consider Moneypenny's role in the franchise and focus on how she negotiates the gendered and aging boundaries between the office and the field.

NEGOTIATING THE OFFICE AND THE FIELD

Moneypenny has been one of the most enduring characters in James Bond franchise. As Tara Brabazon rightly notes,

> Miss Moneypenny has been featured in more James Bond films than any fig-ure except the title role. She is the assistant to M, head of the British Secret Service. All agents, administrators, technicians and scientists must pass through the Moneypenny office and antechamber to reach the Imperial core [M's office]. (489)

The office is a critical space not only for welcoming visitors due to see M but also as a site for encounters involving Moneypenny and Bond. Since the earliest films, these brief and flirtatious exchanges have become emblematic of the narrative arc associated with the Bond films. Namely, after a spectacular opening encounter highlighting his last mission, Bond's return to London is essential for him to be assigned his next mission.

While his time in the office rarely exceeds 10 minutes, these moments contribute to the characterization of Bond as seasoned field agent, office flirt, and largely insolent towards male figures of authority. With M and Q, Bond remains resolutely child-like, either showing off his knowledge of a particular topic or resorting to boyish humor. If Moneypenny is Britain's "last line of defence", she also functions as Bond's last line of professional and personal defense. She will occasionally speak up for him, attempt to collect intelligence on his whereabouts, and forewarn him about M's mood before he enters the office for a meeting. As M's personal secretary, she has access to state secrets but she is not above spying on M in an attempt to help Bond negotiate his way through their office-based encounters. As Moneypenny ages so does the significance of these gestures, from that of a flirtatious young woman with a romantic interest in Bond to more of a mother figure in the films released in the 1980s.

This concern for Bond shifts markedly in the 1990s when Samantha Bond occupies the role. As a thirty-something woman, Moneypenny is paired with a female M who has famously accused Bond of being a "sexist misogynistic dinosaur" in *GoldenEye*. While M berates him, Moneypenny accuses Bond of sexual harassment and mocks his sexualized gestures. While Moneypenny once looked forward to receiving flowers from Bond in *Octopussy,* she seems unimpressed by the empty cigar case he hands her in *The World is Not Enough*. Bond's pathetic attempt at a phallic shaped gift is pointedly disposed of as trash and Moneypenny shows little interest in flirting with Bond, a strategy that no longer gains him traction in a new era of open office space with new social-spatial rules. More importantly, Samantha Bond's Moneypenny walks through the MI6 building and also briefs Bond in the car while he is travelling to the airport in *Tomorrow Never Dies* (Roger Spottiswoode 1997). Under M's leadership, Samantha Bond's character is shown to be more of a confidante than office secretary. While she is not presented a field agent (and there is no hint that she has ever been one), her roles and responsibilities have clearly been enhanced. Under the new leadership of Dench's M, both women are operating in spaces that their male counterparts were never shown to be occupying; working with the Americans in mission control centers, being intimately involved in operations and even fieldwork, and having domestic/personal lives. Moneypenny goes on dates and M is married with children.

After a 10-year absence, Moneypenny played by Naomie Harris returns to the Bond franchise and could remain a staple character in the ongoing re-booting of the series. While *Casino Royale* was Bond's origin story, I would argue that *Skyfall* constitutes Moneypenny's. Although she is initially introduced as a field agent operating in Turkey, her return to the office environment in London is not straightforward. She enters the field again in order to join Bond in China and survives a shoot-out in London. While Bond cannot fathom the idea of ever giving up the field to be re-constituted as an office-worker, Moneypenny is encouraged by Bond to leave the field and her representation from clothing to demeanor changes accordingly.

GENDER AND COMPETENCY
(OR WHY FIELDWORK MATTERS)

Fieldwork is essential to Bond's identity, and his craft depends on his ability to negotiate a diversity of places and contexts in which his physical and social skills will be tested. The fieldwork undertaken is often improvised, and one where he is largely trusted to complete his mission independently. In *Thunderball*, for example, he disobeys an order to travel to Canada and insists on visiting the Bahamas in search of a possible lead. While M queries this insistence, he is allowed nonetheless to deviate from his initial mission instructions. Such autonomy does lead to mistakes and in *Casino Royale* Bond is fitted with a tagging device precisely because his innovative style of fieldwork causes a major diplomatic incident. Notwithstanding reprimands and sanctions, Bond's capacity to undertake fieldwork is not placed in long-term doubt. He may be a "blunt instrument" but there is a basic faith that his physical and emotional attributes remain necessary to work in a fluid and unpredictable world of danger and intrigue.

Such longevity has depended on the continued support of M and Moneypenny. Since adopting the role of M, Dench's character has frequently taken Bond to task for his personal and professional misdeeds and complained about being held accountable by her superiors for his actions. But her reprimands never really stopped Bond from continuing to act as a field agent, even if he has not enjoyed the formal imprimatur of MI6. Unlike her male equivalents, Dench's M has arguably enjoyed a closer relationship with Bond and 007 never visited the home of any other M before Dench (with the only exception being in *OHMSS*, which is considered an outlier film in the Bond canon). Bond's fieldwork has been aided, as *Casino Royale* demonstrated, by hacking into M's computer in order to gain confidential information about potential suspects. Bond's presence around M is quite different in the Craig era. While frequently indignant about Bond's transgressions, including his calculated seduction of women and ruthless use of violence, she is prepared to sanction their usage.

This working flexibility proves crucial to both Bond and M. Despite her seniority, ministerial and parliamentary oversight of MI6 is depicted as far more pressing than in the past. Before *Casino Royale*, it was rare to see any reference to more than an occasional demand for results from ministerial figures. M was trusted to manage the secret agents. It was M who decided who was to be cajoled, prohibited, encouraged, and rewarded. The Craig era marks a shift in political accountability and Bond's legendary autonomy is somewhat constrained. M, Lynd, René Mathis, Fields, Moneypenny, and Gareth Mallory monitor him electronically and personally, albeit with varying degrees of success.

What is arguably at play is two models of governance—on the one hand, Bond's experiential knowledge and risk-taking and, on the other, a more closely monitored form of management with emphasis on accountability, cost-benefit analysis, and risk assessment. Another way to represent this apparent schism is to see Bond's methods as profoundly nostalgic—a man used to thinking, fighting, and sleeping his way through field-based challenges. Both M and Bond dislike any form of managerial oversight. Both revel at the prospect of high levels of autonomy and bridle when questioned by superiors. Although she is not a field agent, M's body, like that of Bond, is an archive of encounters. She does not have the physical scars that mark Bond's body but she proves willing to leave her desk environment if required. Some of those excursions into the field have proven less than ideal (for example being imprisoned in Istanbul in *The World is Not Enough*) and arguably ended up contributing to Bond's difficulties in terms of mission completion. Such experiences, however fleeting, proved vital in her appreciation of Bond's resilience, especially when captured by North Korean forces in *Die Another Day*. But his return also provoked her to send him to the Falkland Islands for a detailed assessment of his suitability for a return to fieldwork. Bond later escapes and evades this testing regime without, as in the case of *Skyfall*, having to rely on M's discretion.

M's decision to deploy a female field agent with Bond on his mission to Istanbul in *Skyfall* is significant, and one of three key moments where fieldwork plays a crucial role in the depiction of Bond as an aging but physically capable field agent. Although her relationship with Bond is not explained at the start of the film, Moneypenny is shown to be a deft driver while in pursuit of Patrice. Her shooting skills, however, appear to be challenged twice. Initially, she misses a fleeing Patrice and then accidentally shoots Bond after being told to "take the shot" by M. In the space of about 10 minutes, Moneypenny's performance and M's competence are questioned. Should M have ordered the shot when Bond was fighting with Patrice on top of a train and would Bond have missed (or even pulled the trigger) if he had faced a similar shot opportunity? What role did fieldwork inexperience and managerial panic play in this particular moment of the mission? Why did the two women, as opposed to any men, make the mistakes? At stake in this opening scene was a missing disk containing details of NATO agents, and M feared that such a loss would destroy her professional reputation and compromise the spying capacities of allies. Interestingly, the victims of that missing disk are all shown to be men; dead MI6 agents and a near-dead Bond.

Later when Dench's M is questioned by a younger female politician, there is a lingering sense that her mistakes and misjudgments have had dreadful consequences for men. No other M has ever been subjected to this level of moral and official scrutiny.

Bond's eventual return to active field service is drawn out and uncertain. In the aftermath of his recovery, Bond's aged and damaged body is the subject of testing. Unlike the situation presented in *Die Another Day*, Bond is a participant in *Skyfall*. Significantly, we are not shown any of the testing regimes that Moneypenny might have undertaken. In his discussion of gender aesthetics, Richard Dyer notes that men accomplish their masculinities by activity (153). The physical development, training, and, if necessary, rehabilitation of the body is critical in that regard. In the case of female characters, as Funnell notes in the representation of Trinity in *The Matrix* (The Wachowskis 1999), their films convey the impression that their training has been carried out off-screen (*Warrior* 176), as if to suggest that it is not worthy of public scrutiny. The audience is lead to presume that Moneypenny underwent extensive training before her Istanbul mission and she emerges in *Skyfall* as a fully-formed field agent.

By not showing the audience Moneypenny's training, it becomes easier to imagine her being transferred away from fieldwork. Because the audience is not shown the institutional scrutiny of her skill set, it is difficult to gauge whether her training was inadequate and/or her task of "taking the shot" was reasonable. Moneypenny takes part in a subsequent fight sequence in Macau and even then her mission, and tentative return to the field, is framed as "watching Bond's back." While Bond might trust Moneypenny, as evidenced by him letting her shave him with a cut-throat razor, the audience is left less certain as they have been given limited information about her competency and professional training. By withholding this information, the narrative sets up her return to the office as being understandable and acceptable.

This lack of narrative information is even more significant in the depiction of a parallel event. When Silva forces Bond to "take the shot," his miss leads to the death of Severine and his mistake is presented within a broader character arc focusing on redemption. The audience sympathizes with Bond because he is struggling with a physical injury and forced to use an old-fashioned pistol. By way of contrast, Moneypenny is able-bodied and equipped with a high-powered sniper rifle. When she misses the shot, the audience does not empathize with her, even though her mistake (unlike Bond's) does not lead to the death of anyone.

While Bond's injured shoulder may have contributed to his inaccuracy, Moneypenny has no obvious injuries to contend with when she shoots Bond in Istanbul. While M lies to ensure Bond's return to the field, she is not prepared to sanction the return of Moneypenny. Her youth is equated with inexperience, while Bond's aging body is judged capable of resurrecting the mission to recover the stolen disk. M and Bond find solace in one another's company due to their shared struggle with age, institutional oversight, and scrutiny of proficiency but it is clear that the kind of relationship that Samantha Bond's Moneypenny enjoyed with M has not been replicated in *Skyfall*. Moneypenny is not a confidante, and M shows little sympathy to her plight post-Istanbul.

AGE AND AGENCY

The role of fieldwork is complicated and the second episode of Bond's aging resilience is to be found in another part of Asia. Bond's physical frailty in Shanghai means that he is unable to prevent his main suspect from literally slipping through his fingers. On arrival, he is greeted by the return of Moneypenny to the field. In a moment of intimacy, Moneypenny shaves Bond's face as if to suggest that Bond remains not only a strongly heterosexual figure (a body to be desired) but also a body that is redeemable (and made youthful again). Dressed in a tuxedo his swagger returns, and while Moneypenny offers to "mind his back" in a casino, his resurrection appears complete when he gambles and flirts with the *femme fatale*, Severine. His love-making, in a steamy shower, echoes earlier films where a series of female characters contribute to affirming Bond's credentials as a fit and heterosexual field agent. Coupled with his time in the casino, the consummation of their mutual lusting appears as a "reward" for his risky behavior in Macau.

Significantly, Moneypenny plays no further role in helping with Bond's field-work—her restorative labor is done as she reinstitutes Bond's sense of purpose. Bond returns to the mission, sleeps with Severine, and the narrative arc moves on without Moneypenny. The audience is left to presume that she returns to London and it is a tracking device attached to Bond's shoe that provides an electronic rather than embodied connection with M back in the office. Later, when Bond decides to take M to his old childhood home in Scotland, he increases his geographical distance from Moneypenny, who is left in London to co-ordinate plans to prevent further carnage. Bond's reconnection with his family home provides him with an opportunity to not only protect M from Silva but also to reclaim his masculinity and sense of purpose. Bond is reunited with Kincade, the old gamekeeper and substitute father figure, who explains to M (and the audience) how Bond coped with the traumatic loss of his parents by hiding in a secret passageway under their family home. Reliving these traumatic experiences appears to consolidate Bond's resolution and provides a more positive impression of his masculinity. In comparison, Moneypenny is not offered narrative space to reclaim her heroic identity, and her mishap in Istanbul continues to trouble her even if she ably supported Bond in Macau.

What the field perhaps proves, in the case of the visit to the Bond family home, is that women like M simply age while men like Bond come back revitalized. M can be taught simple entrapment techniques but ultimately it is her rather than Bond who is hit by an adversary's bullet. Her age and accompanying sense of frailty, compounded by the fact that she is a widow and her children appear absent from her life, is magnified by the time they reach Scotland. It is she who requires comfort, warmth, and reassurance from both Bond and Kincade. Moneypenny's youthful inexperience and M's fragility and ageing render them out of place when it comes to the field. They occupy the extremes of an ageing-gender spectrum. It is Bond and the much older Kincade who repel the attack by Silva and his henchmen. While Bond can survive two bullets to the chest area, the locus of his heroic and muscular masculinity (Funnell, "I Know" 462), M cannot endure a wound to her stomach, the locus of her maternal identity, much like other female characters who die from wounds to the stomach/ womb (Funnell, *Warrior* 50). M, the maternal figure to both Bond and Silva, dies in the arms of Bond. Her death serves as a warning about the suitability of (some) women working in the field, while the film also reflects on Bond's decision to take M away from London. M may have been safer in London with Moneypenny and other colleagues. She might even have killed Silva in a final act of defiance in the face of an impending death but instead she is taken out of the office and it is left to Bond to finish the job and reclaim his masculinity in the grounds of his old family home.

M is used as a trap just as Bond has been in the past in films such as *From Russia with Love* (Terence Young 1963). M goes along with his unconventional decision-making, which she trusts will be effective. What the excursion to his childhood home suggests is the final element of his rehabilitation. As with the *Batman* prequel trilogy (Christopher Nolan 2005, 2008, 2012), this is a field agent, as recognized by Lynd, who lost his parents and decides to become a secret agent. The loss of Lynd traumatizes him initially but then he becomes hardened once more. His rehabilitation is supported by a father substitute figure and later with his childhood home destroyed there is nothing to hold him back from returning to the field. Moneypenny is nowhere to be seen. In the origin stories of iconic male superheroes such as Bond and Batman, there is no space for women to craft their own heroic identities let alone project alternative heroic trajectories.

CONCLUSION

On two occasions while in the field, Craig's Bond has either been killed or assumed to be dead. In each case, women were implicated in his death. In *Casino Royale*, Valenka, the girlfriend of archenemy Le Chiffre, successfully poisons Bond and he is only revived from certain death by Lynd's quick actions. In *Skyfall*, it is assumed that Moneypenny killed Bond after following an order from M to "take the shot." In both cases, the women are punished for their transgression by being removed from the action narrative—while Valenka is killed by Mr. White and his Quantum associates off-screen (a death that is only mentioned in passing conversation), Moneypenny is relegated to the periphery of the space of physical action and does not reappear in key narrative scenes. Moneypenny's disappearance rather than death has consequences for Bond's resurrection and the narrative arc. By the end of the film, two of the three female characters are dead (M dies in Bond's arms and Severine is killed as part of a macabre shooting contest between two men) and Moneypenny is portrayed as uncomfortable with the gendered travails of the field.

Some media reports have suggested that in *Spectre* (Sam Mendes, 2015) Moneypenny might be back in the field and represented as an active sidekick to 007. While Harris is reportedly keen to reprise the role, the speculation about *Spectre* and her character's development might also be a response, on the part of the Bond franchise, to address widespread criticism regarding *Skyfall*'s poor treatment of women. Perhaps *Spectre* will expand on Moneypenny's origin story and provide her with an opportunity to return to the field in order to reclaim her professional competence and heroic identity (much like *Skyfall* did for Bond). *Spectre* might offer a further exploration of how the relationship between the field and the office gets negotiated by an individual who, in various stages of her character development, has been secretary/gatekeeper, personal assistant, confidante, and finally a field agent who not only ensures the safety of M but also aides and abets 007. In *Spectre*, Bond will return to the field and it will be interesting to see if Moneypenny will join him.

CHAPTER 23

"WHO IS SALT?"

The Difficulty of Constructing a Female James Bond and Reconstructing Gender Expectations

Jeffrey A. Brown

"Who Is Salt?" was the tag line used on posters in the months leading up to the 2010 release of director Phillip Noyce's film *Salt*, starring Angelina Jolie. In spite of its vague marketing, *Salt* went on to become the most successful female spy movie in history, earning more than $300 million USD at the worldwide box office. *Salt* was praised by critics and audiences for being a fast-paced action film that follows the exploits of Evelyn Salt, a CIA operative and KGB spy, as she evades both American authorities and Russian terrorists while thwarting a nuclear strike, the assassination of the Russian President, and a coup to overthrow the United States government. The question "Who Is Salt?" is a specific reference to her narrative status as a double-agent. But, as a *female* spy, it is also indicative of the character's uncertain position within the larger genre and traditional gender representations. Women in spy movies are typically cast as seductresses, villainesses, or romantic prizes for the male hero. The infamous "Bond Girl" type tends to overshadow any other female representation in espionage tales. Yet Salt is more like Bond than his Bond Girl. Her atypical status as a female superspy reveals many of the gendered preconceptions inherent in the spy genre that has limited female heroism.

Salt is an interesting case study because the film was a self-conscious attempt by a major studio to create a female equivalent to the Bond franchise. The change of the protagonist's sex exposes the gendered assumptions of several key spy film conventions, such as patriotism, sexuality, and trustworthiness. Much of the press surrounding *Salt* addressed Jolie's assumption of a role usually associated with masculinity. It was widely reported that the role of Edwin A. Salt had been scripted for Tom Cruise. When he backed out studio executives approached Jolie who had previously declined their requests to be a Bond Girl on the grounds that she would rather play Bond himself. The character was changed to Evelyn Salt and with only some minor script adjustments, Jolie found herself playing the closest thing to a female

Bond. Roger Ebert wrote in *The Chicago Sun-Times*: "*Salt* is a damn fine thriller..." (¶ 1) and "Evelyn does everything James Bond did, except backwards and barefoot in the snow" (¶ 6). Richard Corliss, in his *Times* review, claimed that *Salt* effectively honors "the core premise of a Bond or Bourne film—that the main character is bold and resourceful" (¶ 4). By most accounts *Salt* delivered a female superspy as good, if not better, than Bond and other male spies.

SALT AS BOND NOT BOND GIRL

The change of gender did not lessen any of the action sequences or abilities of the protagonist. Salt scales the sides of buildings, jumps from one moving vehicle to another, and fights as well as any male character. In fact, Salt's gender does not seem to be a factor in the film. No blustery villains ridicule her as "just a girl," no sexist agent calls her "butch," and she never has to dress revealingly or flirt with men to disarm them. The increased prominence of action heroines over the last 15 years in film series like *Kill Bill* (Quentin Tarantino 2003, 2004), *Resident Evil* (Paul W.S. Anderson 2002, 2004, 2010, 2012, 2016, Russell Mulcahy 2007), and Jolie's own *Tomb Raider* (Simon West 2001, Jan de Bont 2003) has also normalized cinematic representations of women kicking ass. Audiences no longer perceive action skills as exclusively masculine traits. Discussing early action heroines like Ellen Ripley from *Aliens* (James Cameron 1986) and Sarah Connor from *Terminator 2: Judgment Day* (James Cameron 1991) Elizabeth Hills notes, from the perspective of gender binarism "aggressive women in the cinema can only be seen as phallic, unnatural or figuratively male" (39). Jolie's Salt manages to subvert these outdated conventions and appears to be a heroic character that just happens to be female.

That *Salt* does not emphasize the heroine's femininity marks the film as being significantly different than other action-oriented films and television programs. Strong female characters in contemporary Hollywood continue to be represented as sexually attractive. Embodied by traditionally beautiful actresses like Kate Beckinsale, Milla Jovovich, and Scarlett Johansson, most mainstream films offset the implication that casting women in violent and heroic roles renders them masculine or unfeminine by emphasizing their diminutive physical size, delicate faces, and sexual desirability. As Lisa Purse notes, "female heroes combine their readily apparent strength and skill with a more traditionally feminine, and often emphatically sexualized, physique" ("Return" 187). The standard objectification of the male gaze is in full force when women kick ass. The sexual fetishization of modern heroines is often justified as a form of post-feminist liberation, wherein women can embrace beauty and sexuality as just one of the "girly" pleasures they can employ for their own purposes. *Salt*'s divergence from this tradition is notable since Jolie is clearly recognized by the public as one of the world's most beautiful women. Her established celebrity status predisposes audiences for *Salt* to interpret her character as sexy even if the film itself does not overtly eroticize her. Thus, Jolie as Salt can be sexy despite deemphasizing her femininity as a plot device.

While the action sequences in the film present Salt as an equal to the likes of Bond, the narrative diverges from the Bond formula in notable ways, particularly in relation to sex and nationality. Part of the audience's pleasure in watching Bond has always been his sexual adventures. Bond's sexuality panders to the heterosexual male viewers' fantasy of being irresistible to women. "There was never any question," observe Colleen M. Tremonte and Linda Racioppi, "that Bond would not only vanquish his male enemies but that he would also dominate even the most assertive Bond 'girl'" (184). Bond's sexual exploits carry the weight of ideology in that he repeatedly asserts Western patriarchal authority over other nations through his domination of women. As Tricia Jenkins argues, through "Bond's sexual prowess [...] Britain can subdue even the most powerful, deviant nations in the world" (313). Though the Bond films have struggled to appear less misogynistic in recent years, particularly since Daniel Craig took over the title role in *Casino Royale* (Martin Campbell 2006), his relationships with women are still a key ingredient in the Bond formula. Despite the inclusion of Judi Dench as Bond's female superior M starting with *GoldenEye* (Martin Campbell 1995), and an increase of active roles for Bond's female helpers in recent years, women in the world of Bond are still exotic beauties included for their looks rather than their skills.

The franchise's historic use of sexually available Bond Girls is crucial to Bond's status as a masculine and British ideal. As Lisa Funnell notes, Bond is:

> firmly located within the lineage of British heroes. Envisaged through the lover literary tradition, Bond joins some of Britain's most glamorous literary and early cinematic heroes who were presented as brilliant, witty, urbane, cultivated and sensitive, as well as gentle heroes, men of action who risk everything for a higher cause and the women they love. ("I Know" 458)

Unlike Ian Fleming's novels, in which Bond was rooted in the British tradition of masculine lover, the films have melded the British lover with the American ideal of the brute "everyman" hero. The balance between British and American models of heroic masculinity have varied from film to film, and from actor to actor, but Bond's sexuality has remained a stable indication of his brand of heroism. His sexual conquests confirm his heterosexual masculinity (Black 107), particularly for American audiences that might perceive "witty and urbane" as feminizing traits. Bond's hypersexuality has been somewhat diminished in the Craig era films, with him bedding fewer women and developing more serious romantic relationships. But Bond's virility is still foregrounded and visually bolstered through the display of Craig's muscular body. More than any of the previous Bonds, Craig's masculinity is displayed through his body and its ability to bear the marks of physical pain. This ability to triumph over physical trauma is a marker of American ideals of heroism, the clearest examples of which appeared during the Reagan era films of Sylvester Stallone and Arnold Schwarzenegger.

Still, the long-standing tradition in Bond narratives is that sex is a crucial part of the escapist male fantasy. The persistent double standard in Western culture regarding casual sex means that if a female spy like Salt were to have sex with multiple men she would be perceived as devious and slutty. But where Bond has recently been limited to fewer sexual partners per film, Salt is denied any sexual relationships at all. Despite being portrayed by Jolie, *Salt* does a fairly remarkable job of not eroticizing her. Scenes of her falling in love with her husband are romantic rather than erotic, and an opening sequence showing Salt in her underclothes being tortured is brutal rather than sexual. Likewise, when Salt is trying to evade capture in the CIA headquarters there is a moment when she removes her panties that could have been played up for titillation but is instead presented as utilitarian, as she quickly uses the garment to cover a security camera. The film does not undermine Salt's status as an active protagonist by essentializing her sexually. This is no small accomplishment given that women in Bond narratives "have always been conceived in terms of male desire and pleasure [...and] represented as erotic spectacle" (Woollacott 110). While this is a welcome change in the depiction of strong women in a spy-action film, it also means that she is not allowed to actively engage in sex as Bond does. Salt's only romantic involvement is with her husband, who is unaware that she is a double-agent. Moreover, the character is mostly absent from the narrative, seen only briefly in flashbacks and during his execution. While Salt is certainly attractive, she does not flirt with men in the film.

Salt's avoidance of sexualizing its heroine is an exception to the spy genre rule that female agents have to be seductresses. Female spies have had more success headlining their own adventures on television, but even there women are overwritten by sexuality. Series like *Alias* (2001-06), *Nikita* (2010-13), and *Covert Affairs* (2010-14) focus on strong and competent women who are often presented as more Bond Girl than Bond. These heroines—Sydney Bristow, Nikita, and Annie Walker respectively—are exceptionally skilled agents but often have to rely on their beauty in order to dupe men. In almost every episode they are called upon to perform an exaggerated feminine stereotype as part of their mission. Sultry guests at formal parties, high-end prostitutes, and damsels in distress are regular undercover assignments. This convention is an example of what Mary Anne Doane refers to as a masquerade of femininity (*Femmes* 25). In contrast, exaggerated sexuality is not part of Salt's spy skills. When she infiltrates the White House, she impersonates a male soldier rather than a stunning female party guest. Salt's masculine masquerade, while surprising, is employed in a practical sense to gain access to a restricted level rather than to suggest that she is a masculinized heroine.

Because female sexuality and espionage are so closely linked in popular culture, these small screen super-spies have to strike a balance between appearing sexy and being sexually compromised. While Bristow, Nikita, and Walker are routinely fetishized by their narratives, they never employ copulation to achieve their missions. They use the lure of sex as an effective tool of the trade, but as good American heroines they would never actually prostitute themselves to accomplish their goals. In her discussion of sexuality and nationality in *Alias*, Miranda J. Brady argues that the series presents:

> foreign and minority female spies as single-minded vixens who apparently place personal and national interests above family. Conversely, Sydney Bristow, the white American female spy, desperately clings to familial normalcy and wants nothing more than to reproduce the heteronormative familial structure. While foreign female spies will shamelessly enter into a sexual contract (including marriage) to gain information, Sydney Bristow will only emulate the use of sex for espionage, saving copulation for meaningful, conjugal relations. (113-4)

Given cultural values about gender and sexuality, for a female spy to actually use sex would be un-American and un-heroic. By this cultural logic, Salt's status as a genuine heroine is far more precarious than her small screen counterparts. Through flashbacks, the audience learns that Salt initially targeted her husband as part of a mission. But it is also revealed that Salt fell in love with him before they were married and her main concern is for his safety after her cover is blown. Salt's love for her husband renders her actions heroic even when her national allegiance is drawn into question.

TRUSTING SALT

Despite the narrative's best efforts to present a gender-neutral action/thriller in the Bond tradition, *Salt* does have to contend with perceptions of female spies as untrustworthy. Salt's status as a Russian sleeper agent continuously puts her national allegiances in doubt. Male film spies like James Bond, Jason Bourne, and Jack Ryan, as well as those from television such as Jack Bauer from *24* (2001-14) and Michael Westen from *Burn Notice* (2007-13) may have disputes with their superiors or question their governments' decisions, but their loyalty to a greater national cause is never placed in doubt. Jack Ryan can yell at the President for his costly mistakes in *Clear and Present Danger* (Phillip Noyce 1994) but viewers know it is because Ryan is the real patriot.

Female spies are almost always depicted as suspicious and unknowable. The stereotypical fear of female sexuality as untrustworthy takes on far greater importance in fictional espionage. As Estella Tincknell argues in her discussion of post-feminism in spy stories:

> female agents are almost always double-agents. Their untrustworthiness for the state is, then, systemically linked to their availability to the central male character and to the threat desire poses for him. This anxiety, although represented in the terms of the genre's overt concern with protecting national (or Western) power interests, can also be understood as a symptom of the threat femininity poses to the stability of masculinity. The female double-agent's "doubleness" is constituted in her apparent lack, her fragmented subjectivity, rather than the wholeness of masculinity. (101-2)

For Tincknell, the female double-agent is a crucial threat the male hero must overcome. She is a sexual lure that can lead to the hero's downfall, either by delivering him to the central villain or, worse yet, trapping him into mundane domesticity.

Salt avoids being cast as a sexual lure used to compromise a heroic male agent. But as a female spy, and a Russian sleeper agent with questionable loyalties, Salt is still over-determined by her "doubleness." Her lack of a true national identity or allegiance tempers her heroism by leaving her intentions ungrounded. Bond may be many things, but above all else he is always a symbol of unwavering British (and Western) fortitude. Even when Bond goes rogue and renounces his official status to pursue vengeance, as he does in both *Licence To Kill* (John Glen 1989) and *Quantum of Solace* (Marc Forster 2008), viewers know that his personal motives coincide with national concerns. There is never a possibility that Bond could be a traitor to his country even when he chooses to ignore direct orders. Bond embodies national stability and a conception of masculinity as steadfast and dependable. Salt, on the other hand, despite all of her actions, is still an enigma. There are no voice-overs or private moments that reveal Salt has converted to Western ideals. Jolie plays her as stoic and emotionally unrevealing of her state allegiances. There is only what Ben Child describes as "a stone-cold stare," while "playing both sides for fools" (¶ 6). The masculine Bond is iconic while the feminine Salt remains a question mark. Bond's perennial catchphrase, "Bond. James Bond" is a statement of firm identity while Salt's defining tagline is the question "Who is Salt?" Longstanding misogynistic stereotypes of women as unknowable, mysterious, and duplicitous compound Salt's status as an ungrounded heroine.

This disjuncture in stability between male and female spy identities parallels gendered preconceptions about nations themselves. Tremonte and Racioppi argue that Craig's hypermasculine body in *Casino Royale* reinforces the idea that national and international security is coded in gendered terms:

> Men [symbolically] are the main agents of the state and the international sys-
> tem of states; women, as some feminist scholarship has argued, are positioned
> as subordinate helpmeets and often embodied as symbols of the "nation." [...]
> National identities, such as Britishness, therefore have been constructed with-
> in the context of a binary gender/political order; they are differentiated for
> men and women and reflect and direct gender roles. Historically, men protect
> and defend the nation-state, if necessary sacrificing their own lives; women
> serve the nation through reproducing and socializing its children and sup-
> porting militarized men who may be away from home. (187)

The preconception is that men are protectors of the state and women are akin to the
state itself, a romanticized haven in need of protection. Bond is ultimately heroic
not just because of his exciting adventures, but because he is always a champion of
Western culture. The franchise is premised on the notion that in a complex and ever-
changing world Bond will remain an unflinching warrior against the forces of chaos
that seek to undermine the state. But Salt's status as a female spy with an unknown
political agenda denies her the level of iconic heroism afforded Bond. Salt's actions
save the world but we are never really certain of why. She has no allegiance to the West
and her heroism is coincidental to her own quest for vengeance.

Salt's unknown political and national concerns reflect the difficulty of presenting
a Cold War themed spy film in a post-Cold War era. Russia is no longer a clear ideological opposite to America, which opens up the possibility that Salt is free to become
an American hero, but it also implies an uncertain agenda. In Cold War era Bond
films like *From Russia with Love* (Terence Young 1963), it was clear that agent Tatiana
Romanova was acting under orders from her Russian superiors to entrap Bond. It was
also clear that Bond could assert British virility and defeat the Russians in large part
by romantically winning over Romanova. As a Russian female spy, Salt taps into the
convention of sexy communist fatales that could threaten Western democracy through seduction. In her discussion of Bond and Cold War sexual politics, Tricia Jenkins
describes the cultural fear that communism might literally seduce weak-willed men:
"heterosexual men who were 'slaves to their passions' could be easily duped by seductive women working for the communists" (312). Thus, Bond represented a counter
to this fear by not only being strong enough to resist seduction, but by being able to
seduce women away from communism. Salt has no American counterpart to convert
her to the West (even her husband is not American), nor is it exactly clear what she
wants for Russia. As a Cold War sleeper agent activated in a post-Cold War environment, Salt is the epitome of a liminal character. While Romanova had a clear
choice between Mother Russia and British Bond, Salt has no political choice to make.
Moreover, audiences knew they could not trust Romanova until Bond won her over,
but they could trust Bond. Viewers are never permitted this definitive trust with Salt;

as a double-agent she remains an enigma and there are no indications that she even has sides to choose from.

WHO IS EVELYN SALT?

According to the "binary gender/political" logic, only heroic male bodies are capable of protecting the state. Part of the success of Craig's version of Bond is the more realistic depiction of violence and the evidence of physical struggle marked on his body. Unlike earlier Bonds who rarely wrinkle their tuxedos, this Bond is constantly bruised, bloodied, and in need of time to heal. Bond, like the state itself, may be battered but never beaten. Conversely, while the real world settings of *Salt* ground the film in a realistic *mise-en-scène*, the action is pure fantasy. Salt's noticeably thin body never shows the signs of struggle. She dispatches hordes of enemies without breaking a sweat, engages in gun fights and jumps from moving cars with barely a scratch. Roger Ebert describes the action in *Salt* as "gloriously absurd. The Laws of physics seem to be suspended here the same way as in a Road Runner cartoon" (¶ 5). Lisa Purse points out that *Salt*, like science fiction and superhero films, provides "a space in which female physical power is permitted" (*Contemporary* 81). But where the fantastical settings of science fiction "underlines its [female physical power] real-world impossibility," in *Salt* "Jolie performs her powerful physicality in a relatively real-seeming rendering of New York; that is, a fictional universe that looks uncomfortably close to the real world" (ibid. 81). The use of fantastic settings for many action heroines is a type of containment strategy that implies women can only perform their heroic feats in the realm of fantasy. *Salt* blurs the lines of this containment by letting a heroine undertake astonishing acts without any lasting injury in an otherwise realistic setting. But in comparison to the new model of Bond that emphasizes his painful struggles as heroic perseverance, Salt's remarkable exploits and her ability to carry on when wounded seem less genuinely heroic. Salt's action is fun to cheer on, but it does not carry the same level of gravitas that the current version of Bond does.

While Jolie's Salt may not bear the physical injuries that Craig's Bond does, Salt does perform her action sequences in a far grittier way than most other action heroines do. Salt can be understood as liminal politically, caught between Russia and America, but she is also liminal in a sense that she straddles the conventional divide between female and male action heroes. The typical modern heroine may be violent but she rarely musses up her hair, let alone gets extremely bloody. The heroines' conventionally beautiful face, in particular, needs to stay attractive. This is notable in a film like *Aeon Flux* (Karyn Kusama 2005) in which "Aeon's face remains undamaged, undirtied, and carefully made-up; where injuries do happen they are minor and occur on other parts of the body" (Purse, "Return" 185). According to Purse, action films of the 2000s, including those starring Jolie, "re-imagine the traditional heroic qualities of toughness and determination in ways that uphold conventional notions of gender, emphasizing the female action hero's 'feminine' grace, dignity, and (well-maintained) appearance" (ibid. 190). Unlike most contemporary action heroines, *Salt* does not foreground Jolie's beauty at the expense of physical action. Salt may not need months of hospitalization to recover from a sustained beating and torture like Bond does in *Casino Royale*, but she does endure a brutal torture scene of her own at the beginning of the film, when her North Korean captors force oil down her throat. Likewise, near the end of *Salt*, we see the strain of her efforts on her blood-streaked face as she chokes Ted Winter to death with the chain she is shackled by. Audiences may not be ready to see a beautiful face like Jolie's bloody and swollen beyond recognition, but the film does mark its violence on her famous features, albeit strategically, in an effort to offer physical proof of her heroic efforts.

The question of the relative physical abuse marked on the bodies of Craig's Bond and Jolie's Salt may be the clearest example of culturally acceptable gender differences between the characters. Action film audiences expect to see the battered and beaten body of heroic men endure to defeat the villain. The iconic image of the badly wounded John McClane limping to the rescue on bloody feet in *Die Hard* (John McTiernan 1988) typifies the American model of masculinity as physically strong and resilient. This is the fantasy of masculinity that Craig's Bond taps into as he battles on despite the obvious damage done to his body. But audiences do not seem ready for the same type of realistic violence to be visited upon female heroines. Patriarchal notions about female vulnerability, and real world epidemics of violence against women, lead to an environment where excessive violence visible on a female body is unforgiveable in a way it is not for men. Moreover, action film violence carries with it a thinly veiled element of sexual assault that registers differently depending on the victim's gender. When naked men are tortured, like the way Bond is in *Casino Royale*, the sexualized threat is clear but the body endures and avoids penetration. A similar scene with a female as victim implies the possibility of rape, which is taboo in the fun fantasy of action movies. This difference explains *Salt*'s brief glimpses of torture versus the prolonged scenes of Bond being tortured. The challenges of creating a female equivalent of Bond are not restricted to issues of sexuality and trustworthiness, they also include navigating different gender expectations regarding acceptable levels of violence.

As an attempt to create a female version of Bond, *Salt* delivers on the thrills of action cinema and wisely avoids the gratuitous sexual exploits that are central to the masculinist Bond fantasy. On the surface of it, *Salt* seems to present a gender-neutral version of a superspy adventure. Anyone can identify with Salt's exploits and her personal motivation for revenge. But at a deeper level, the film is mired in misogynistic fears about women as untrustworthy, and grounded in preconceptions about female agents as duplicitous. *Salt* is a fun adventure film and the character of Salt is intriguing, complex, and infinitely capable without having to resort to sexuality.

And while all of these characteristics contribute to a progressive depiction of female heroism, the film's core premise limits Salt's ability to equal the larger heroic and cultural status of Bond. Salt may not be a Bond Girl but she is not really Bond either, at least not in the sense of being a cultural hero. If Salt is a female Bond, she is the Bond of the recent past rather than present. The retro Cold War politics of *Salt*, and the unrealistic nature of the action sequences, are more in line with a version of Bond as embodied by Roger Moore or Pierce Brosnan than the updated Bond of Craig. *Salt* is relatively more serious-minded than the Moore or Brosnan eras of Bond, but in a post-9/11 world even Bond has to treat espionage as more than just a series of fantastic action sequences. Salt's actions do save the world but her aloof nature and her lack of national identity makes the film feel like *just* a fun fantasy.

On the bright side, *Salt* was a blockbuster hit by any financial standard. While Salt may not yet have the cultural cache of Bond she was embraced as a desirable female alternative to him. And Salt certainly has the potential to become a heroine who stands for larger state concerns. The film ends with Salt's escape and her vow to hunt down other Russian sleeper agents. Salt could easily be set up in sequels as an agent of Western protection, an immigrant who embraces Western cultural values. The delay in producing a sequel has left the character of Salt as an enigma and the potential for a female-driven franchise in limbo. Even before the film was released, director Phillip Noyce talked about long-term plans for a series of *Salt* movies, but his subsequent departure from the project has stalled a studio commitment. Bond is a fantasy of ideal masculinity and Western heroism, and while Salt is fun escapism she may not yet be enough of an ideal archetype to really challenge the Bond dominated formula of feature film super-spies.

Section 6

JUDI DENCH'S TENURE AS M

CHAPTER 24

FROM MASCULINE MASTERMIND TO MATERNAL MARTYR

Judi Dench's M, *Skyfall*, and the Patriarchal Logic of the James Bond Films

Peter C. Kunze

When Judi Dench assumed the role of M in *GoldenEye* (Martin Campbell 1995), the response stateside varied widely from indifference to derision. Some critics like Roger Ebert (1995) noted Dench's arrival but did not remark on the casting decision, as if to suggest that it was a routine move one might expect for the first Bond film of the 1990s. Others offered more sexist and homophobic responses to the representation of a female M. Todd McCarthy of *Variety* called Dench's M an "iron maiden" (¶ 7), a term generally reserved for a torture device, whereas Peter Stack of the *San Francisco Chronicle* casually refers to her as a "butch-looking woman" (¶ 5). In *Time*, Richard Schickel harshly described Bond's new boss as having "a butch hairdo, a brusque Thatcherite manner and a license to kill with unkindness" (92). While none of these critiques demean Dench's acting ability, M's appearance and demeanor face scorn, insult, and backhanded praise. Collectively, these reviews illustrate, either in their ambivalence towards or petty snickering about M, the rise of postfeminism in contemporary Anglo-American popular culture. Postfeminist discourse believes the concerns of feminism are no longer relevant as women assume positions of power within the public and private spheres. One might think that the casting of a female M reflects greater gender equality in the Bond series and, more generally, in Hollywood film and society at large. Such gestures imply feminism has succeeded—but has it?

The latest Bond film, *Skyfall* (Sam Mendes 2012), marks Dench's exit from the franchise, therefore affording critics the opportunity to appraise her tenure as M. Focusing on her final performance, this chapter reads Dench's M through the lens of feminist critiques of postfeminist discourse and culture. While a female M gestures toward productive revision of the traditionally sexist franchise, the move ultimately fails to support a worldview where gender inequities are properly addressed. In an age where identity trumps ideology, a female M pays lip service to calls for greater representation while still perpetuating an ideology that, in the words of Tania Modleski, threatens to take us "back into a prefeminist world" (3). Through a close reading of *Skyfall*, this chapter challenges the progressivism of certain recent representations of women while demonstrating the patriarchal logic that persists in the so-called updated Bond films.

POSTFEMINISM AND ITS DISCONTENTS

Like feminism itself, postfeminism escapes easy definition. Rosalind Gill and Christina Scharff identify three different strains of postfeminism: postfeminism as "*epistemological break within feminism*" against the dominance of Anglo-American feminism, postfeminism as "*an historical shift after their height of Second Wave feminism*" that views feminism as passé or complete, and postfeminism as a "*backlash against feminism*" that romanticizes and longs for masculine dominance (3).[1] Modleski suggests postfeminism exuberantly declares its arrival, but "actually engag[es] in negating the critiques and undermining the goals of feminism" (3). Postfeminist, like postracialist discourse, announces false social progress as a conservative backlash against the radical potential of progressive politics. Angela McRobbie observes how "the new female subject is, despite her freedom, called upon to be silent, to withhold critique, to count as a modern sophisticated girl, or indeed withholding of critique is a condition of her freedom" (260). Yvonne Tasker and Diane Negra observe that while postfeminism emphasizes "educational and professional opportunities for women and girls; freedom of choice with respect to work, domesticity, and parenting; and physical and particularly sexual empowerment," it fails to explain the relationship between gender and power (2). Despite its inconsistencies, postfeminism remains seductive because of its individualist emphasis on personal choice and its pervasiveness across media (ibid. 2). While the ability of a female protagonist to select her own partner, career, and lifestyle may suggest the futility of contemporary feminism, her complicity in the power structures that subjugate herself and other women undermine the seemingly progressive ethos of the film.

While M may be a beneficiary of feminist progress in the workplace, the Bond films featuring Dench largely skirt gender issues inherent to a female authority figure supervising a largely male workforce. This oversight, or possibly even silencing of the issue, represents a postfeminist ethos in the recent Bond films. Postfeminism, as Tasker and Negra explain, concerns itself with the "'pastness' of feminisms, whether that supposed pastness is merely noted, mourned, or celebrated" (1). McRobbie contends postfeminism represents "the co-existence of neo-conservative values in relation to gender, sexuality and family life [...] with processes of liberalization in regard to choice and diversity in domestic, sexual and kinship relations" (255-6). These understandings limit postfeminism to concerns of personal identification, interpersonal relationships, and market participation. How might postfeminism play out in the professional world or even geopolitically? Over seven films, the gender of Dench's M becomes increasingly irrelevant as her position and mission objectives take precedent. M's focus on national security and the maintenance of geopolitical dominance supersedes her personal concerns. Her children are only alluded to in passing conversation and her husband is seen only once sleeping with his back turned; by *Skyfall*, the audience learns he has died without explanation. What matters in the world of Bond is not love, but sex, and not self, but country. M, as a representative of country, sacrifices any sense of self in favor of professional competence. This move has ramifications not only for how we understand women in this diegetic space, but perhaps how we discuss gender in film more generally.

ENTER JUDI DENCH

Primarily known as a stage actress, Dench made her first appearance as M in *GoldenEye*, and by her second film, *Tomorrow Never Dies* (Roger Spottiswoode 1997), she had won international acclaim as Queen Victoria in *Mrs. Brown* (John Madden 1997). Dench's casting was doubly interesting: on one hand, it is in the tradition of casting a seasoned, classically-trained British actor, and, on the other, it represents a crude modernization of the Bond franchise. When Dench's M first meets Bond and refers to him as a "relic of the Cold War," she speaks to him as a metonym for an aggressive, masculinized British nationalism and, by extension, the film series built around this persona. Dench's appearance attempts to revise the franchise's trademark sexism, where the Bond Girl represents submission and the female Bond villain embodies non-normative sexuality that is threatening to Bond. As Lisa Funnell has argued, "female villainy not only serves to strengthen Bond's heroic masculinity but also offers a perfect opportunity to demonize feminism as lesbian, deviant, threatening, monstrous, excessive, and other" ("Negotiating" 210). As neither sex kitten nor *femme fatale*, Dench's M challenges the series' reductive understanding of women, yet her role is neither wholly progressive nor conservative. Perhaps Dench's M may best be viewed as a feminist character operating in a postfeminist narrative. The diegesis certainly resists such alleged progressiveness, and by the conclusion of Dench's tenure in the series, it recuperates the gender normativity that has become characteristic of the franchise.

 GoldenEye introduces not only Dench as M, but Pierce Brosnan as the new Bond. Brosnan's Bond is characteristically attractive and debonair, and his humor is suggestive, even crass, delivered with a cheeky overtone that showcases his playful nature. M, however, is not wooed by Bond's tricks, and in their first encounter, the film ably navigates between traditional models of femininity and masculinity. In her analysis of *Working Girl* (Mike Nichols 1988), Tasker keenly observes that "advancement is presented as a form of masculinization" (*Working* 41). M draws upon masculinist metaphors to assuage any concern regarding her competency. "If you think I don't have the balls to send a man to his death," she warns Bond, "you're wrong." The metaphorical testicles move the character of M beyond male embodiment, and though Zukovsky mocks Bond for being supervised by a "lady," the franchise predominantly minimizes the relevance of M's gender. The question remains if such a move progressively eradicates any hesitancy about a female leader or conservatively obscures any of the real world challenges a female leader in this position may face. The nationalist agenda of the Bond franchise as a beacon of Britishness for the global stage suggests the latter, and the film may further be seen as postfeminist in its inattention to these nuances. Just as conservatives have ineffectively touted the alleged progress of "post-racialism" in the United States, the concept of a "postfeminist" workspace and nation in the Bond world echoes the thorny governance of the "Iron Lady," Margaret Thatcher, whose supposed symbolic triumph over sexism is marred by her reactionary social policies, aggressive foreign policy, and austere economic measures.

Tomorrow Never Dies finds M's authority in question as Admiral Roebuck claims she does not have the balls for the job. "Perhaps," she muses. "The advantage is I don't have to think with them all the time." Though not yet explicit, a maternal interpretation of her relationship with Bond is building as M shows concern for his well-being in the face of danger and possible nuclear annihilation. The audience sees the softer side of M again in *The World is Not Enough* (Michael Apted 1999), as her friend Sir Robert King becomes the target of an assassin. Reliant on her top agent, she strategically avoids admitting Bond's excellence: "He's the best we have, though I'd never tell him that." Bond's role in the death of an American agent in *Die Another Day* (Lee Tamahori 2002) shakes M's confidence in him, and the relationship between the two remains tense as Craig assumes the role in *Casino Royale* (Martin Campbell 2006).

As in Ian Fleming's book series, *Casino Royale* is a prequel and presents the origin story of Bond. He has just received his 00 status, and much to the dismay of M, Bond has blown up an embassy. After breaking into M's apartment—a move he repeats in *Skyfall*—Bond is advised to "take [his] ego out of the equation and judge the situation dispassionately." This decision to rewind the series to the moment that Bond is promoted demonstrates retroactive continuity, an approach commonly employed in comic books, in which the creative team modifies the existing storyline developed throughout the franchise as new lead actors take over the title character. Since all of these "Bonds" are the same character in the same universe, the setting of *Casino Royale* in the uncertain present and the inclusion of a female M noticeably disrupts any sense of narrative time or historical accuracy in the series. More importantly, Craig's assumption of the iconic lead role marks a turn towards a more serious and mysterious Bond, in defiance of the "campy persona made famous by his predecessors" (Funnell, "I Know" 455). This return to a more traditional model of masculinity, informed by violence, stoicism, and secrecy, speaks to a post-9/11 world where the "campy" Bond and the feminized/queered male figure in general is seen as a sign of weakness and where the enemy is no longer "on the map," as M says, but instead lurks "in the shadows." Like *The Dark Knight Rises* (Christopher Nolan 2012), *Skyfall* illustrates how state officials must go to extreme measures to protect the interests of their citizens in a post-9/11 world. This shift in national security efforts poses issues for social concerns such as feminism, where issues of gender equality get dismissed against the urgency of survival. While the importance of homeland security in protecting the safety of citizens cannot be negated, the hawkish discourse that accompanies these initiatives often marginalizes the concerns of social activism domestically. In *Skyfall*, this same rhetoric that validates M's persistence and potency counteracts any sense of progress we might find in the casting of a woman in the role. Ultimately, as Tasker notes, "images and narratives are more ambivalent and more evocative than [the 'progressive']" (*Working* 204).

M'S LAST STAND

In the opening sequence of *Skyfall*, M possesses a dispassionate focus that typifies her rejection of traditional feminine virtues that reduce the social understanding of women, including compassion, sensitivity, and emotion. Unfazed by the shooting of Ronson and Bond's appeals to assist his wounded colleague, M directs Bond and his fellow agent Eve Moneypenny to continue the pursuit of the stolen hard drive across rooftops, through the marketplace, and eventually on top of a moving train. M stares ahead with steely resolve, her hands flat on her desk, as her subordinates, most noticeably her assistant Tanner, look on in a mixture of respect for M and anxiety about the situation. With a choice of taking a shot or allowing Bond to continue the struggle with Patrice, M orders Moneypenny to shoot, even though it risks Bond's life and leads to his fall off the train into the water below. The news of Bond's injury causes M to spin away from her subordinates and stare out over the Thames River, but she shows no emotion; the London rain symbolizes the tears M must contain for Britain's fallen son. Typical of the fast-paced sequences that begin the Bond films, the opening of *Skyfall* reinforces the competency of both M and her top agent, though Bond's inability to stop Patrice, M's bad call, and Moneypenny's poor shot ultimately reveal the imperfections of these characters. It is this opposition—the mythic vulnerability and inevitable fallibility—that structures each character, and the flux between the two points informs the narrative as well as clears the path for Dench's exit from the franchise with her assuming the role of mother to Bond and martyr for Great Britain.

As I suggested earlier, the Bond films featuring Dench are often ambivalent about M's gender. In *Quantum of Solace* (Marc Forster 2008), Bond jokes that M "likes to think" she is his mother, but the only sign of such a symbolic relationship lies underneath M's exasperated scolding and Bond's boyish smirking. Otherwise, M demonstrates a focus and severity necessitated by her position. Her cold, calm demeanor sharply contrasts with the hyperbolic performance of femininity by Bond Girls, who often yield to Bond's seductive faculties to reward him with sexual favors he will accept and affection he will inevitably spurn. Unlike Moneypenny, M generally remains impervious to Bond's charm, and any sense of fondness towards him results from his proficiency rather than his personality. Nevertheless, the sheer age difference between Craig and Dench encourages viewers to see the relationship in terms of mother and son, and Silva underscores this reading in his efforts to manipulate Bond and exact revenge on his former boss.

The film also perpetuates the "M as mother" interpretation: her agents addressing her as "Ma'am" can almost be heard as "Mom," and when Silva bombs MI6 headquarters—her symbolic home—M must take charge to protect her subordinates/children. In a stunning visual, M reflects on events near the flag-draped coffins of her fallen employees. Though she does not cry, her blank stare suggests a level of sorrow, contemplativeness, and conviction evocative of the "stiff upper lip" demeanor that has become so characteristically British in the cultural lexicon. M may not be the classic British gentleman, but as a member of the women's liberation generation, she can hold her own in the workplace, even if it means adopting a traditionally masculine stoicism. Of course, the masculinization of women serves at best as a problematic example of equality.

The sheer power wielded by a silver-haired stoical woman points to a commentary on Queen Elizabeth II and, by extension, the state of the monarchy and what remains of the British Empire. For Paul Stock, the character of M in the Bond films represents "administrative England" in comparison to Bond's role as colonizer (224). Though M dismissed Bond and his nationalist machismo as a "relic of the Cold War," the intelligence service she runs has its origins in the early twentieth century and the beginning of the end of the Empire. Silva underscores this ongoing descent when he alternately taunts Bond with "You're still clinging to your faith in that old woman" and "England. Empire. MI6. You're living in a ruin as well, you just don't know it yet. At least here there are no old ladies giving orders." Of course the "old lady" alternately refers to M and the Queen. Bond, therefore, defends not only the integrity and mission of MI6, but both the imperial goals of Great Britain and the nation-building objectives of cultural products like the Bond franchise itself.

Silva unfortunately continues the odious cinematic convention of the queered villain, an apt figure to antagonize the hyper-heterosexual Bond, who is wholly absorbed in id-associated drives towards sex and violence. In a game of psychological warfare that Bond strives to resist, Silva caresses Bond's cheek and chest, perhaps hoping to inspire a homosexual panic that will agonize the restrained 007. Yet by flirting with Bond and referring to M as "Mother," Silva intricately navigates between roles as Bond's symbolic brother (as "children" of M and fellow agents) and a potential lover.

The complex eroticism of this interchange speaks not only to Silva's skill at psychological manipulation, but also to the fraught relationship he has with M that seems intensified by her gender and, therefore, the composite he forges of her as mother, boss, and betrayer.

Silva disturbs the psyche of the seemingly invincible M, ironically from within his holding cell. Initially M comports herself with indifference, referring to her former employee as "Mr. Silva" and insisting, "Soon your past will be as nonexistent as your future." When Silva tells her of what she allegedly did to him and then removes his prosthetic mandible and denture, M cannot help but look on in horror, even concern. (Noticeably Bond is unmoved by Silva's story.) M later admits to Bond she gave up Silva when he went rogue, yet this cold admission does not negate the fact that her vulnerability has been revealed and, in turn, the compassion she so often suppresses has made itself known.

The film continues to waver between vulnerability and infallibility, and this fluctuation makes it nuanced in its characterizations and necessitates close textual analysis. In a particularly revealing scene, M goes to testify before a government panel including her new supervisor Gareth Mallory, who has previously suggested she transition out of her current position; M sternly informs him she will leave when the job is done. During M's testimony, a minister berates her for being "almost single-handedly responsible" for the breach of security and loss of agent lives. The minister's gender and age deserve comment: a female minister further represents the increasing visibility of women in government, but as a noticeably younger woman than M, her scolding comes off as disrespectful and unrelenting. Furthermore, as Klaus Dodds notes, M's resistance to and resentment of the hearing effectively ages her (127). Any sense of progress regarding another female superior in the Bond world is undermined by Mallory's suggestion to the Minister that they hear from the witness, which implies the woman needs to stop talking so much—yet another gross female stereotype. M appreciates the opportunity and reiterates her belief that feeling safe and being safe are different states, and the nation-state in the current era is vulnerable to attacks from the shadows—a space, coincidentally, which yields figures like Bond and Silva. Rogue individuals rather than belligerent nation-states are Britain's greatest threat, which reinforces the film's nationalism and collectivism against vigilante individualism. Invoking Tennyson, M seems to reject a vision of oneself as sensitive and reflective, qualities that are often gendered feminine and consequently of little purpose to one in her position. Soon after, Silva and his men enter the room and attack. M stands up and stares her attacker in the eyes, ready to face her "son." Whether she does so as a representative of the dauntless Great Britain or as a "mother" seeking redemption for her "sins" is unclear, but certainly both readings warrant consideration. What becomes evident to M is her need to accept responsibility for fixing what has befallen her agency, even if it brings her harm. By situating Silva and Bond as her children, the film legitimates M's decision to pursue Silva personally—and ennobles her sacrifice. Personalizing the battle humanizes M, but it also casts her in a familiar, regressive manner as the selfless maternal figure.

Oddly, even though the film moves M into a more traditional female role of mother, it conversely makes her the first M to be a true action hero. In the film's climatic scene, M moves from wielding power behind a desk to taking action in the field. Escaping to Bond's family manor of Skyfall, M and Bond, with the help of the irascible Scottish groundskeeper Kincade, begin planning a counterassault against the advancing enemy. Of course the return to Skyfall is ripe with symbolism, and Bond bringing M to his home only reinforces the impression that she is a mother figure. M feigns interest in Bond's early life, but Bond knows M is aware of his past, to which she matter-of-factly observes, "Orphans always make the best recruits." Indeed M admits MI6 depends on a symbolically familial structure for its functioning—not only to encourage loyalty among members, but to sever ties between the agency and the world outside. At Skyfall, the drama of the family returns for Bond, thus Kincade, M, and Silva respectively take on roles as father, mother, and brother. In a struggle reminiscent of Cain and Abel, Bond and Silva's conflict is fraught with jealousy and the sin of fratricide seems the inevitable conclusion. M, in turn, will only find her redemption as head of MI6 and *de facto* mother figure at the hands of Silva—either in his death or her own.

The moment of reckoning comes in the chapel where Kincade and a bleeding M have fled. The symbolism of the location should not be lost on the viewer, of course, as it intensifies the scene's theatricality while underscoring the religious implications of martyrdom. With his teeth clenched in anger, Silva prepares to shoot M, but realizes she must pull the trigger and kill them both. M finally relents on her withholding of emotion, revealing her vulnerability as she whimpers in fear. The tension defuses, though, as Bond throws a knife into Silva's back, thereby killing him. Her attacker dead, M regains her composure and asks Bond what took him so long. Even though she has just been saved, she must repress any notions of her own vulnerability and maintain her administrative power over Bond. Staggering, M falls and Bond catches her. As the "mother" who allowed her children to perish under her watch, M must pay for her sins. She muses that it is too late to make a run for it: "I did get one thing right." Her valediction suggests remorse and a belief that her impending death may absolve her of her transgressions. In a pose reminiscent of Michelangelo's *Pietà* (1498-99), M dies in Bond's arms although here, of course, the son agonizes over his martyred mother. Bond reveals his own vulnerability and openly weeps for his fallen leader. M, who once threatened to send Bond to his death, dies trying to save him and her other "children," a sacrifice made all the holier by its parental overtones. By emphasizing M's role as surrogate mother to the orphaned Bond, her death shifts from being a minor casualty of national security efforts to an emotionally resonant personal tragedy.

CONCLUSION

In his review of *Skyfall*, Roger Ebert remarks Dench "is all but the co-star of the film, with a lot of screen time, poignant dialogue, and a character who is far more complex and sympathetic than we expect in this series" (¶ 5). Yet the substantial development in her character comes at a cost. Ultimately, Dench's portrayal of M foregrounds the necessity to distinguish between (post)feminist characters and (post)feminist narratives. While M certainly embodies a feminist ethos to the extent that she is a woman who garners control over a powerful government agency and holds her own against both male and female superiors in *Skyfall*, the thrust of the narrative remains decidedly conservative and, by extension, anti-feminist in its leanings, as it recuperates a traditional model of femininity to bid farewell to the current M and usher in the new (male) M, Gareth Mallory. In the process, it upholds a masculinized nationalism that underscores the virility and vitality of the Great Britain in a post-empire world, one that sees Great Britain greatly reduced in land holdings and monarchial power, yet still commanding considerable influence on the world stage. Therefore, while M's professional success underscores the film's postfeminist notion of second-wave feminism's contemporary irrelevance, *Skyfall* perpetuates a patriarchal logic that works against her persona and predilections to ultimately work her into a maternal model that redeems her not so much for her power and capabilities, but her willingness to sacrifice herself for her "sons" and her country. This (neo)conservative message serves both to undo the impression of progress promoted by Dench's introduction into the franchise as a strong, capable woman whose faculties are beyond her figure and her sexuality and instead work her into a mold that would yield maximum emotional response to her departure in its rather brilliant exploitation of melodramatic convention. Since M's final validation comes from her maternal martyrdom, her value as a woman and as a boss lies in her sacrifice to causes beyond the self and, in turn, deems any antagonism she faces as a woman as negligible. While this turn of events upsets the complexity of representational politics in the film, it nevertheless maintains the (neo) conservative bend that has made the Bond films box-office blockbusters for millions and perpetual headaches for the socially conscious and progressively minded. Even more disturbingly, it contributes to a postfeminist discourse that "can easily lead us back into our 'pregendered' past where there was only the universal subject—man" (Modleski 163).

NOTE

1   Emphasis in original.

CHAPTER 25

M, 007, AND THE CHALLENGE
OF FEMALE AUTHORITY IN
THE BOND FRANCHISE

Brian Patton

The enduring appeal of the Bond film franchise can be attributed in part to the staging of familiar elements that are recalled with each new entry in the series: the image of the man in the gun barrel, the ordering of a martini, the hero's self-identification as "Bond. James Bond," and so on. At the same time, the series has been continuously responding to the changing circumstances of the world it represents in fantasy form. From the outset, the films signaled a partial withdrawal from the Cold War context in which Ian Fleming's Bond was born, eschewing SMERSH, a Soviet counter-spy organization, in favor of SPECTRE, an unaligned haven for megalomaniacs. The films have since adjusted to the end of the Cold War, collapse of the Soviet Union, and emergence of global terrorism. Changes have also been required in the area of sexual politics, as the sexism of the Bond novels was woven into the fabric of the films they inspired, as the term "Bond Girl" clearly indicates. However, the series has also featured, albeit on its margins, a limited critique of its own prevailing sexist ethos. The arrival of Judi Dench in the role of M in *GoldenEye* (Martin Campbell 1995) was a remarkable innovation and arguably an explicit attempt to confront the Bond series' fraught relationship with feminism in the 1990s. This chapter maps the transformation of M as well as the Bond/M relationship at this crucial point in the series and considers Dench's M in relation to her novel and film predecessors. The introduction of a female M brings to the fore a new emphasis on female authority as the films work to situate Bond in a world where a woman in a position of power might be greeted with something other than contempt.

All representations of Bond, from Fleming's onward, are characterized by a tension between the agent's heroic individuality and his obedience to the government from whence his license to kill derives. The royal authority behind the famous license is never more than a dim presence in either the novel or films. Rather, the fullest visible embodiment of that licensing authority is M. Thus, the Bond/M nexus is the site where the shifting relationship between official authority and its secret agent has been most precisely defined, and where that inevitable tension comes most clearly into view, from the hints of unruliness apparent in *Dr. No* (Terence Young 1962) to the open conflict of *Licence to Kill* (John Glen 1989), in which M revokes Bond's "00" status, only to have him turn rogue and pursue his revenge plot anyways.

Fleming's M can be every bit as grumpy as his screen equivalents, but his absolute authority is never questioned, though his subordinates may inwardly rail against it. M bears a heavy burden of responsibility, and he does it well. He is firmly rooted in a pre-war world of Empire with a clear social distinction and deference to (masculine) authority, but it never occurs to Fleming's Bond that these institutions and values are un-hip or that his superior is a bit of a fuddy-duddy. 007's relationship with M is severely strained at times, but it is arguably the most important love relationship in Fleming's books. In *Diamonds Are Forever* (1956)[1] Bond explains to Tiffany Case that he is "almost married already. To a man. Name begins with M" (246). His greatest moments of satisfaction in his work come not from the royal or public recognition he avoids, but from seeing approval in "the weatherbeaten face he knew so well and which held so much of his loyalty" (*Moonraker* 1955, 15). The final chapter of *Moonraker* includes the following moment shared by the two men: "M gave one of the rare smiles that lit up his face with quick brightness and warmth. Bond smiled back. They understood the things that had to be left unsaid" (242). A similar moment occurs in the closing pages of *The Man with the Golden Gun* (1965), where Bond fails to conceal his pleasure at M's commendation (196). For Fleming's Bond, nobody does it better than M.

Fleming's novels and the early films are not far removed from each other: the first film, 1962's *Dr. No*, adapted Fleming's 1958 novel, and the next three films were based on books published in 1957 (*From Russia, with Love*), 1959 (*Goldfinger*), and 1961 (*Thunderball*). However, in bringing Fleming's 1950s spy to 1960s screens, producers felt the need to reconstitute this relationship by placing some ironic distance between Bond and his boss. In the films, Bond's meetings with his superior have largely been comic scenes whose function is to distance 007, the "hero of modernisation" (Bennett and Woollacott, *Bond* 19), from the office-bound establishment man who sends him on his missions. The basic pattern was set in *Dr. No*: in the outer office, Bond is flirtatious with Miss Moneypenny, M's secretary, who is complicit in the game. Their playful moment is interrupted by a buzzer and signal light above the leather-covered door, an abrupt summons into M's (Bernard Lee) inner sanctum. From the start, M's tone is marked by a rudeness apparently licensed by his authority. Bond stands before his superior's desk until he is told to sit. M replies to Bond's polite "Good evening, sir," with a brusque "It happens to be 3:00 a.m.," never looking up from some important bit of paper on which he is scribbling. In the space of minutes, M outlines the situation and informs Bond that he is booked on the next plane to Kingston at 7:00 a.m. Throughout the encounter, M's tone is authoritarian: he speaks in imperatives—"Take off your jacket. Give me your gun"—and feels no need to introduce a third man who enters carrying a new gun, a Walther PPK, which Bond does not want, but which M requires him to take in place of his preferred Beretta. When he is dismissed by M, Bond quietly retrieves his old gun, only to have his attempt thwarted by M—who, again, does not bother to look up as he calmly reasserts his authority. Back in Moneypenny's office, Bond opens his mouth to continue their flirtation, only to be silenced by the apparently omniscient M, who calls through on the intercom instructing her to "forget the usual repartee." In a final rebellious gesture before he departs, Bond hands the unwanted Walther to Moneypenny and bids her "*ciao.*"

Dr. No introduces a comic quality to the Bond/M encounter that becomes more prevalent over time. Connery's Bond is careful to appear respectful of M's authority, but he is inwardly playfully rebellious against it. The generational difference between the two men is emphasized, and viewers are invited to view that difference through the ironic perspective of the younger man, Bond, along with his co-conspirator, Moneypenny. By *Live and Let Die* (Guy Hamilton 1973), this comedy has come fully into view. Here, the initial meeting between Bond (Roger Moore) and M (Bernard Lee) unfolds as bedroom farce, with M arriving unannounced at Bond's apartment in the early morning, prompting Moneypenny to collude with 007 to spare M a vision of Bond's naked female companion—which might, presumably, finish the old fellow off. The scene flirts with the broad humor of *Carry On Spying* (Gerald Thomas 1964) or *The Benny Hill Show* (1955-89), and the joke unfolds at the expense of M and his implicitly delicate, Victorian sensibilities.

The defiance in these encounters between the government agent and his spymaster amplifies the insistent, heroic individuality of the literary 007, a quality that reveals something of the anachronistic nature of Fleming's portrait of a Cold War spy. As many have observed, Bond is something of a throwback to the early twentieth century world of the imperial thriller, a figure reminiscent of John Buchan's Richard Hannay or Sapper's Bulldog Drummond. Michael Denning and others have noted that the imperial thriller had its roots in the imperial adventure stories of the later nineteenth century, and it carried on the heroic tradition of those ripping yarns, featuring a lone man or an intrepid band of male adventurers whose secret doings change the course of history. In his study of the British spy thriller, Denning locates this recurring narrative pattern in a broad historical context. Borrowing from Georg Lukács' account of the modernist novel, Denning suggests that the spy novel offers a magical solution to our sense as individuals that we are enveloped by historical forces too great to control or even comprehend. The spy becomes "the link between the actions of an individual [...] and the world historical fate of nations and empires [...] The secret *agent* returns human *agency* to a world which seems less and less the product of human action" (*Cover* 14).[2] At the same time, "an incomprehensible political situation" is re-imagined in terms of "the ethical categories of masculine romance, the battle of hero and villain becoming one between Good and Evil, the forces of light and the forces of darkness" (14). The Bond mythos is rooted in the tradition of masculine romance. From time to time, Fleming explicitly equates his hero with England's dragon-slaying knight, St. George and the irony that is usually present at those moments does not quite undo the comparison. Bond battles monsters (Blofeld, Dr. No, Goldfinger) at nearly impossible odds, and he always wins.

However, Denning's yoking of the secret agent to the notion of "agency" also brings to light the potentially self-contradictory meaning of the word "agent." An agent may be an efficient cause, a prime mover, a significant and autonomous force in the world; this is clearly what Richard Hannay and his companions are, as is Bond in the guise of St. George. However, an agent may also be someone who acts on another's behalf ("agent" n.p.)—as a deputy, emissary or instrument of an absent figure who is the true bearer of power and authority, such as a real-estate agent, for instance. In short, the word "agent" may connote both *autonomy* as well as its effective opposite, *instrumentality*. For all his masculine heroics, even 007 cannot be entirely isolated from this threat of instrumentality—he is, after all, not only a secret agent, but a secret *servant*.

During a tense face-to-face encounter in *Casino Royale* (Martin Campbell 2006), M (Judi Dench) refers disparagingly to 007 (Daniel Craig) as "a blunt instrument," attempting to bring the unruly 007 to heel by emphasizing her authority over him. This phrase belongs to Fleming and points toward the author's own divided conception of his famous spy. Andrew Lycett suggests that Fleming had "not worked out whether Bond was a 'blunt instrument', as he had often claimed, or a mythical hero" (402). Fleming also described his intention to create "an ordinary character to whom extraordinary things happen," rather than "a paragon or a freak. I wanted him to be an entirely anonymous instrument and let the action of the book carry him along" (qtd. in Fishman 13). It is not surprising, then, that metaphors suggesting the instrumentality of her Majesty's secret servant recur in Fleming's novels. In the climactic scene of *You Only Live Twice* (1964), Bond's arch-enemy Blofeld taunts him with the accusation that he is "a common thug, a blunt instrument wielded by dolts in high places" (246). Related passages from other novels indicate that Blofeld's insult is not entirely unfounded. In *The Man with the Golden Gun* (1965), M thinks, "James Bond, if aimed straight at a known target [...] was a supremely effective firing piece" (26). Earlier, in *From Russia, with Love*, Fleming's narrator describes M's telephone summons as "the signal that had fired him, like a loaded projectile, across the world to some distant target of M's choosing" (134). The phallic simile is particularly apt in this case, since Bond is about to be dispatched to Istanbul "to pimp for England" (148)—this is his own sardonic description of his assignment, which involves seducing and escorting a Russian agent who has supposedly fallen in love with him and is willing to turn over a coveted Soviet cypher machine if Bond accompanies her. It is clearly

M who is in possession of the phallus here—he is the big gun who fires the projectile Bond across the world. As if to underscore the point, as Bond departs, M remarks, "It's up to you to see that you *do* come up to her expectations" (143). Bond is a hero of romance, certainly, but his individual agency is always under pressure from the state authority that directs and licenses his actions, an authority represented throughout the series by M.

This phallic contest, which structures both the novels and the films, becomes complicated with the arrival of a woman, Dame Judi Dench, in the role of M beginning with 1995's *GoldenEye*. Dench enters the revived franchise—on hiatus since 1989 and also featuring a new actor, Pierce Brosnan, in the lead role—unable to fit into the established masculine dynamic in any of its forms (father/son, headmaster/schoolboy) and threatening to loosen state authority from its familiar, masculine moorings. Initially hostile to the sexist ethos that has always been a defining feature of the series, Dench's M is a new figure of modernization and feminist critique whose presence reveals an attempt to accomplish a very difficult end: to balance continuity with change and secure a place for credible female authority within the insistently masculine mythos of Bond.

At the time of *GoldenEye*'s release, much was made of the casting of a woman, and a highly regarded actor, in the role of Bond's superior, and the filmmakers followed through with a deeply ambivalent attempt to address some well-founded feminist concerns, most notably by having Dench's M blast Bond as a "sexist, misogynist dinosaur" in their first private meeting. *GoldenEye*'s explicit condemnation of Bond's sexism is one of several features intended to bring the franchise into a more comfortable alignment with the contemporary world. The film self-consciously looks backward to the series' history, while also stressing its own novelty and currency. It begins in familiar territory with an expected cold opening, but the scene's spectacular quality signals the filmmakers' acknowledgment that the action-film game has intensified in the six years since *Licence to Kill* was released: Bond bungee-jumps his way into a Soviet chemical weapons facility, causes some impressive mayhem, and makes an impossible mid-air leap from a motorcycle to an airplane en route back to England.

A cluster of early scenes suggests a new interest in turning a critical eye on the series' uneasy relationship with feminism, but the resulting message is mixed at best. In the sequence immediately following the credits, Bond, behind the wheel of an Aston Martin DB5, tells a woman sent to evaluate him that he has "no problem with female authority," but his words are heavily ironic, and there is little indication that her authority poses any challenge to his own. Her evaluation of him gives way to his seduction of her: "James, you're incorrigible. What am I going to do with you?" Variations on this question have been posed repeatedly in the series, and the answer is well known. Arguably more interesting, in terms of this ambivalent attempt at feminist critique, is a conversation between Bond and Moneypenny, where their anticipated flirtation takes an unaccustomed turn—into a joking suggestion by Moneypenny that Bond's conduct "could qualify as sexual harassment." The remark is unmistakably ironic: the penalty, she adds, is that "someday you have to make good on your innuendoes." Still, the phrase is a remarkable one to hear in a Bond film, an indication, Tara Brabazon suggests, that "the power imbalance between them is narrowing" (494). Perhaps less cause for optimism is afforded, however, by the "playful" workplace harassment perpetrated by the considerably less suave Boris Grishenko on Natalya Simonova. The two are computer programmers at an isolated Russian space weapons control center whose relationship is characterized by adolescent, sexist pranks and comments on his part, and a mixture of patient indulgence and mild irritation on hers.

The introduction of Dench's M follows these scenes, which serve to establish a context of feminist critique, however partial—but the explicit critique voiced by M herself is also muddled in that it cannot be extricated from the film's ambivalent representation of other striking manifestations of change that invite a mixed—or openly negative—response. Of all the film's innovations, surely the casting of a woman as Bond's superior is the most dramatic, and its strongest claim to having embraced, if only tentatively, a more progressive stance with respect to women. When Russian gangster Valentin Zukovsky taunts Bond, he suggests that, in the modern world, 007 is an anachronism and the British Secret Service is poised somewhere between irrelevance and absurdity—adding, to his minions' amusement, "I hear the new M is a lady." Turning a spotlight on her gender, Zukovsky implies that the eccentricity of a "lady" M is symptomatic of a more general malaise at MI6, and his view is shared to a significant degree by Bond himself. Significantly, though, M's newness resides not only in her being a woman, but in her being a representative of the increasing bureaucratization of the secret service, in which clueless desk-jockeys now wield authority over knowledgeable and competent field agents such as 007. Paul Stock contends that the introduction of Dench is arguably less remarkable for the fact of her being a woman than for the character's make-over into "the evil queen of numbers," a bean-counting bureaucrat no longer bound in any obvious way to the pre-war world of the Empire. Gone is the old imperial flavor of "Universal Exports"; in its place is the new, hyper-modern SIS headquarters at Vauxhall Cross. Where M's office had always been a miniature naval museum—"a cluttered antique shop, and heart of Empire" (226), in Stock's words—it is now anonymously modern. "The Admiral," he concludes, "[has] been replaced by an accountant" (226).

Owing to M's close association with a new order of accountancy, statistics, and inexpert "experts," the obvious hostility that greets her in her introductory scenes cannot be attributed exclusively, or even primarily, to her being a woman in a position of authority in the traditionally male-dominated world of espionage and counter-terrorism. What might otherwise be read as mere antifeminist resentment is instead mingled with a resistance to a dangerous, creeping bureaucratization. The first encounter between Brosnan's Bond and Dench's M bears some similarity to that of Connery's and Lee's in *Dr. No* in its pairing of an annoyed, older authority figure with a subordinate who is not entirely so. However, the differences, beginning with M's gender, are noteworthy: the encounter takes place not in M's private office but in an MI6 situation room whose other occupants, save one woman glimpsed briefly in the back of one shot, are male, and M must face the barely submerged disapproval of not one man but a like-minded pair, Bond and Bill Tanner, while other men in the room listen with clear interest. Also, M, though officially at the helm, is new on the job, not yet well established, and associated with a suspect new order at MI6 of which neither of these seasoned agents approves. The narrative form undermines her as well: her entrance into the film is cued by Tanner's disparaging reference not only to "the evil Queen of numbers," but also to her having misjudged in not allowing Bond to play a "hunch" that turned out to be correct. She enters the room as Tanner speaks, out of clear view, and is revealed to Tanner and the film's viewers at the same moment, when Bond's subtle throat-clearing provides a late warning as to her presence—so the audience is invited to share with Bond some pleasure in the embarrassing moment. The one person left out of the conspiratorial circle is the stone-faced M. Tanner, slightly disheveled, his collar open and tie askew, looks like a discomfited schoolboy, and the dialogue casts him as such and her as the humorless teacher who has overheard what the children say when she steps out of the classroom: "You were saying?" is Dench's inauspicious first line of dialogue as M. Tanner sputters an incoherent reply, to which M responds, "Good, because if I want sarcasm, Mister Tanner, I'll talk to my children, thank you very much." This is authority, but of the sort that demands obedience in the absence of respect.

The antipathy that marks Bond's exchanges with M is barely suppressed in this first scene and erupts during their private conversation shortly thereafter. M voices both Bond's objection to her—that she is "an accountant, a bean-counter, more interested in my numbers than your instincts"—and hers to him: that he is, among other things, a "sexist, misogynist dinosaur." Her accusation asserts a hitherto unspoken feminist interpretation of the hostile atmosphere surrounding her at MI6, shifting attention from her offending association with "numbers" to the specifically gendered nature of the epithet "evil queen." While there is much evidence to support her interpretation, though, it is not one that the film itself is keen to sustain. After all, he is James Bond; his hunches are proved correct and her statistical analyses are not. A simple camera movement in their first scene together subtly but clearly indicates the film's affirmation of Bond as the necessary masculine hero in a troubled world, regardless of developments in either feminism or statistical analysis: as GoldenEye's electro-magnetic pulse is released and the surveillance screen goes blank, a shallow-focus close-up of M's concerned face gives way, via a pan right and an upward tilt that gradually moves her down and out of the frame, to a close-up of Bond, front and center. The diagonal movement is necessitated by Brosnan's greater stature, but it also conveys Bond's greater importance in the world of the film. Having registered her complaint, M bows out after these two scenes. The battle and the victory will be his, and the reward—in the form of another Bond girl, Natalya Simonova—will confirm once again that the "boyish charm" disdained by M is better appreciated by younger women.

Dench's role in *GoldenEye* as the new M—the "lady" M—is a thankless one that carries the burden of innovation in a series with over three decades' worth of beloved tradition. Brosnan was, of course, every bit as new to the series as Dench at the time of the film's release, but he wears the tuxedoes, wields the weapons, and espouses the traditional values of masculine heroism with an ease that she cannot match in her performance of her role. The M template is less accommodating to her than the Bond one is to him. Where Brosnan can prompt memories of his precursors, from Connery through Dalton, the unsmiling M recalls less favorable figures from the past: the aberrant female villains Rosa Klebb and Irma Bunt. Lisa Funnell's description of those characters as "short, stocky, middle-aged white women who are conservatively dressed and appear androgynous in their films," with their hair "cut short to emphasize age over aesthetics" ("Negotiating" 203) might well be applied to Dench's M in her debut.

Fortunately, none of Dench's six subsequent appearances in the series cast her quite so firmly in the trying role of the standard-bearer for innovation. The Bond/M tension remains, as it must, but her second film, *Tomorrow Never Dies* (Roger Spottiswoode 1997), aligned her more closely with 007 in opposition to the clueless button-pushers, represented in this film by Admiral Roebuck, and that pattern has generally repeated since. When the series was effectively restarted in 2006 with *Casino Royale*, Dench's M became the primary link between the old continuity and the new, and our first sight of her in that film is of a furious woman storming through the tall doorway of an elegant "Committee Room" in Whitehall where some unnamed committee ("a bunch of self-righteous, arse-covering prigs," as M describes them) has apparently hauled her onto the carpet because one of her agents, Bond (Daniel Craig), has just killed a man and set off an explosion in a foreign embassy. Dench's final film in the series, *Skyfall* (Sam Mendes 2012) is nearly as much hers as it is Craig's, and it presents her as a venerable figure of authority—not only respected, but loved, especially by Bond, now explicitly cast in the role of surrogate son. This maternal role—embodying a wholly feminine form of authority—is paired with those of unlikely action hero, as she finds herself in the midst of one fire fight after another, and also spokesperson for the nation, as she delivers an eloquent defense of the shadowy work of the SIS in a post-imperial England. An odd little table ornament, a Royal Doulton bulldog draped in the Union flag, is the emblem of Churchillian resolve she bequeaths to Bond after her death, and which he recognizes as her directive to keep calm and carry on.

If the promises of this most recent film are kept, he will carry on in a world that has restored many of the familiar landmarks jettisoned from the past few entries in the series, including Q and Moneypenny, who begins the film at Bond's side as a field agent and ends it situated behind a secretarial desk outside the office of the new M, Gareth Mallory. The adjoining door, with its leather padding, is immediately recognizable as a replica of the one Sean Connery and subsequent Bonds walked through en route to the old-fashioned, masculine sanctum of M prior to the innovations of *GoldenEye*— and that office has also been carefully restored, down to the wall sconces, fireplace, floor globe, and a naval painting that recalls Trafalgar and Britain's days as a great world power. Outside the story world, Bond's accentuated use of the title "M" in the film's final moment is a revelation; within that world, it signals his warm acceptance of his new superior, a former SAS man still sporting an arm sling after being hit by a bullet while trying to protect his predecessor. The film's penultimate shot depicts the two men standing, facing each other across M's old-fashioned wooden desk with the old naval painting clearly visible in the background. After some brief, friendly banter that brings a rare smile to Bond's face, M turns to business, dropping a folder marked "top secret" on the desk as he says, "So, 007, lots to be done. Are you ready to go back to work?" Bond replies, his face now conveying a respectful seriousness, "With pleasure... M. With pleasure," as the familiar 007 theme introduces the end credits. The moment could not be more different from the initial encounters between Brosnan's Bond and Dench's M in *GoldenEye*. Rather, the tone is reminiscent of a Fleming portrait of the spy with his spymaster: "M gave one of the rare smiles that lit up his face with quick brightness and warmth. Bond smiled back. They understood the things that had to be left unsaid" (*Moonraker* 242). Among the things left unsaid in the final scene of *Skyfall* is that it marks the end of an extended experiment testing the possibility of a woman exercising authority over a man whose exploits embody a valued fantasy of masculine heroism and autonomy. The gradual revelations of these final scenes, capped by Bond's identifying his new, male superior as "M" in the film's final line, have the effect of bringing us back to a treasured, familiar, and unequivocally masculine place.

NOTES

1   References are from the novels published by Penguin.
2   Emphasis in original.

CHAPTER 26

"M" (O)THERING

Female Representation of Age and Power in James Bond

Lori Parks

With the release of *Casino Royale* (Martin Campbell 2006), the Bond franchise has been effectively rebooted and the audience has been introduced to a darker and grittier Bond (Daniel Craig) who has just earned his 00 status. Bond's first mission is to investigate Le Chiffre, a banker for terrorists, and this leads to their confrontation in a high stakes poker game in Montenegro. During this time, Bond engages in a love affair with Vesper Lynd who has been sent to oversee the money bankrolling Bond's mission. The death of Lynd leads Bond into his next assignment in *Quantum of Solace* (Marc Forster 2008) where, fueled by anger at the betrayal of Lynd, he attempts to track down the mastermind behind Mr. White's sinister organization.

Unlike Lynd, Judi Dench's M is a constant figure in Bond's life and her role offers an interesting contrast to the Bond Girl character. As a strong-willed matriarch, she provides a complex representation of female authority in a franchise that is known for emphasizing the sexuality of its female characters. Although she is older and occupies a position of power, her authority is challenged in *Skyfall* (Sam Mendes 2012) by Gareth Mallory, the new Chairman of the Intelligence and Security Committee. It is later revealed that the villain, Silva, has a personal vendetta against M and she is presented as a surrogate mother over whom Bond and Silva fight. M transitions from a secondary/supportive character in the earlier films into an important site of psychological and social conflict by *Skyfall*.

This chapter seeks to examine the roles and representations of women within the context of Bond's origin story in the reboot trilogy and explore how the female body is defined in the new framework of the Bond franchise. I am most interested in exploring the intersection of age and gender. I will discuss how the representation of M, an aging woman, contrasts with the typical representation of the Bond Girl and how the introduction of Eve Moneypenny as an inexperienced agent who trades fieldwork for a desk job influences the perception of Dench's M.

THE WOMEN OF BOND

The Bond film universe taps into a prevalent theme within Western culture: the ongoing relationship between pleasure and violence through the objectification of the female body. The films have a 50-year history of spectacular staging that draws on a specific formula of espionage, technology and gadgetry, fast cars, memorable villains, and the protagonist Bond who is celebrated for his aggressive heterosexual masculinity and power. Bond women are instrumental to the momentum of the storyline. There are always multiple attractive female characters that tempt, support, and hinder Bond over the course of his missions. Steven Woodward argues that Bond's relationships are central to the creation of meaning, because "both Bond and his adversary have been carefully maintained as symbols rather than individuals, symbols that take their meaning from their relationship with each other rather than from any iconic or indexical ground of truth" (174). Not only is Bond symbolic, but so too are the women who interact with him. They are always presented superficially with their position being a reflection of their physical attributes. Thus, women are often portrayed as disposable characters in the franchise.

In his discussion of sex and sexuality in the Bond films, Jeremy Black posits that Bond's copulation with women functions as a tipping point in the narrative. It not only helps to guarantee the success of his missions but also works to validate his heroism by confirming his phallic masculinity (Black 109). However, Lisa Funnell makes an important distinction between the Bond Girl and other female characters:

> The term Bond Girl refers to a particular female character type of the Bond
> film. She is a non-recurring character and lead female protagonist, central to
> the plot of the film and instrumental to the mission of James Bond. However,
> the defining feature of the Bond Girl is the strong, intimate, and intense rela-
> tionship she builds with Bond. ("From English" 63)

Although Bond (sexually) interacts with a variety of women, both good and bad, only one can be considered the Bond Girl. The others can be subdivided into other categories such as the Bond Girl Villain, secondary women, Moneypenny, and M.

Attractive female characters are central to the formation of the Bond fantasy world where the Bond Girl is a pivotal figure in the narrative and the secondary women contribute to the overall *mise-en-scène* of the film. In an unforgettable scene from *Dr. No* (Terence Young 1962), the viewer is presented with an exotic island where Bond first glimpses Honey Ryder, the original Bond Girl played by Ursula Andress, rising out of the surf in a white bikini. Ryder asks Bond: "What are you doing here? Looking for shells?" Bond replies with: "No, I'm just looking." Between the lingering camera on her body and the dialogue between Bond and Ryder, this scene epitomizes the role of the Bond Girl who functions as a mainstay of the series along with the attending issues of gender and power through "the gaze." This iconic scene is replayed again in *Die Another Day* (Lee Tamahori 2002), this time with Jinx emerging out of the water wearing a similarly styled orange bikini as a *homage* to *Dr. No*.

Laura Mulvey has notably explored the gaze and its significance in film studies. Mulvey draws on Freud's reference to the infantile, in particular the notion of sco-pophilia (the pleasure one experiences by looking at other people's bodies as erotic objects), and applies it to the pleasure of viewing a film. The darkness of the theater creates a voyeuristic viewing situation where one can look without being seen by the figures on the screen or the other viewers in the audience. Mulvey argues, "in their traditional exhibitionist role women are simultaneously looked at and displayed, with their appearance coded for strong visual and erotic impact so that they can be said to connote *to-be-looked-at-ness*" ("Visual" 837). This notion draws upon the way that film can both naturalize and manipulate through the gaze. For Mulvey, there is a "triple gaze" from the camera, the spectator, and the gaze between the characters within the film. In addition, narrative and editing work to reinforce an active male perspective as owner of the gaze. From that iconic moment on the beach, there is an overt nod to the gaze as an active and powerful form of exchange between Bond and the women he interacts with in the films. This interaction further reflects Mulvey's notion of the gaze by the implied male perspective of the audience as they actively look along with Bond.

The casting of a female M is an interesting contrast to the Bond Girl and the stereo-typical treatment of periphery females in the films. Dench was featured in *GoldenEye* (Martin Campbell 1995) and her character quickly makes a strong impression by asserting that she regards Bond as little more than a "relic of the Cold War." As an older female in a powerful position, M is able to subvert the stereotypes associated with the "aging female" who is often considered "sick, sexless, uninvolved except for church work, and alone" (Payne and Whittington 488). Instead, M is presented as a competent professional woman who is the keeper of state secrets and holds the lives of many in her hands. She must make decisions that could potentially have major ramifications, not just for her agents, but for her country and its global position. The viewer does not question her ability to make the difficult decisions that are often at the expense of one of her agents. Through the characterization of Dench's M, the franchise offers an alternative representation of female identity that is not subject to the "triple gaze."

REVISIONING FEMALE/FEMININE CHARACTERS

In *Casino Royale*, M must contend with a new and more corporeal Bond, who exudes a chaotic, carnal, and barely controllable presence. Colleen M. Tremonte and Linda

Racioppi argue that it is through the "hypervisibility of Bond's body—in motion, specularised, under threat [...that] helps reinforce the role of masculinity in the international and gender orders" (185). Craig's Bond has an edge that is still discernable when he is wearing his tuxedo. Instead of gadgetry he uses his fists and the sheer physicality of his body. And yet, he seems to defy many of the characteristics that have long defined the role. In one scene, his body is objectified as he rises out of the sea, using the iconography associated with the Bond Girl. This body is symbolic of a masculine ideal and a prelude to more successful action for the benefit of Britain. Lisa Funnell makes an interesting argument for Bond as a hybrid of both Bond and Bond Girl. She asserts that

> Craig's Bond [is] youthful, spectacular, and feminized relative to the gaze through the passive positioning of his exposed muscular body in scenes where he is disengaged from physical activity. Moreover, through intertextual referencing of renowned Bond Girl iconography, exemplified through Bond's double emergence from the sea, Craig's Bond is positioned as a visual spectacle and aligned with the Bond Girl character type rather than with his Bond predecessors in the filmic franchise. ("I Know" 456)

Character hybridity extends beyond Bond to Lynd, who is presented as a questionable ally. She does not easily fit within the past models of Bond Girls. She represents the British Treasury and as such has some control over Bond through the purse strings ("I'm the money"). Tremonte and Racioppi suggest that the women in *Casino Royale*, much like those who came before them in the franchise, "remain 'out of place' in relationship to the international security and gender orders and still need to be 'put in place' by Bond" (188).

Lynd is "out of place" because her allegiance is split between Bond and another man; as a result, she cannot entirely be considered a Bond Girl. She works as a double-agent for Quantum, a secret villainous organization, in order to secure the release of her lover, Yusef Kabira. As it turns out, Kabira is a member of Quantum who manipulates women with valuable intelligence connections. This renders Lynd more of a *femme fatale* than a devious villain or henchperson who willingly acts in service of the villain. As Elisabeth Bronfen astutely points out:

> To focus on the *femme fatale*, of course, also means introducing the question of gender difference into a discussion of tragic sensibility, in the sense that, while she comes to acknowledge her responsibility for her fate, the hero she involves in her transgressive plot is characterized by the exact opposite attitude, namely, a desire to stave off knowledge of his own fallibility at all costs. (105)

At the end of *Casino Royale* Bond resigns from the service to start a life with Lynd. During a phone call with M, he learns that the government money has not been returned and believes that Lynd has betrayed him. Bond tracks her down and engages in a dramatic gun fight with a group of armed men. During this encounter, Lynd becomes trapped in an elevator and ultimately makes the choice to not be saved by Bond; by drowning, Lynd takes personal responsibility for her betrayal of Bond and her country. As a *femme fatale*-Bond Girl hybrid, Lynd's suicide serves a key narrative purpose: it inspires Bond to recommit to his job as he channels his emotions towards attacking the next task at hand. Although Bond is clearly bitter towards Lynd, remarking that "the bitch is dead," M serves as a voice of reason when she explains to Bond that Lynd "must have known she was going to her death." It is M who recognizes Lynd's sacrifice within her betrayal.

Much like Bond and the Bond Girl who are revisioned in the Craig era, M is also reconceptualized as a character. This is most interesting given the fact that Dench continues on in the role. In the Craig era, M has her authority undercut numerous times over the course of three films. Bond breaks into her home in *Casino Royale* and hacks into her personal computer in his quest to pursue his mission at all costs, despite her directives. M is also depicted on a few occasions in a more intimate space: she is presented in bed with a man who is presumably her husband, and another time is interrupted by the office as she readies for a bath. One could argue that these scenes work to humanize M, offering viewers the impression that she has a life beyond MI6; the Craig era, after all, presents the deepest and most earnest depictions of Bond. On the other hand, there has never been this level of personal revelation with her predecessors. The viewer's knowledge of this figure of authority is through the leather-padded door with Moneypenny overseeing external access to this inner sanctum. The bath scene has long been a visual trope for representing the female nude in art and became especially popular in the nineteenth century as a subject that reflected modern life through the ordinary or mundane. It is also voyeuristic as it presents the subject at their most vulnerable and private. Moreover, bedrooms in Bond films are typically spaces where his seduction plays out. These intimate scenes focused on M are a reflection of the shifting power dynamics between age and gender, which culminate in *Skyfall*.

M as a figure of power is tenuous in the Craig era. This becomes explicit in *Skyfall* when her credibility and ability to command MI6 comes under scrutiny. The theme of aging and power is played out on the bodies of M and Bond. The significance of these personal scenes is revealed by the way they contrast with Mallory's backstory. Monneypenny defends Mallory to Bond by alluding to his past as something that makes him more than simply a bureaucrat. His past is not personal in the context of interior spaces and bodily relationships, but instead serves to reinforce his ability to be a credible leader. Moments like these also reference the direction that this reboot is moving towards: traditional gender roles. Much like Lynd, M is transformed into a tragic figure that has to die in order for Bond to reach his full potential as 007. This is a form of Othering that has an impact on establishing male identity and highlights the underlying fear of becoming Othered through age and loss of authority within the social structure. This is something that is highlighted in the "mothering" of M as her past (in the form of Silva) literally collides with the present (Bond) and she becomes the casualty—the body on which this is played out on. M is a complex figure that reflects the Bond Girl trope in that she and Bond share a close and emotional relationship; this is especially evident in *Skyfall* where she becomes the locus of the power struggle between Bond and Silva. M's fate highlights the instability of these various roles and their impact on her position as an older woman in power. *Skyfall* becomes a collision of gender, her professional position, and the choices she has made and must make, along with the secrets she keeps.

"TAKE THE BLOODY SHOT!"

The opening of *Skyfall* thrusts the viewer in the midst of a dynamic chase scene that ultimately has Bond on top of a moving train, fighting against an opponent as he attempts to retrieve an important hard drive loaded with a list of covert agents. This sequence is intercut with scenes of another agent, Moneypenny, who is also in pursuit. M is monitoring from a control room in Britain and making decisions from a limited perspective based on Moneypenny's reporting. The view switches between the dynamic space of action and the institutionalized space that M occupies. M's command for Moneypenny to shoot even though it is not a clean shot leads to Bond's "death" and the subsequent failure to secure the hard drive. It also sets into motion overarching themes focused on age, power, and the maternal figure.

In modern society power is enacted through the body. Michel Foucault argues that the way we understand our bodies is through a series of disciplinary practices that socially categorize bodies and place them in hierarchal distinctions. For Foucault, the body occupies a central place in the historical configuration of power, knowledge, and society. His analysis highlights the location of the body within a political field of power relations, and, in particular institutions, that seek to discipline the body and thus render it "docile" and ultimately productive and economically useful. What defines Foucault's work is the focus on the socially constructed nature of the body as it is lived, and its malleability because of the power/knowledge relationship (*Discipline* 136). In their assessment of the construction of female politicians in the European media, Iñaki Garcia-Blanco and Karin Wahl-Jorgensen note:

> The representation of women in the highest political offices is not only a
> matter of political equality but also relevant to the general pursuit of a more

egalitarian society. The low presence of women in positions of political power demonstrates the persistence of patriarchal power, perpetuating the secondary political role to which women have traditionally been relegated. Despite significant gains made in recent decades, gender still remains an issue when it comes to standing for office or being appointed to official positions. (422)

Regardless of capability and positional gains within the societal hierarchy of power, the female is still connected to her gender in a way that the male is not. In *Skyfall*, M is confronted with a series of cyber invasions and the demolition of the MI6 headquarters that leads to a challenge of her authority by Mallory who is gunning for her position. Mallory admonishes: "Three months ago, you lost the computer drive containing the identity of almost every NATO agent embedded in terrorist organizations across the globe. A list which, in the eyes of our allies, never existed. So if you'll forgive me, I think you know why you're here." Dench's M radiates an offended dignity as she refuses to explain herself or apologize except when she absolutely must. In one instance when it is suggested that she should get out of the game she angrily replies, "Oh, to *hell* with dignity! I'll leave when the job's done!"

The dualist legacies of the past have been influential though limiting in the definition of the body. In her discussion of identity in the western imagination, Margrit Shildrick writes, "To be a self is above all to be distinguished from the other, to be ordered and discrete, secure *within* the well-defined boundaries of the body rather than actually being the body" (50). The body is always socially formed and located. What it is to be a man or woman is a social definition, since even physiology is mediated by culture. One could argue that the aging body is subject to its own kind of disciplined activity quite separate from other aspects of adulthood. Thus, to age successfully can become a full-time job central to one's identity, and for the female, who is already often viewed through her body, the female becomes the embodiment of aging. As Susan Sontag has argued, there is a "double standard of aging," where women suffer scorn and exclusion as they age, "a humiliating process of gradual sexual disqualification" (102). Richard Leppert discusses the importance of the gaze: "The sense of sight is a fundamental means by which human beings attempt both to explain and to gain control of the reality in which they find themselves" (16). The power inherent in sight impacts how one is perceived as viable in powerful positions or weak and unproductive. M is typically presented in a neutral palette. There is even less variation in *Skyfall* when she is dressed in either black or grey. The most saturated color near her is in the form of the kitschy porcelain English Bulldog draped in a brightly painted Union Jack flag. This costuming washes her out, emphasizes her age, and makes her appear overly tried and burdened by the crisis at hand. It contributes to the impression that M's ability to manage and maintain secrets and secure Britain's safety has been compromised.

"MUM'S" THE WORD...

In *Skyfall*, Bond makes his way back into the fold of MI6 when he hears about the attacks on the news. He reveals himself to M by breaking into her home yet again. "Where the hell have you been?" she barks out as a haggard looking Bond sarcastically replies "enjoying death." There is an undercurrent of tension between the two that seems to speak volumes. Bond is a returning ghost from the past and this will be referenced many times throughout the film. Bond, we are told, is past his prime—he cannot shoot straight, he's hooked on pills and booze, and he looks weak and haggard. During a word association test at MI6 the doctor says "M" and Bond quickly replies "Bitch." Herein lies another major theme within the film: the mother/son relationship between M and Bond. This becomes more complicated as we learn that the reason for the attacks on MI6 is because of a past 00 agent who also has a problematic relationship with M and is acting out feelings of abandonment and vengeance.

When Bond finally meets Silva, it is at the expense of Severine. Bond's initial interaction with her at the club reveals her entanglement as a sex slave who is now indebted to Silva of whom she is very afraid. He nevertheless makes a promise to assist her for her help in leading him to Silva. Bond's use of her body by slinking into her bathroom while she is taking a shower and seducing her (a nod to the sexualized horror of the shower scene in Hitchcock's 1960 film *Psycho*) does not really serve any narrative purpose as he is already on the boat making its way towards his adversary. She is a disposable female much like Solange in *Casino Royale*; they are simply a means to an end in Bond's missions. In both cases, Bond's reaction to their deaths indicates a detachment that is further emphasized by his lover Lynd, who suggests that Bond sees women as "disposable pleasures rather than meaningful pursuits," which would render him a "cold-hearted bastard."

Silva takes great pleasure in taunting Bond, much like he has been doing with M and MI6. During their initial meeting, Silva strokes Bond's upper thigh as he tells a story about rats. He taunts Bond by stating, "She sent you after me, knowing you're not ready, knowing you would likely die. Mommy was very bad." In another statement he boasts that he was a better agent than Bond and when Bond responds "Are you sure this is about M?" Silva snaps back that "it is about her, and you and me. We are the last two rats." The dynamic that Silva sets up between himself and Bond is of competitive brothers vying for their mother's attention and affection. The actual and implied violence within the film serves as a signifier of masculinity—Bond's in particular—because Silva is presented to us as deranged, broken, effeminate, and ultimately second best (this is even referenced in his name Silva/Silver). Silva's masculinity is questionable and becomes a way for Bond's character to put to rest the rising doubts that he (like M) was simply an embodiment of a traditional model of international espionage; one that is premised on national borders and reflects white-Western entitlement through excessive consumption of alcohol and women. Underpinning the relationship between Bond and Silva is the contrast between whole vs. broken and hero vs. monster. For Rosi Braidotti, "the monster is the bodily incarnation of difference from the basic human norm; it is deviant, an a-nomaly; it is abnormal" (62). Violence serves as a signifier of masculinity and is also integral to the formation of social identity. Violence and the ability to be violent has been one of the main ways that the male and masculinity is differentiated from the female and her femininity. As René Girard astutely puts it, "only violence can put an end to violence, and that is why violence is self-propagating. Everyone wants to strike the last blow, and reprisal can thus follow reprisal without any true conclusion ever being reached" (26).

Steven Woodward identifies the presence of a female M as "unsettling the Oedipal dynamics of the narratives," which for Bond means "trouble orienting himself" (184); this is played out between the "brothers" and through the institution of MI6. The female defined and limited by her reproductive function is not a new concept. Society has historically viewed the female body in relation to patriarchal ideology. Where she was once valued for her reproductive ability she is now devalued as a product. This reflects the impact of consumerism and social constructions as applied to the body. Although M is past her reproductive prime she is reduced to a reference of Mother when she becomes the pawn between Bond and Silva.

Yet, it is through the damaged body of Silva, the aging body of M, and the road-weary body of Bond that psychological and social conflicts are played out. Bond fails to protect M, much like he fails to protect Lynd in *Casino Royale*. Lynd chooses not to be rescued by Bond, and his dramatic attempt to protect M at the decrepit ancestral home on barren land in Scotland is laughable at best. Silva seems to have a never ending supply of henchmen and guns to come after them, while their arsenal consists of homemade bombs and other diversionary tactics found around his mostly empty home. Are we to be convinced that this is the best course of action, given Bond's prowess and previous interactions with villains along with his remarkable skill for breaking into M's home? Silva has been one step ahead of M, Bond, and the whole agency from the beginning. He has infiltrated and attacked MI6 from within. His deformity and dexterity place him as the Other and as such he enjoys a certain level of freedom. Silva represents a destabilizing force that disrupts the status quo only for it to be firmly re-established again. Bond provides the climactic release of re-establishing the status quo by taking the battle against Silva over M (who is experiencing a profoundly professional Othering of her power and position) to the desolate outer world of Scotland. Bond's battle is a literal enactment of Freud's oedipal complex as it has shifted between "brothers." M becomes a sacrifice that allows Bond to re-establish his masculine prowess within the established framework of MI6.

CONCLUSION

The reboot of Bond began with a number of complex and multi-dimensional characters that do not easily fit into the previous templates of Bond, the Bond Girl, Moneypenny, and M. The body is a presence that can be symbolic in many ways, and for M it ultimately becomes a signal of limitation and vulnerability, and her demise is directly related to Bond and his power struggle with Silva. While M is not completely disempowered, she is perceived as different (Other) and thus a hindrance because of her so-called "advanced" age. Ultimately *Skyfall* is not a reboot but instead takes us full circle back to the Bond of the past. The audience is left with a new and mysterious location of MI6 where Mallory is the new (male) M, who is ensconced behind a leather padded and studded door, and Moneypenny has given up fieldwork to take over as his secretary and occupy a space that is on the periphery of power while re-establishing the precedent for flirtatious taunts with Bond. Bond nostalgia is not just a reference or an echo within the film, it is the standard from which Bond is reincarnated at the expense of the female M. M now stands for male.

CHAPTER 27

MOTHERING THE BOND-M RELATION IN *SKYFALL* AND THE BOND GIRL INTERVENTION

Christopher Holliday

The casting of Judi Dench as M, the high-ranking government official and administrative Head of MI6, in the Bond franchise helped revise the character; M shifted away from the curt, cold, and crusty admiral of Ian Fleming's original novels, played by Bernard Lee and Robert Brown in the official Eon films, and was presented as an explicitly maternal figure. A successful stage actress, but with few cinema credits, Dench was the first female performer to be cast as Bond's institutional authority, upturning the male-dominated tradition by grafting new familial dynamics onto the hitherto all-male Bond-M relation. Tony Garland observes that in Dench's debut in *GoldenEye* (Martin Campbell 1995), "M combines condemnation that extends beyond the criticism of a senior manager with an almost maternal concern: after telling Bond she has no compunction to send him to his death, she tells him to come back alive" (184-5). The matriarchal coding of M consolidated throughout the Pierce Brosnan era (1995-2002) has accelerated since the Irish actor's departure from the role. The reboot of the Bond franchise with *Casino Royale* (Martin Campbell 2006) has continued to spotlight the maternal vicissitudes of the Bond-M relationship. Since Daniel Craig inherited the role of Bond, 007 has emerged as a greater conduit through which the maternal qualities of M have been rendered visible. As a result, M lives up to "the connotations associated with her initial M, [and] has officially become Bond's mother" (Savoye 55).

With Dench being the only cast member carried over from the Brosnan era, M has been envisaged through an increasingly maternal lens across this contemporary revisionist Bond period, perhaps prompted by the greater age gap between Dench and Craig (34 years) than the actress shared with Brosnan (19 years) during his tenure. The increased agency and mobility of M across the Craig era films has further contributed to her textual figuration as a surrogate mother to Bond. Paul Stock argues that in Bernard Lee's portrayal of the character, for example, M "seldom leaves" the confines of the office in his defense of the boundaries of the nation (217). Being relocated away from the secure, stable office space diminishes ex-admiral M's authority and ability to successfully participate in the preservation of the Empire. In comparison, Dench's M is rarely protected by the leather-padded, soundproofed door behind which lies the "administrative core of the British secret service" (Stock 215). In *Casino Royale*, and again in *Quantum of Solace* (Marc Forster 2008), it is Bond's unsanctioned access into M's private sphere and their verbal jousting away from the office space that provides a glimpse into his female boss's domestic milieu. Increasingly marked by her home space, Dench's M has been repeatedly associated with the trappings of domesticity. Glimpsed in her nightgown and shown sleeping alongside her husband, it is Craig's second outing as 007, *Quantum of Solace*, that most forcefully awards spectators unprecedented admittance into M's "motherliness."

The more substantial engagement in the Craig era with M's home space (not seen since *On Her Majesty's Secret Service* [Peter Hunt 1969]) counterpoints to the fleeting glimpses of Bond's own domestic context across the franchise. Yet the increasingly frequent visits to M's home by Craig's Bond also recall those moments whereby M has interfered into Bond's personal sphere, not least M's nocturnal house-call to 007's flat in *Live and Let Die* (Guy Hamilton 1973) that inadvertently catches Bond in a romantic tryst. But in both *Casino Royale* and *Quantum of Solace*, it is now Bond who actively collapses the distinction between domestic and administrative spaces in ways that strengthen Bond-M's familial dynamic. Discussing Bond's infiltration of M's modern penthouse in *Casino Royale*, Katharine Cox notes that "Like a mother, she scolds him for his arrogance and immaturity, and chastises him for flaunting the boundaries of the relationship" (6). If M's intervention into Bond's personal space cements his fatherly relationship to Bond, then it is the reverse intrusion of Bond into M's home in the more recent Craig era films that renders her connection to Bond as increasingly motherly.

The plotting of the Bond-M relationship from professional to familial has, however, gained particular momentum in *Skyfall* (Sam Mendes 2012), a film that relocates the orphaned 007 to the center of such mounting (M)otherly attitudes. Not only does Bond once more intrude into M's domestic realm, but he also actively brings her to his childhood home, the eponymous Skyfall Lodge. The narrative of *Skyfall* leans heavily on Bond's origin story, with a pronounced emphasis on 007's lack of biological parents as the film recalls the events leading up to Bond being orphaned. The stress placed upon Bond's ancestry allows the film to further develop the Bond-M relationship in son/mother terms, as M is strongly positioned as his adoptive mother. M becomes symbolically rooted within Bond's personal history; she is associated both with his deceased mother, another "M"— Monique Delacroix—and father, whose identity, like the Head of M16, is manifest through initials—A.B. Yet Bond is not the only character in *Skyfall* who lays claim to M as his mother, as she is subject to the threats, matricidal in nature and tone, of ex-MI6 agent Raoul Silva. Silva refers to M as "Mummy" and

"Mother" throughout the film, and he competes with Bond like a jealous brother for the attentions and affections of their surrogate mother.

While M is increasingly presented as a maternal figure, her character is far more multifaceted and complex. This chapter aims to interrogate the Bond-M relationship by exploring how M also functions as a Bond Girl in the Craig era films. Central to the ideology of the series, the Bond Girl character type has been strikingly absent, or at least notably decentered, in the reboot trilogy, as *Casino Royale* focuses predominantly on the early career of Bond and the acquisition of his double-O status. But *Skyfall's* portrayal of M seems to evoke Umberto Eco's structuralist analysis of Bond women in Fleming's novels, where the narratives end as 007 "rests from his great efforts in the arms of the woman, though he is destined to lose her" (qtd. in Bondanella 63). This chapter argues that the narrative agency and formal presentation of M throughout *Skyfall* develops her affiliation with Bond in a manner traditionally reserved for 007's female conquests, in particular the secret agent's ill-fated monogamous relationships with the Bond Girl and especially Tracy di Vicenzo (*On Her Majesty's Secret Service*) and Vesper Lynd (*Casino Royale*). *Skyfall* cues a terminal exchange of M's characteristics (dominant, knowledgeable, moderated, recurring) with several Bond Girl qualities (dominated by villain, rescued, possessed, transient). M's alignment with the Bond Girl archetype ultimately works to overwhelm her matriarchal coding, conflating and collapsing the Bond-M and Bond-Women relationships that Eco argues structure the Bond narratives. It is this irresolvable tension between M's maternal weight and her iconography as "lover" that instigates the character's demise in *Skyfall*, and marks the culmination of Dench's seven films and 17 years in the role.

M AS "ENGLISH PARTNER"

Framed by the shifting cultural attitudes towards women and sex, contemporary Bond films have been enlivened by a cycle of increasingly progressive female protagonists. Jeremy Black acknowledges how "the women in the recent films have been achievers, rather than the emotional victims of the novels," adding that there is a "wider sense that attitudes to the role and position of women had changed" (160). Despite Vesper Lynd's accusation that Bond merely views women "as disposable pleasures rather than meaningful pursuits" in *Casino Royale*, the franchise has paired him with visibly empowered allies as the series has progressed.

In their examination of gender in series, Colleen M. Tremonte and Linda Racioppi argue that the presence of Dench's M is foundational to this pantheon of new Bond femininity as the series maneuvers away from discourses of misogyny and chauvinism (195-6). They discuss the characterization of Bond Girls Natalya Simonova in *GoldenEye*, Wai Lin in *Tomorrow Never Dies* (Roger Spottiswoode 1997), Christmas Jones in *The World is Not Enough* (Michael Apted 1999) and Jinx in *Die Another Day*

(Lee Tamahori 2002) directly in relation to M: like M, each of these women "possesses official or professional capabilities that not only help Bond defeat the enemy but that reflect contemporary gender politics" (ibid. 187). Tremonte and Racioppi identify a connection between Dench's M and the Bond Girl archetype developed in the Brosnan era, a blueprint founded on M's service as a government agent (in the mold of Lin and Jinx) and a sustained techno-literacy (shared by Simonova, Lin and Jones).

The revisionist trilogy—*Casino Royale, Quantum of Solace,* and *Skyfall*— reintroduces, reworks, and at times even conflates many of the generic Bond conventions, not least within the mobilization of familiar Bondian identities. In her examination of *Casino Royale,* Lisa Funnell notes a displacement of the Bond Girl as the locus of "visual spectacle," arguing that the muscular body of Craig's Bond becomes the object of desire implicated firmly within a scopic regime usually reserved for Bond's heterosexual desires ("I Know" 456). Cox has similarly elaborated on what she sees as the merging of Bond with Bond Girl iconography, spotlighting *Casino Royale*'s "mannish women and womanish men" (8). She argues "it is Bond's physique that is being viewed and evaluated, at the expense of the Bond 'girl'" (9). Such feminization of a heroic male taps into the lack of a "hegemonic masculinity," and the pluralizing of male identities, within a contemporary postfeminist culture, which manifest in a Bond franchise shaping 007 to be polysemous in his gender signifiers (Hamad 1).

Within the self-enclosed world of the Bond series, however, M's occupation of Bond Girl territory brings into relief how character signifiers are altogether more shifting and shifty in Craig-era Bond. M represents another merging of typical Bondian roles, and the conflation between traditional Bond characters (in this case the heroic ally and romantic interest). Indeed, the characterization of M in *Skyfall* is heavily informed by Bond Girl iconography. M is located squarely at the center of the narrative as Bond's primary female relationship. Bond does not develop a deep emotional attachment to any of the women who appear sporadically throughout the film: an unnamed sexual conquest who appears briefly on screen, Severine who dies at the hands of Silva midway through the film, and Moneypenny who disappears from the narrative for prolonged periods of time. In *Skyfall,* then, it appears as though many of the Bond Girl characteristics, which have been fragmented and redistributed in the Craig era, have been (re)assigned to the figure of M. If, as Funnell argues, the Bond Girl is defined by the deep and intimate relationship she develops with Bond ("From English" 63), then M (and not these other women) is positioned as the Bond Girl of the film.

The emergent status of M as a potential hybrid figuration of Mother and Bond Girl is further borne out by Funnell's analysis charting the trajectory in representations of Bond Girls. Funnell argues that Bond Girls first emerged under the guise of the

Anglicized sidekick role or "English Partner," a character type closely allied to the franchise's roots as a British imperialist spy thriller ("From English" 63). Running contrary to the discourses of international diversity that generically marks the exoticism of the Bond Girl archetype, Funnell promotes a model of Bond femininity that, through particular casting choices and dubbing practices, align early Bond Girl(s) "with English culture and present her as an English protagonist working alongside Bond" (ibid. 64-6). This template of the "English Partner" prevailed during the Connery and Lazenby eras (1962-69), before it gave way to the "American Sidekick" period of Connery, Moore and Dalton (1971-89) and the "American Action Hero" (1995-2002) phase of the Brosnan era, embodied by women who match Bond intellectually and physically (ibid. 77). The partnering of Craig with Dench in *Skyfall* evokes something of the British "male-female team" that inaugurated the Bond franchise, serving to re-establish an English national and cultural identity between Bond and his Bond Girl.

Skyfall certainly taps into the mythology of Britishness typically surrounding 007, demonstrating a strong patriotic allegiance as it negotiates its own home-grown British identity. At several junctures, the film regularly trades on the reproducible and culturally familiar iconography of a London hitherto unseen in the franchise, from governmental Whitehall and the Houses of Parliament to the interior of the National Gallery on the North-West side of Trafalgar Square for the Bond-Q exchange. Yet it is ultimately M's Britishness, rather than that of Bond, which is most at stake in *Skyfall*, in a manner that reinforces the view of M as Bond's "English Partner." Indeed, part of Silva's cyber-terrorist plot involves co-opting M into the Queen Mother: an image that intertextually references Dench's earlier screen roles as the head of sovereign state in *Mrs. Brown* (John Madden 1997) and *Shakespeare in Love* (John Madden 1998). M's pervasive "Britishness" in *Skyfall* is further registered through two complementary sequences involving the Union Jack flag, whose appearances play across the poles of life and death. First, as M stands solemnly over the bodies of those killed in the explosion at MI6, a row of flags are draped over the coffins in what is a macabre portrayal of the character's associations with nationhood. Second, the Union Jack forms part of the decorative design of the porcelain bulldog, a keepsake that resides on M's office desk but which is ultimately bequeathed to Bond by M following her death. A symbol of the dogged determination of Britons during World War II, the porcelain dog was manufactured by the notable English pottery company, Royal Doulton. The durability of the figurine, as it is passed from M to Bond via Moneypenny against the sun-drenched London skyline, works to reconcile M as Bond's "English Partner" through their shared association to the nation. So just as Bond travels with M "back in time" to Skyfall Lodge in his Aston Martin DB5 (introduced in *Goldfinger* [Guy Hamilton 1964]), the film's portrayal of M maps out the Bond Girl's own origin story too, and transports the franchise back to its own English roots.

"THE BITCH IS DEAD."
TRANSIENCE, ROMANCE AND THE FINAL CLINCH

The murder of Bond's English bride, Tracy di Vicenzo, immediately following their marriage in the final scenes of *On Her Majesty's Secret Service*, signals the downfall (or death) of the "English Partner" archetype, and ushers in a new phase of representation for Bond femininity, the "American Sidekick," which would prevail across the franchise until *GoldenEye* (Funnell, "From English"70). The violent death of Tracy Bond offers some insight into how the Bond franchise has commonly negotiated marital relationships. Multiple Bond Girls have adopted marital aliases while working undercover with Bond. Tatiana Romanova becomes Mrs. Somerset in *From Russia with Love* (Terence Young 1963); Tiffany Case assumes the role of Mrs. Jones in *Diamonds are Forever* (Guy Hamilton 1971), and Anya Amasova is Mrs. Sterling in *The Spy Who Loved Me* (Lewis Gilbert 1977). Even the marriage ceremony between Kissy Suzuki and Bond in *You Only Live Twice* (Lewis Gilbert 1967) is framed as a fictional cover story, with Bond posing as a local Japanese fisherman. Although Bond and Suzuki's business arrangement blossoms into a sexual relationship, the "false" image of wedlock regularly provides the only sustainable mode of marital existence for a secret agent. *On Her Majesty's Secret Service* presents real marriage as being untenable, and thus for Bond the pursuit of a civilian life outside the secret service will remain unobtainable. Marriage, for Bond, can only operate within the institutional confines of a designated mission.

The death of Tracy Bond in *On Her Majesty's Secret Service* also works against the conventional trajectory of the Bond film narrative. Bond's missions typically end in success (with a primary villain being killed), and 007 rewards himself for a "job well done" by making love to his Bond Girl; his masculinity is confirmed by his heroic actions and ability to sexually satisfy his woman. None of the Eon-produced Bond films have concluded without the inevitable embrace between Bond and his Bond Girl, and locations for the final tryst have ranged from a romantic gondola ride (*From Russia with Love*) and an inflatable raft (*Thunderball* [Terence Young 1965] and *You Only Live Twice*) to a submarine-style escape pod (*The Spy Who Loved Me*) and even a ship in outer space (*Moonraker* [Lewis Gilbert 1979]). In *Tomorrow Never Dies*, Bond and Chinese Secret Agent Wai Lin even eschew any rescue by military forces as they float amid the wreckage of Elliot Carver's stealth boat, opting instead to preserve the romance of their union rather than confirm to their superiors their survival ("They're looking for us, James", "Let's stay undercover"). The final scene of *Tomorrow Never Dies* makes explicit the narrative of romance (personal) as both a satisfactory and necessary coda to the fulfilment of the mission (professional).

What distinguishes the Craig era Bond films is their renegotiation of the climactic

Bond-Bond Girl romantic clinch to reinforce the emotional connection between Bond and M. Whereas the Bond-M confrontation traditionally occurs early in the narrative, normally at a briefing when Bond is given his assignment, the Craig era films are structured to include multiple briefings and moments of contact between the two characters. It is this pluralizing of scenes between Bond and M that aligns the latter with the iconography of the Bond Girl. Following the death of Vesper Lynd at the end of *Casino Royale*, Bond has a telephone conversation with M in which she states: "Get back as soon as you can. We need you." During the final scenes of *Quantum of Solace*, a similar exchange takes place only this time in person. Standing outside an apartment complex in Russia, M divulges her personal desire for Bond—speaking on behalf of herself rather than MI6—when she says, "Bond, *I* need you back," to which 007 confirms his own willingness to resume his duty in equally personalized terms ("I never left"). In *Quantum of Solace*, Bond's relationship with female ally Camille Montes never turns sexual, and they part ways prior to this climactic Bond-M exchange. This sequence of events draws attention to the fact that Bond has a strong(er) emotional attachment to M; she is the woman he is connected to at the end of the film, and she reciprocates by expressing how much she needs him. Despite Savoye observing that in *Quantum of Solace* "the function of M as the Mother has never been so explicit" (55), the narrative works to place M within the throes of the ulterior Bond Girl archetype. Indeed, by privileging the intimate Bond-M relationship rather than reverting to images of 007's sexual exploits at its conclusion, *Quantum of Solace* hints that this Bond is incapable of a meaningful connection to another woman all the while he remains emotionally loyal to M.

Although M is the woman who ends up with Bond at the end of both *Casino Royale* and *Quantum of Solace*, she must compete with Vesper Lynd and Camilla Montes for Bond's affections. In *Skyfall*, however, M remains the central female protagonist and person with which Bond develops the strongest and most intimate relationship. M's engagement with the established iconography of Bond's lovers, and her elevation into Bond Girl status, is ultimately achieved in *Skyfall* through her death. Fatally wounded by Silva, M lies in Bond's arms in the church where his parents are buried. On the one hand, this works to symbolically connect M to Bond's parents and position her in a maternal role: Bond is orphaned once more. On the other hand, the staging of M's death is reminiscent of the murder of Tracy Bond in *On Her Majesty's Secret Service*. After getting married (in a church), she is killed in a drive-by shooting. The film ends with Bond weeping as he cradles his wife's lifeless body in his arms.

Through the death of M, *Skyfall* foregrounds the notion that Bond's personal and professional lives cannot be connected, combined, or reconciled. By intertextual referencing the ending of *On Her Majesty's Secret Service*, *Skyfall* (re)introduces the theme of love versus duty, which has long been a staple of the franchise. Just as Irma Bunt's assassination of the new Mrs. Bond sends a message about the viability of marriage within the film series, the killing of M due to her emotional proximity to Bond fore-grounds the dangers for a woman who gets too close to Bond. Women, who, in the words of Paris Carver in *Tomorrow Never Dies*, "get too close...for comfort," risk divi-ding Bond's loyalty and diverting his attention away from queen and country, and so they must be reprimanded accordingly.

In this way, the intensity of the Bond-M clinch that culminates *Skyfall* also evo-kes (within Craig's ongoing tenure at least) the demise of Lynd. Much like Lynd, M develops a strong relationship with Bond while she is still married. It is only in *Skyfall* that M divulges that she is widowed, thus sustaining the wounded dignity of Lynd and even the "damaged" vulnerability of Montes, sharing with them the severing (or, perhaps, the Severine) of traditional family ties. The alignment between Lynd and M is further corroborated through notable parallels in dialogue. Both Lynd ("MI6 looks for maladjusted young men") and M ("orphans always make the best recruits") make explicit verbal reference to Bond's troubled childhood, while confirming their indivi-dual roles in Bond's rehabilitation at the forefront of British national security. No less significant is Bond's vengeful line regarding Lynd's suicide in *Casino Royale* that "the bitch is dead." In its most ominous form, this riposte anticipates Bond's derogatory description of M as "bitch" in *Skyfall*, revealed during a word association exercise as part of his psychiatric evaluation at MI6. It is this verbal slippage that momentarily brings Lynd and M together, unified and defined even in death under the Bond Girl umbrella through their relationship with Bond himself.

"HE IS DESTINED TO LOSE HER"

From a structural standpoint, the familiar mechanisms of the romantic clinch across Bond films work in conjunction with the necessarily fleeting nature of Bond Girls as one of the series' elementary "moves." Umberto Eco has described Fleming's novels according to a series of binary, oppositional pairs which, when fixed in variance and combination, "plot" the narrative structure in ways that closely resemble a game of chess. Gesturing towards the fulfilment of the romantic narrative as an erotic epi-logue to Bond's assigned mission, Eco describes how in a typical Bond novel "Bond defeats the Villain, who dies horribly, and rests from his great efforts in the arms of the woman, though he is destined to lose her" (qtd. in Bondanella 63). Bond Girls are certainly marked by features of impermanence, and their "destiny" of non-recurrence is an important element of the underlying logic of the Bond franchise.

The ephemeral feature of Bond women supports many female characters across the series, including the archetype of the "bad" Girl or villainous Bond Girl as a figure against which the "good" Bond Girl has routinely been aligned. On the one hand, female antagonists, as both Funnell and Garland have acknowledged, are typically *punishable* and *punished* through their sexual association with 007. These characters (which Garland equates to the *femme fatale* characters of *film noir*) typically perish at the hands of the villains, their romantic entanglement with Bond keying their demise by sealing their fate. When discussing Fiona Volpe in *Thunderball*, Garland explains that "her duplicity produces an inherent contradiction between her mission and her desire," and it is this negotiation of profession and emotion that ultimately leads to Volpe's death (182). Villainous Bond Girls are thus branded by a *textual* failure to live, often disposed of in a particularly violent manner that befits their sudden expendability. Yet those heroic Bond Girls demonstrating a virtuous fidelity to 007's mission, and who operate with (rather than against) him, are marked by an *extratextual* inability for survival, insofar as they are sexual partners not carried over between narratives. Such transience is also a necessary feature of their definition: a Bond Girl is "a non-recurring character and lead female protagonist" (Funnell, "From English" 63). The disposability of secondary women that procure their status as short-lived romantic conquests thus runs contrary to other kinds of characters found in the Bond films, who are defined through their repeating presence and charge the franchise with a degree of narrative coherency.

M's conflation of mother figure and Bond Girl in *Skyfall* precipitates her downfall by posing a challenge to the standardized ideology contained within the series. Cox argues the initial decision in *GoldenEye* to cast a woman as M, and the coercion of M as a "pseudo-mother" actually "accentuates Bond's inability to sleep with her, and places her as the only unavailable, inaccessible and taboo woman he meets" (6). Noting the emergent "Oedipal prohibition" that now marks the Bond-M relation, Luke Hockley speculates over whether this will prove to be a "good development" (118). However, M's development into Bond Girl in *Skyfall* proves to be a fatal deviation from the regulating principles of the familiar Bond structure, a framework that up to now has successfully marshalled her position. For M, the identities of Bond Girl and Mother are not separate but in dangerous conversation throughout *Skyfall*, and it is this confrontation that does not go unchecked. M's death is cued by her progressively intimate relationship with Bond, himself a hero who is far from innocent in undertaking a liaison "with a woman old enough to be (of course) his mother" (Martinson ¶ 10). *Skyfall* ultimately overwhelms M through the imposition of a Bond Girl status onto her, and the untenable collaboration between mother and lover expresses what happens when being a matriarch to British intelligence is simply not enough.

CHAPTER 28

PROPERTY OF A LADY

(S)Mothering Judi Dench's M

Michael W. Boyce

GoldenEye (Martin Campbell 1995) stands as a significant film in the Eon Bond franchise for being the first film since *Dr. No* (Terence Young 1962) to introduce new actors in the roles of both James Bond (Pierce Brosnan) and his boss, M (Judi Dench). It also marks the first time that M is presented as a new character, a female superior who challenges the perceptions of Bond (and, by extension, the audience) regarding women. In *GoldenEye*, M is set up as a strong female character within the traditionally stereotypical and limited gender framework of the Bond film. M is neither Bond Girl nor Bad Girl. She establishes her own complex female identity, defying attempts by Bond, other characters, and the audience to categorize and define her.

As Dench is the only actor to survive the 2006 franchise reboot, *Casino Royale* (Martin Campbell), her character makes an interesting subject for an examination of the changing attitudes towards women, particularly women in authority, in the series. Despite the presence of Dench's M in the first three Craig era films, there is a noticeable change in her characterization and her relationship to the younger, less experienced, and more petulant Bond. In *Casino Royale, Quantum of Solace* (Marc Forster 2008), and *Skyfall* (Sam Mendes 2012) M's initial strength, which I argue comes by defying attempts to categorize her, disappears and is replaced with uncertainty about herself and her abilities. This chapter will examine the shift in the representation of Dench's M from an unusually complex female character in the Brosnan era to a domesticated, neutered mother-figure in the Craig era. By exploring how the Brosnan films initially draw M as one who challenges the limited gender identities of the Bond world and how that characterization is undone by "domesticating" her in the Craig films, I will show how M's relationship to Bond shifts from employer to mother. Although it is Silva, the main villain of *Skyfall*, who takes great delight in calling M, "Mummy," the previous two films lay the groundwork for this change. The plot of *Skyfall* and Bond himself conspire to label M "mother" by altering the nature of her relationship to Bond and reinforcing her association with domestic spaces. In creating this identifiable label for her, one not traditionally associated with the Bond franchise, M is reduced to "understandable" and simple. She is subject to a similar violent backlash experienced by Tracy Draco/di

Vicenzo in *On Her Majesty's Secret Service* (Peter Hunt 1969) when she becomes Mrs. Bond. Within the limited gender perspective of the Bond world, mothers (like wives) are unnecessary and undesirable, and so her exit is foreshadowed and required.

LIMITED OPTIONS?
ROLES FOR WOMEN IN THE BOND FILMS

There has been an oversimplification in critical literature considering the role of women in the Bond films. Through this limited perspective, female characters in the franchise are viewed primarily as sexualized objects upon whom Bond, the strong sexual adventurer, preys. In their detailed quantitative content analysis of female characters in Bond films, Kimberley A. Neuendorf et al. coded 195 female characters from 20 Bond films (from *Dr. No* to *Die Another Day* [Lee Tamahori 2002]) to determine such things as importance to narrative, age, ethnicity, hair length and color, body type, and sexual contact with Bond: "One of the most striking findings of this content analysis resides in the fact that despite societal progression of feminist ideology, the women of Bond continue to be portrayed in a rather limited and sex-stereotyped manner" (758). After the first 40 years of cinematic Bond, the majority of female characters—whether good, bad, good-then-bad, or bad-then-good—are still young, attractive, and sexually desirable.

Despite the admittedly limited roles for females in the Bond films, considerable interest remains in these characters. Scholars such as Christine Bold, Tony W. Garland, and Lisa Funnell have broadened the understanding of women and the more nuanced role of gender in Bond films. Bold's against the grain reading of Fleming's narratives sees women as "the enabling mechanism" (171) for Bond and the British Secret Service. While early filmic Bond Girls such as Honey Ryder (1962), Pussy Galore (1964), Kissy Suzuki (1967), and Tiffany Case (1971) are presented as sexualized objects of desire, they also provide Bond with assistance that aids in the success of his missions. Garland and Funnell have each explored the nuances of those sexually desirable female characters who seek to harm or kill Bond, what Garland labels the Bond girl villain (179) and Funnell differentiates as a separate category, the "Bad" Girl ("Negotiating" 199). Yet there remains a desire to describe/categorize all women in the series as Bond Girls, which leads us to overlook the variety of female characters such as Bond Girls, Bond Girl Villains (or Bad Girls), secondary female roles, Miss Moneypenny, and M.

THE NEW HEAD OF MI6: M'S INTRODUCTION

The prologue sequence of *GoldenEye* (1995), in which Bond (Pierce Brosnan) believes colleague Alec Trevelyan dies, takes place nine years before the main narrative.

This gap makes it hard to situate these events in terms of continuity within the Bond franchise. *GoldenEye* was released six years after Timothy Dalton's final outing as Bond in *Licence to Kill* (John Glen 1989). The idea of lost time is interesting in that it allows the film to address the "changing world" and values. The nine year gap also serves to distance the new M from the failed mission. The introduction of Dench as M, which occurs more than a third of the way through the film, highlights societal changes in terms of women's roles in positions of leadership, particularly the espionage community, and provides a unique female character within the Bond canon who can voice criticism of the male dominated world of the Bond films while allowing Bond to continue his womanizing ways. Dench's M is presented as a complex character, a strong and independent older woman who resists the charms of Bond, unlike Moneypenny, and refuses to be placed into categories by Bond or anyone else.

In her first scene, in the situation room with Bond and MI6 Chief of Staff Bill Tanner, Dench portrays M as staid, self-restrained, and authoritative. Before her appearance, Tanner refers to M as "the Evil Queen of Numbers" and states that she will not trust Bond's instinct over solid evidence. Bond's cough alerts Tanner to M's presence right behind him and certainly within earshot. Tanner's face shows his awareness of his blunder and he steps aside to reveal Dench. Immediately M carries herself as stoic and unemotional, contrasting her with the two other women Bond has had contact with at this point: his panicked driving evaluator and the sexually lethal Xenia Onatopp. Tanner's comment, which is never mentioned again, is a rather juvenile and sexist attempt to categorize M as a stereotypical "Wicked Queen," a female figure of fright from fairy tales or an unreasonable adversary/authority figure to be feared. The comment attempts to dismiss M as a creditable superior and instead turns her into a figure of parody for the men of MI6 who are not used to a woman in charge. M faces similarly sexist comments from men in the military and espionage community. In *Tomorrow Never Dies* (Roger Spottiswoode 1997), when Admiral Roebuck argues against M's recommendation for an investigation and for a strong naval response, he tells M, "With all due respect, M, sometimes I don't think you have the balls for this job." M's response subverts the implications of her lacking the male-ness necessary for her profession with her retort, "Perhaps. But the advantage is I don't have to think with them all the time." In *Die Another Day*, American CIA agent Damian Falco tells M that she needs to "get [her] house in order," a colloquial expression implying she is a failed homemaker.

In *GoldenEye*, M's response to Tanner's comment establishes her understated authority by its coolness and anticipates the other feminine/domestic label that could be applied to her—that of mother: "If I want sarcasm, I'll talk to my children." In other words, M has children of her own and will not act as a surrogate mother for a bunch of immature schoolboys in the workplace. Stephen B. Tippins Jr. argues that the relationship between Bond and the male M suggests a paternal one:

And if you read carefully between the lines—or listen closely to the give-and-take on screen—you'll notice that Bond's relationship with his superior "M" always plays much more like the relationship between a headstrong adolescent and a stern, hard-of-praise father, as if [...] Bond [strains] for fatherly guidance. (36)

In this introductory scene, M rejects the idea that her character will be fulfilling a maternal role for Bond or for anyone else in her professional capacity. Later, in *The World is Not Enough* (Michael Apted 1999), M again stresses her unwillingness to act "like a mother," telling Bond that she repressed all of her maternal instincts to convince her friend, Sir Robert King, not to pay the ransom for his kidnapped daughter, Elektra King, for professional reasons: to draw the criminals out. M refuses to define her power by her reproductive abilities or what Welldon calls "the power of the womb" (40). Neither does she attempt to falsely enact what Funnell describes in *Warrior Women* as "maternal masculinity"—muscular action woman who "temporarily employs physical force to protect her children" and who is "frequently (mis) interpreted by audience and critics as enacting masculinity" (166). M shows no discernible characteristics of the "caring mother" or the muscular female hero.

The cultural significance of Dench's role as M becomes much more apparent when considering research on the (under)representation of older women in popular film. In their 1997 study (published just two years after *GoldenEye*), Bazzini et al. discovered that in film "[80] percent of characters over the age of 35 were male, whereas only 20% were female" (541). These older women were typically "cast in a particularly negative light [...] less friendly, less intelligent, less good, possessing less wealth, and being less attractive" (ibid. 541). According to Lauzen and Dozier, in terms of positions of power and authority, "male characters are more likely than female characters to be employed and hold" such positions, and "female characters were more likely to be found in relatively powerless household occupations" (439). Tara Brabazon described Moneypenny, who had, until *Skyfall*, functioned solely as M's assistant, where "she can view power, but wields little" (490) in similar terms. Played by Lois Maxwell in 14 films (1962-85), Moneypenny shifts from Bond's partner in an innocuous flirtation to an "Old Maid" caricature—a woman sexually past her prime, "ragged, over-painted and old" (Brabazon 493).

From her first scene in *GoldenEye* M establishes that she is in control. Even the framing during the cross-cut dialogue between Bond, Tanner, and M places her in the position of authority (Bond and Tanner are framed together; M is in a close up). She allows Tanner to do his job and continue briefing Bond, but feels comfortable interrupting when she has something to add, showing herself to be intelligent and well briefed. Similarly, her clothing is reserved and practical, but authoritative. She wears what will be her standard costume throughout the Brosnan films: a solid color (usually dark blue) pant suit set with her collarless jacket buttoned to the neck. She does not attempt to look overtly masculine, especially when compared to the various uniformed men that surround her with medals and distinctions, artefacts that function as outward signs of military success. M lacks the naval credentials of her predecessor. She does not look, or act, feminine, as defined by the Bond films, with form-fitting dresses or showy jewelry. As Welldon notes, "[s]uch is the bitter power of that the feminine body and femininity have been assigned as opposed to the lack of power of accorded to [the female] intellect" (24). M's power, however, derives from her intellect and cold reason.

The professional spaces that M occupies in the Brosnan era films also establish her authority, most notably her place in the various professional spaces. The situation rooms show her leadership skills and ability to make difficult decisions (usually surrounded by men questioning her decisions), but it is her office space, the traditional locus for the M-Bond briefing, that is the most significant space. Paul Stock has explored the importance of M's office space in terms of colonialism and empire. Before 1995, M's office was a clustered monument to his naval career and the larger history of British imperialism: paintings of sailing ships, model ships and "an antiquated world globe, with Britain's Imperial conquests pretty in pink" (216). When M briefs Bond for the first time in *GoldenEye,* her office is sparsely but tastefully furnished with an off-white couch, a glass-top coffee table, black swivel chairs, and many lamps. Vertical blinds replace the luxurious green curtains over the window. The walls retain their wood paneling, but the tone of the wood is much lighter. Uniformly sized pictures are hung on every other panel. Her floor to ceiling book case is neatly organized; while full it is not cluttered with books and decorative objects. When she asks Bond if he would like a drink, he replies, "Thank you. Your predecessor kept some cognac in the top…" M cuts him off before he can finish with a sharp, "I prefer bourbon." The redecoration of the office and stocking of her preferred alcohol serves as an act of marking her own territory. This space visually differentiates her from her predecessor even before she bluntly asserts that she is a unique character, unlike any Bond has encountered before:

You don't like me, Bond. You don't like my methods. You think I'm an accountant, a bean counter more interested in my numbers than your instincts… Because I think you're a sexist, misogynist dinosaur. A relic of the Cold War, whose boyish charms, though lost on me, obviously appealed to that young girl I sent out to evaluate you… If you think I don't have the balls to send a man out to die, your instincts are dead wrong. I've no compunction about sending you to your death. But I won't do it on a whim. Even with your cavalier attitude towards life.

This new M, with her own tastes, preferences, and ideas, proves to be a formidable challenge to Bond. She is neither charmed nor impressed with her top agent, and will not be manipulated by him or anyone else.

M IN THE CRAIG ERA: OLD GUARD AND MUMMY

In the 2006 reboot *Casino Royale*, Craig's Bond moves from experienced secret agent to novice, portraying his early adventures as a double-0 agent. The film omits the over-the-top gadgets and lightheartedness of even the best Brosnan films and introduces a much darker tone into the franchise. The action sequences, though elaborate, are much more violent and gritty. Craig's portrayal of Bond stretches the limits of accep-table masculinity in a Bond film as he not only bleeds (something rare in previous films), but is presented with bruises and cuts that serve as visual reminders of this violence. While Craig's Bond is the most bloodied and battered in the series, he is also emotionally vulnerable, visibly shaken by his own capacity for violence. Moreover, this Bond is on display. As Funnell argues, *Casino Royale* emphasizes Craig's "exposed muscular torso" and muscular masculinity instead of Bond's "sexuality, libido, and conquest" ("I Know" 462). Visually, Funnell argues, in recreating the Honey Ryder bikini scene from *Dr. No*, Craig is linked to the "iconography" of the Bond Girl, "as spectacular, passive, and feminized" (ibid. 467). *Skyfall* further complicates the tradi-tional heterosexual Bond masculinity when Bond responds to Silva's sexual advances with the allusions to his own history of bisexual or homosexual experimentation: "What makes you think this is my first time?"

Just as the Craig films re-imagine Bond and his heroic masculinity, they also pre-sent a re-framing of M, one that works to undermine the position she established in the Brosnan films. In *GoldenEye*, Bond represents the old boys' Secret Service of the past and M represents a modern woman, valued for her expertise and professiona-lism, but assumed to be in over her head by most of the men she encounters, including Bond. In the Craig reboot, M is increasingly defined by her age, and is presented, in the words of Silva, as "an old woman." Throughout *Casino Royale*, *Quantum of Solace*, and *Skyfall* implicit and explicit emphasis is placed on M's age and her inability to do her job; she occupies and conducts business from clearly domestic spaces and assumes a more overtly maternal relationship with Bond.

When M first appears in *Casino Royale*, her costume suggests an alteration in her characterization. While dressed in her typical dark colored suit, her jacket is open at the chest, revealing her cleavage and a gold necklace hangs from her neck. Later, while in the Bahamas, she wears an off-white jacket and a dark brown skirt. In the visual medium of film, costuming sends powerful messages about the identity of a character and so the differences are subtle but noticeable. M dresses more overtly "feminine" as defined within the context of the Bond films. This is reinforced by M's emotional ranting after having been called in to explain Bond's unauthorized actions: "I report to the Prime Minister and even he's smart enough not to ask me what we do." Her words suggest changes in political climate and ways of doing business, the length of her experience, and being somewhat out of touch (not knowing where Bond is currently located); her tone and volume suggest a flustered emotionalism unseen in the Brosnan era films.

M's long years of service are again foregrounded more pointedly in *Skyfall* when the government holds her responsible for losing files with the identities of undercover NATO operatives, and Bond blames her for not trusting him to complete the job and getting shot. On her way to meet with Gareth Mallory, her eventual replacement, M remarks, "It's like being summoned to the headmaster's study." The comment, which infantilizes her, is reinforced by the image of a diminutive M walking alongside her much taller Chief of Staff. The interview with Mallory does indeed resemble a school disciplinary meeting: the taller, confident Mallory leans back in his chair; M sits forward, uneasy and nervous, both hands clutching a glass in her lap. As the conversation quickly turns to "retirement planning," the visual indicators of childlikeness, smallness, and fragility underscore the assertion of M's unfitness for duty. M herself questions her own suitability while at Skyfall Lodge, telling Bond, "I fucked this up, didn't I?"

While M's office space in the Craig era films is nearly identical to her office in the Brosnan era films, she is not as closely associated with it, or any professional space. When Bond calls M from the Miami airport in *Casino Royale*, she answers in her office. As she stands to take the call, demanding to know what Bond is up to, Bond hangs up abruptly, leaving M standing alone, powerless, in her office. In *Skyfall*, her office blows up, but the physical destruction is only the final manifestation of M's waning career and authority. When MI6 is forced to relocate to new temporary headquarters, M's departure is already foreshadowed.

M's most significant interactions with Bond take place in her home and the domestic space becomes the location for her briefings with Bond. She returns home in *Casino Royale* to find Bond in her living room on her computer. Her response to this invasion lacks the appropriate gravitas: "You've got a bloody cheek." As she scolds him, M sounds more like a parent who has found an adult child back in the family home unannounced after having moved out. This domestic scene is repeated in *Skyfall* when M returns home to find Bond waiting for her in the dark. Later, in *Casino Royale*, when MI6 tracks Bond's computer usage, M is contacted at home where she is in bed for the night. Not only does her red nightgown further undermine her carefully constructed appearance of professionalism, this clear and consistent invasion of her professional life into her home life works to (re)situate her in the domestic sphere and emphasizes her age: while exciting events are happening, she is at home in bed with her husband.

Silva also mentions the unfitness of M in *Skyfall,* during his interrogation of Bond. He connects her explicitly with Mother, gleefully exposing "Mummy's" lies to Bond about his fitness for duties, "You're still clinging to your faith in that old woman when all she does is lie to you." As Silva reads off Bond's actual evaluation and his failure to meet acceptable standards, Bond sits silently, first staring off to his left, then looking at Silva. When Silva gets to "Pathological rejection of authority based on unresolved childhood trauma," the film cuts back to Bond, who looks almost shaken. Silva interprets this as evidence of M's betrayal and recklessness with the lives of her agents: "She sent you after me, knowing you're not ready, knowing you'll likely die. Mummy was very bad." While Silva considers Bond as his brother through their shared connection to M, Bond's association with M as a mother-figure develops across the three Craig films. As a result, Bond disregards any sudden fraternal connection to Silva.

When M finds Bond in her living room in *Casino Royale,* her initial scolding gives way to a strange exchange that can best be described as counseling. Her tone changes and she sits down across from Bond, after pacing the room. She talks about lost trust and how she needs space from him because she's so angry. M again expresses the need to be able to trust Bond in *Quantum of Solace.* This conversation, when considered in relation to others she has with Bond, points towards her overtly maternal feelings for Bond. After Vesper Lynd's death, for example, Bond coldly reports to M, "The bitch is dead." Without comforting or coddling Bond, M makes clear the obvious truth that the betrayed and heart-broken Bond cannot see: Lynd must have tried to save his life. A similar conversation takes place in *Quantum of Solace* in which M's concern for Bond is more pronounced, "You look like hell. When is the last time you slept?" M acknowledges her understanding of Bond's desire for revenge and how it is motivating his actions. She tries to make Bond see how much Lynd loved him. M assumes the role of concerned parent as if Bond was a hurt teenager. The Bond-M relationship described by Tippins as a "headstrong adolescent and a stern hard-of-praise father" (36) has been transformed into an angry and lovesick boy and his compassionate mother.

The representation of M as mother culminates in *Skyfall* when Bond takes her to his childhood home. In returning to the dilapidated space of memory and occupying the domestic space of Bond's childhood, M allows Bond to settle the unresolved "childhood trauma" Silva mentioned. Playing this part strips M of any remaining identifiers of her professionalism. The grizzled groundskeeper Kincade mishears her title and calls her "Emma," her title turned into a first name, the Italianate "-a" ending further feminizing her. She surrenders completely to Bond's plans for preparing the house for battle, her own years of tactical expertise ignored in favor of the role of supporter. Even when she assists in removing dust covers, the dirt makes her cough and spit comically. Preparing baggies with glass and screws, M sits at the large dining room table, small piles of domestic materials in front of her like an arts and craft project. She looks small, almost childlike in the large chair. While Kincade and Bond use tools, fit booby-traps, and test weapons, M's tasks seem almost quaint by comparison. When Silva's men attack, M carries a small hand gun and springs booby-trapped baggies of glass and screws by turning on lights. When she finally does shoot, she misses completely.

M's final descent into the priest's closet, where the young Bond hid for two days after being told of his parents' death, more completely connects her with his mother. Although she has not displayed such maternal characteristics before, there remains a commonly held assumption "that [the] 'maternal instinct' will come to the fore and will perform miracles" (Welldon 18). When Silva's helicopter approaches, Bond orders Kincade and M first to the kitchen (another domestic, motherly space) and then, after machine gun fire all but destroys the walls to the place he hid to mourn his dead parents, he instructs them to "Get to the chapel. Use the tunnels." Leaving Bond to fight on alone, Kincade leads M to the door of the tunnel. Unaware of the injury slowing M down, he leads the way, holding the lamp head to light the path. M stumbles, holding the support beams for balance. When they exit and see the destruction of the house, Kincade wraps his arms around the frail woman and guides her towards the chapel and her eventual death, as she has been shot in the stomach or womb.

After Silva is killed by Bond, M is not permitted a heroic, self-sacrificing death. M initiates the expected professional banter with Bond, even using his code name: "007, what took you so long?" Before she can respond to Bond's excuse, M collapses into Bond's arms. He cradles her, watching as she looks up at him and gasps out her final words, "I did one thing right." The words function as an appraisal of her success in "bringing up Bond;" no matter what other failures she leaves behind, she has raised a good Secret Agent. In the close up of Bond, only part of M's head is visible at the bottom of the screen as if she is slipping from the frame as she is slipping from life. When she dies, Bond, overcome with grief and emotion, carefully closes her eyes. He tenderly kisses her forehead, not as a lover or even a friend, but as a son. As the camera pulls back down the aisle of the chapel, Bond continues to hold her in his arms.

Dench's presence in seven Bond films, spanning both the Brosnan and Craig eras, makes her a worthy subject when examining the changing role of female characters in the Bond films. Between 1995 and 2012, Dench's M showed a marked change: from a strong, authoritative leader and representative of contemporary societal attitudes of women to a frail old mother, out of place and past her prime. In death, M does not receive the titles and honors befitting her years of service and promised by Mallory. Her title is assumed by her successor—who immediately redesigns the office to something from a private English gentlemen's club. Although her death, according to Dodds, "has played a vital role in making Bond's [and Britain's] resilience possible" (119), the only lasting legacy is the ceramic bulldog she leaves Bond in her will. Her exit from the franchise suggests a broader re-identification with attitudes about women more closely associated with the Connery era. With a man back in charge of MI6 and Moneypenny "safely" behind a desk again—or what Brabazon describes as "the women behind the man (M) behind the legend (Bond)" (490)—*Skyfall* does not end with the melancholic tone one might expect following the death of a major character. Rather, when Bond enters the new M's office, meets Miss Moneypenny, and accepts the Top Secret 007 file "with pleasure," the familiar sound of the Bond theme plays suggesting all is right with the world.

BIBLIOGRAPHY

"agent, n.1 and adj." *OED Online*. Oxford University Press, March 2014. Web. 2 May 2014.

Alexander, John T. *Catherine the Great: Life and Legend*. New York: Oxford University Press, 1989.

Allison, Deborah. "Innovative Vorspanne und Reflexivität im klassischen Hollywoodkino." *Das Buch zum Vorspann: "The Title is a Shot."* Eds. Alexander Böhnke, Rembert Hüser, and Georg Stanitzek. Berlin: Vorwerk, 2006. 90-101.

____. "Novelty Title Sequences and Self-Reflexivity in Classical Hollywood Cinema." Trans. Andrea Kirchhartz. *Title Design Project*. 28 January 2015 <http://www.titledesignproject. com/2012/04/novelty-title-sequences-and-self-reflexivity-in-classical-*hollywood*-cinema/>.

Althusser, Louis. *Lenin and Philosophy and Other Essays*. New York: Monthly Review Press, 1971.

Altman, Rick, Jones McGraw and Sonia Tatroe. "Inventing the Cinema Soundtrack: Hollywood's Multi-plane Sound System." *Music and Cinema*. Eds. James Buhler, Caryl Flinn, and David Neumeyer. Hanover, NH: Wesleyan University Press, 2000. 339–59.

Amacker, Anna Katherine, and Donna Ashley Moore. "'The Bitch is Dead': Anti-feminist Rhetoric in *Casino Royale*." *James Bond in World and Popular Culture: The Films are Not Enough*. 2nd ed. Eds. Robert G. Weiner, B. Lynn Whitfield and Jack Becker. Newcastle upon Tyne: Cambridge Scholars, 2011. 144-55.

Amis, Kingsley. *The James Bond Dossier*. London: Jonathan Cape, 1965.

"An Extremely Engaging Affair." *The Times Literary Supplement*. 17 April 1953: 249.

Antony, Paul, and Jacqueline Friedman. *Ian Fleming's Incredible Creation*. Chicago: Novel Books, 1965.

Ardizzone, Heidi. "Catching Up With History: Night of the Quarter Moon, the Rhinelander Case, and Interracial Marriage in 1959." *Mixed Race Hollywood*. Eds. Mary C. Beltran and Camilia Fojas. New York: New York University Press, 2008, 87-112.

Arp, Robert and Kevin S. Decker. "'That Fatal Kiss': Bond, Ethics and the Objectification of Women." *James Bond and Philosophy: Questions are Forever*. Eds. James B. South and Jacob M. Held. Chicago, IL: Open Court, 2006. 201-14.

Barnes, Alan, and Marcus Hearn. *Kiss Kiss Bang! Bang! The Unofficial James Bond Film Companion*. London: B.T. Batsford, 1997.

Barrett, Thomas M. "Mingling Pearl Powder with Nitroglycerin: Russian Nihilists in American Popular Culture." *Association Slavic, East European, and Eurasian Studies*. Boston Marriot Copley Place, Boston, MA. 21 November 2013.

Basinger, Jeanine. *A Woman's View: How Hollywood Spoke to Women, 1930-1960*. Middletown, CT: Wesleyan University Press, 1995.

Baudrillard, Jean. *Symbolic Exchange and Death*. Trans. Iain Hamilton Grant. London: SAGE

Publications, 1993.

Bazzini, Doris G., William D. McIntosh, Stephen M. Smith, Sabrina Cook, and Caleigh Harris. "The Aging Women in Popular Film: Underrepresented, Unattractive, Unfriendly, and Unintelligent." *Sex Roles* 36.7/8 (1997): 531-43.

Bear, Andrew. "Intellectuals and 007: High Comedy and Total Stimulation." *Dissent* (Winter 1966): 23-7.

Beaulieu, Elizabeth Ann. *Writing African American Women: An Encyclopedia of Literature By and About Women of Color. Volume 1: A-J.* Westport, CT: Greenwood Press, 2006.

Beckman, Karen. *Vanishing Women: Magic, Film, and Feminism.* Durham: Duke University Press, 2003.

Bennett, Tony. "James Bond as Popular Hero." *U203 Popular Culture: Unit 21.* Milton Keynes: The Open University, 1982.

____. "James Bond in the 1980s." *Marxism Today* 27.6 (1983): 37-9.

Bennett, Tony, and Janet Woollacott. *Bond and Beyond: The Political Career of a Popular Hero.* London: Macmillan, 1987.

____. "The Moments of Bond". *The James Bond Phenomenon: A Critical Reader.* Ed. Christoph Lindner. Manchester: Manchester University Press, 2003. 13-33.

Benson, Raymond. *The Facts of Death.* New York: Jove Books, 1999.

____. *High Time to Kill.* London: Hodder and Stoughton, 1999.

____. "Introduction." *James Bond: Choice of Weapons.* New York: Pegasus, 2010. vii-x.

____. *Tomorrow Never Dies.* London: Hodder and Stoughton, 1997.

____. *Zero Minus Ten.* London: G.B. Putnam, 1997.

Berger, John. *Ways of Seeing.* London: BBC and Penguin Books, 1972.

Bergonzi, Bernard. "The Case of Mr. Fleming." *Twentieth Century* (March 1958): 220-8.

Biskind, Peter. *Easy Riders, Raging Bulls: How the Sex, Drugs, and Rock 'n' Roll Generation Saved Hollywood.* New York: Simon and Schuster, 1998.

Black, Jeremy. *The Politics of James Bond: From Fleming's Novels to the Big Screen.* Westport CT: Praeger, 2001.

Bold, Christine. "Under the Very Skirts of Britannia: Re-Reading Women in the James Bond Novels." *The James Bond Phenomenon: A Critical Reader.* Ed. Christoph Lindner. Manchester: Manchester University Press, 2003. 169-83.

Bolton, Lucy. *Film and Female Consciousness.* London: Palgrave MacMillan, 2011.

Bondanella, Peter. *Umberto Eco and the Open Text: Semiotics, Fiction, Popular Culture.* Cambridge: Cambridge University Press, 1997.

Botticelli, Sandro. *The Birth of Venus/Nascita di Venere.* 1486. Uffizi Gallery, Florence.

Boucher, Anthony. "On Assignment with James Bond." *New York Times.* 25 August 1963: BR4.

Bourdieu, Pierre. *Masculine Domination.* Trans. Richard Nice. Stanford, CA: Stanford University Press, 2001.

Boyd, Nan Alamilla. "Lesbian feminism" *The Reader's Companion to U.S. Women's History.* Ed. Wilma Mankiller et al. New York: Houghton Mifflin Company, 1998. 213-14.

Brabazon, Tara. "Britain's Last Line of Defence: Miss Moneypenny and the Desperations of Filmic Feminism." *Women's Studies International Forum* 22.5 (1999): 489-96.

Brady, Miranda J. "The Well-Tempered Spy: Family, Nation and the Female Secret Agent in *Alias*." *Secret Agents: Popular Icons Beyond James Bond.* Ed. Jeremy Packer. New York: Peter Lang Publishing, 2009. 111-32.

Braidotti, Rosi. "Mothers, Monsters, & Machines." *Writing on the Body: Female Embodiment and Feminist Theory.* Eds. Katie Conboy, Nadia Medina, and Sarah Stanbury. New York: Columbia Press, 1997. 59-79.

Britton, Wesley. "007 on the Turntable: The Bond Music Off-screen." *James Bond in World and Popular Culture: The Films are Not Enough.* 2nd ed. Eds. Robert G. Weiner, B. Lynn Whitfield, and Jack Becker. Newcastle upon Tyne: Cambridge Scholars, 2011. 88-101.

Bronfen, Elisabeth. "*Femme Fatale*—Negotiations of Tragic Desire." *New Literary History* 35.1 (2004): 103-16.

Brown, Helen Gurley. *Sex and the Single Girl.* New York: Bernard Geis, 1962.

Bruzzi, Stella. *Undressing Cinema: Clothing and Identity in the Movies.* London: Routledge, 1997.

Buchanan, Paul D. *Radical Feminists: A Guide to an American Subculture.* Santa Barbara, CA: ABC-CLIO, 2011."

Burlingame, Jon. *The Music of James Bond.* Oxford and New York: Oxford University Press, 2012.

Bussey, Brenda, and J.B. Whipple. "Weaving the Past into the Present: Understanding the Context of Domestic Violence Against Native American Women." *Domestic Violence: Intersectionality and Culturally Competent Practice.* Eds. Lettie L. Lockhart and Fran S. Danis. New York: Columbia University Press, 2010. 286-317.

Butler, Judith. *Das Unbehagen der Geschlechter.* Trans. Kathrina Menke. Frankfurt: Suhrkamp, 1991.

Canby, Vincent. "The Ten Worst Films of 1969." *New York Times.* 4 January 1970: 81.

Cannadine, David. "James Bond and the Decline of England." *Encounter* 53.3 (November 1979): 46-55.

Caplen, Robert A. *Shaken & Stirred: The Feminism of James Bond.* Bloomington, IN: Xlibris, 2010.

Case, Ken. "Cinema Scene." *Ludington Daily News.* 23 August 1965: 12.

Castañeda, Antonia. "Women of Color and the Rewriting of Western History: The Discourse, Politics and Decolonization of History." *Pacific Historical Review* 61.4 (1992): 501–533.

Castle, Robert. "The Revolutionary James Bond Movie: *On Her Majesty's Secret Service.*" *Bright Lights Film Journal* 43 (2004): n.p. 28 January 2015 <http://brightlightsfilm.com/the-revolutionary-james-bond-movie-on-her-majestys-secret-service/>.

Cawelti, John G. "The Concept of Formula in the Study of Popular Literature." *Journal of Popular Culture* 3 (1969): 381-90.

Chapman, James. "Bond and Britishness." *Ian Fleming & James Bond: The Cultural Politics of 007.* Eds. Edward P. Comentale, Stephen Watt, and Skip Willman. Bloomington, IN: Indiana University Press, 2005. 129-43.

____. *Licence to Thrill: A Cultural History of the James Bond Films.* 2nd ed. London and New York: I.B. Tauris, 2007.

Chatterjee, Choi. "Transnational Romance, Terror and Heroism: Russia in American Popular Fiction, 1860-1917." *Comparative Studies in Society and History* 50.3 (2008): 753-77.

Child, Ben. "Will Angelina Jolie's *Salt* be a Seller?" *The Guardian.* 29 July 29 2010. 28 January 2015 <http://www.theguardian.com/film/filmblog/2010/jul/29/angelina-jolie-salt>.

Chin, Frank, and Jeffery Paul Chan. "Racist Love." *Seeing Through Shuck.* Ed. Richard Kostelanetz. New York: Ballantine Books, 1972. 65-79.

Citron Marcia J. "The Operatics of Detachment: *Tosca* in the James Bond Film *Quantum of Solace.*" *19th-Century Music* 34.3 (2011): 316-40.

Clarke, Deborah. *Driving Women: Fiction and Automobile Culture in Twentieth Century America.* Baltimore, MD: Johns Hopkins University Press, 2007.

"Communistic?" *Duncanville Suburban.* 11 June 1964: 10.

Conley, Jim. "Automobile Advertisements: The Magical and the Mundane." *Car Troubles: Critical Studies of Automobility and Auto-Mobility.* Eds. Jim Conley and Arlene Tigar McLaren. London: Ashgate, 2009. 37-58.

Cook, Nicholas. *Music: A Very Short Introduction.* 2nd ed. Oxford: Oxford University Press, 2000.

Cook, Pam. "No Fixed Address: The Women's Picture from *Outrage* to *Blue Steel.*" *Contemporary Hollywood Cinema.* Eds. Steve Neale and Murray Smith. London: Routledge, 1998. 229-46.

Coon, David Roger. "Two Steps Forward, One Step Back: The Selling of *Charlie's Angels* and *Alias.*" *Journal of Popular Film and Television* 33.1 (2005): 2-11.

Coppa, Francesca. "The Body Immaterial: Magicians' Assistants and the Performance of Labor." *Performing Magic on the Western Stage.* Eds. Francesca Coppa, Lawrence Hass, and James Peck. New York: Palgrave Macmillan, 2008. 85-106.

Corliss, Richard. "Angelina Jolie: Worth Her *Salt*" *Time.* 2 August 2010. 28 January 2015 <http://content.time.com/time/magazine/article/0,9171,2005859,00.html>.

Cowgill, Rachel, and Hilary Poriss. *The Arts of the Prima Donna in the Long Nineteenth Century.* New York: Oxford University Press, 2012.

Cox, Katharine. "Becoming James Bond: Daniel Craig, Rebirth, and Refashioning Masculinity in *Casino Royale* (2006)." *Journal of Gender Studies* 23.2 (2013): 1-13. < http://www.tandfonline.com/doi/abs/10.1080/09589236.2013.783462#.VMkA8misWSp >.

Cross, Robert. "Ian Fleming's Refashioning of the English Gentleman in *From Russia, with Love.*" *James Bond in World and Popular Culture.* 2nd ed. Eds. Robert G. Weiner, B. Lynn Whitfield, and Jack Becker. Newcastle upon Tyne: Cambridge Scholars, 2011. 310-23.

"Daniel Craig in Conversation with Brian D. Johnson." *Maclean's* 125.42 (29 October 2012): 14-6.

Dassanowsky, Robert von. "A Caper of One's Own: Fantasy Female Liberation in 1960s Crime Comedy Film." *Journal of Popular Film and Television* 35.3 (2007): 107-18.

Darby, William, and Jack Du Bois. *American Films Music: Major Composers, Techniques, Trends, 1915-1990.* Jefferson: McFarland & Company, 1990.

de Beauvoir, Simone. *The Second Sex.* New York: Alfred A. Knopf, 2010.

____. *The Second Sex.* Trans. H.M. Parshley. London: Vintage Books, 1997.

Denning, Michael. *Cover Stories: Narrative and Ideology in the British Spy Thriller.* London: Routledge & Kegan Paul, 1987.

____. "Licensed to Look: James Bond and the Heroism of Consumption." *The James Bond Phenomenon: A Critical Reader.* Ed. Christoph Lindner. Manchester: Manchester University Press, 2003. 56-75.

Dittmer, Jason, and Klaus Dodds. "The Geopolitical Audience: Watching *Quantum of Solace* (2008) in London." *Popular Communication* 11 (2013): 76-91.

Doane, Mary Ann. *The Desire to Desire: The Woman's Film of the 1940s.* Bloomington: Indiana University Press, 1987.

____. *Femmes Fatales: Feminism, Film Theory, Psychoanalysis.* New York and London: Routledge, 1991.

____. "Film and the Masquerade: Theorising the Female Spectator." *Feminist Film Theory: A Reader.* Ed. Sue Thornham. New York, NY: New York UP, 1999. 131-45.

Dodds, Klaus. "Shaking and Stirring James Bond: Age, Gender and the Resilient Agent in *Skyfall* (2012)." *Journal of Popular Film and Television* 42.3 (2014): 116-30.

Dow, Bonnie. *Prime-Time Feminism: Television, Media Culture, and the Women's Movement Since 1970*. Philadelphia, PA: University of Pennsylvania Press, 1996.

Drake, Alicia. *The Beautiful Fall: Fashion, Genius, and Glorious Excess in 1970s Paris*. London: Bloomsbury, 2006.

Dresner, Lisa M. "'All Mixed Up': James Bond's World of Mixing, Displacement, and Boundary Crossing." *James Bond in World and Popular Culture*. 2nd ed. Eds. Robert G. Weiner, B. Lynn Whitfield, and Jack Becker. Newcastle upon Tyne: Cambridge Scholars, 2011. 271-87.

Dutz, Britni. "James Bond and the Evolution of the Gaze though Female Spectatorship." *James Bond in World and Popular Culture: The Films Are Not Enough*. Eds. Robert G. Weiner, B. Lynn Whitfield, and Jack Becker. 2nd ed. Newcastle upon Tyne: Cambridge Scholars, 2011. 183-92.

Dyer, Richard. *White*. London: Routledge, 1997.

Ebert, Roger. Rev. of *GoldenEye*, dir. Martin Campbell. *RogerEbert.com*. 17 November 1995. 28 January 2015 <http://www.rogerebert.com/reviews/goldeneye-1995>.

____. Rev. of *Skyfall*, dir. Sam Mendes. *RogerEbert.com*. 7 November 2012. 28 January 2015 <http://www.rogerebert.com/reviews/skyfall-2012>.

____. "Salt." *The Chicago-Sun Times*. 21 July 2010. 28 January 2015 <http://www.rogerebert.com/reviews/salt-2010>.

Eco, Umberto. "Narrative Structures in Fleming." *The James Bond Phenomenon: A Critical Reader*. Ed. Christoph Lindner. Manchester: Manchester University Press, 2009. 34-55.

____. *The Role of the Reader: Explorations in the Semiotics of Texts*. Bloomington: Indiana University Press, 1979.

Elliot, Andrew J., and Daniela Niesta. "Romantic Red: Red Enhances Men's Attraction to Women." *Journal of Personality and Social Psychology* 95.5 (2008): 1150-64.

Espiritu, Yen Le, "Ideological Racism and Cultural Resistance: Constructing Our Own Images." *Contested Images: Women of Color in Popular Culture*. Ed. Alma M. Garcia. Plymouth, UK: AltaMira Press, 2012. 3-26.

Evans, Dylan. *An Introductory Dictionary of Lacanian Psychoanalysis*. New York, Routledge, 1996.

Everett, Wendy. "Songlines. Alternative Journeys in Contemporary European Cinema." *Music and Cinema*. Eds. James Buhler, Caryl Flinn, and David Neumeyer. Hanover, NH: Wesleyan University Press, 2000. 99-117.

"Fall Fashion Rumors Are Spiked." *Ada Evening News*. 7 July 1964: 6.

Faludi, Susan. *Backlash: The Undeclared War Against American Women*. New York: Random House LLC, 2006.

Fiegal, Eddi. *John Barry, a Sixties Theme: From James Bond to Midnight Cowboy*. London: Boxtree, 2001.

Fishman, Jack. "Jack Fishman Presents 007 and Me by Ian Fleming." *For Bond Lovers Only*. Ed. Sheldon Lane. New York: Dell, 1965. 9-34.

Fleming, Ian. *Casino Royale*. 1953. Penguin Classics ed. London: Penguin, 2004.

____. *Casino Royale. A James Bond Novel*. 1953. Las Vegas: Thomas & Mercer, 2012.

____. *Diamonds Are Forever*. 1956. London: Penguin, 2004.

____. *Diamonds are Forever*. 1956. London: Vintage Books, 2012.

____. *Dr. No*. 1958. Penguin Classics ed. London: Penguin, 2004.

____. *For Your Eyes Only.* 1960. Penguin Classics ed. London: Penguin, 2006.

____. *From Russia, With Love.* 1957. Penguin Classics ed. London: Penguin, 2004.

____. *From Russia with Love.* New York: Signet, 1957.

____. *From Russia With Love, Dr. No, Goldfinger.* London: Penguin, 2002.

____. *Goldfinger.* 1959. Penguin Classics ed. London: Penguin, 2004.

____. *Goldfinger.* 1959. London: Vintage, 2012.

____. "How To Write A Thriller." *Books and Bookmen,* May 1963: 14-16.

____. *Live and Let Die.* 1954. Las Vegas: Thomas and Mercer, 2012.

____. "The Living Daylights." *Octopussy and the Living Daylights.* 1966. New York: Penguin Group, 2004.

____. *The Man with the Golden Gun.* 1965. London: Penguin, 2006.

____. *Moonraker.* 1955. Penguin Classics ed. London: Penguin, 2004.

____. *On Her Majesty's Secret Service.* 1963. Penguin Classics ed. London: Penguin, 2004.

____. *On Her Majesty's Secret Service.* New York: Signet, 1963.

____. *The Spy Who Loved Me.* 1962. Penguin Classics ed. London: Penguin, 2006.

____. *Thunderball.* 1961. Penguin Classics ed. London: Penguin, 2004.

____. *You Only Live Twice.* 1964. Penguin Classics ed. London: Penguin, 2004.

Foucault, Michel. *Discipline and Punish: The Birth of the Prison.* Trans. Alan Sheridan. New York: Penguin, 1977.

____. *History of Madness.* New York: Routledge, 2006.

Freud, Sigmund. *On Metapsychology.* Trans. James Strachey. London: Penguin Books, 1991.

____. *On Sexuality.* Trans. James Strachey. London: Penguin, 1977.

Friedan, Betty. *The Feminine Mystique.* New York: W.W. Norton & Company Inc., 2013.

"From Greece with Love." *New York Times.* 13 April 1964: 19.

"From Russia." *The Progress Index.* 19 December 1965: 4.

Funnell, Lisa. "Assimilating Hong Kong Style for the Hollywood Action Woman." *Quarterly Review of Film and Video* 28.1 (2011): 66-79.

____. "From English Partner to American Action Hero: The Heroic Identity and Transnational Appeal of the Bond Girl." *Heroines and Heroes: Symbolism, Embodiment, Narratives and Identity.* Ed. Christopher Hart. Kingswinford, UK: Midrash, 2008. 61-80.

____. "'I Know Where You Keep Your Gun': Daniel Craig as the Bond-Bond Girl Hybrid in *Casino Royale*." *Journal of Popular Culture* 44.3 (2011): 455-72.

____. "Negotiating Shift in Feminism: The 'Bad' Girls of James Bond." *Women on Screen: Feminism and Femininity in Visual Culture.* Ed. Melanie Waters. Basingstoke: Palgrave Macmillan, 2011. 199-212.

____. *Warrior Women: Gender, Race, and the Transnational Chinese Action Star.* Albany, NY: SUNY Press, 2014.

Gaines, Jane. "Costume and Narrative: How Dress Tells the Woman's Story." *Fabrications: Costume and the Female Body.* Eds. Jane Gaines and Charlotte Herzog. New York: Routledge, 1990. 180-211.

____. "Introduction: Fabricating the Female Body." *Fabrications: Costume and the Female Body.* Eds. Jane Gaines and Charlotte Herzog. New York: Routledge, 1990. 1-27.

Garcia-Blanco, Iñaki, and Karin Wahl-Jorgensen. "The Discursive Construction of Women Politicians in the European Press." *Feminist Media Studies* 12.3 (2012): 422-41.

Gardies, André. "Am Anfang war der Vorspann." *Das Buch zum Vorspann: "The Title is a Shot."* Eds. Alexander Böhnke, Rembert Hüser, and Georg Stanitzek. Berlin: Vorwerk, 2006.

21-33.

Garland, Tony W. "'The Coldest Weapon of All': The Bond Girl Villain in James Bond Films." *Journal of Popular Film and Television* 37.4 (2009): 179-88.

Gardner, John. *COLD*. London: Coronet, 1996.

____, *GoldenEye*. New York: Boulevard Books, 1995.

____. *Win, Lose or Die*. London: Coronet, 1990.

Gavron, Hannah. *The Captive Wife: Conflicts of Housebound Mothers*. London: Routledge and K. Paul, 1966.

Gerhard, Jane F. *Desiring Revolution: Second-wave Feminism and the Rewriting of American Sexual Thought, 1920 to 1982*. New York: Columbia UP, 2001.

Giammarco, David. *For Your Eyes Only: Behind the Scenes of the James Bond Films*. Toronto: ECW Press, 2002.

Gill, Rosalind, and Christina Scharff. "Introduction." *New Femininities: Postfeminism, Neoliberalism and Subjectivity*. Eds. Rosalind Gill and Christina Scharff. New York: Palgrave Macmillan, 2011. 1-18. Print.

Girard, René. *Violence and the Sacred*. Baltimore: Johns Hopkins University Press, 1972.

"The Girls of Russia and the Iron Curtain Countries." *Playboy*. March 1964: 104-16, 136-40.

Goldie, Terry. "The Representation of the Indigine." *The Post-colonial Studies Reader*. Eds. Bill Ashcroft, Gareth Griffiths, and Helen Tiffin. London: Routledge, 1995. 232-236.

Gorbman, Claudia. *Unheard Melodies: Narrative Film Music*. Indianapolis: Indiana University Press, 1987.

Grant, Donald. "Prof. Fedorenko Lectures at the U.N." *New York Times*. 16 July 1967: 172.

Greiner, Wilhelm. *Kino macht Körper: Konstruktionen von Körperlichkeit im neueren Hollywood-Film*. Alfeld (Leine): Coppi-Verlag, 1998.

Grella, George. "James Bond: Culture Hero (Book)." *New Republic* 150.22 (1964): 17-20.

Grosz, Elizabeth. *Jacques Lacan: A Feminist Introduction*. London: Routledge, 1990.

Guerrero, Ed. "The Black Image in Protective Custody: Hollywood's Biracial Buddy Films of the Eighties." *Black American Cinema*. Ed. Manthia Diawara. New York & London: Routledge, 1993. 237-46.

Gunther, John. *Inside Russia Today*. New York: Harper, 1957.

Hamad, Hannah. *Postfeminism and Paternity in Contemporary US Film: Framing Fatherhood*. New York: Routledge, 2014.

Hartmann, Susan. "Gender and the Transformation of Politics." Ed. Mark C. Carnes. *The Columbia History of Post WWII America*. New York: Columbia University Press, 2007. 285-310.

Haskell, Molly. *From Reverence to Rape: The Treatment of Women in the Movies*. 2nd ed. Chicago: University of Chicago Press, 1987.

Haworth, Catherine. "Introduction: Gender, Sexuality and the Soundtrack." *Music, Sound and the Moving Image* 6.2 (2012): 113-35.

Hediger, Vinzenz. "Now, in a World where: Trailer, Vorspann und das Ergebnis des Films." *Das Buch zum Vorspann: "The Title is a Shot."* Eds. Alexander Böhnke, Rembert Hüser, and Georg Stanitzek. Berlin: Vorwerk, 2006. 102-22.

Hesford, Victoria. *Feeling Women's Liberation*. Durham, NC: Duke University Press, 2013.

Heung, Marina. "Representing Ourselves: Films and Videos by Asian American/Canadian Women." *Feminism, Multiculturalism, and the Media: Global Diversities*. Ed. Angharad N. Valdivia. Thousand Oaks, CA: SAGE Publications, 1995. 82-104.

Hills, Elizabeth. "From 'Figurative Males' to Action Heroines: Further Thoughts on Active Women in the Cinema." *Screen* 40.1 (1999): 38-50.

Hindus, Maurice. *House without a Roof*. Garden City, NY: Doubleday, 1961.

Hines, Claire. "Entertainment for Men: Uncovering the Playboy Bond." *The James Bond Phenomenon: A Critical Reader*. Ed. Christoph Lindner. Manchester: Manchester University Press, 2003. 169-77.

Hockley, Luke. "Shaken, Not Stirred: James Bond and the Puer Archetype." *Perpetual Adolescence: Jungian Analyses of American Media, Literature, and Pop Culture*. Eds. Sally Porterfield, Keith Polette and Tita French Baumlin. Albany, NY: State University of New York Press, 2009. 105-22.

hooks, bell. *Black Looks: Race and Representation*. Boston: South End Press, 1992.

____. *Reel to Real: Race, Sex, and Class at the Movies*. New York: Routledge, 1996.

Hollows, Joanne. *Feminism, Femininity and Popular Culture*. Manchester: Manchester University Press, 2000.

Hovey, Jaime. "Lesbian Bondage, or Why Dykes Like 007." *Ian Fleming & James Bond: The Cultural Politics of 007*. Eds. Edward P. Comentale, Stephen Watt, and Skip Willman. Bloomington, IN: Indiana UP, 2005. 42-54.

Hubai, Gergely. "Recapturing the Midas Touch: A Critical Reading of the Bond Songs' Chart Positions." *James Bond in World and Popular Culture: The Films are Not Enough*. Eds. Robert G. Weiner, B. Lynn Whitfield, and Jack Becker. 2nd ed. Newcastle upon Tyne: Cambridge Scholars, 2011. 129-41.

Hulko, Wendy. "The Time- and Context-Contingent Nature of Intersectionality and Interlocking Oppressions." *Affilia*, 24.1 (2009): 44-55.

"'In' Fashions to Make the Scene." *Kingsport Times-News*. 22 September 1968: 2d.

"James Bond Double Bill Set for Manor Theater." *San Mateo Times*. 18 May 1965: 15.

Jeffords, Susan. *Hard Bodies: Hollywood Masculinity in the Reagan Era*. New Jersey: Rutgers University Press, 1994.

Jenkins, Tricia. "James Bond's 'Pussy' and Anglo-American Cold War Sexuality." *Journal of American Culture* 28.3 (2005): 309-17.

Jennings, Ros. "It's All Just a Little Bit of History Repeating: Pop Stars, Audiences, Performance and Ageing — Exploring the Performance Strategies of Shirley Bassey and Petula Clark." *Rock On: Women, Ageing and Popular Music*. Eds. Ros Jennings and Abigail Gardner. Aldershot: Ashgate, 2012. 35-52.

Jiwani, Yasmin. "The Eurasian Female Hero(ine): Sydney Fox as *Relic Hunter*." *Journal of Popular Film and Television* 32.4 (2005): 182-91.

Jones, Alan. "Interview with Michael Apted." *Cinefantastique* 31.9 (1999): 36-8.

Johnson, Paul. "Sex, Snobbery and Sadism." *New Statesman* 5 April 1958: 431.

Johnson, Allan G. "The Social Construction of Difference." *Readings for Diversity and Social Justice*. 2nd ed. Eds. Maurianne Adams et al. New York: Routledge, 2010. 15-20

Kackman, Michael. *Citizen Spy: Television, Espionage, and Cold War Culture*. Minneapolis: University of Minnesota Press, 2005.

Kael, Pauline. *Reeling*. Boston: Little and Brown, 1976.

Kamitsuka, Margaret. *Feminist Theology and the Challenge of Difference*. New York: Oxford University Press, 2006.

Klein, Renate and Susan Hawthorne. "Reclaiming Sisterhood: Radical Feminism as an Antidote to Theoretical and Embodied Fragmentation of Women." *Desperately Seeking Sisterhood: Still*

Challenging and Building. Eds. Magdalene Ang-Lygate, Chris Corrin and Millsom S. Henry. New York: Taylor and Francis, 1997. 57-70.

Koestenbaum, Wayne. *The Queen's Throat: Opera, Homosexuality, and the Mystery of Desire*. New York: Vintage, 1993.

Krainitzki, Eva. "Judi Dench's Age-Inappropriateness and the Role of M: Challenging Normative Temporality." *Journal of Aging Studies* 29 (2014): 32-40.

Krueger, John. "Which Beauty Will Be Bonded?" *Stars and Stripes*. 22 March 1963: 11.

Kyriazi, Paul. "A Bond Girl Threatens Suicide to Keep Her Part." *AuthorsDen.Com* 17 May 2014. 28 January 2015 <http://www.authorsden.com/visit/viewarticle. asp?AuthorID=5687&id=71472>.

Lacan, Jacques. *The Psychoses: The Seminar of Jacques Lacan Book III*. Trans. Russell Grigg. New York: W.W. Norton & Company, Inc., 1993.

____. "The Signification of the Phallus." *Écrits: The Complete Collection*. Trans. Bruce Fink. New York: W.W. Norton & Company, Inc., 1996. 575-84.

Ladenson, Elisabeth. "Pussy Galore." *The James Bond Phenomenon: A Critical Reader*. Ed. Christoph Lindner. Manchester: Manchester University Press, 2003. 184-201.

Laing, Heather. "Emotion by Numbers: Music, Song and the Musical." *Musicals: Hollywood and Beyond*. Eds. Bill Marshall and Robynn Stilwell. Exeter and Portland: Intellect, 2000. 5-13.

Landis, Deborah Nadoolman. *Screencraft - Costume Design*. Burlington: Focal Press, 2003.

Lauzen, Martha M., and David M. Dozier. "Maintaining the Double Standard: Portrayals of Age and Gender in Popular Films." *Sex Roles* 52.7/8 (2005): 437-46.

Leach, Jim. "'The World Has Changed': Bond in the 1990s-and Beyond?" *The James Bond Phenomenon: A Critical Reader*. Ed. Christoph Lindner. Machester: Manchester University Press, 2003. 248-58.

____. "The Spymaster who Loved Me: M and the Gender Dynamics of the Bond Phenomenon." *Beauty and the Abject: Interdisciplinary Perspectives*. Eds. Leslie Boldt-Irons, Corrado Federici, and Ernesto Virgulti. New York: Peter Lang, 2006. 225-33.

Lenoir, Jean-Pierre. "Spying behind the Curtain." *New York Times*. 18 September 1965: BR56.

Leppert, Richard. *The Nude: The Cultural Rhetoric of the Body in the Art of Western Modernity*. Boulder: Westview Press, 2007.

Lindner, Christoph, ed. *The James Bond Phenomenon: A Critical Reader*. Manchester: Manchester University Press, 2003.

____. *Revisioning 007: James Bond and Casino Royale*. London: Wallflower, 2009.

London, Justin. "Leitmotifs and Musical Reference in the Classical Film Score." *Music and Cinema*. Eds. James Buhler, Caryl Flinn, and David Neumeyer. Hanover, NH: Wesleyan University Press, 2000. 85-96.

Lorde, Audre. *Sister Outsider: Essays and Speeches*. Trumansburg, NY: Crossing, 1984.

Lu, Sheldon H. *China, Transnational Visuality, Global Postmodernity*. Stanford: Stanford University Press, 2001.

Lukas, J. Anthony. "Withholding of 'Zhivago' Film Stirs Indian Storm." *New York Times*. 21 June 1966: 3.

Lupton, Deborah. "Monsters in Metal Cocoons: 'Road Rage' and Cyborg Bodies". *Body and Society* 5.1 (1999): 57-72.

Lycett, Andrew. *Ian Fleming: The Man Behind James Bond*. London: Weidenfeld & Nicolson, 1995.

Lynch, Annette. *Porn Chic: Exploring the Contours of Raunch Eroticism*. New York: Berg, 2012.

Macey, David. *Dictionary of Critical Theory*. London: Penguin, 2000.

MacColl, René. *Just Back from Russia: 77 Days Inside the Soviet Union*. London: Daily Express, 1960.

Madden, Karl. "The Melancholy Touch: Romantic Shades of John Barry's Bond." *James Bond in World and Popular Culture: The Films are Not Enough*. Eds. Robert G. Weiner, B. Lynn Whitfield, and Jack Becker. 2nd ed. Newcastle upon Tyne: Cambridge Scholars, 2011. 118-28.

Manatu, Norma. *African American Women and Sexuality in the Cinema*. Jefferson, NC: McFarland, 2003.

Marchetti, Gina. *Romance and the "Yellow Peril": Race, Sex, and Discursive Strategies in Hollywood Fiction*. Los Angeles: University of California Press, 1993.

Martinson, Jane. "Is *Skyfall* a Less Sexist Bond Film?" *The Guardian: The Woman's Blog*. 30 October 2012. 29 January 2015 <http://www.theguardian.com/film/the-womens-blog-with-jane-martinson/2012/oct/30/skyfall-less-sexist-bond-film>.

Marwick, Arthur. *The Sixties: Cultural Revolution in Britain, France, Italy and the United States, c.1958-c.1974*. Oxford: Oxford University Press, 1998.

Matheson, Sue. "He Who Eats Meat Wins: Appetite, Power, and Nietzsche in the Novels of Ian Fleming." *James Bond and Philosophy: The Questions Are Forever*. Eds. James B. South and Jacob M. Held. Chicago: Open Court, 2006. 63-78.

Mazower, Mark. *Dark Continent: Europe's Twentieth Century*. New York: Knopf, 1998.

McCarthy, Todd. Rev. of *GoldenEye*, dir. Martin Campbell. *Variety* 15 November 1995. 29 January 2015 <http://variety.com/1995/film/reviews/goldeneye-1200443796/>.

McClary, Susan. *Feminine Endings: Music, Gender, & Sexuality*. 2nd ed. Minneapolis: University of Minnesota Press, 2002.

McDermot, Mark K. "'He Strikes Like Thun-n-n-nder-r-r-r-BALL-L-L-L-L-L!': The Place of the James Bond Theme Song." *James Bond in World and Popular Culture: The Films are Not Enough*. Eds. Robert G. Weiner, B. Lynn Whitfield, and Jack Becker. 2nd ed. Newcastle upon Tyne: Cambridge Scholars, 2011. 102-17.

McKay, Sinclair. *The Man with the Golden Touch: How the Bond films Conquered the World*. New York: Overlook Press, 2010.

McNeely, Tom L. "The Feminization of M: Gender and Authority in the Bond Films." *James Bond in World and Popular Culture: The Films are Not Enough*. 2nd ed. Eds. Robert G. Weiner, B. Lynn Whitfield, and Jack Becker. Newcastle upon Tyne: Cambridge Scholars Press, 2011. 156-61.

_____. "Somebody Does it Better: Competent Women in the Bond Films." *James Bond in World and Popular Culture*. Eds. Robert G. Weiner, B. Lynn Whitfield, and Jack Becker. Cambridge: Cambridge Scholars Publishing, 2011. 178-82.

McRobbie, Angela. "Post-Feminism and Popular Culture." *Feminist Media Studies* 4.3 (2004): 255-64.

Mera, Miguel. "Invention/re-invention." *Music, Sound, and the Moving Image* 3.1 (2009): 1-20.

Miller, Daniel. "Driven Society." *Car Cultures*. Ed. Daniel Miller. Oxford: Berg, 2001. 1-33.

Miller, Martin. "Letter from Max." *Portsmouth Times*. 18 November 1963: 6.

Miller, Toby. "Cultural Imperialism and James Bond's Penis." *Spyscreen: Espionage on Film & TV from the 1930s to the 1960s*. Oxford: Oxford University Press, 2003. 122-53.

Modleski, Tania. *Feminism without Women: Culture and Criticism in a "Postfeminist" Age*. New York: Routledge, 1991.

Moniot, Drew. "James Bond and America in the Sixties: An Investigation of the Formula Film in Popular Culture." *Journal of the University Film Association* 28.3 (Summer 1976): 25-33.

Montgomery, Fiona. *Women's Rights: Struggles and Feminism in Britain c.1770-1970.* Manchester: Manchester University Press, 2006.

Mulvey, Laura. "Hitchcock's Blondes and Feminist Film Theory: A Cinema of Voyeurism or a Cinema of Self-Reflexivity?" University of St. Andrews. Arts Lecture Theatre, Fife, Scotland. 15 October 2013.

Mulvey, Laura. "Visual Pleasure and Narrative Cinema." *Film Theory and Criticism: Introductory Readings.* Eds. Leo Braudy and Marshall Cohen. New York: Oxford UP, 1999. 833-44.

Neuendorf, Kimberly A., et al. "Shaken and Stirred: A Content Analysis of Women's Portrayals in James Bond Films." *Sex Roles* 62.11/12 (2010): 747-61.

"New Film Costume." *Coshocton Tribune.* 25 July 1963: 12.

Norton, Howard. *Only in Russia.* Princeton: D. Van Norstrand, 1961.

O'Connell, Sean. *The Car and British Society: Class, Gender and Motoring, 1896-1939.* Manchester: Manchester University Press, 1998.

O'Day, Marc. "Of Leather Suits and Kinky Boots: *The Avengers*, Style and Popular Culture." *Action TV: Tough Guys, Smooth Operators and Foxy Chicks.* Eds. Bill Osgerby and Anna Gough-Yates, London: Routledge, 2001. 221-35.

"*On Her Majesty's Secret Service.*" Review. *Variety* 31 December 1968. 29 January 2015 <http://variety.com/1968/film/reviews/on-her-majesty-s-secret-service-1200421871/>.

"Oswald Read Assassination, Kennedy Books." *Wisconsin State Journal.* 29 November 1963: 1.

Palmer, William J. *The Films of the Eighties.* Carbondale, IL: Southern Illinois University Press, 1995.

Parker, Barry. *Death Rays, Jet Packs, Stunts, and Supercars: The Fantastic Physics of Film's Most Celebrated Secret Agent.* Baltimore: Johns Hopkins University Press, 2005.

Paulin, Scott D. "Richard Wagner and the Fantasy of Cinematic Unity: The Idea of *Gesamtkunstwerk* in the History and Theory of Film Music." *Music and Cinema.* Eds. James Buhler, Caryl Flinn, and David Neumeyer. Hanover, NH: Wesleyan University Press, 2000. 58-84.

Payne, Barbara, and Frank Whittington. "Older Women: An Examination of Popular Stereotypes and Research Evidence." *Social Problems* 23.4 (1976): 488-504.

Pearson, John. *The Life of Ian Fleming.* New York: McGraw-Hill, 1966.

Pelrine, Eleanor and Dennis. *Ian Fleming: The Man with the Golden Pen.* USA: Swan Publishing Co., 1966.

Perkin, Harold. *The Rise of Professional Society: England Since 1880.* London: Routledge, 1989.

Pfeiffer, Lee, and Dave Worrall. *The Essential Bond: The Authorized Guide to the World of 007.* 2nd ed. London: Boxtree, 2000.

Potts, Annie. "The Mark of the Beast: Inscribing 'Animality' through Extreme Body Modification." *Knowing Animals.* Eds. Laurence Simmons and Philip Armstrong. Boston: Brill, 2007. 131-52.

Powell, Dilys. Rev. of *Thunderball*, Dir. Terence Young. *Sunday Times* 2 January 1966: 33. Powledge, Fred. "F.B.I. Studying Oswald's Stay in New Orleans." *New York Times.* 29 November 1963: 21.

Prendergast, Roy M. *Film Music: A Neglected Art. A Critical Study of Music in Films.* New York: New York University Press, 1977.

Price, James. "Our Man in the Torture Chamber: The Novels of Ian Fleming." *London Magazine* July 1962: 67-70.

Purse, Lisa. "Return of the 'Angry Woman': Authenticating Female Physical Action in Contemporary Cinema." *Women on Screen: Feminism and Femininity in Visual Culture.* Ed. Melanie Waters. New York: Palgrave Macmillan, 2011. 185-98.

_____. *Contemporary Action Cinema.* Edinburgh: Edinburgh University Press, 2011.

Redshaw, Sarah. *In the Company of Cars: Driving As a Social and Cultural Practice.* Aldershot: Ashgate, 2008.

Reich, Charles A. *The Greening of America.* New York: Bantam Books, 1970.

Reid, Susan E. "Cold War in the Kitchen; Gender and the De-Stalinization of Consumer Taste in the Soviet Union under Khrushchev." *Slavic Review* 61.2 (2002): 211-52.

Richards, Mark. "John Barry's James Bond Scores (Part 6 of 6): Barry's Changing Bond Style." Film Music Notes: *Analysis, Style, Technique, and More.* 30 June 2013. 29 January 2015 <http://www.filmmusicnotes.com/john-barrys-james-bond-scores-part-6-of-6-barrys-changing-bond-style/>.

Richler, Mordecai. "James Bond Unmasked." *Mass Culture Revisited.* Eds. Bernard Rosenberg and David Manning White. New York: Van Nostrand Reinhold, 1971. 341-55.

Rogers, Michael. "Book Reviews: Classic Returns." *Library Journal* 128.16 (2003): 123.

Roof, Judith. "Living the James Bond Lifestyle." *Ian Fleming and The Cultural Politics of James Bond.* Ed. Edward Comentale, Stephen Watt and Skip Willman. Bloomington: Indiana University Press, 2005. 71-86.

Rubin, Steven Jay. *The James Bond Films.* New York: Arlington House, 1981.

Rudy, Kathy. "Radical Feminism, Lesbian Separatism, and Queer Theory." *Feminist Studies* 27.1 (Spring 2001): 190-222.

Ryall, Tom. *Britain and the American Cinema.* New York: SAGE Publications, 2001.

Ryan, Kathleen M., and Deborah A. Macey, eds. *Television and the Self: Knowledge, Identity, and Media Representation.* New York: Lexington, 2013.

Salisbury, Harrison. *To Moscow—And Beyond: A Reporter's Narrative.* New York: Harper, 1959.

Sarris, Andrew. "Diamonds Are Forever." *Village Voice.* 16 December 1971. 79.

Savoye, Daniel Ferreras. *The Signs of James Bond: Semiotic Explorations in the World of 007.* Jefferson, NC: McFarland, 2013.

Scheibel, Will. "The History of *Casino Royale* On (and Off) Screen." *Revisioning 007: James Bond and Casino Royale.* Ed. Christoph Lindner. London: Wallflower, 2009. 11-32.

Schjeldahl, Peter. "Bond is Back and Diamonds Got Him." *New York Times* 26 December 1971: D15.

Schickel, Richard. "Shaky, Not Stirring." Rev. of *GoldenEye*, dir. Martin Campbell. *Time* (1995): 92.

Schößler, Franziska. *Einführung in die Gender Studies.* Berlin: Akademie Verlag, 2008.

Shapira, Michal. "Psychoanalysts on the Radio: Domestic Citizenship and Motherhood in Postwar Britain." *Women and Gender in Postwar Europe: From Cold War to European Union.* Eds. Joanna Regulska and Bonnie G. Smith. New York: Routledge, 2012. 82-97.

Sharpe, Jenny "Figures of Colonial Resistance." *The Post-Colonial Studies Reader.* Eds. Bill Ashcroft, Gareth Griffiths, and Helen Tiffin. London: Routledge, 1995. 99-103.

Shildrick, Margit. *Embodying the Monster: Encounters with the Vulnerable Self.* London: Sage, 2002.

Sikov, Ed. *Mr Strangelove: A Biography of Peter Sellers.* New York: Hyperion, 2002.

Silverman, Kaja. *The Acoustic Mirror: The Female Voice in Psychoanalysis and Cinema.* Bloomington and Indianapolis: Indiana University Press, 1988.

Silverstein, Shel. *Playboy's Silverstein around the World*. New York: Simon & Schuster, 2007.

Singh, Chandra. *Radical Feminism and Women's Writing*. New Delhi: Atlantic Publishers, 2007.

Sked, Alan and Chris Cook. *Postwar Britain: A Political History*. New York: Penguin Books, 1990.

Smith, Jeff. "Unheard Melodies?: A Critique of Psychoanalytic Theories of Film Music." *Post-Theory: Reconstructing Film Studies*. Eds. David Bordwell and Noël Carroll. Wisconsin: Wisconsin University Press, 1996. 230-47.

_____. *The Sounds of Commerce: Marketing Popular Film Music*. New York: Columbia University Press, 1998.

Smith, Jim, and Stephen Lavington. *Bond Films*. London: Virgin Books, 2002.

Sontag, Susan. "The Double Standard of Aging." *On the Contrary: Essays by Men and Women*. Eds. Martha Rainbolt and Janet Fleetwood. Albany, NY: State University of New York Press, 1983. 99–112.

Soter, Tom. *Investigating Couples: A Critical Analysis of the Thin Man, the Avengers, and the X-Files*. Jefferson, NC: McFarland, 2002.

Souriau, Etienne. "Die Struktur des filmischen Universums und das Vokabular der Filmologie." *Montage AV* 6.2 (1997): 140-57.

Spender, Dale. *Man Made Language*. 2nd ed. London: Pandora Press, 1990.

Spicer, Andrew. *Typical Men: The Representation of Masculinity in Popular British Cinema*. London: I.B. Tauris, 2001.

Spivak, Gayatri Chakravorty. *Can the Subaltern Speak?* Basingstoke: Macmillan, 1988.

Stack, Peter. "New Bond More Action Than Style." Rev. of *GoldenEye*, dir. Martin Campbell. *San Francisco Chronicle* 17 November 1995. 29 January 2015 <http://www.sfgate.com/movies/article/FILM-REVIEW-New-Bond-More-Action-Than-Style-3019862.php>.

Stanitzek, Georg. "Vorspann (*titles/credits, générique*)." *Das Buch zum Vorspann: "The Title is a Shot."* Eds. Alexander Böhnke, Rembert Hüser, and Georg Stanitzek. Berlin: Vorwerk, 2006. 8-20.

Starkey, Lycurgus Monroe. *James Bond's World of Values*. Nashville: Abingdon Press, 1966.

Sterling, Martin, and Gary Morecambe. *Martinis, Girls and Guns: 50 Years of 007*. London: Robson Books, 2003.

Stock, Paul. "Dial 'M' for Metonym: Universal Exports, M's Office Space and Empire." *The James Bond Phenomenon: A Critical Reader*. Ed. Christoph Lindner. Manchester: Manchester University Press, 2003. 215-31.

Street, Sarah. "Contemporary British Cinema." *The Cinema Book*. 3rd ed. Ed. Pam Cook. London: British Film Institute, 2007. 185-7.

_____. *Costume and Cinema: Dress Codes in Popular Film*. London: Wallflower, 2001.

Sutherland, John A. *Fiction and the Fiction Industry*. London: Athlone Press, 1978.

Tasker, Yvonne. *Spectacular Bodies: Gender, Genre and the Action Cinema*. New York: Routledge, 1993.

-----. *Working Girls: Gender and Sexuality in Popular Cinema*. New York: Routledge, 1998.

Tasker, Yvonne, and Diane Negra. "Feminist Politics and Postfeminist Culture." *Interrogating Postfeminism: Gender and the Politics of Popular Culture*. Eds. Yvonne Tasker and Diane Negra. Durham, NC: Duke University Press, 2007. 1-25.

Tasker, Yvonne, ed. *Action and Adventure Cinema*. London: Routledge, 2004.

Taylor, Verta and Nancy Whittier. "Collective Identity in Social Movements Communities: Lesbian Feminism Mobilization." *Waves of Protest: Social Movements Since the Sixties*. Eds.

Jo Freeman and Victoria Johnson. Lanham, MD: Rowman & Littlefield, 1999. 169-94.

"Teen Spy Party." *Press-Courier*. 3 July 1965: 11.

Teltsch, Kathleen. "Fedorenko to Mix Politics and Humor in TV Appearance." *New York Times*. 11 January 1967: 8.

"This Party Is Spy Special." *Fairbanks Daily News-Miner*. 27 August 1965. 5.

Tincknell, Estella. "Double-0 Agencies: Femininity, Post-Feminism and the Female Spy." *Revisioning 007: James Bond and Casino Royale*. Ed. Christoph Lindner. New York: Wallflower Press, 2009. 99-113.

Tippins, Stephen B. "007's Masculine Mystique." *The American Conservative*. 17 October 2012: 34-7.

Tremonte, Colleen M., and Linda Racioppi. "Body Politics and *Casino Royale*: Gender and (Inter) national Security." *The James Bond Phenomenon: A Critical Reader*. 2nd ed. Ed. Christoph Lindner. Manchester: Manchester University Press, 2009. 184-204.

"Wai Lin's Cut Role from *Die Another Day*." *M16: The Home of James Bond 007*. 1 May 2003. 29 January 2015 <http://www.mi6-hq.com/sections/articles/bond_20_wai_lin.php3?t=&s=articles>.

Wallace, Jo-Ann. "De-scribing *The Water Babies*: 'The Child' in Post-colonial Theory." De-Scribing Empire: Post-Colonialism and Textuality. Eds. Chris Tiffin and Alan Lawson. London: Routledge, 1994. 171-84.

Walser, Robert, "The Rock and Roll Era." *The Cambridge History of American Music*. Ed. David Nicholls. Cambridge: Cambridge University Press, 1998. 345-87.

Watts, Stephen. "On Britain's Bustling Film Scene." *New York Times* 1 November 1964: X13.

Weiler, A.H. "New James Bond: George Lazenby Follows the Connery Pattern." Review of *On Her Majesty's Secret Service.*, *New York Times*. 19 December 1969. 29 January 2015 <http://www.nytimes.com/movie/review?res=9F07E5DC1131EE3BBC4152DFB4678382679EDE>.

Weiner, Robert G., B. Lynn Whitfield, and Jack Becker, eds. *James Bond in World and Popular Culture: The Films are Not Enough*. Newcastle upon Tyne: Cambridge Scholars Publishing, 2010.

Weiss, Penny A. "Feminist Reflections on Community." *Feminism and Community*. Eds. Penny A. Weiss and Marilyn Friedman. Philadelphia: Temple University Press, 1995. 3-20.

Welldon, Estella V. *Mother, Madonna, Whore: The Idealization and Denigration of Motherhood*. London: Karnac Books, 1992.

Westad, Odd Arne. *The Global Cold War: Third World Interventions and the Making of our Times*. New York: Cambridge University Press, 2007.

Wheelwright, Julie. "Poisoned Honey: The Myth of Women in Espionage." *Queen's Quarterly* 100.2 (1993): 291-309.

White, Rosie. *Violent Femmes: Women as Spies in Popular Culture*. London: Routledge, 2007.

Willis, Martin. "Hard-Wear: The Millennium, Technology, and Brosnan's Bond." *The James Bond Phenomenon: A Critical Reader*. Ed. Christoph Lindner. Manchester: Manchester University Press, 2003. 151-68.

Willman, Skip. "The Kennedys, Fleming, and Cuba: Bond's Foreign Policy." *Ian Fleming & James Bond: The Cultural Politics of 007*. Eds. Edward P. Comentale, Stephen Watt, and Skip Willman. Bloomington IN: Indiana University Press, 2005. 178-201.

_____. "The Politics of James Bond: From Fleming's Novels to the Big Screen (review)." *Symploke* 13.1 (2006): 350-52.

Wilson, Earl. "It Happened Last Night." *The Progress Index*. 3 April 1964: 17.

Wong, Eugene Franklin. *On Visual Media Racism: Asian in the American Motion Pictures.* New York: Arno, 1978.

Wood, Julia T. *Gendered Lives: Communication, Gender, and Culture.* 9th ed. Boston: Wadsworth, 2011.

Woodward, Steven. "The Arch Archenemies of James Bond." *Bad: Infamy, Darkness, Evil, and Slime on Screen.* Ed. Murray Pomerance. Albany: SUNY Press, 2004. 173-86.

Woolf, Virginia. *A Room of One's Own.* Peterborough, ON: Broadview Press, 2001.

Woollacott, Janet. "The James Bond Films: Conditions of Production." *The James Bond Phenomenon: A Critical Reader.* Ed. Christoph Lindner. Manchester: Manchester University Press, 2003. 99-118.

Wright, Robin Redmon. "*The Avengers* and Feminist Identity Development: Learning the Example of Critical Resistance from Cathy Gale." *Television and the Self: Knowledge, Identity, and Media Representation.* Eds. Kathleen M. Ryan and Deborah A. Macey. New York: Lexington, 2013. 189-204.

Young, Iris Marion. "The Ideal of Community and the Politics of Difference." *Feminism/Postfeminism.* Ed. Linda J. Nicholson. New York: Routledge, 1990. 300-23.

"The Young Generation Presents Fashion Flickers '68." *Lowell Sunday Sun.* 4 August 1968: 2.

Zeiger, Henry A. *Ian Fleming, the Spy Who Came in with the Gold.* New York: Duell, Sloan and Pearce, 1965.

Žižek, Slavoj. "The Desert and the Real." *Lacan.com.* 1 September 2001. 29 January 2015 <http://www.lacan.com/zizek-welcome.htm>.

"Zulus Can't See 'Zulu' in South Africa." *New York Times.* 17 November 1969: 25.

INDEX